POLICY ANALYSIS IN TURKEY

Edited by Caner Bakır and Güneş Ertan

International Library of Policy Analysis, Vol 14

First published in Great Britain in 2018 by

Policy Press
University of Bristol
1-9 Old Park Hill
Bristol BS2 8BB
UK
+44 (0)117 954 5940
pp-info@bristol.ac.uk
www.policypress.co.uk

North America office:
Policy Press
c/o The University of Chicago Press
1427 East 60th Street
Chicago, IL 60637, USA
t: +1 773 702 7700
f: +1 773 702 9756
sales@press.uchicago.edu
www.press.uchicago.edu

© Policy Press 2018

British Library Cataloguing in Publication Data
A catalogue record for this book is available from the British Library.

Library of Congress Cataloging-in-Publication Data
A catalog record for this book has been requested.

ISBN 978-1-4473-3895-6 hardcover
ISBN 978-1-4473-4721-7 ePub
ISBN 978-1-4473-4722-4 mobi
ISBN 978-1-4473-3896-3 ePdf

The right of Caner Bakır and Güneş Ertan to be identified as editors of this work has been asserted by them in accordance with the Copyright, Designs and Patents Act 1988.

All rights reserved: no part of this publication may be reproduced, stored in a retrieval system, or transmitted in any form or by any means, electronic, mechanical, photocopying, recording, or otherwise without the prior permission of Policy Press.

The statements and opinions contained within this publication are solely those of the editors and contributors and not of the University of Bristol or Policy Press. The University of Bristol and Policy Press disclaim responsibility for any injury to persons or property resulting from any material published in this publication.

Policy Press works to counter discrimination on grounds of gender, race, disability, age and sexuality.

Cover design by Qube Design Associates, Bristol
Front cover: image kindly supplied by istock
Printed and bound in Great Britain by CPI Group (UK) Ltd, Croydon, CR0 4YY
Policy Press uses environmentally responsible print partners

POLICY ANALYSIS IN TURKEY

International Library of Policy Analysis

*Series editors: Iris Geva-May and Michael Howlett,
Simon Fraser University, Canada*

This major new series brings together for the first time a detailed examination of the theory and practice of policy analysis systems at different levels of government and by non-governmental actors in a specific country. It therefore provides a key addition to research and teaching in comparative policy analysis and policy studies more generally.

Each volume includes a history of the country's policy analysis which offers a broad comparative overview with other countries as well as the country in question. In doing so, the books in the series provide the data and empirical case studies essential for instruction and for further research in the area. They also include expert analysis of different approaches to policy analysis and an assessment of their evolution and operation.

Early volumes in the series will cover the following countries:

Australia • Brazil • China • Czech Republic • France • Germany •
India • Israel • Netherlands • New Zealand • Norway •
Russia • South Africa • Taiwan • UK • USA

and will build into an essential library of key reference works. The series will be of interest to academics and students in public policy, public administration and management, comparative politics and government, public organisations and individual policy areas.
It will also interest people working in the countries in question and internationally.

In association with the ICPA-Forum and *Journal of Comparative Policy Analysis*.
See more at http://goo.gl/raJUX

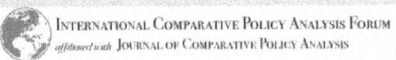

Contents

List of tables and figures   vii
Notes on contributors   ix

one   Pushing the pendulum from politics to policy: the state of policy analysis in Turkey   1
Caner Bakır and Güneş Ertan

Part One: Historical roots, styles and methods of policy analysis in Turkey   17

two   The past, present and future of policy analysis in Turkey   19
Akif Argun Akdoğan, Göktuğ Morçöl, Gökhan Orhan and Mete Yıldız

three   'Boomerang effect': the bottleneck of public policy analysis in Turkey   35
Akif Argun Akdoğan

four   Methods of policy analysis: the US and Turkish cases   51
Hüseyin Gül and Muhittin Acar

Part Two: Policy analysis by governments   67

five   Policy analysis in Turkey's central government: current practices and future challenges   69
Uğur Sadioğlu

six   Territorial policy-making and administrative reform in Turkey   87
Can Umut Çiner

seven   Policy-making at local level: an analysis of Turkish municipalities   105
Ulaş Bayraktar

Part Three: Experts, international actors and public opinion   121

eight   Beyond developmentalism: the role of experts and expertise in Turkey's environmental policy disputes   123
Gökhan Orhan

nine   Europeanisation of policy-making in Turkey and its limits   143
H. Tolga Bölükbaşı, Ebru Ertugal and Saime Özçürümez

ten   Public opinion and public policy in Turkey   163
Sedef Turper

Part Four: Parties and civil society-based policy analysis   181

eleven   Political parties and public policy in Turkey   183
Selim Erdem Aytaç

twelve	Policy analysis in civil society organisations *Güneş Ertan*	199

Part Five: Academic, bureaucratic and advocacy-based policy analysis   **213**

thirteen	Policy analysis and capacity in the Central Bank of Turkey *Caner Bakır and Mehmet Kerem Coban*	215
fourteen	Think tanks and policy analysis in Turkey *Göktuğ Morçöl, Özer Köseoğlu, Mehmet Zahid Sobacı and* *Ömer Faruk Köktaş*	235
fifteen	Public policy and media in Turkey *Başak Yavçan and Hakan Övünç Ongur*	255
sixteen	Public policy education in Turkey *Mete Yıldız and Cenay Babaoğlu*	271
Index		289

List of tables and figures

Tables

4.1	A classified list of methods of social inquiry and policy research	58
4.2	Methods and techniques of policy research in Turkey	60
4.3	Methods of policy analysis in Turkey	61
6.1	Local administrations	91
10.1	Political interest over time by gender, education and age (mean, SD)	165
10.2	Most important problems in Turkey (%)	167
10.3	Most important economic problems in Turkey (%)	167
10.4	Public evaluation of income inequality in Turkey (raw numbers, %)	168
10.5	Public evaluation of tax policies in Turkey (raw numbers, %)	169
10.6	Public preferences for business ownership (raw numbers, %)	170
10.7	Satisfaction with healthcare services by gender, education and age (mean, SD)	172
10.8	Confidence in the educational system in Turkey (raw numbers, %)	173
10.9	Public evaluation of the government's educational policies (%)	174
11.1	Vote shares and seats in Parliament of the major political parties in Turkey, 2002–15	185
11.2	Seven major policy domains and categories in the Manifesto Project	186
12.1	CSOs by legal status	204
12.2	Number of CSOs in select countries	204
12.3	Election process of executive board members in CSOs	207
14.1	Think tanks included in the study	240
15.1	Basic data on newspapers selected	259
15.2	Distribution of public policy news by subject area (1995–2013)	261
15.3	Framing public policy news across five newspapers (1995–2013)	265
16.1	List of public policy workshops organised in Turkey	277
16.2	New Master's programmes and sub-departments/concentrations of public policy in Turkey	280

Figures

2.1	Policy-related articles in AID (1968–2015)	27
5.1	Hierarchy of a prime ministerial government system	77
11.1	Distribution of manifesto statements across policy domains for AKP, CHP, MHP and DTP/BDP/HDP, 2002–15	187
11.2	Distribution of manifesto statements across policy categories for AKP, 2002–15	190
11.3	Distribution of manifesto statements across policy categories for CHP, 2002–15	191
11.4	Distribution of manifesto statements across policy categories for MHP, 2002–15	192
11.5	Distribution of manifesto statements across policy categories for DTP/BDP/HDP, 2007–15	193

12.1	Membership of CSOs, OECD vs Turkey	203
12.2	Associations by membership numbers	205
12.3	Profiles of CSO executive board members in Turkey	206
12.4	Approaches to evaluation	209
14.1	Papers published per year, 2002–15	242
14.2	Policy areas covered in 94 papers	243
14.3	Trends in more popular policy areas	243
14.4	Geographic loci of papers	244
14.5	Institutional affiliations of authors	244
14.6	Academic degrees of authors	245
14.7	Use of abstract/executive summary in papers by think tank	246
14.8	Use of statement of purpose in papers by think tank	246
14.9	Use of problem definition in papers by think tank	247
14.10	Descriptive and normative analyses in papers by think tank	247
14.11	Retrospective and prospective forms of policy analysis in papers by think tank	248
14.12	Data collection methods used in papers	248
14.13	Data analysis methods used in papers	249
14.14	Number of secondary sources used in papers	249
15.1	Distribution of public policy news over 19 years	262
15.2	Five specific subcategories of public policy with political content across 19 years	263
15.3	Distribution of criticism towards public policy across five newspapers over 19 years	266
15.4	Distribution of criticism towards public policy by subject area, 1995–2013	267
16.1	Policy-related articles in Amme İdaresi Dergisi, 1969–2014	273
16.2	Courses and graduate programmes of public policy, 1990–2017	275
16.3	Master's and PhD theses about public policy in the Turkish Higher Education Council Thesis Catalogue	279

Notes on contributors

Editors

Caner Bakır is Associate Professor of Political Science, with a special focus on International and Comparative Political Economy, and Public Policy and Administration at Koç University, Istanbul, Turkey. He received his PhD in Political Science from Monash University in Melbourne, Australia. He is Co-director of the Center for Globalisation, Peace and Democratic Governance (GLODEM). His work relates to political economy and public policy with a special emphasis on comparative institutional analysis and policy change. He has published articles in leading journals such as *Policy Sciences*, *Governance*, *Public Administration*, *Development and Change* and *New Political Economy*. He has authored and co-edited eight books, most recently with Darryl Jarvis, *Policy entrepreneurship and institutional change* (Palgrave, 2018). He is the recipient of the 2010 Scientific and Technological Research Council of Turkey (TUBITAK) Incentive Award, and TUBITAK Early Career Award in 2008. He has been the principal investigator of various TUBITAK-funded projects and his recent research has been linked with the Cooperation on Science and Technology (COST) project entitled 'The emergence of southern multinationals and their impact on Europe' (*ISCH COST Action IS0905*). Caner is national member of the Management Committee of the COST Action CA15207 Professionalization and Social Impact of European Political Science. He is the Associate Editor of *Policy Sciences*, editorial board member of *Journal of Comparative Policy Analysis*, *Journal of Economic Policy Research* and *International Journal of Emerging Markets*. Recently, he has been the editor and co-editor of two themed issues of *Policy and Society*.

Güneş Ertan is an Assistant Professor of International Affairs at Koç University, Istanbul, Turkey. She received her PhD from the Graduate School of Public and International Affairs at the University of Pittsburgh, USA, in 2013 with a specialisation in Public Policy. Her research focuses on the relationship between social networks and collective action. More specifically she studies the role of social networks in shaping collective action outcomes within the context of policy processes and social movements. Her articles have appeared in journals such as *Social Networks*, *Safety Science*, *Public Organization Review* and *Earthquake Spectra*.

Contributors

Muhittin Acar is Professor of Public Administration in the Department of Political Science and Public Administration at Hacettepe University in Ankara, Turkey. He holds a BA from Ankara University, an MPM from Carnegie Mellon University and a PhD from the University of Southern California, USA.

Professor Acar's main research interests include transparency, accountability and integrity in governance; collaboration, partnerships and networks; and public policy and management. He has been frequently consulted on these subjects by various national and international organisations, and his work on these themes has appeared in journals such as *Nonprofit and Voluntary Sector Quarterly*, *International Review of Administrative Sciences* and *American Review of Public Administration*.

Akif Argun Akdoğan is a Professor at the Public Administration Institute for Turkey and the Middle East. He completed his BA in the Political Science and International Relations Department of Bogazici University, and followed his MA in the Peace Studies Department of Bradford University and in the Public Policy and Management Graduate Programme of the Institute of Social Studies in the Netherlands. He undertook his PhD degree in the Middle East Technical University in the field of Political Science and Public Administration. His current research interests are focused on public policy analysis and policy transfer.

Selim Erdem Aytaç is an Assistant Professor in the Department of International Relations at Koç University, Turkey. He received his PhD from the Department of Political Science at Yale University, USA, in 2014. His research areas include comparative political behaviour, political economy and economic voting. His academic articles have appeared in *Comparative Political Studies*, *Comparative Politics*, *European Political Science Review* and *Democratization*. In addition, he is the author of two book chapters on the political economy of Turkey during the AKP era and public support for presidentialism in Turkey ahead of the June 2015 general elections.

Cenay Babaoğlu is a Researcher at the Grand National Assembly of Turkey and Nigde University. He received his PhD from Hacettepe University in 2016. His research interest centres on Turkish administrative history, public policy, information and communication technology use in public administration and public administration education. He has articles published in journals such as the *Journal of Public Affairs Education* and the *International Journal of Public Administration in the Digital Age*.

Ulaş Bayraktar is an independent researcher. He was previously an Associate Professor of Political Science at Mersin University, Turkey. He received his undergraduate degree in Public Administration at Galatasaray University and graduate degrees (MA in 2002 and PhD in 2006) in Political Science at the Institute of Political Sciences of Paris. He has worked and published on local politics, local governments and public policies. He represents Turkey within the Group of Independent Experts on the European Charter of local self-government of the Council of Europe.

Notes on contributors

H. Tolga Bölükbaşı is an Assistant Professor of Political Science and Public Administration at Bilkent University, Turkey. He holds a PhD from McGill University, Canada. His current research interests include the political economy of macroeconomic policies, the Europeanisation of socioeconomic governance and emerging welfare states. His articles have appeared in *South European Society and Politics*, *Comparative European Politics*, *Journal of European Public Policy*, *European Political Science*, *Uluslararasi Iliskiler-International Relations* and *Current Politics and Economics of Europe*. He is co-editor of a special issue of *South European Politics*, which was reprinted with the title *Europeanization of public policy in Southern Europe: Comparative political economy from the 2000s to the crisis* (published by Routledge). Bölükbaşı has also authored book chapters on the political economy of Turkey, Turkey's neighbourhood policies and elite attitudes in Turkey towards Turkey–EU relations. He has been part of numerous research projects on the Europeanisation of Turkey's macroeconomic and employment policies and mapping the Turkish welfare state within emerging welfare states.

Can Umut Çiner is an Associate Professor at Ankara University, Turkey, where he gained his PhD. His research explores how administration works, how it is structured and how it shapes policy and is shaped by politics. His publications include two co-authored books – *Metropolitan administration* (2009) and *Boundaries of the municipalities* (2013), both published by the Public Administration Institute for Turkey and the Middle East – as well as articles in a wide variety of journals, including the *International Journal of Public Administration*, *La Revue Administrative* (*The Administrative Review*) and *Amme İdaresi Dergisi* (*Public Administration Journal*). Dr Çiner's current research focuses on imperialism, especially colonial administration. The Galatasaray Education Foundation awarded him the Dr Besim Üstünel Research Award for his article, 'Training of public administrators: From colonialism to cooperation: A different outlook on the practice of national administration school experience'.

Mehmet Kerem Çoban is a PhD candidate at Lee Kuan Yew School of Public Policy (LKYSPP), National University of Singapore (NUS) and Visiting Researcher at the Center for Globalisation, Peace and Democratic Governance (GLODEM) at Koç University, Turkey. His research interests include the political economy of development, financial liberalisation, bank regulation and development aid. Kerem obtained his Master's degree in Development Studies at the Graduate Institute of International and Development Studies (IHEID), Geneva, in 2013, and his Bachelor's in International Relations in Kadir Has University, Istanbul, in 2011. He interned at the UNDP Office in Geneva and the General Consulate of Turkey in Geneva.

Ebru Ertugal is Associate Professor in the Department of Political Science and Public Administration at Baskent University, Turkey. She holds a PhD from Katholieke Universiteit Leuven, Belgium. Ertugal conducts research on comparative public policy, regional policy and multi-level governance, social and employment policy, the Europeanisation of public policies and the political economy of Southern Europe. Her articles have been published in *Policy & Politics, Europe-Asia Studies, Southeast European and Black Sea Studies, South European Society and Politics* and *Uluslararasi Iliskiler-International Relations*. She is co-editor of *Europeanization of public policy in Southern Europe: Comparative political economy from the 2000s to the crisis* (Routledge) and *Bridging the real divide: Social and regional policy in Turkey's EU Accession Process* (METU Press). She has authored book chapters on social and economic development in Turkey and Turkey's central administration in historical and comparative perspective. She has taken part in research projects on comparative European research, absorption capacity of EU funds, Europeanisation of Turkey's employment policies and regional development policy.

Hüseyin Gül is a Professor in the Department of Public Administration at Süleyman Demirel University, Turkey. He gained his PhD in Urban and Public Administration (2000), MPA (1999) and MA in Urban Affairs (1996) from the University of Texas at Arlington, USA. He received his undergraduate degree from the Faculty of Political Sciences at Ankara University in 1991. During 1999 and 2000 he worked as a researcher in the Front-Line Management Practices Study, a study on welfare reform in the US conducted by the Rockefeller Institute of Government. His research interests include urban and public policy, urban poverty, local economic development, reform in public administration and the welfare state. Dr Gül has published articles in several Turkish and international journals, as well as books in Turkish and English. He edited and/or co-authored *Local administrations and local politics in Turkey* (Detay, 2014), *Turkey in the new millennium: A critique of social, political and economic transformation* (Lambert Academic Publishing, 2013), *Leadership in public administration and governorship* (Detay, 2013) and *Basic principles of scientific research* (Süleyman Demirel University Publications, 2007). Since 2007 he has also served as the editor and general coordinator of *Toplum ve Demokrasi Dergisi (Journal of Society and Democracy)*.

Ömer Faruk Köktaş is a Research Assistant in the Department of Political Science and Public Administration, at Sakarya University, Turkey. He received his MA from the Institute of Social Sciences at Sakarya University in 2015, and has continued his research as a PhD candidate at the same university since 2015. His research interests are public policy analysis, think tanks and evidence-based policy-making.

Özer Köseoğlu is an Associate Professor in the Department of Political Science and Public Administration at Sakarya University, Turkey. He received his PhD in Public Administration from Sakarya University. He is the co-editor of *In search of a paradigm in public administration: New public management and beyond* (2015) (in Turkish). He is also the co-author of *Organizational performance management in municipalities* (2011) (in Turkish) and *Social media in municipalities: New opportunities* *for change* (2015) (in Turkish). His studies mostly focus on public policy, public management reform, social media in government, public value and performance management. He is the author of many journal articles and book chapters published in national and international academic journals and books.

Göktuğ Morçöl is a Professor of Public Policy and Administration at Penn State Harrisburg, USA. His research interests are complexity theory, metropolitan governance, business improvement districts and research methodology. He has authored, edited and co-edited seven books, most recently *Challenges to democratic governance in developing countries* and *A complexity theory for public policy*. His articles have appeared in journals including *Public Administration Review*, *Administration and Society*, *Administrative Theory and Praxis*, *Policy Sciences*, *Public Administration Quarterly*, *Politics & Policy*, *International Journal of Public Administration*, *Journal of Urban Affairs* and *Emergence*. He is an editor-in-chief of the journal *Complexity, Governance & Networks*.

Hakan Övünç Ongur is an Assistant Professor in the Department of Political Science and International Relations at TOBB University of Economics and Technology, Turkey. He is the author of *Consumer society, neurotic culture and Fight Club* (Ayrıntı) and *Minorities of Europeanization: The new others of European social identity* (Lexington Press). He also has several research articles and book chapters across his research interests, which include critical theory, media criticism, biopolitics and identity politics.

Gökhan Orhan is a Professor of Public Administration at the Bandırma Onyedi Eylül University, Turkey. He received his BSc (Hons) from the METU and MA (Politics) and PhD (Government) degrees both from the University of Essex. His academic studies focus on public policy analysis, interpretive policy analysis and environmental policy and politics in Turkey. Dr Orhan has published in journals such as *Policy & Politics* and *Critical Policy Studies*, and has contributed to edited volumes on policy analysis and environmental policy. His research focuses on the impact of international regimes, institutions and policy discourses on countries' environmental policies and the efforts of local governments and cities in mitigating climate change.

Saime Özçürümez is an Associate Professor in the Department of Political Science and Public Administration at Bilkent University, Turkey. She holds a PhD from McGill University, Canada. Özçürümez publishes on migration policy and politics in the EU, Turkey and Canada, health and immigration, gender and immigration, citizenship and integration, deliberative democracy and Europeanisation. Her articles have been published in *International Migration*, *Journal of Balkan and Near Eastern Studies*, *Turkish Studies*, *Comparative European Politics*, *Journal of Common Market Studies*, *Uluslararasi Iliskiler-International Relations*, *Women's Studies International Forum* and *European Political Science*. She is co-editor of *States, rights and social closure* (Palgrave) and *Asylum, international migration and statelessness: Concepts, theories and politics* (in Turkish, UNHCR Publications). She has co-authored several book chapters on the immigration policy process, Turkish foreign policy and access to healthcare by ethno-cultural groups. Özçürümez has run research projects on cultural diversity and healthcare systems, collective identities in Europe, migrants' media representation and the Europeanisation of Turkey's immigration policy.

Uğur Sadioğlu is an Associate Professor in the Department of Political Science and Public Administration at Hacettepe University in Ankara, Turkey. He is currently the Vice-Chairman of the Local Governments Application and Research Centre of the same university, and Vice-Editor in Chief of the *Journal of Hacettepe University Faculty of Economics and Administrative Sciences*. He studied political science and public administration at Hacettepe University (gaining his BSc in 2006). He received his PhD degree from Hacettepe University in 2012. He was a Visiting Fellow at the University of Cologne, Germany, the Cologne Centre for Comparative Politics, between 2015 and 2016. His research interests are public administration theory, new trends in public administration, local government and politics, urban policy and affairs, e-government and development studies. He has acted as a researcher on various administrative reform projects in Turkey and Germany. His four books were published in the area of local government. He has recently presented papers at national and international conferences and published extensively in national and international journals on local governments and administrative reform outcomes in Turkey.

Mehmet Zahid Sobacı is an Associate Professor of Public Administration at Uludağ University, Turkey. He received his PhD in Public Administration from Uludağ University. His research interests are public policy, policy transfer, public management reform and social media in government. He has authored, edited and co-edited eight books, most recently *Administrative reform and policy transfer: The diffusion of the new public management* (in Turkish), *Public policy: Theory and practice* (in Turkish), *Social media and local governments: Theory and practice, E-Parliament and ICT-based legislation* and *In search of a paradigm in public administration: New public management and beyond* (in Turkish). He is also the author of many journal articles and book chapters published in national and international journals and books.

Sedef Turper is an Assistant Professor of International Relations at Koç University, Turkey. She received her doctorate from the University of Twente for her thesis on European attitudes towards political institutions and immigration policies. Her main research interests are in public opinion of immigration policies and political processes in modern democracies. Her articles have appeared in journals such as *Journal of Ethic and Migration Studies* and *International Journal of Public Opinion Research*.

Başak Yavçan is an Assistant Professor in the Department of Political Science and International Relations at TOBB University of Economics and Technology in Turkey. She received her PhD from the University of Pittsburgh, USA, with a focus on comparative politics and international relations. She specialises in comparative political behaviour, mostly in relation to inter-group relations in the forms of attitudes toward immigration and the EU in Europe and immigrant acculturation attitudes in Europe. Some of her current research focuses on criticism of Turkish politics in the press and the effect of newspaper frames on attitudinal change, and the integration attitudes of Syrian displaced people in Turkey. Her latest works have appeared in the *International Journal of Communication*, *Journal of Comparative Policy Analysis* and *Turkish Studies*.

Mete Yıldız is a Professor of Public Administration and Policy in the Department of Political Science and Public Administration at Hacettepe University, Turkey. He received his PhD from Indiana University, Bloomington's School of Public and Environmental Affairs, in 2004. Among his research topics are government reform, e-government, public policy, comparative public administration and governance issues.

Editors' introduction to the series

Professor Iris Geva-May and Professor Michael Howlett, ILPA series editors

Policy analysis is a relatively new area of social scientific inquiry, owing its origins to developments in the US in the early 1960s. Its main rationale is systematic, evidence-based, transparent, efficient, and implementable policymaking. This component of policymaking is deemed key in democratic structures allowing for accountable public policies. From the US, policy analysis has spread to other countries, notably in Europe in the 1980s and 1990s and in Asia in the 1990s and 2000s. It has taken, respectively one to two more decades for programmes of public policy to be established in these regions preparing cadres for policy analysis as a profession. However, this movement has been accompanied by variations in the kinds of analysis undertaken as US-inspired analytical and evaluative techniques have been adapted to local traditions and circumstances, and new techniques shaped in these settings.

In the late 1990s this led to the development of the field of comparative policy analysis, pioneered by Iris Geva-May, who initiated and founded the Journal of Comparative Policy Analysis, and whose mission has been advanced with the support of editorial board members such as Laurence E. Lynn Jr., first co-editor, Peter deLeon, Duncan McRae, David Weimer, Beryl Radin, Frans van Nispen, Yukio Adachi, Claudia Scott, Allan Maslove and others in the US and elsewhere. While current studies have underlined differences and similarities in national approaches to policy analysis, the different national regimes which have developed over the past two to three decades have not been thoroughly explored and systematically evaluated in their entirety, examining both sub-national and non-executive governmental organisations as well as the non-governmental sector; nor have these prior studies allowed for either a longitudinal or a latitudinal comparison of similar policy analysis perceptions, applications, and themes across countries and time periods.

The International Library for Policy Analysis (ILPA) series fills this gap in the literature and empirics of the subject. It features edited volumes created by experts in each country, which inventory and analyse their respective policy analysis systems. To a certain extent the series replicates the template of *Policy Analysis in Canada* edited by Dobuzinskis, Howlett and Laycock (Toronto: University of Toronto Press, 2007).

Each ILPA volume surveys the state of the art of policy analysis in governmental and non-governmental organisations in each country using the common template derived from the Canadian collection in order to provide for each volume in the series comparability in terms of coverage and approach.

Each volume addresses questions such as: What do policy analysts do? What techniques and approaches do they use? What is their influence on policymaking in that country? Is there a policy analysis deficit? What norms and values guide the work done by policy analysts working in different institutional settings? Contributors focus on the sociology of policy analysis, demonstrating how analysts working in different organisations tend to have different interests and to utilise different techniques. The central theme of each volume includes historical works on the origins of policy analysis in the jurisdiction concerned, and then proceeds to investigate the nature and types, and quality, of policy analysis conducted by governments (including different levels and orders of government). It then moves on to examine the nature and kinds of policy analytical work and practices found in non-governmental actors such as think tanks, interest groups, business, labour, media, political parties, non-profits and others.

Each volume in the series aims to compare and analyse the significance of the different styles and approaches found in each country and organisation studied, and to understand the impact these differences have on the policy process.

Together, the volumes included in the ILPA series serve to provide the basic data and empirical case studies required for an international dialogue in the area of policy analysis, and an eye-opener on the nuances of policy analysis applications and implications in national and international jurisdictions. Each volume in the series is leading edge and has the promise to dominate its field and the textbook market for policy analysis in the country concerned, as well as being of broad comparative interest to markets in other countries.

The ILPA is published in association with the International Comparative Policy Analysis Forum, and the *Journal of Comparative Policy Analysis*, whose mission is to advance international comparative policy analytic studies. The editors of each volume are leading members of this network and are the best-known scholars in each respective country, as are the authors contributing to each volume in their particular domain. The book series as a whole provides learning insights for instruction and for further research in the area and constitutes a major addition to research and pedagogy in the field of comparative policy analysis and policy studies in general.

We welcome to the ILPA series Volume 14, *Policy Analysis in Turkey*, edited by Caner Bakır and Güneş Ertan, and thank the editors and the authors for their outstanding contribution to this important encyclopedic database.

Iris Geva-May
Professor of Policy Studies, Baruch College at the City University of New York, Professor Emerita Simon Fraser University; Founding President and Editor-in-chief, International Comparative Policy Analysis Forum and *Journal of Comparative Policy Analysis*

Michael Howlett
Burnaby Mountain Professor, Department of Political Science, Simon Fraser University, and Yong Pung How Chair Professor, Lee Kuan Yew School of Public Policy, National University of Singapore

ONE

Pushing the pendulum from politics to policy: the state of policy analysis in Turkey

Caner Bakır and Güneş Ertan

Public policy as a discipline and a practice is predominantly concerned with the decision-making processes that are aimed at addressing societal problems. Policy analysis relates to tools of public policy implementation (for example, regulations) and formulation (for example, scenarios, cost-benefit and cost-impact analyses) (Jordan and Turnpenny, 2015). The most cited definition of policy analysis describes it as '… the activity of creating knowledge *of* and *in* the policy making process' (Dunn, 1994, p 1, from Lasswell, 1970). Analysis *of* policy processes comprises scholarly research that aims at theorising policy-making processes and empirically evaluating the performance and consequences of existing policies. Analysis *in* policy denotes use of analytic techniques, mostly by expert practitioners, with the immediate aim of providing policy recommendations to policy-makers. We discuss why the research and practice in policy analysis is in its infancy and skewed towards the analysis *of* the policy process in Turkey.

Modern policy analysis is a recent discipline that emerged in the US as a result of successful collaboration between the military and scientific communities during the Second World War (deLeon, 2008). Soon this model of policy-making spread to other government departments, becoming a novel discipline and profession in the 1960s with the establishment of professional graduate schools of public policy akin to medical and law schools (Allison, 2008). Unlike most social sciences disciplines, policy analysis can be both normative, explicitly stating policy goals that 'create and critique knowledge claims about the values of public policies' (Dunn, 1994, p 3), as well as descriptive, in using the traditional tools of political science to decipher policy processes. Policy analysis is also problem-driven and relies on collaborations from multiple disciplines, since intractable policy problems consist of interactions of various sub-problems that frequently require expertise from more than one discipline (deLeon, 2008).

Considered one of the founders of policy analysis, Harold Lasswell (1951), who coined the term 'policy sciences' and characterised this new discipline as the 'policy science of democracy', argued that policy-making based on scientific evidence would be instrumental in eroding authoritarian regimes around the world. But many scholars criticised his vision, which dismissed the role of politics and ignored the inevitable clash of values, but nevertheless his vision included fundamental traits of democratic societies (see, for example, deLeon, 1997; Fischer and Gottweis, 2012). For example, Dryzek (1989, p 98) warned against the 'policy science of tyranny' indicating the domination of an 'elite controlled policy process that overrules the desires and aspirations of ordinary people.' One of the pressing questions for both scholars and practitioners of public policy remains how to balance technical expertise, using the tools of policy analysis, with responsiveness to popular political demands in policy-making processes. If we were to consider this balance as a pendulum, swinging between technocratic tyranny at one end and populism and politics at the other, the pendulum in Turkey has been too close to politics and far from policy capacity and analytic techniques.

In other words, policy analytic approaches to policy problems, in public and other policy-relevant non-governmental organisations (NGOs) in Turkey, remain relatively underdeveloped. Similarly, both academic works on public policy studies and undergraduate and graduate programmes involving policy analysis-relevant coursework remain rather scant, despite increasing interest from academic and practitioner communities in the last few decades.

There are various explanations for Turkey's delay in catching up with policy analysis in policy-making and academia. Many scholars agree that the Turkish administrative system is characterised overall by 'generality, bureaucratism, elitism, over-centralization, formalism, legalism, commandism and traditionalism' (Fişek, 1982, p 117). A strong and highly centralised state tradition that is the legacy of the Ottoman era, the dominance of patrimonial values, a very weak civil society that has limited power to shape policy-making and the bureaucracy's lack of autonomy from the executives are usually considered to be some of the major factors that historically inhibited the emergence of policy analysis in the Turkish context (Heper, 1976, 1982, 2000; Kalaycıoglu, 2002). On the whole, the strong hierarchical power structure in the state prevents the emergence of a capable and rigorous stock of technical expertise that can contribute to policy-making. In a similar vein, nepotism, favouritism and partisanship is at the centre of Turkish political and policy traditions (Parlak and Sobacı, 2012).

Formally, there are many permanent personnel positions in the executive government that resemble policy analyst types of appointments, such as consultants to members of parliament and consultancies for ministries. However, a limited number of studies indicate that these positions may be filled in a nepotistic way in order to provide employment for relatives or fellow countrymen (hemşeri) of politicians; these types of personnel's day to-day tasks very much look like those of personal assistants', such as running errands (Abakay, 2008). In some other instances, these positions are reserved for demoted public officials or retiring politicians with minimal to zero work expectations (Abakay, 2008). Unsurprisingly, there is not much evidence indicating that the policy analyst types of positions in government are occupied by the modern policy analyst, described by Radin (2000) as the multi-method, problem-oriented policy wonk.

Results of a rare empirical study on the use of scientific evidence in policy-making in Turkey also indicate that policy-makers rarely utilise scholarly research in decision-making and that most of the time they rely on their own experiences, their political party programme and their own perception of the public's expectations of politicians (TÜBA, 2005). Based on elite interviews with policy-makers, politicians and various other policy-relevant actors, the Turkish Science Academy (TÜBA, 2005) report identifies several factors inhibiting change in modes of policy-making, such as cumbersome policy institutions, lack of collaborative tradition and an overall political culture that does not value criticism and shows no tolerance for opposition.

According to Akdoğan (2011), there have been some major policy windows that could foster the adoption of policy analytic approaches, such as Turkey's residence invitation to John Dewey to help the Ministry of Education redesign education policies in the 1920s, the establishment of the State Planning Organisation in 1960 as an independent agency to promote modern budgeting techniques with significant powers to have oversight over public agencies, and advancement of social sciences and operations research in universities. However, all these opportunities failed to make a significant impact, either due to conflict with political interests or because of lack of resources, infrastructure or trained specialists.

Despite this overall bleak picture, until recently international organisations have been increasingly pushing public sector actors to adopt policy analytic approaches to policy design and decision-making. An elite group of well-trained bureaucrats are also acting as policy entrepreneurs (Bakır, 2009) to move the pendulum towards adoption of policy analytic decision-making processes, especially in public organisations that rely on high levels of technical expertise (see Chapter Thirteen, this volume). Specifically, the 2001 Turkish economic and financial crisis opened a window of opportunity for a policy entrepreneur with multiple identities that enabled him to perform institutional entrepreneurship in various stages of public policy-making processes.[1] Some of the examples include the legal reform supplying independence to the Central Bank of the Republic of Turkey in 2001 (Bakır, 2009) and the Public Financial Management and Control Law (5018) in 2003 that strengthened the policy capacity in the Undersecretariat of the Treasury by reinforcing the introduction of a substantive set of policy tools in policy formulation and analysis (Bakır, 2012a, b).[2]

In addition to the structural constraints of a strong and centralised administrative tradition, nepotism, favouritism and partisanship, there are several institutional and agency-level constraints in policy analysis in Turkey. For example, although a growing number of academics who were either trained in international policy schools or are students of such scholars are likely to influence the education and research practices of policy sciences in academia, there are several limitations in the supply side of policy analyses and analysts. First, public policy education and training is in its infancy in Turkey. This is because public policy departments are non-existent, and education and training in the field are mostly marginalised in public administration and political science departments with limited resources and audiences. Second, already existing public policy programmes mostly offer policy process-related education and training rather than formal policy analysis. Thus, policy actors engaged in public policy formation, design and implementation in public bureaucracies and government include policy generalists rather than policy analysts who, for example, are not exposed to policy analysis tools such as risk, impact, scenario and cost and benefit analyses. Despite the fact that more students are graduating equipped with some public policy relevant skills, the relevance of their knowledge and skills to the challenges posed by complex and politically contestable policy issues remain limited. The broader long-term risk for the public policy field and policy analysis in Turkey is the over-reliance on policy analysis methods and preferences from the economics discipline, which is informed by narrow, rationalist assumptions utilising abstract econometric models that are detached from context. Third, in academia, most policy-focused scholarly work tends to concentrate on particular policy issue areas, and most of the time lack strong theoretical framing and methodological rigour. A majority of policy research focuses on social policy and uses critical theory to describe and decipher how a particular policy functions within the constraints of capitalistic economies. Finally, political scientists and public administration scholars' interest in the public policy field in general, and public policy and analysis in particular, is rather limited.

Nevertheless, with increasing competition for funding and sustainability, and due to growing concerns for evidencing social impact, large numbers of non-governmental policy actors are also embracing policy analysis techniques to guide their management and project implementation. As such, it should also be noted that there are venues of policy analysis beyond the public sector, and politicians and bureaucrats are increasingly dependent on policy analysis by non-governmental policy actors (Craft and Howlett, 2012); increasingly, consultants supplant in-house policy analysis and analysts (Howlett and Migone, 2013), and the boundary between the supply of policy advice from 'within' and 'outside' government is blurring (Craft and Wilder, 2017). Turkey is no exception. This is due mainly to the esoteric (technical, private and closed) rather than exoteric (political, public and open) nature of some of the internationalised policy domains such as monetary and fiscal policy, ideological commitment to the principles of New Public Management, and the weak or uneven distribution of policy capacity across bureaucratic agencies (see Bakır, 2012a, b).

Consequently, the caricatured image of policy-making in Turkey as a uniform, strictly top-down hierarchical process that is solely shaped by politics does not represent the more complex decision-making mechanisms, which vary significantly among policy-making actors. Therefore, with this book we aim to go beyond these simplistic views of policy analysis in Turkey and intend to open the black box of decision-making and analysis in both public organisations and NGOs, while paying special attention to the Turkey-specific context and crucial policy actors embedded in public policy-making, such as the European Union (EU), International Monetary Fund (IMF), The World Bank and the Organisation for Economic Co-operation and Development (OECD). By bringing together a small group of dedicated Turkish policy scholars, we also see this book as part of the larger movement to push the pendulum towards policy analysis-based decision-making in all policy relevant organisations.

Emerging themes

There are a number of emerging themes across the chapters that highlight some of the characteristics of policy analysis practices in the Turkish context, including chronic implementation failures, inability of organisations to coordinate common policy goals, and salient policy issue areas in public opinion, political parties, academia and in the media.

Implementation challenges

Implementation has been a major sub-discipline of public policy since the publication of Pressman and Wildavsky's (1984) ground-breaking book. Implementation studies are mainly concerned with understanding the factors that contribute to implementation failures and developing policy recommendations to ensure successful outcomes on the ground. Not surprisingly, barriers to implementation and significant gaps between the stated policy and actual behaviour of policy actors is a major theme in various chapters of the book.

A number of chapters underline that despite the presence of formal policies and institutions to ensure participation in decision-making, there is a lack of participatory processes. For example, Akdoğan et al, in Chapter Two, highlight that while the Directive of Methods and Principles of Legislative Process clearly indicates that participatory processes are mandatory for strategic planning and regulatory impact assessment, in practice, participation is very limited. Similarly, Bayraktar, in Chapter Seven, indicates that municipal councils are supposed to be the main decision-making body at municipal level by law. These councils usually represent different political groups and are expected make decisions through deliberation. However, as Bayraktar shows, in practice these councils operate under the supervision of a mayor and can hardly make decisions that contradict the preferences of the mayor. Bayraktar also states that city councils, which were designed to give a voice to civil society actors in local matters, are essentially dysfunctional and do not go beyond acting as 'participatory tokens'. Moreover, these councils exclusively represent the interests of the political elite and lack representation from diverse social groups. Similarly, in Chapter Twelve, Ertan shows that while most civil society organisations state their commitment to representation and participatory mechanisms, in fact, top-down decision-making dominates civil society as well. While analysing the EU's influence on regional development policy in Turkey in Chapter Nine, Bölükbaşı et al indicate that participatory mechanisms enacted in policy-making in order to transfer the multi-level governance model of the EU are almost never implemented on the ground. Similarly, Chapter Eight by Orhan also states that despite the presence of formal structures to ensure participation in environmental policy-making, decision-makers never utilise these venues.

Overall, these examples suggest that the above-mentioned characteristics of Turkish political culture, such as hierarchy and paternalism, can easily triumph over formal policies and structures. Structural and institutional contexts and their interactions with various agents matter in policy formulation and implementation (Bakır and Jarvis, 2017, 2018). Successful policy implementation within the Turkish context is less likely when policies clash with dominant ideas and interests. In this respect, the well-known leadership cult tradition in Turkish politics (Heper and Sayari, 2000) can also be considered a crucial contributing factor in explaining the systematic failure of implementation when participatory mechanisms are required.

Akdoğan, in Chapter Three, provides a lengthy discussion of the failure of implementation of policy analytic tools such as strategic planning and performance auditing. Akdoğan provides a multitude of explanations for implementation failures. First of all, he states that organisations with supervision responsibilities lack the power to impose sanctions on organisations that fail to implement regulations. He also raises the role of administrative culture and the importability of policy analytic tools that were developed to address the needs of the Anglo-Saxon countries to the Turkish context to further explain acute barriers to implementation. Finally, Akdoğan also questions the fitness of private sector-born practices to the public sector, and suggests that implementation problems regarding strategic planning or performance auditing are not unique to Turkey due to inherent compatibility problems.

Coordination

Some contributors also underline the well-known coordination challenges when there are a large number of implementing organisations (Comfort, 2007). For example, Orhan (Chapter Eight) depicts the Turkish administrative system as 'centralised, but fragmented and disjointed', and considers the limited capacity of policy actors for cooperation and coordination as one of the main reasons for problems with the implementation of environmental legislation. Bölükbaşı et al (Chapter Nine) also underline coordination problems in relation to implementation of regional policy, accompanied with limited resources.

Predominant policy issues

This book is not about understanding the dynamics of specific policy sectors in Turkey. Instead, in line with the series theme, our main goal is to reveal the dominant modes of policy analysis in various policy-relevant organisations and to show the effect of formal and informal institutions on decision-making structures. Nevertheless, across chapters it is possible to see the supremacy of certain policy issue areas over others. For example, Turper's Chapter Ten, which is on public opinion, clearly indicates that economic issues have been the main policy concern among the public for the last 15 years in Turkey. Security/terrorism issues rank second to economic issues, but the difference between the two issues is considerably large, showing that the economy alone is the chief concern for a majority of Turkish citizens. Not surprisingly, economy has also overwhelmingly dominated the agendas of major political parties in Turkey since 2002, except for the Kurdish parties, indicating the responsiveness of political parties to the policy priorities of the larger public. Interestingly enough, Morçöl et al's content analysis of policy documents produced by the major think tanks in Turkey in Chapter Fourteen show that international relations is the dominant policy issue, followed by education policy.

This mismatch of dominant policy issues between political parties and public opinion, and think tanks and newspapers is an interesting one that may require further investigation to provide meaningful explanations. When we look at policy issues that were most commonly covered by mainstream newspapers in Turkey between 1995 and 2013, from Yavçan and Ongur's analyses in Chapter Fifteen we can see that security and terrorism issues dominated policy-related coverage, except for the year 2001, when Turkey faced one of the most alarming economic crises in the history of the modern Turkish Republic. However, Yavçan and Ongur's data consist of only the first pages of the papers. Considering all the major papers dedicated to the economy alone, their analysis may be deflating the economy coverage, to a certain extent.

Summaries

Part One, *Historical roots, styles and methods of policy analysis in Turkey*, sets the stage by providing an overview of the state of policy analysis in Turkey. In Chapter Two, Akif Argun Akdoğan, Göktuğ Morçöl, Gökhan Orhan and Mete Yıldız first provide an overview of policy analysis for readers who may not be familiar with this discipline. They underscore the critical events in history that gave rise to policy analysis, such as the development of the scientific method, rise of logical positivism, innovations in data collection and analyses and exacerbation of complex social problems such as poverty with increasing urbanisation and changes to the social structure of capitalistic societies. Contrary to conventional wisdom, they demonstrate that the Ottoman Empire relied heavily on advice to rulers from bureaucrats who were recruited solely on the merit principle. Akdoğan et al also deliver an extensive overview of key organisations and events that facilitated the development of policy analysis in Turkey, such as the intensification of ties with international organisations, the establishment of Public Administration at the Faculty of Political Science at Ankara University, and Public Administration Institute for Turkey and the Middle East (TODAİE). Akdoğan et al recognise most of the previously mentioned challenges for the advancement of policy analysis in Turkey, such as the domination of politics at the expense of technical knowledge during policy-making processes, a centralised administrative structure and limited academic interest in policy analytic approaches. Akdoğan et al conclude that policy studies have made significant progress in the last few decades in Turkey, despite still having a long way to go, and offer some pathways towards advancement such as promoting participatory mechanisms in policy-making and state-of-the-art analytical tools.

In Chapter Three, Akif Argun Akdoğan poses an interesting and important question: Why did the Justice and Development Party invalidate public policy tools such as strategic planning, performance auditing, regulatory impact analysis and performance budgeting despite being very committed to the administrative reforms that imported these tools to Turkey in the 2000s? Policy analytic tools were mostly transferred to the Turkish administrative system with the initiation and guidance of international and regional organisations such as the IMF, World Bank, EU and OECD. The overarching goal of the public administration reform that enabled the introduction of these policy analytic approaches was to ensure efficient and effective use of public resources in order to ensure accountability, transparency and increased performance in public organisations. However, various evaluative studies show that implementation of these tools has been mostly inadequate due to limited support from the government, as well as capacity and public service culture-related issues. By using the illustrative metaphor of a boomerang effect, borrowed from communication studies, Akdoğan focuses on the case of one particular organisation, the Court of Accounts, the main public organisation charged with performance auditing. Akdoğan traces the processes through which the Court of Accounts lost its scrutinising authority as its audits started to make the government vulnerable to criticism and revealed inherent inefficiencies and unlawful practices in various public organisations. This chapter is also crucial in terms of deciphering lingering policy implementation challenges in Turkey.

Chapter Four, Hüseyin Gül's and Muhittin Acar's contribution, presents an overview of the major methods and techniques that are commonly used in policy-oriented research. This chapter first provides a more universal discussion of positivist and post-positivist traditions in policy analysis and research. In order to demonstrate the major methodological trends and styles of policy research within the Turkish context, the authors conduct a content analysis of academic works produced by Turkish scholars, including scholarly journal articles, theses, dissertations, book chapters, conference proceedings and professional reports. Gül and Acar identify education, health, urbanisation, environment and gender as the leading policy issue areas examined by Turkish policy scholars. This chapter also shows that political scientists and public administration scholars produce most policy-oriented academic studies, a stark contrast with the US where a large number of economists tend to study numerous policy issue areas. The major finding of this chapter is very bleak; about 75 per cent of the documents analysed are basically deprived of any specific methodology, and most of the studies are based on simple literature reviews or reviews of existing policies through examinations of laws and regulations. However, a small number of studies use more rigorous techniques such as case studies, content analysis and regression analysis. Gül and Acar foresee mixed methodology and multidisciplinary research as the most adequate approach to address the complex and deepening social problems of the 21st century.

In Part Two, *Policy analysis by governments*, the contributors focus on recent administrative reforms and legislative changes, as well as policy analysis by different levels of government including central and local governments. These chapters provide a meticulous account of both the formal and informal institutional environments that shape policy-making and policy analysis in the most powerful executive governmental units in Turkey. Uğur Sadioğlu in Chapter Five analyses changes to the structure of central government in Turkey with an emphasis on the recent transition to the presidential system. Sadioğlu starts with a review of amendments to the constitution since the early Republic in order to demonstrate the shifts in policy-making power among the President, Prime Minister, Council of Ministers and Parliament. This historical examination indicates a trend towards centralisation and transfer of power to presidency since the early 1980s. Next Sadioğlu assesses the legal and institutional changes expected as a result of the 2017 referendum that was won by the 'yes' votes (51.4%) and passed Law no 6771 to amend the constitution towards a full presidential system. According to Sadioğlu, whether the new system will promote or hinder democracy cannot yet be determined since the institutional design of policy-making structures highly interacts with other factors such as political culture, political party system, election system and state of the economy.

In Chapter Six, Can Umut Çiner goes beyond the prevailing analysis of the Turkish administrative system that relies on strong central government–weak local government duality. While acknowledging the predominance of central governments over local bodies, Çiner reveals a more dialectical relationship between these two main levels. More specifically Çiner identifies organisations and mechanisms that facilitate collaboration between central and local governments with special emphasis on the conditions under which a local government's capacity to influence policy-making, both at the local and central level, is significantly augmented. Accordingly, this chapter provides a thorough analysis of special bodies in the Turkish administrative system, such as Special Provincial Administrations, Presidencies for Investment Monitoring and Coordination and Directorates for City Planning and Coordination. Çiner also discusses various other policy interaction mechanisms between central and local government such as Transportation Coordination Centres and Project Support Centres for Village Infrastructures that are mostly ignored in the existing literature on the Turkish administrative system. Çiner situates his argument on the relationship between central and local administrations within a comprehensive overview of the major changes to the administrative system since 2002, including legislative changes in public finance, local administration, public administration, public personnel management and ongoing changes towards the presidential system.

In Chapter Seven, Ulaş Bayraktar zooms in on major modes of policy analysis in Turkish municipalities using a critical perspective and Lasswell's policy cycle framework. Bayraktar mainly argues that elected mayors dominate all stages of policy analysis regardless of their political party affiliation, and characterises each stage basically as 'a one man show'. Bayraktar acknowledges the decentralisation of administrative structures since the 1980s that has furnished Turkish municipalities with increased powers and resources. However, he warns against a simplistic interpretation of these processes as giving more voice to local actors since decision-making within the municipalities is still a very top-down process without any well-functioning surveillance or evaluation mechanisms that may ensure accountability and democratic participation. Bayraktar is also very critical of recent changes to the service delivery functions of municipalities that include privatisation and sub-contracting and raise questions about generating public value and render elected mayors akin to CEOs (chief executive officers). With regard to agenda setting, Bayraktar emphasises the increasing predominance of mega projects among Turkish municipalities such as gigantic statues or the artificial waterway project, Istanbul Canal, which will connect the Black Sea with the Marmara Sea. According to Bayraktar, these types of projects have very poor cost-effectiveness but nevertheless are still very prevalent across most municipalities since they assist the over-empowered mayors in strengthening their populist policies. While delineating mayor-dominated stages of policy analysis, Bayraktar also portrays the mechanisms that render existing power-sharing institutions, such as the municipal councils, non-operational.

In Part Three, *Experts, international actors and public opinion*, the chapters focus on various actors that shape policy-making in Turkey. Chapter Eight by Gökhan Orhan analyses the role of experts in policy analysis in Turkey. This chapter first provides a historical and theoretical overview of the main scholarly debates on the role of experts in policy-making. Orhan's perspective on the role of experts in policy analysis is shaped by the interpretivist tradition. This chapter normatively recognises the essential role played by the experts and science in policy-making; however, Orhan also argues that both societal problems and recommended solutions are socially constructed, to a certain extent. Thus he contends that scrutiny over experts should be an indisputable practice in democratic societies. Orhan's main argument regarding the role of experts in policy-making is very much in line with the common themes across the chapters of the book: there is an evident proliferation of interest in experts since the 1980s as a result of the emergence of investigative journalism, independent researchers and consultancy firms, the rise of new social movements, professionalisation of political parties' electoral campaigns and intensified cooperation with international organisations. However, the use of expert knowledge in policy-making in Turkey is still quite limited due to the previously mentioned dominance of political decision-making. Orhan provides a number of revealing examples on the problematic relationship between experts and policy-makers, such as the bypassing of public experts on issues such as the urban renewal of historical sites, recent radical reforms to compulsory education and legislative changes to metropolitan municipalities. Orhan does not suggest that there is no expert involvement in these examples; he asserts that only a small group of *embedded experts* are involved in policy issues of critical importance, without any input from public experts or public opinion in general. Finally, Orhan reviews some recent examples of environmental disputes in Turkey, and states that not only experts whose views conflict with the government, but also citizens may be harmed as a result of ignoring certain projects and repression by policy-making agencies and companies that partner with those agencies in carrying out disputed projects.

One of the major cross-cutting themes across all chapters is the role of international organisations, more specifically, the EU's role in triggering policy change and shaping the formulation of domestic policies in Turkey. In Chapter Nine, Tolga Bölükbaşı, Ebru Ertugal and Saime Özçürümez and, go beyond simplistic accounts of the EU's role in shaping public policy in Turkey. Instead, they first analyse recent policy changes within three policy domains based on content analyses of policy-relevant documents and elite interviews. These policy domains include macroeconomic policies, regional development policies and immigration and asylum policies. For each domain, the authors trace the critical policy changes and study the extent to which these changes are attributable to the EU. They identify significant changes in macroeconomic policies since the early 2000s, but state that the IMF has been the leading international organisation that has shaped macroeconomic policy-making. With regard to regional development policy, the EU stands out as the main international actor in both triggering and shaping policy-making. However, the authors underline the fact that these changes have remained mostly regulative and implementation-related problems have inhibited significant outcomes on the ground. Finally, the EU has also been instrumental in determining recent immigration policies. Based on the analyses of these three cases, Bölükbaşı et al argue that there have been major policy changes in all domains, both in terms of policy density and policy intensity. With regard to the EU's direct role in these changes, they are cautious at making simplistic causal claims. While the transformative role of the EU is undisputable, it is very difficult to tease out its net causal effect, as other international actors tend to affect policy in similar directions in all policy domains discussed, and these changes cannot happen without the motivations and actions of domestic institutions and policy actors.

In Chapter Ten, the final chapter of Part Three, Sedef Turper examines the policy preferences of Turkish citizens for the period between 1990 and 2015 by combining data from various public opinion studies. Turper's chapter relies on well-established literature regarding the relationship between voters' policy preferences and the responsiveness of political parties and governments to those preferences. Assuming that such responsiveness is also present in the Turkish case, Turper first identifies salient policy issues areas for Turkish citizens and examines the policy preferences within those salient policy domains. In the first section of her analyses, Turper identifies significant gaps across demographic groups with regard to interest in politics. According to World Values Survey data, males and higher educated groups are consistently more interested in politics. Next, Turper shows that economic problems were the most salient policy problem for Turkish citizens between 2004 and 2013. More specifically, Turper's analysis shows that indirect taxes, unemployment, economic crises and inflation are the most pressing issues for citizens. With regard to policy preferences, Turper demonstrates that there is major demand for tax reform and considerable public support for privatisation.

Part Four of the book, *Parties and civil society-based policy analysis*, investigates salient issues and decision-making practices in political parties and civil society organisations. In Chapter Eleven, Selim Erdem Aytaç also builds his work on the literature indicating a positive relationship between voters' preferences and government responsiveness. Aytaç is mainly concerned with understanding dominant policy issue areas within political parties, points of convergence and divergence, and changing trends over time. For his study, Aytaç is using data from the election manifestos of four major parties in the Turkish political system: the Justice and Development Party (Adalet Kalkinma Partisi, AKP), Republican People's Party (Cumhuriyet Halk Partisi, CHP), Nationalist Movement Party (Millliyetci Hareket Partisi, MHP) and People's Democratic Party (Halklarin Demokratik Partisi, HDP and previous Kurdish parties that were banned by the constitutional court). Aytac's analyses reveal economy, welfare and quality of life as the dominant themes across all manifestos. While AKP, MHP and CHP manifestos emphasise increased public spending and expansion of social services, HDP has a limited focus on economy but underlines democracy, human rights and equality. Finally, emphasis and proposals on bureaucratic administration and inefficiencies seem to have declined steadily in AKP, MHP and CHP manifestos since 2002. This finding suggests the responsiveness of political parties to public demands since the effects of the economic crises have been slowly dwindling since the mid-2000s.

In Chapter Twelve, Güneş Ertan provides an overview of some of the policy analysis practices in civil society organisations (CSOs). Ertan first discusses the roots of weak civil society in Turkey with associated factors, and empirically shows the extent of limited civic participation in comparison with OECD countries. Using various secondary data on CSOs in Turkey, Ertan first shows that administrative structures of CSOs tend to be dominated by middle-aged, married males. Moreover, most CSOs barely meet the minimum number of members that is legally required to establish an association or foundation; this raises important questions about the representativeness of CSOs of the larger citizenry and their ability to mobilise for collective action. With regard to decision-making processes, Ertan argues that top-down decision-making is common in most CSOs, and states that the Tocquevillian idea that CSOs act as schools of democracy through participation and deliberation-based decision-making does not hold true in the Turkish case. With regard to agenda setting, Ertan asserts that most advocacy and service delivery-based CSOs rely on international funds, and donors of these funds have a significant impact on the prioritisation of certain societal problems over others. Ertan recognises the problematic aspects of international donors, such as the domination of project culture, but concludes overall that these funds have had a positive effect on Turkish CSOs in terms of pushing organisations to adopt policy analytic techniques such as strategic planning, input output analysis and programme evaluation.

Part Five of the book, *Academic, bureaucratic and advocacy-based policy analysis*, concentrates on public policy education in Turkey, the nexus of public policy and media, and policy analysis in bureaucracies and think tanks. In Chapter Thirteen, Caner Bakır and Mehmet Kerem Çoban focus on macroeconomic stability and financial stability-related proactive policy formulation and implementation by the Central Bank of the Republic of Turkey in response to a surge in capital inflows into Turkey between 2010 and 2011. Based on triangulation of various data, they illustrate the utility of interrelated policy design, analysis, learning and capacity literatures in understanding *analysis in policy*. They find that internal sources of policy capacity of the Central Bank in policy analysis also highlight the significance of the much-neglected political support given to the Central Bank in its policy design and implementation, enhancing its policy capacity. They argue that proactive behaviour in policy design and implementation at organisational level is most likely when a central bank has a strong policy capacity.

In Chapter Fourteen, Göktuğ Morçöl, Özer Köseoğlu, Mehmet Zahid Sobacı and Ömer Faruk Köktaş examine think tanks operating in Turkey. They first investigate the historical roots of think tanks in Turkey and identify the liberal political environment in the 1960s and initiation of economic integration with the European Economic Community as critical factors that led to the emergence of the first generation of think tanks such as the Turkish Economic and Social Studies Committee, Economic Research Foundation and Economic Development Facility. Swift adoption of neoliberalisation in the early 1980s also fostered the establishment of think tanks that may do research and represent the interests of the private sector. Accelerated integration with the EU in the late 1990s generated an imminent need for a new generation of thinks tanks to analyse the implications of rapidly progressing reform processes. Next, they provide their findings of content analysis of policy documents produced by major think tanks in Turkey. Their main goals are to examine the dominant policy issue areas studied by think tanks, and the extent to which these policy documents rely on policy analytic tools and methodologies. The analyses by Morçöl et al show that international relations by far is the most common topic studied by think tanks in Turkey, followed by politics and education policy. With regard to geographical concentration, a majority of analysed documents focus on Turkey and the Middle East region, especially following the Arab Uprisings in 2010, with very few papers relating to other geographies such as Europe, Africa and Central Asia. Finally, Morçöl et al demonstrate that a majority of policy papers do not rely on any data or analysis. Common sources of data among a minority of papers are interviews or secondary data. Finally, among papers that rely on data, the most common analyses techniques include descriptive statistics with very few cases of modelling or other inferential methods.

In Chapter Fifteen, Başak Yavçan and Hakan Övünç Ongur aim to demonstrate the variation in the salience of different policy issue areas in ideologically different media outlets as well as how these issues are framed differently. Yavçan and Ongur's analysis is based on content analysis of five major newspapers – mainstream centrist papers *Hürriyet*, *Milliyet* and *Sabah*, the leftist paper *Cumhuriyet* and conservative paper *Zaman* – for the period between 1995 and 2015. In their analysis Yavçan and Ongur show that domestic political/ideological issues constitute the predominant category of content. However, with regard to policy issues, the economy is the major policy domain covered across all papers. Security/terror-related issues are also noticeable. In terms of the agenda-setting functions of the media, coverage of corruption is evident; however, Yavçan and Ongur argue that the agenda-setting functions of Turkish media is rather limited. Instead, they observe a disproportionate focus on reporting in media on what the government does or says. Yavçan and Ongur also provide some evidence for the declining critical tone of the Turkish media outlets over time, a trend that further suggests the agenda-setting powers of Turkish media may be weakening.

The final chapter of the book, Chapter Sixteen by Mete Yıldız and Cenay Babaoğlu, traces the evolution and current state of public policy education in Turkey. Yıldız and Babaoğlu provide dramatic data on the exponential increase in courses and graduate programmes in public policy since the late 2000s in Turkey. While both courses and graduate programmes could be counted on the fingers of one hand in the early 1990s, there were about 50 undergraduate courses and 35 Master's level courses by 2016. According to Yıldız and Babaoğlu, the dramatic increase in recent years is mostly due to increases in the number of new faculty returning to Turkey with degrees in policy-focused PhD programmes from North American and European countries. In their analyses of newly emerging graduate programmes and policy majors since 2010, Yıldız and Babaoğlu consider the weak link between theory and real life applications/case studies, superficial application of quantitative methodologies, lack of qualified instructors and students' lack of knowledge on the discipline as major limitations that impede the growth and institutionalisation of these new programmes and majors. They conclude that despite the positive trends in public policy education in Turkey, these developments have mostly been driven by supply; the demand for policy education does not appear as strong, and more research is needed to understand the demand aspect.

Notes

[1] Policy entrepreneurs couple multiple streams and capture influential politicians setting the governmental agenda (Kingdon, 1995), while institutional entrepreneurs move beyond this policy work. They have multiple identities, strong discursive skills and operate in all stages of public policy-making processes to deliver institutional and policy changes (for a detailed discussion, see Bakır, 2009, 2013, chapter 4; Bakır and Jarvis, 2017, 2018).

[2] It is interesting to note that the Turkish Treasury did not have the knowledge of the amount, maturity and cost of the public debt it was supposed to manage before the 2001 crisis due to its poor administrative and policy capacity. The collection, mining and analysis of data, coupled

with the use of forecasting and risk management tools contributing to policy formulation and analysis were introduced following this law (see Bakır, 2012a, chapter 6). An institutional policy entrepreneur was in close coordination and collaboration with the IMF and its interlocutors at the Treasury in this bureaucratic capacity-building (Bakır, 2012a, chapter 6).

References

Abakay, A. (2008) *Bakan Danismaninin Not Defteri* [*Notes of a minister's analyst*], Ankara: Imge Yayinevi.

Akdoğan, A.A. (2011) 'Türkiye'de kamu politikası disiplinin tarihsel izleri' ['Historical roots of public policy discipline in Turkey'], in F. Kartal (ed) *Türkiye'de Kamu Yönetimi ve Kamu Politikaları* [*Public administration and public policy in Turkey*], Ankara: TODAİE.

Allison, G. (2008) 'Emergence of schools of public policy: Reflections by a founding dean', in M M. Moran, M. Rein and R.E. Goodin (eds) *The Oxford handbook of public policy*, Oxford: Oxford University Press, pp 58–79.

Bakır, C. (2009) 'Policy entrepreneurship and institutional change: Multilevel governance of central banking reform', *Governance*, vol 22, no 4, pp 571-98.

Bakır, C. (2012a) 'Organizational change in economic bureaucracy in Turkey, 1980-2010: Interactions with national and global dynamics', TUBITAK Project No 108K511, Unpublished report.

Bakır, C. (2012b) 'Maliye burokrasisinde orgutsel degisim ve vergi denetim Kurulu Baskanliginin Kurulmasi' ['Organisational change in fiscal bureaucracy and the establishment of Tax Inspection Board'], *Amme Idaresi Dergisi* [*Journal of Public Administration*], vol 45, no 2, pp 81-102.

Bakır, C. and Jarvis, D. (2017) 'Institutional entrepreneurship and institutional change in public policy: linking ideas, actors and institutions', *Policy and Society*, vol 36, no 4, pp 465-631.

Bakır, C. and Jarvis, D. (2018) *Institutional entrepreneurship and policy change: Theoretical and empirical explorations*, Basingstoke: Palgrave.

Craft, J. and Howlett, M. (2012) 'Policy formulation, governance shifts and policy influence', *Journal of Public Policy*, vol 32, no 2, pp 79-98.

Craft, J. and Wilder, M. (2017) 'Catching a second wave: Context and compatibility in advisory system dynamics', *Policy Studies Journal*, vol 45, no 1, pp 215-39.

Comfort, L.K. (2007) 'Crisis management in hindsight: Cognition, communication, coordination, and control', *Public Administration Review*, vol 67, no 1, 189-97.

deLeon, P. (1997) *Democracy and the policy sciences*, New York: SUNY Press.

deLeon, P. (2008) 'The historical roots of the field', in M. Moran, M. Rein and R.E. Goodin (eds) *The Oxford handbook of public policy*, Oxford: Oxford University Press, pp 39-57.

Dryzek, J.S. (1989) 'Policy sciences of democracy', *Polity*, vol 22, no 1, pp 97-118.

Dunn, W.N. (1994) *Public policy analysis*, Upper Saddle River, NJ: Prentice Hall Inc.

Fischer, F. and Gottweis, H. (2012) *The argumentative turn revisited: Public policy as communicative practice*, Durham, NC: Duke University Press.

Fişek, K. (1982) 'The Bonapartist origins and failings of Central and Provincial State Administration in Turkey: A case study in administrative transplantation', in *Public administration and management: Problems of adaptation in different socio-cultural contexts*.

Heper, M. (1976) '*Traditional tendencies* in the upper reaches of the bureaucracy in a changing Turkey', *Turkish Public Administration Annual*, no 2, pp 121-53.

Heper, M. (1982) 'Bürokrasi' ['Bureaucracy'], in *Cumhuriyet Dönemi Türkiye Ansiklopedisi* [*Encyclopaedia of Republican era Turkey*], İstanbul: İletişim, vol 2, pp 290-7.

Heper, M. (2000) 'The Ottoman legacy and Turkish politics', *Journal of International Affairs*, pp 63-82.

Heper, M. and Sayari, S. (2002) *Political leaders and democracy in Turkey*, Lanham, MD: Lexington Books.

Howlett, M. and Migone, A. (2013) 'The permanence of *temporary services*: The reliance of Canadian federal departments on policy and management consultants', *Canadian Journal of Public Administration*, vol 56, no 3, pp 369-90.

Jordan, A. and Turnpenny, J. (eds) (2015) *The tools of policy formulation: Actors, capacities, venues and effects*, Cheltenham: Edward Elgar Publishing.

Kalaycıoglu, E. (2002) *Civil society in Turkey: Continuity or change? Turkish transformation: New century, new challenges*, Huntingdon: Eothen Press.

Kingdon, J.W. (1995) *Agendas, alternatives, and public policies* (2nd edn), New York: Longman.

Lasswell, H.D. (1951) 'The policy orientation', in D. Lerner and H. Lasswell (eds) *The policy sciences: Recent developments in score and methods*, Stanford, CA: Stanford University Press.

Lasswell, H.D. (1970) 'The emerging conception of the policy sciences', *Policy Sciences*, vol 1, no 1, pp 3-14.

O'Toole, L.J. (1986) 'Policy recommendations for multi-actor implementation: An assessment of the field', *Journal of Public Policy*, vol 6, no 2, pp 181-210.

Parlak, B. and Sobacı, Z. (2012) *Ulusal ve Küresel Perspektifte Kamu Yönetimi Teori ve Pratik* [*Public administration theory and practice in national and global perspective*], MKM Yayıncılık, Bursa, Mart.

Pressman, J.L. and Wildavsky, A. (1984) *Implementation* (3rd edn), Berkeley, CA: University of California Press [earlier editions published in 1973, 1979].

Radin, B.A. (2000) *Beyond Machiavelli: Policy analysis comes of age*, Washington, DC: Georgetown University Press.

TÜBA (Türkiye Bilimler Akademisi [Turkish Academy of Sciences]) (2005) *Scientific research and policy*, Ankara [in Turkish].

Part One
Historical roots, styles and methods of policy analysis in Turkey

TWO

The past, present and future of policy analysis in Turkey

Akif Argun Akdoğan, Göktuğ Morçöl, Gökhan Orhan and Mete Yıldız

Historical and global context of policy analysis in Turkey

In this chapter we trace the evolution of policy analysis in Turkey. The roots of policy analytical practices and thinking in today's Turkey can be traced back to the administrative traditions of the Ottoman Empire, when there were some practices that would fit the most general definition of policy analysis: giving advice to rulers or policy-makers for decision-making. There were efforts by Ottoman intellectuals to adopt the European scientific knowledge and practices to produce policy-relevant knowledge in the late 19th and early 20th centuries. The European and American influences continued in the Republican era, as the leaders made more systematic efforts to apply scientific knowledge and methods in policy-making. The knowledge transfer from Europe and the US was accelerated in the 1990s by Turkish academics who gained their advanced educational degrees abroad. They then began to teach courses on policy analysis at universities, organising public policy conferences in this and following decades.

Harold Lasswell, in his conceptualisation of the 'policy sciences of democracy' (Lasswell, 1951, 1971), most cogently articulated the body of knowledge the Turkish academics transferred. As Dunn (2012) points out, Lasswell's articulation followed centuries of developments in giving advice to the rulers of human societies. These rulers sought advice from 'symbol specialists' (that is, shamans, the clergy and the educated) before making decisions about when to plant crops, when to go to war against a rival tribe, and so on. These forms of advice were based on mysticism – they were not 'scientific' in the sense we would use the term today. Later in human history, the practice of advice giving was codified in major texts such as the Code of Hammurabi and Confucius and Kautilya's treatises, in Mesopotamia, China and India respectively. Centuries after these developments – with the Enlightenment thinking in the late 17th and early 18th centuries and the developments in scientific methods in the 19th and early 20th centuries – systematic and empirical information collection and analysis became possible, which constituted the foundations of Lasswell's articulation of the policy sciences.

The backdrop of the period of Enlightenment and the development of scientific methods led to a series of social and economic transformations in Europe and the US. The Industrial Revolution created the conditions for massive migrations to cities and the ensuing social problems, such as sharpening social class divisions and increasing poverty and health epidemics in cities. The new means of transportation and communication (rail systems and nationwide postal services), combined with advances in data collection methods (for example, surveys) and quantitative analytical methods enabled European and US governments to conduct nationwide population censuses and surveys on such social problems – the first systematic and nationwide censuses in the US were carried out in 1790 and in England in 1801 (Dunn, 2012, p 35). The surveys of social problems that were conducted by the Manchester and London Statistical Societies in England were enabled by innovations in data collection and quantitative analytical methods (Dunn, 2012, p 36). Consequently, some European countries such as England managed to alleviate the problems of poverty, crime and contagious diseases by applying quantitative and statistical methods (Porter, 2008, p 240; Yeo, 2008, p 83).

Belief in science and advances in survey methods and quantitative analyses during the Enlightenment culminated in the formulation of positivism by Auguste Comte in the 19th century. Logical positivist philosophers (Vienna Circle of Logical Empiricism), such as Rudolf Carnap, Otto Neurath and Moritz Schlick, codified positivism in the early 20th century. Parallel to this development, the US federal government made significant efforts to collect and analyse information about social conditions, and employed social scientists to generate policy-relevant knowledge. These efforts intensified after the First World War, particularly during the Great Depression, as the social and economic problems and conflicts became more acute, and the American people turned increasingly to federal government in search of solutions for their problems.

Lasswell's formulation of the 'policy sciences of democracy' was an attempt to articulate a conceptual framework for the developments in the early 20th century. His formulation reflected a key concern of his and many other political scientists of his time: what should be the role of expert knowledge in policy-making in a democratic society? Lasswell (1971, p 15) wrote: 'policy sciences of democracy ... is directed toward knowledge needed to improve the practice of democracy', whose ultimate goal would be a 'fuller realization of human dignity' (1951, p 5). With his formulation, Lasswell created a conceptual problem and potential dilemma that has kept many theorists of policy analysis busy to this day. In essence he posited that policy sciences would have two potentially conflicting aims: that of generating objective knowledge through empirical scientific thinking and methods, on the one hand, and that of 'improving democracy' and 'realisation of human dignity', which is necessarily value-laden. Farr, Hacker and Kazee (2006, p 585) argue that the inner contradiction in Lasswell's formulation has continued to confound academics and practitioners. They ask, are political scientists (or policy analysts) obligated to serve democratic values? And what are those values anyway?

There are two implicit assumptions in Lasswell's conceptualisation that affected the practice and thinking in policy analysis in the following decades: humans are capable of making rational decisions and the government is capable of solving social problems. Without rational thinking, no science would be possible. Lasswell's policy scientists have to be rational, by definition. 'The government' is a unified actor that can act rationally. This conceptualisation of 'the government' as a unified actor is reflected in major textbooks in the field. Dye (2017, p 1) defines public policy as 'whatever governments choose to do or not to do.' According to Simon (2007, p 1), 'Public policy is ... what government ought or ought not do, and does or does not do.'

Lasswellian assumptions of objective knowledge generation through rational thinking and analysis, pursuit of democratic ideals and human dignity and the primary role of the government in solving social problems did not meet major challenges in the 1960s, but were questioned as the practice and theory of policy analysis evolved in the following decades (Radin, 2013). In the 1960s, the federal government in the US expanded, a few federal governmental agencies (for example, the US Department of Defense) formed their units of policy analysis, federal agencies designed and implemented programmes to address social problems such as poverty and policy analytical methods such as cost-benefit analysis and programme budgeting were developed and refined. The practice of policy analysis spread to other countries in the 1970s and 1980s, particularly in the 1990s, as part of the globalisation of the world economy.

Radin (2013) notes that during this geographic expansion, policy analysts began to realise that the 'boundaries' of the systems they studied and the 'targets' of policies and programmes they designed could no longer be defined clearly. The boundaries between 'domestic' and 'international' issues and between the 'private' and 'public' realms were blurred. In the 1990s, as the policy think tanks proliferated, the federal government's policy analysis units lost their near monopoly in producing policy-relevant information.

The blurring of boundaries and the loss of federal government's monopoly over policy analysis challenged the notion that policy advice was supposed to be objective and based on rational analyses. It became more difficult to differentiate between 'objective analysis' and 'value-laden politics'. Radin (2013) observes that the world of policy analysis has become even more complex in the early 21st century, as public policies are made and implemented in networks of governmental and non-governmental actors.

The developments in the environment and practice of policy analysis in the 1990s and 2000s instigated theoretical challenges to the Lasswellian vision of policy sciences. The first line of challenges was directed at the assumptions of rationality and scientificity in policy analysis. Critical theorist Mark Fischer (1990, 1995, 2009) lauded Lasswell's goals of furthering democracy and realising human dignity, but he criticised the deceptive image of scientificity the 'policy sciences' created. Fischer argued that the practice of policy analysis masked the power relations in societies and helped reproduce the existing inequitable distribution of resources.

Another line of challenges came from rational choice (public choice, polycentrism and institutional rational choice) theorists, who did not critique the rationality assumption, but the role attributed to the government in solving society's problems (see, for example, Ostrom, 1990; Friedman, 1996; Mueller,

1997; McGinnis, 1999). In this theoretical framework, governmental units and agencies are viewed as actors who play roles in policy processes, together with many others. Public choice theorists particularly challenge the view of 'government' as a unified actor that can make cohesive decisions and take actions; instead, they argue, governments are composed of multiple 'self-seeking' actors. Rational choice theorists in general also challenge the notion that 'the government' represents the 'public interest' as opposed to 'private interests', and thus they question the validity of the distinction between the 'public' and 'private' realms.

The developments in Europe and the US since the 17th century affected the evolution of the policy analysis education, research and practice in Turkey. However, those effects were mediated by the country's own history and traditions. Both in the Ottoman and Republican periods, several attempts were made to bring European and US knowledge and practices in policy analysis to the country, but were not adopted easily or fully, sometimes because of the lack of organisational capacity and other times because of the resistance of politicians and bureaucrats. We now turn to this history.

Policy analysis practice in Turkey's history

The Ottoman Empire had its own tradition of policy analysis in the broadest sense of the term: giving advice to rulers. The governmental institutions of the Empire were more advanced in producing polity-relevant knowledge compared to its contemporaries in Europe and the Middle East. During its earlier centuries, the Ottoman government was admired by European thinkers such as Trajano Boccalini (1556-1613) as a living example of the ideal polity of the Renaissance: 'an artificial construction which had been concisely and purposely built up, a State mechanism which was arranged like a clock, and which made use of the various species and strengths and qualities of men as its springs and wheels' (quoted in Gordon, 1991, p 11). This clockwork was based on the principles of merit in recruiting military and civilian bureaucrats. Austrian ambassador Ogier Ghiselin de Busbecq declared in 1694: 'Turks esteem no men for their birth, but only for their own performed accomplishments' (quoted in Çırakman, 2001, p 52).

The fortunes of the Ottoman Empire began to turn after the consecutive defeats its armies faced against European forces in the later centuries of its 600-year existence, particularly in the 19th century. The rulers of the Empire then began to implement a series of policy reforms inspired by developments in Europe – the major reason for this was the thinking that the successes of European countries in the battlefields had resulted from advancements in science and scientific methods.

Inspired by European practices, the Ottoman bureaucrats began using scientific data collection methods to compile information about the population of the Empire. A few decades after the censuses conducted in the US and England, a nationwide census was conducted in the Ottoman Empire in 1831. The aim was to determine how many soldiers could be recruited for military service, and to make an inventory of goods belonging to peasants to find out their tax collection potentials. In the late 19th century the bureaucrats of the Empire expanded the scope of their data collection to include information about foreign trade, the general population, agriculture, education and industry. The lack of qualified personnel for data collection, organisational problems in the governmental agencies and technical difficulties limited the accuracy and quality of the data collected; consequently, the data were not used to formulate or evaluate policies (İnalcık and Pamuk, 2000, p iv).

The founders of the Republic of Turkey made more systematic efforts to use data collected using scientific methods in policy-making. They came from ranks of the military and civilian bureaucrats of the Empire, who were well versed in the European and US ideals and the trends of the late 19th and early 20th centuries (Köker, 1992, p 114). An example of the influence of these trends and one of the early signs that the Modern Turkish Republic was determined to use scientific methods of policy analysis in making policies was Mustafa Kemal Atatürk's invitation to US pragmatist philosopher John Dewey[1] to Turkey in 1924. Dewey proposed that the educational system in Turkey should be based on problem-solving and scientific thinking (Ata, 2000, p 127).

The US influence on Turkish public administration and policy-making gained pace in the 1950s, with the ascension of the pro-US Democrat Party to power. In this decade, a series of US experts who were invited to Turkey drafted reports about the reorganisation of Turkish public administration (for example the Dorr (Hilts) Report, the Neumark Report, the Barker Report, and the Thornburg Report, as cited in Yayman, 2008) and how to use modern policy analytical techniques (Sözen, 2003, p 203).

More serious and systematic efforts in adopting and applying policy analytical methods were made in the 1960s. The State Planning Organisation (SPO) was established in 1960, with the help of Dutch economist Jan Tinbergen (1903-94). SPO prepared the consecutive five-year development plans in this and in following decades. Governmental institutions were required to use policy instruments such as input-output analysis and cost-benefit analysis in preparations of their investment proposals. SPO reviewed these proposals for their compatibility with five-year plans and it had the authority to reject them on technical/analytical grounds (Sezen, 1999, p 221). This was too much power granted to a technical organisation, the Parliament and government thought later; consequently, the powers of SPO were diminished with amendments in its enabling law in the 1970s. The experience of SPO illustrates that attempts to use analytical methods in the formulation and evaluation of public policies in Turkey were frustrated by some politicians who did not want to yield some of their policy-making powers to technocrats and the sections of bureaucracy that held on to their legalistic traditions.

After the military coup in 1980, another series of efforts was made by political leaders to apply policy analytical methods in policy-making. These efforts were also demanded by the International Monetary Fund (IMF) and The World Bank, from which the Turkish government had requested financial and technical assistance. In 1983 Turgut Özal (1927-93), who became the first Prime Minister after the first parliamentary elections after the coup, believed in expert knowledge in policy-making and sought to replace political with technocratic decision-making. Like the leaders of the 1950s Democrat Party, Özal thought that bureaucracy was too slow, cumbersome and unresponsive to people's demands, or it was ideologically too committed to state intervention, and was not market-oriented (Heper and Sancar, 1998, p 151). In order to overcome the resistance by traditional bureaucracy, Özal created new agencies. Policy analytical methods were applied in some sections of these new agencies, such as the enclaves of the Undersecretaries of Treasury and Foreign Trade, and to a lesser extent in the more traditional Ministry of Finance. The new agencies had more qualified personnel (Heper and Keyman, 1998, p 267), and many of the directors of these agencies were graduates of US universities.

The political instability and economic problems the country faced in the 1990s prevented the implementation of the earlier IMF and World Bank recommendations, which included the introduction of policy analytical methods in decision-making (Çetin, 2010, p 7). The intense competition between political parties to seize power in a fragmented political party system and the populist policies of the successive coalition governments made it difficult to apply any analytical methods in policy-making.

The populist policies led the country to a major economic crisis in 2001. The loss of trust in the established political parties shifted the votes to the newly established Justice and Development Party (JDP) led by Recep Tayyip Erdoğan in the 2002 elections. In order to end the economic crisis, JDP sought the help of The World Bank and IMF, and adopted the neoliberal reform policies they required. Turkey then became able to access foreign loans, which were conditioned on the initiation of public sector reforms and the use of policy analytical tools. Another factor that contributed to the applications of these tools was the European Union's (EU) confirmation in 1999 of Turkey becoming a candidate country for full membership.

In the first decade of the 21st century the pace of the applications of the tools was mixed, particularly after the loosening of ties with the EU and the end of stand-by agreements with the IMF. The government's requirement that each government agency prepare a regulatory impact analysis report before submitting a draft bill to the prime ministry has been largely ignored, however: very few draft bills included any analyses. A report published by the Turkish Academy of Sciences showed that scientific data were rarely used in the formulation of public policies in Turkey, with policy-makers mostly choosing to use personal observations and experience instead (TÜBA, 2005).

The Ministry of Development (former SPO) publishes guidelines for preparing investment proposals for all public organisations in Turkey every year (see www.kalkinma.gov.tr/Pages/YatirimProgramiHazirlamaEsaslari.aspx). For investment proposals costing over 10 million Turkish liras, the organisation that proposes the investment should follow the guidelines for feasibility analysis. In the feasibility report, the organisation should justify the project by presenting a needs analysis, estimates the costs, inputs and ouputs of the project, and, in some cases, sensitivity and risk analyses. These requirements are only occasionally met, however. Because the requirements for funding public programmes and projects in Turkey are very loose, their administrators are not motivated to apply modern public policy tools and techniques. Political support for an investment project seems to be more important then sound policy analysis for its approval.

The public programmes conducted under EU guidelines carry out policy analyses more systematically. These organisations are required to follow the EU's project preparation, implementation and evaluation guidelines to be eligible for these funds. Examples of such organisations are İnsan Kaynaklarının Geliştirilmesi Program Otoritesi (Human Resources Development Programme Authority) and Tarım ve Kırsal Kalkınmayı Destekleme Kurumu (TKDK) (Agriculture and Rural Development Institution). Both organisations use modern public policy monitoring and evaluation tools to execute the programming, budgeting and implementation phases of projects that are outsourced by EU programmes. Both have their own monitoring information systems in which they can follow the projects' inputs, outputs and outcomes. The Agriculture and Rural Development Institution issued an impact evaluation report about the results of the projects and the funds distributed to agricultural entrepreneurs in 2015 (TKDK, 2015).

Policy analysis education in Turkey

Despite the reluctance of the Turkish bureaucracy and politicians in applying policy analytical methods, there is a growing interest in policy studies and policy analysis in the higher education institutions. The study of public policy analysis in Turkey can be traced back to the foundation of the first Public Administration Department in the Faculty of Political Science at Ankara University in 1953, which was recommended in the Barker Report of 1950. The department was founded and managed initially by US professors, who were also influential in setting the course schedules, giving lectures and conducting research in the field of public administration. This arrangement was part of a protocol between the US Department of State and Ankara University to send Turkish students to study public administration at New York University in exchange for temporarily assigning this university's faculty members to Ankara University (Adolfson, 1958, p 232).

A parallel development was the founding of the Public Administration Institute for Turkey and the Middle East (Türkiye ve Orta Doğu Amme İdaresi Enstitüsü, TODAİE) in 1952, as a result of a protocol signed between the United Nations (UN) and Turkish Government. The Institute's goal was to train civilian servants to use policy analytical methods, but it did not fulfil that mission due to lack of interest in the government for such methods (Tural, 2014). The governing Democrat Party was interested in introducing policy analysis methods only when they enabled the government to attract more foreign aid, investments, credits and loans. Consequently, Turkish civil servants continued to formulate policies in their traditional and most legalistic ways.

The teaching of policy analysis in Turkish universities at undergraduate and graduate levels began in earnest in the early 1990s; since then, the numbers of policy analysis courses and programmes have increased substantially (Yıldız et al, 2011). These are discussed in detail in Chapter Sixteen, later in this volume. Chapter Sixteen shows that there was only one graduate programme on public policy in 2011 in Turkey (at Sabancı University). Four others have been added since then: at Hacettepe University (2013), Marmara University (2103), Gazi University (2014), and Nevşehir University (2014) (Yıldız et al, 2017).

The first documented courses on policy analysis were taught at TODAİE, the Middle East Technical University and Galatasaray University in the 1990s (Yıldız et al, 2011). As explained in detail in Chapter Sixteen, the 2000s witnessed a continuous increase in the number and diversity of policy analysis courses at both undergraduate and graduate levels. Yıldız et al (2011) found that policy analysis courses were taught almost exclusively in political science and public administration departments and/or institutes. Policy analysis courses may also be offered in other social science departments (for example, education, social services, economics, foreign policy and finance), but we were unable to find any documents verifying their existence at the time of the writing this chapter.

Yıldız et al's (2011, pp 353-4) analysis of the syllabi of the public policy/policy analysis courses taught at universities in Turkey and their interviews with the course instructors indicate that five factors can help explain their increase. First, the Turkish public administration students who received their Master's and PhD degrees from US and European universities in the 1980s and 1990s transferred their knowledge of public policy to the courses they taught after they returned to Turkey as new faculty members. Second, Turkish public administration faculty members who visited US and European institutions during their sabbatical leaves observed the policy-related courses at their host institutions and then brought back the idea of teaching a similar course in Turkey. Third, the PhD students of the first generation of policy analysis instructors graduated and became the second generation of public policy instructors at their institutions. Fourth, some public administration scholars found the public policy analysis process and concepts useful to analyse the recent global changes in public administration systems and their reflections in Turkey. Finally, the academic exchange programmes between Turkey and the EU countries contributed to the synchronisation of the curricula, including policy analysis courses, in Turkey.

Academic activities

There has been an increase in academic publications about policy analysis in Turkey. Olgun's (2015) analysis of papers published in *Amme İdaresi Dergisi* (AID), the flagship journal of the Turkish public administration academic community, identified relevant articles beginning with the first issue of the journal in 1968.

She identified three groups of articles. The first is the early articles that aimed to introduce the general theories and concepts of policy analysis to Turkey. They covered topics such as 'decision-making', 'system theory', 'planning-programming-budgeting system', 'cost-benefit analysis' and 'the use of mathematical techniques in public administration'. The second group of articles, which were published between 1998 and 2010, introduced the basic 'disciplinary knowledge' of policy analysis studies, such as the main theories of policy analysis, approaches, methods and actors. The third group includes applications of policy analytical methods, approaches, techniques, and so on, on different topics and areas. The earliest of these articles were published in 1979, and their numbers increased during the 1990s and 2000s. The increase in the overall number of policy-related articles in AID during the period of 1968 to 2015 is documented by Olgun (2017, p 84), and the results of her analyses are presented in Figure 2.1.

Figure 2.1: Policy-related articles in AID (1968–2015)

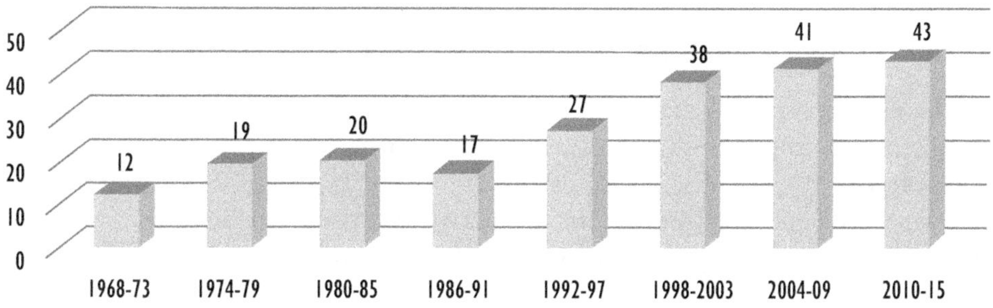

Period	Articles
1968-73	12
1974-79	19
1980-85	20
1986-91	17
1992-97	27
1998-2003	38
2004-09	41
2010-15	43

Source: Olgun (2017, p 84)

In addition to the journal articles, Turkish language policy analysis textbooks have been published, particularly in the 2000s. Examples are books by Çevik and Demirci (2015), Erkul and Gökdemir (2006), Kartal (2011), Kaptı (2011) and Yıldız and Sobacı (2013). These provided the teachers and students of public policy courses the much-needed Turkish language content by including the translation of at least parts of classical studies on public policy, summaries of theoretical developments in various book chapters and the applications of these theories and concepts in specific policy areas such as education, health and technology policies in Turkey.

Conferences and workshops have added strength to the academic activities in policy analysis in Turkey. There have been an increasing number of presentations on policy analysis-related papers at the Public Administration Forum (KAYFOR), the oldest and most well-established annual public administration conference of Turkey, since its establishment in 2003. The increasing importance of policy analysis was reflected in KAYFOR's 2012 theme: 'Transformation in public policy'.

In addition to participating in KAYFOR conferences, public policy researchers have been meeting at Public Policy Workshops since 2009 (detailed information about these is provided in Chapter Sixteen). These increased the awareness of the existence and development of policy studies in the general public and in the practitioner community in Turkey. The academics' output is likely to be positively affected by these workshops, which also provide a medium in which younger scholars receive feedback and encouragement for future studies.

An academic community of policy researchers in Turkey also created a knowledge repository, under the leadership and management of Hasan Engin Şener of Yıldırım Beyazıt University, and funded by researchers. This repository, named the 'Public Policy Analysis Study Group', is available at http://kamupolitikalari.org/index.php/Ana_Sayfa, and includes rich content regarding the past developments and current state of the policy analysis academic community, information about past Public Policy Workshops, exemplary syllabi, contact information for the academics, and so on.

Future of policy analysis in Turkey

As the previous sections have shown, policy analysis has a relatively long history in Turkey. In the Turkish public sector there have been repeated attempts to use policy analytical methods since the 1950s, but many of these efforts were frustrated by resistance from politicians who did not want to share their powers with technocrats and by bureaucrats who did not want to change their old ways of conducting business. The public sector has become more receptive to using policy analytical methods since the early 2000s. In academia, there is a growing interest in policy studies, which is reflected in the increase in numbers of courses taught, articles and books published, and conferences organised.

All these developments indicate that there is a vibrant environment for policy studies and the use of policy analysis in the country, and that we can be optimistic about the future of the field. However, there are also problems in the applications of policy analysis and the use of policy-relevant knowledge in the policy-making and implementation processes. We address these issues and discuss what they mean for the future next.

Problems in teaching and research

The most common forms of publications are theoretical pieces and descriptive studies on the historical development and methods of policy analysis. The translations of theoretical discussions contribute to the accumulation of knowledge in the Turkish literature (Kaptı, 2011; Çevik and Demirci, 2015), but there are limited applications of policy analysis (Kartal, 2011; Yıldız and Sobacı, 2013).

If we consider Lasswell's (1971) two categories of policy scientific studies, we can observe that there is far more emphasis in the Turkish literature on public policy studies (studies about how policies are actually made) than studies in policy-making (policy analysis and planning or policy and programme evaluation). The emphasis on the former in itself would be fine, but a common problem is that most of these studies simply summarise and describe historical developments in a chronological manner, without conducting detailed analyses of the relationships or factors that create social problems and possible points of interventions (Erkul and Gökdemir, 2006; Kartal, 2011). The models of policy processes that are described in major textbooks (see, for example, Dunn, 2012; Dye, 2017; Weible and Sabatier, 2018) are rarely applied in these studies.

Methods of policy analysis, planning or evaluation (for example, problem structuring, forecasting, cost-benefit analysis and experimental and quasi-experimental designs) are mainly taught in some industrial engineering departments at universities, but not in public administration or political science departments (see the syllabi at http://kamupolitikalari.org/index.php/Dersler). Because of the lack of teaching such courses at universities, future practitioners are not being trained in using them; consequently, policy studies and policy analysis may lose their relevancy in the policy-making processes and even in academia in Turkey.

Public policy problems are complex. The context of policy analysis has become even more complex in the early 21st century, with the globalisation of economies, increased interactions among human societies through the internet and through increased worldwide travel (Radin, 2013). Policy problems emerge as a result of complex interactions among a number of variables, and their solutions require the involvement of an ever-increasing number of players from several levels and sectors. Experts, officials from almost every level of government and non-state players have increasingly become involved in defining policy problems and making and implementing policies. There are theoretical frameworks that recognise the complexity of policy problems and the multiplicity of players: the advocacy coalition framework, the rational choice framework (more specifically, the institutional rational choice framework), the complex network governance framework and others (see Weible and Sabatier, 2018). These frameworks are not studied in depth at educational institutions in Turkey, and nor are they applied systematically in empirical studies.

Radin (2013) reminds us that it has become more difficult in the last few decades to differentiate between 'objective analysis' and 'value-laden politics' because of the proliferation of policy analysis done in think tanks around the world. This development forces policy scholars to take into account the roles of values (ideology, worldview) in policy-making. Interpretivist and critical policy scholars like Fischer (1990, 1995, 2009) critiqued technocratic perspectives and practices in policy analysis for ignoring values, and brought the critique of societal norms in to the centre of policy analysis. They also argued that policy analysis and policy-making practices should be participatory and deliberative. Participatory practices do not simply promote participants' subjective value positions, but they also encourage participants to work together in solving social problems, and hence they enhance democratic practices. There are only few critical policy studies that offer an alternative to technocratic approaches to policy-making and implementation in Turkey (Orhan, 2006, 2007, 2013).

Although Turkish government documents such as the Directive on Methods and Principles of Legislative Processes (Mevzuat Hazırlama Usul ve Esasları Hakkında Yönetmelik, see www.mevzuat.gov.tr/MevzuatMetin/3.5.20059986.pdf) require that participatory processes be used in the strategic planning process, regulatory impact assessments and the like, actual participatory practices are rare in Turkey. They are either limited to a certain stage of policy process to comply with procedures or are completely overlooked, and there are a number of problems in maintaining stakeholder participation (Yerlikaya, 2015, pp 84-110).

Good participatory practices require sound evidence that is generated by policy analysts to be presented to participants. The evidence used in these practices should be interdisciplinary and problem-oriented and policy-relevant. As noted above, the quantitative and qualitative analytical methods developed by researchers are not regularly taught at universities or used in policy-making processes. In the absence of sound analyses, ideological priorities and dominant interests are likely to shape the policy process.

Because policy problems are complex, their analyses require interdisciplinary research. In Turkey there are only rare examples of interdisciplinary research or policy integration or coordination. This is especially evident in the case of environmental policy. Instead of addressing the environmental consequences of investment projects and integrating environmental concerns into policy-making and the implementation process, policy-makers only make investment decisions on the basis of ensuring rapid economic returns.

Summary and conclusions

The discussions in this chapter provide a picture of the past, present and prospects for policy analysis and policy studies in Turkey. There is a long, indigenous tradition of providing policy-relevant information to rulers in Turkish history, but more systematic applications of policy analysis are recent. Ottoman intellectuals and bureaucrats used the data collection methods they learned from Europeans in the late 19th century. US scholars brought ideas of using scientific analyses in public decision-making to Turkey as early as in the first decades of the Turkish Republic. There were multiple attempts to apply analytical methods in policy-making between the 1950s and 1980s, and an academic literature on policy analysis and policy studies emerged in the 1970s in Turkey. All these developments came to a climax in the 1990s and 2000s. Turkish academics who gained their doctoral degrees in the US and Europe began teaching policy-related courses at their institutions in the 1990s. The political environment in the 2000s, particularly the prospects for Turkey's ascension to EU memberships, and the laws that were passed to comply with membership requirements, increased the number and extent of applications of analytical methods in public policy-making.

Policy analysis and policy studies have come a long way in Turkey, but they also have a long way to go. The increased numbers of courses taught at educational institutions, the papers published in academic journals and the applications of analytical methods in public decision-making in recent years are promising, although these courses do not cover advanced theories of policy processes or analytical methods sufficiently. Many of the publications are descriptive, but there were few applications of the methods such as cost-benefit analysis and social network analyses in recent publications. The legal requirements imposed on public agencies to conduct strategic planning and use of analyses in the early 2000s have not been implemented fully.

The traditions of Turkish politics and public bureaucracy have been resistant to analytical thinking and using evidence in policy-making. The centralised system of governance in Turkey has not been conducive to deal with the ever-increasing complexities of policy problems. The system has not made it easy for information to flow freely among policy stakeholders, and nor has it allowed them to participate in the policy-making processes systematically and effectively.

Many social theorists like Manuel Castells (2000) and Bob Jessop (1990) remind us that our world has become multi-centred and its problems more complex. Policy and governance scholars like Hubert Heinelt (2010) and Jacob Torfing et al (2012) demonstrate that not only governments, but also many other actors have to take part in trying to solve our collective problems, such as poverty, global warming and worldwide health epidemics. Applications of sophisticated analytical methods and meaningful participation by all stakeholders are needed to deal with these problems. It is yet to be seen whether and to what extent the Turkish governmental system will be able to evolve to meet these needs.

Note
[1] Torgerson (2007, pp 16-17) argues that Lasswell proposed his methods of social problem-solving following the direction set by John Dewey.

References
Adolfson, L.H. (1958) 'Üniversitelerin dış öğretim ve teknik yardım faaliyetleri', *SBF Dergisi*, vol 13, no 2, pp 235-9.

Ata, B. (2000) 'The influence of an American educator (John Dewey) on the Turkish educational system', *Turkish Yearbook of International Relations*, vol 31, pp 119-30.

Castells, M. (2000) *The rise of the network society*, Oxford: Blackwell.

Çetin, T. (2010) 'The role of institutions over economic change in Turkey', in T. Çetin and F. Yilmaz (eds) *Understanding the process of economic change in Turkey: An institutional approach*, New York: Nova Science Publishers, pp 21-39.

Çırakman, A. (2001) 'From tyranny to despotism: The Enlightenment's unenlightened image of the Turks', *International Journal of Middle East Studies*, vol 33, no 1, pp 49-68.

Çevik, H.H. and Demirci, S. (2015) *Kamu politikası* [*Public policy*] (2nd edn), Ankara: Seçkin.

Dunn, W.N. (2012) *Public policy analysis* (5th edn) Boston: Pearson.

Dye, T.R. (2017) *Understanding public policy* (15th edn), Boston, MA: Pearson.

Erkul, H. and Gökdemir, L. (eds) (2006) *Türkiye'de cumhuriyetin kuruluşundan günümüze uygulanan kamu politikaları*, Ankara: Detay.

Farr, J., Hacker, J. and Kazee, N. (2006) 'The policy scientist of democracy: The discipline of Harold D. Lasswell', *The American Political Science Review*, vol 100, no 4, pp 579-87.

Fischer, F. (1990) *Technocracy and the politics of expertise*, Newbury Park, CA: Sage.

Fischer, F. (1995) *Evaluating public policy*, Chicago, IL: Nelson-Hall Publishers.

Fischer, F. (2009) *Democracy and expertise: Reorienting policy inquiry*, Oxford: Oxford University Press.

Friedman, J. (ed) (1996) *The rational choice controversy: Economic models of politics reconsidered*, New Haven, CT: Yale University Press.

Gordon, C. (1991) 'Governmental rationality: An introduction', in G. Burchell, C. Gordon and P. Miller (eds) *The Foucault effect: Studies in governmentality*, Chicago, IL: University of Chicago Press, pp 1-51.

Heinelt, H. (2010) *Governing modern societies: Towards participatory governance*, New York: Routledge.

Heper, M. and Keyman, F. (1998) 'Double-faced state: Political patronage and the consolidation of democracy in Turkey', *Middle Eastern Studies*, vol 34, no 4, pp 259-77.

Heper, M. and Sancar, M.S. (1998) 'Is legal-rational bureaucracy a prerequisite for rational productive bureaucracy?', *Administration and Society*, vol 30, no 2, pp 143-65.

İnalcık, H. and Pamuk, Ş. (2000) Giriş [Introduction], In H. İnalcık and Ş. Pamuk (eds) *Osmanlı devleti'nde bilgi ve ıstatistik* [*Information and statistics in the Ottoman state*] Ankara: DİE Yayınları.

Jessop, B (1990) *State theory: Putting capitalist states in their place*, University Park, PA: The Pennsylvania State University Press.

Kaptı, A. (ed) (2011) *Kamu politikası süreci*, Ankara: Seçkin Yayıncılık.

Kartal, F. (ed) (2011) *Türkiye'de kamu yönetimi ve kamu politikaları* [*Public administration and public policies in Turkey*], Ankara: TODAİE.

Köker, L. (1992) *Demokrasi üzerine yazılar* [*Essays on democracy*], Ankara: İmge.

Lasswell, H.D. (1951) 'The policy orientation'. in D. Lerner and H. Lasswell (eds) *The policy sciences: Recent development in scope and method*, Stanford, CA: Stanford University Press, pp 1-17.

Lasswell, H.D. (1971) *A preview of policy sciences*, New York: American Elsevier.

McGinnis, M.D. (ed) (1999) *Polycentricity and local public economies: Readings from the workshop in political theory and policy analysis*, Ann Arbor, MI: University of Michigan Press.

Mueller, D.C. (ed) (1997) *Perspectives on public choice: A handbook*, Cambridge: Cambridge University Press.

Olgun, B. (2015) '*Amme İdaresi Dergisi*'nde kamu politikası çalışmalarının izini sürmek' ['Tracking public policy studies in the *Journal of Public Administration*'], Paper Presented at the 6th Public Policy Workshop, Sakarya University.

Olgun, B. (2017) 'Türkiye'de kamu politikaları çalışmalarının gelişiminin Amme Idaresi Dergisi'nde yayımlanmış makaleler üzerinden analizi: 1968-2015', Unpublished Master's thesis, Ankara: Hacettepe University.

Orhan, G. (2006) 'The politics of risk perception in Turkey: Discourse coalitions in the case of Bergama gold mine dispute', *Policy & Politics*, vol 34, no 4, pp 691-710.

Orhan, G. (2007) 'Institutions and ideas in the institutionalisation of Turkish environmental policy', *Critical Policy Analysis*, vol 1, no 1, pp 42-61.

Orhan, G. (2013) 'Türkiye'de çevre politikaları: Değişen söylemler, değişmeyen öncelikler', *Memleket Siyaset Yönetim Dergisi*, 19-20, 1-24.

Ostrom, E. (1990) *Governing the commons: The evolution of institutions for collective action*, Cambridge: Cambridge University Press.

Porter, T.M. (2008) 'Statistics and statistical methods', in T.M. Porter and D. Ross (eds) *The Cambridge history of science: The modern social sciences*, vol 7, Cambridge: Cambridge University Press, pp 238-50.

Radin, B.A. (2013) *Beyond Machiavelli: Policy analysis reaches midlife* (2nd edn), Washington, DC: Georgetown University Press.

Sezen, S. (1999) *Devletçilikten özelleştirmeye Türkiye'de planlama* [*Planning in Turkey from etatism to privatization*], Ankara: TODAİE.

Simon, C.A. (2007) *Public policy: Preferences and outcomes*, New York: Pearson/Longman.

Sözen, S. (2003) 'Administrative reforms in Turkey: Imperatives, efforts and constraints', *Ankara Universitesi SBF Dergisi*, vol 60, no 3, pp 196-214.

TKDK (2015) *Tarım ve Kırsal Kalkınmayı Destekleme Kurumu, desteklenen projeler etki değerlendirme raporu* [*Agriculture and Rural Development Support Institution, supported projects impact assessment report*], Ankara: TKDK Publications (www.tkdk.gov.tr/Content/File/Yayin/TKDKEtkiDegerlendirmeRaporu.pdf).

Torfing, J., Peters, G.B., Pierre, J. and Sørensen, E. (2012) *Interactive governance: Advancing the paradigm*, Oxford: Oxford University Press.

Torgerson, D. (2007) 'Promoting the policy orientation: Lasswell in context', in F. Fischer, G.J. Miller and M.S. Sidney (eds) *Handbook of public policy analysis: Theory, politics and methods*, New York, CRC Press, pp 15-28.

TÜBA (Türkiye Bilimler Akademisi) (2005) *Bilimsel araştırma ve politika ilişkisi* [*Scientific research and politics relations*], Ankara: TÜBA Yayınları.

Tural, E. (2014) *Türkiye'de kamu yönetimi eğitiminin tarihi: 1940-1990* [*A history of public administration education in Turkey: 1940-1990*], Ankara: TODAİE.

Weible, C.M. and Sabatier, P.A. (eds) (2018) *Theories of the policy process* (4th edn) New York: Westview Press.

Yayman, H. (2008) *Türkiye'nin idari reform tarihi* [*The history of administrative reform in Turkey*] Ankara, Turkey: Turhan Kitabevi.

Yeo, E.J. (2008) 'Social surveys in the eighteenth and nineteenth centuries', in T.M. Porter and D. Ross (eds) *The Cambridge history of science: The modern social sciences*, vol 7, Cambridge: Cambridge University Press, pp 83-99.

Yerlikaya, H. (2015) *Kamu politikalarının oluşturulmasında katılımcılık ve bilgi ve iletişim teknolojileri* [*Participation and knowledge and communication technologies in public policymaking*], Ankara: Kalkınma Bakanlığı [Professional degree thesis] (www.bilgitoplumu.gov.tr/wp-content/uploads/2015/11/Kamu_Politikalarinin_Olusturulmasinda_Katilimcilik_ve_BIT.pdf).

Yıldız, M. and Babaoğlu, C. (2012) 'Türkiye'de lisansüstü düzeyde kamu politikası öğretimi konusunda düşünce ve öneriler' ['Propositions on teaching public policy education in Turkey'], in H. Kavruk (ed) *Kuram ve yöntem açısından kamu yönetimi* [*Public administration from the perspectives of theory and method*], Ankara: TODAİE, pp 415-25.

Yıldız, M. and Sobacı, M.Z. (eds) (2013) *Kamu politikası: Kuram ve uygulama* [*Public policy: Theory and applications*], Ankara: Adres.

Yıldız, M., Babaoğlu, C. and Tuğan, E.N. (2017) 'Türkiye'de kamu politikaları öğretiminde kurumsallaşma örnekleri' ['Examples of the institutionalisation of public policy education in Turkey'], *Ankara Üniversitesi Siyasal Bilgiler Fakültesi Dergisi*, vol 72, no 3, pp 669--88.

Yıldız, M., Demircioğlu, M.A. and Babaoğlu, C. (2011) 'Teaching public policy to undergraduate students: Issues, experiences, and lessons in Turkey', *Journal of Public Affairs Education*, vol 17, no 3, pp 343-65.

THREE

'Boomerang effect': the bottleneck of public policy analysis in Turkey

Akif Argun Akdoğan

Introduction

A boomerang is a thin, hardwood missile that was originally designed to kill animals and return in a circle to its thrower. If thrown without skill, however, it can recoil on the thrower, wounding them. This boomerang metaphor can be used to explain why the Turkish Justice and Development Party (AKP) has disregarded or even prevented the use of public policy methods and techniques that it introduced in the first period of its rule, when it was enthusiastic in introducing policy tools such as strategic planning and performance audits to increase the efficiency, effectiveness and economy of Turkish public organisations. Soon after their implementation, the published evaluation reports of the Court of Accounts revealed the government's poor performance. Opposition groups in Turkey have criticised the government on the basis of the evidence provided in these reports. Thus, the AKP took legal measures to restore or even reverse the public policy evaluation system within a very short period of time.

When the AKP, led by Recep Tayyip Erdoğan, took office in 2002 ending the long period of coalition governments, the government promised to undertake the most comprehensive public administration reform in the history of Turkey. Although most of its cadres were part of the Islamic political movement, the party declared itself as conservative democratic, representing the Turkish centre right (Celenk, 2009, p 49; see also Akdoğan, 2003). Supported by broad segments of society, the party's first goal was to end the economic crisis. For this purpose AKP welcomed the technical and financial assistance of international economic organisations such as The World Bank and the International Monetary Fund (IMF). It undertook a neoliberal reform policy that enabled Turkey to access foreign loans that it desperately needed.

International financial loan agreements signed with the IMF and World Bank assisted the transfer of public policy analysis tools and instruments (Koçak, 2010, p 13). These loans were conditional on the realisation of public administration reforms and the transfer of public policy tools associated with these reforms such as strategic planning, performance auditing, regulatory impact analysis, and so on (Celenk, 2009, p 49). AKP full-heartedly accepted a new reform paradigm in public administration, and attempted to create a flexible, market-based form of public management by transforming the 'rigid, hierarchical, bureaucratic form of public administration' (Hughes, 1994, p 1). In line with the demands of a neoliberal economy, a full-scale reform in state administration and in public policy formation was deemed necessary to attract more foreign investment to Turkey.

International organisations welcomed the acquiescent attitude of the AKP, and financially supported the government's reform attempts. For instance, project credits were received from The World Bank in 1995 and 2002 for reforming financial administration. Half of the credit amount, which totalled around 2.3 billion US$, has been used to reform the Turkish public administration and justice system (Güler, 2003, p 4). The Organisation for Economic Co-operation and Development (OECD), in line with these organisations, encouraged the reform process in Turkey through its regulatory reform programme. Most of the reforms were to reduce public spending and to increase accountability by emphasising output-oriented 'responsiveness' or 'performance' (Mulgan, 2000, pp 568-9; Papadopoulos, 2003, pp 482-6).

The declaration of Turkey as a candidate country by the European Union (EU) for membership in 1999 further stepped up the AKP's reform attempts in order to obtain a date for the beginning of accession talks (Patton, 2007, p 344; Şener, 2009). The demands of the EU from Turkey have been set out in an accession partnership report and are monitored by progress reports published each year. The EU clearly supported administrative reforms for 'rationalizing the administration and increasing the responsiveness and transparency of the system vis-à-vis the citizens' (Celenk, 2009, p 53). These reforms are justified by the targets of 'facilitating economic development, increasing administrative efficiency in accordance with the EU norms and establishing a stable political structure' (Celenk, 2009, p 49).

In line with the demands of the international and regional organisations, AKP took steps to transfer and implement public policy analysis methods and techniques frequently used in most OECD countries. Several reports had already indicated that the first and most important need for public reform is the more rational and effective use of scarce public resources (TODAİE, 1991; TUSİAD, 2002). For this purpose, the new Public Finance Management and Control Law (PFMCL) introduced new public policy techniques such as strategic planning and performance budgeting that mainly belong to the new public management movement in 2003.

The need to reorganise the Turkish public sector and to create new procedures for policy formulation and evaluation were deemed necessary to shift accountability from policy processes to policy outcomes. The new public management approach was quite influential in the recommendations of international finance organisations and the EU. In fact, these organisations cooperated in their technical and financial assistance to Turkey for the realisation of public administration reform, encouraging the Turkish government to realise reforms to control results rather than more than rules and regulations to increase efficiency, responsiveness and accountability. These reforms intended to encourage entrepreneurial behaviour among bureaucrats to manage results and thus to change the culture within which public managers conduct their duties. The transition to performance measurement is considered as an important step to make public accountability more transparent (Romzek, 2000, p 21).

Public policy tools such as strategic planning and performance budgeting have now been in use for more than 10 years in use in Turkish public administration. Several studies demonstrate, however, that these policy tools are poorly implemented in public organisations and weakly supported by government (Songür, 2008; Karacan, 2010). Not surprisingly, the implementation results of these policy tools were far from reaching the initial goals of the law, that is, making public service delivery more efficient, effective and accountable.

This chapter seeks to propose some possible reasons for the poor performance of public policy tools in Turkey on the basis of strategic planning and performance auditing benefiting from the concept of the 'boomerang effect' that is mainly used in communication studies. It follows the steps of the heuristic public policy cycle model for the analysis. After clarifying the transfer process of strategic planning and performance auditing to the Turkish administrative system, it focuses on implementing these policy tools. Demonstrating the poor performance of these tools with reference to some empirical studies, the aim is to discuss the reasons for non-implementation.

Design and transfer of new policy tools

The public administration reform series of the AKP government started in 2003 when the PFMCL law was enacted in the Turkish Grand National Assembly. It introduced the system of performance-based budgeting to discipline public expenditure for reducing the public deficit, leading to major economic crises in 2000 and 2001 (Övgün, 2010, p 150). The law was inspired from the performance-based budgeting system implemented in the US where public institutions have prepared strategic plans and performance reports since the introduction of the Government Performance Results Act in 1993. The PFMCL law intended to improve public policy formulation and evaluation in Turkey by inserting strategic planning and performance auditing into the Turkish administrative system. It is clearly inspired from the new public management approach emphasising the need for tangible and measurable results in public service delivery (Jos and Tompkins, 2004, p 268).

The issue of public sector performance management came on to the agenda in the late 1980s, with a research project titled 'Measurement of output and performance in central government'. The sixth five-year development plan (1996-2000) set goals for a transition to performance management in the public sector. The real push for enacting the law, however, was the signing of the Programmatic Financial and Public Sector Adjustment Loan Agreement (PFPSAL-1) with The World Bank in 2001 (Güler, 2003, p 4). The transition to performance-based budgeting and the introduction of strategic planning were among the conditions of the agreement for the release of financial credits (Köseoğlu and Şen, 2014, p 128).

The law requires each public organisation to define the public services they will deliver in the coming five years. Each need to set yearly performance goals and indicators so that the state's auditing agencies can monitor and evaluate to what extent they have been successful in achieving the goals they previously set. The idea was is to increase the accountability of public organisations and to rationalise public expenditure. According to the law, each public organisation should define its strategic aims and goals in line with the five-year development plans, government programme and other related macro policy documents and plans. Each public organisation would develop strategic plans in which they specify their aims, goals and specific set of activities to reach the goal. They should specify performance indicators based on the results of their activities and set yearly performance targets. At the end of each budget year they should publish their performance reports indicating to what extent they were successful in reaching their targets. Internal control units had to be established in each organisation to monitor the quality and quantity of the public services delivered.

The Court of Accounts was assigned to control not only the legality of public expenditure but also to assess the performance of the public organisations. The Court, being set up during the Ottoman Empire rule in 1862, is Turkey's supreme audit institution. It decides whether or not the accounts and transactions of the public organisations are in accordance with the legal arrangements. As with its counterparts in many countries, it used to carry out two types of regularity controls on all public organisations and decide any losses to the public purse. While the financial audits consist of an evaluation and an opinion on the accuracy of the financial reports and statements, compliance audits examine whether the revenue, expenditure and assets of public organisations comply with legal regulations. The performance audit system introduced with the Court's new organic law was enacted in 2010. The new mission of the Court is to evaluate whether or not public resources have been used effectively, efficiently and economically. Performance audit reports prepared for each public organisation by the Court of Accounts are an essential part of the system as they objectively evaluate each public organisation's performance (Övgün, 2010, p 150). This system seeks to rationalise the allocation of budget to each public organisation by the Ministry of Finance on the basis of previous years' performance measured by objective and quantifiable indicators. Furthermore, this policy tool is supposed to increase the accountability of the Turkish Grand National Assembly since budget proposals for each public organisation can be discussed in the Plan and Budget Committee, and then approved by the General Assembly on the basis of performance reports provided by the Court of Accounts.

As a result of this mechanism the idea is to allocate and use limited public resources in a more efficient, effective and economic way. In other words, the idea of this reform is to change compliance-oriented control to performance-based auditing. The administrative behaviour of Turkish bureaucrats is usually defined by their motive to follow laws, rules and regulations, reflecting inputs and process orientations (Heper, 1991, p 8). PFMCL seeks to create an administrative culture in which public managers will no longer be assessed by whether they follow legal rules but on the performance of their organisations measured by their output and outcome, which are set out in their strategic plan (Romzek, 2000, p 32). Each public organisation therefore has to justify its success in using public resources. The monitoring and review of results by the Court of Accounts will not only lead to rational use of budgets but also enhance the accountability of the public sector in Turkey (Jos and Tompkins, 2004, p 256).

The judicial powers of the Court of Accounts have always been an important deterrence mechanism for Turkish bureaucrats to use the budget in line with legal regulations. PFCML empowered the Court of Accounts with the authority to assess public organisations in terms of their effectiveness and efficiency. Thus it enhanced the legal control authority of the Court with a performance audit. The managers of Turkish public organisations are supposedly not only accountable as to whether their decisions and acts are in line with legal regulations, but also whether they have efficiently and effectively used public resources in line with the goals and targets they have determined in their organisations' strategic plan.

Policy implementation

Strategic plan

Strategic planning was to be implemented in eight pilot public organisations selected by the State Planning Organization (SPO, today, the Ministry of Development).[1] On the basis of the first implementation results, SPO published its *Strategic planning guide for public administration* in 2003. Local governments started to prepare their strategic plans system after local elections held in March 2009. Most of the public institutions are now currently drafting their strategic plans for 2018-22. Several studies on the preparation and implementation of strategic plans highlight that there is a clear gap between the theory and reality of strategic planning in Turkish public institutions.

A survey conducted in 27 central government agencies found that only 18 of them defined performance indicators measuring outputs, and only half defined them quantitatively (Karaca, 2010, pp 172-3). A similar survey conducted among municipalities showed that only 35 per cent of them have measurable performance indicators in their strategic plan (Songür, 2008, p 70). In both studies, almost no public organisations defined performance indicators for outcomes (results). These studies do not question whether the inability of these organisations to define measurable indicators stem from their incapacity or reluctance. Whatever the reasons for this failure, the lack of measurable indicators for either output or outcome of the activities set in the strategic plan indicates that there is no reliable reference point to monitor or audit the performance of these organisations.

Karaca found that only 13 organisations of central government established a direct link between performance indicators and budget, although the SPO guidebook on strategic planning specifically indicates that each activity should have a measurable target to be achieved for each year. Fourteen public organisations requested their budget from the Ministry of Finance by calculating each budget item on the basis of the yearly performance indicators and unit price of the activities that they foresee for each year, as indicated in the guidebook. However, Karaca (2010, p 174) notes that budgetary figures for these 14 organisations were not based on cost estimate models, but on intuition.

SPO is well aware of the problems in the implementation of strategic planning, but it lacks the power to impose sanctions on government agencies and local governments that do not prepare their strategic plans in accordance with the guidebook. SPO undertook research for developing the administrative capacity in strategic planning with the financial support of the European Commission in 2013. The results of this study showed that strategic plans, performance programmes and yearly activity reports of central and local government organisations do not provide enough data to be able to assess their performance. Furthermore, most of the performance programmes were not prepared in line with strategic plans. Thus, the goals and targets that were set in the strategic plan could not be monitored through performance programmes. The report also found that there was no mechanism of enforcement or penalty for poorly performing institutions, mainly due to the lack of an overall policy strategy for the development of strategic planning and performance measurement systems.

The strategic management working group established by the SPO for analysing the implementation of strategic plans had similar findings. The report published by this group classified the problems of implementation into two – macro and micro. Lack of ownership, poor accountability, poor functioning of the internal and external audit, poor association between strategic plans and macro policy documents were some of the macro problems. Weak support by managers, training and consulting needs, symbolic participation of internal and external stakeholders, poor information and experience sharing within the organisation were among the findings in the micro problems (Ministry of Development, 2012, p 3).

The failure in most strategic plans prepared by Turkish central and local government organisations to define measurable performance criteria for their activities has two interrelated consequences. First of all, the auditors are bound to make organisational assessments within the limits of a poorly defined set of targets that are mostly irrelevant, unspecific and non-measurable. Second, the Parliament does not have any reliable data related to public organisations in allocating budgets. Although PFMCL, with the strategic plan, brought the requirement to establish a link between the goals of the public institution and the budget, performance budgeting has not been realised. Most public institutions continue to ask the Ministry of Finance to increase their budgets without proving that they have reached the outputs or outcomes set in their strategic plan. So, the failure of public organisations to prepare strategic plans as required by the law has made the performance-based budgeting system dysfunctional.

Performance audit

Instead of taking policy measures to tackle these problems, the AKP government has decided to change the organic law of the Court of Accounts, making it *de facto* impossible for the Court to conduct performance audits. The Court of Accounts has been preparing since the beginning of the 2000s to change its law and to increase its capacity in performance auditing, which required a total change in its approach to budget control. For instance, INTOSAI's (International Organization of Supreme Audit Institutions) audit standards and guidelines for leading countries in performance auditing have been translated into Turkish.[2] A twinning project was conducted with the Court of Accounts of England to prepare the transition to performance auditing.

The Court of Accounts undertook several pilot performance audits while waiting the legal changes made in its organic law.[3] The reports of these audits were different from the previous reports prepared by the Court of Accounts in the sense that they were assessing the results obtained in a specific public issue rather than legally controlling the expenditure of a particular public organisation. However, these pilot studies were not performance audits in the strict sense of the term, as performance criteria for these public services have not yet been defined. The results of these reports attracted immediate media attention when they were published on the Court of Accounts' website.

All of these reports showed the poor performance of AKP in delivering efficient and effective public services. For instance, the report on *The planning and control of seashores* published in 2006 highlighted coordination problems between the public agencies responsible for seashore management and overlapping responsibilities. An important finding was that public organisations that are legally responsible for controlling seashores are themselves violating seashore law. The report mentioned some public organisations that have established recreational facilities on the seashore in direct violation of seashore law. According to the Court of Accounts' report, these recreational facilities, which were exclusively open to the personnel of these organisations, were harming the natural environment, preventing people accessing the beaches and restraining citizens' rights to freely and equally benefit from the seashore (Court of Accounts, 2006, p 54).

The report furthermore stated that most of the local governments are either ignoring the occupation of public spaces or using mesne profits[4] as a revenue source for the budget (Court of Accounts, 2006, p 55). The auditors found 334 cases of illegal occupation of seashores in Maltepe, Kartal, Tuzla and Pendik municipalities – in all these municipalities the mayors had been elected from the AKP. In 75 of these cases, public areas under illegal occupation have been gradually increasing every year. In 156 of the cases, illegal occupation of public areas had been going on for over five years. Local governments have illegally rented 34 of these public areas that were supposed to be open to the public. Perhaps the most striking observation of the report is that in 11 cases, public land had been illegally occupied by these municipalities (Court of Accounts, 2006, p 56). Thus, the report clearly demonstrated that the public organisations were using seashores illegally, harming the natural habitat and limiting the rights of citizens to enjoy these public areas freely and equally.

Just after the publication of the report, the main opposition party of Turkey demanded a general debate to be opened in Parliament about the use of seashores. A leading and effective non-governmental organisation (NGO) in Turkey, the Chambers of Turkish Architects and Engineers, criticised the government's policies on seashore management by referring to the Court of Accounts' report, and many articles and opinions have been published in newspapers blaming the government.[5]

So performance audit reports prepared by the Court of Accounts became the reference point for opposition groups in Turkey to direct their political attacks against the government. Thus, AKP prepared a draft law seeking to change the organic law of the Court of Accounts' law in 2010. In the new law, the government deprived the Court of Accounts from using its own criteria and indicators for assessing the efficient, effective and economic use of public resources by public organisations. It can only audit the activities of public organisations on the basis of the goals and indicators specified by these organisations in their respective strategic plan. Nonetheless, as Songür (2008) and Karaca (2010) show, most public organisations in Turkey do not formulate measurable performance indicators. So, the Court of Accounts cannot prepare audit reports claiming that public services delivered by an organisation are ineffective, inefficient or uneconomical unless these services are in line with the goals and indicators defined by the organisation. When the main opposition party brought this issue to Constitutional Court, the Court annulled the article and opened the way for the Court of Accounts for auditing the performance of organisations. Still, the Court of Accounts has not publicly published any performance audit report since the beginning of 2017.

The political move that really crippled the power of the Court of Accounts to audit the performance of a public organisation came with a motion of law given by the AKP MPs during the parliamentary debates to change the article of the law specifying the legal and financial liabilities of public managers. According to this motion, the performance audits of the Court of Accounts would not bring any financial and legal liability for public managers. This motion has been accepted in Parliament, although the proposed change was claimed to be against the constitution that states that the Court of Accounts is the ultimate adjudicative authority in the financial decisions of public managers. Still, according to the law in effect, public managers are immune from any financial and legal liability from issues that may arise from performance audits.

AKP's attempt to render the Court of Accounts' legal control and performance audits dysfunctional continued in 2013 with a proposal to amend the law enacted in 2010. According to the proposal, legal control and performance audit reports prepared by the Court of Accounts shall not be submitted to Parliament before budgetary discussions. The proposal has been taken to the agenda of Parliament, but it has been blocked in the Plan and Budget Committee due to reactions of opposition MPs who demonstrated that the proposal was in direct violation of power of the purse.[6] Just a few months after this attempt to eliminate the power of the purse, the government issued a by-law that retroactively annulled the obligation of public institutions to submit their detailed financial data and tables to the Court of Accounts for legal control. All these obstructive legal moves demonstrate that the concern of the AKP government is not to strengthen the Court of Accounts in auditing the performances of public organisations but to undermine the power of the Court to conduct legal controls.

Policy evaluation of the boomerang effect

The concept of the 'boomerang effect' can be used to explain why the AKP government disregarded or even prevented the use of public policy methods and techniques that it introduced in the first period of its rule. The boomerang can be a deadly weapon, not only for the animal being hunted, but also for the hunter. The person who throws the boomerang can also be the target.

Metaphorically speaking, the AKP government (hunter) dealing with a financial crisis and trying to prove itself as a Western-type conservative party (desire to hunt) attempted to seize the opportunity to gain the support of international organisations and the EU by transferring the policy tools and instruments widely used in OECD countries (decision to use the boomerang). When these policy tools and instruments were implemented (throwing the boomerang), international organisations and the EU financially and technically supported the AKP government (hunting the animal). However, the long-term results of using these tools have demonstrated the ineffectiveness of government policies, making the government vulnerable to criticism and political attack from opposition groups (recoiling of the boomerang). In other words, the government strategy to disregard or restrain the implementation of strategic planning and performance auditing stems from the fact that results of these policies may be used to discredit and criticise the government.

The new Court of Accounts law enacted in 2010 has not only *de facto* inhibited performance audits, but also trimmed the conventional legal controls of the Court. The boomerang metaphor can be further used to explain the reverse effect of strategic planning and performance audits in impairing legal controls. In communication studies, the concept of the boomerang effect is used to demonstrate the 'change within an individual due to message exposure, or in comparison to other individuals who were exposed to an alternative message, or no message at all' (Byrne and Hart, 2009, p 4). For instance, while a media literacy campaign 'seeks to *reduce* a child's desire for products that are advertised in television commercials, a boomerang effect would entail an *increase* in the child's desire for the product beyond that which would have occurred without the intervention' (Byrne and Hart, 2009, p 4, emphasis in original).

While strategic plans are intended to increase efficiency, effectiveness and the economy in public spending, performance audits are designed to assess public organizations' success in reaching the goals and aims set out in their strategic plans. A performance system would theoretically strengthen the conventional legal controls of the Court of Accounts. However, this policy evaluation tool that is designed for improving the rationale in public spending and increasing audit capacity has led to a regression in both of these goals, which would not have occurred without the intervention. This deterioration indicates the presence of the boomerang effect of these public policy tools, as conceptualised in communication studies. While international organisations would like to create positive change in the Turkish administrative system by transferring these policy tools, the government has become aware of their potential disruptive effects. This has led the government to take measures that not only render the implementation of the new policy ineffective, but also impair conventional and well-established policy.

Four arguments for the boomerang effect

Four arguments are now put forward to explain the boomerang effect. The first is that the strategic plans and performance audits may not be the best policy tools to solve the problems faced in the Turkish public administration system. The incompatibility of using private sector methods in public administration is a common critique in the literature (Hedley, 1998; Mashaw, 2009). Private sector companies may rather easily define tangible results in their strategic plans as they can clarify ambiguities and resolve potential conflicts between their goals and priorities by focusing mainly on profitability. Nonetheless, public organisations do not take public policy decisions and implement them merely on the basis of the three famous slogans of the new public management movement, that is, efficiency, effectiveness and economy. Other public values and duties of the public sector, such as treating each citizen equally, protecting the environment, preserving culture, and so on, inevitably create conflict between the diverse goals that the government should achieve. Most public organisations are required to fulfil more than one goal and criteria at once due to the inherent nature of the public services that they provide. Nonetheless, according to strategic planning methodology, each organisation should define only one mission statement and specify non-conflicting goals to be accomplished for the coming five years.

The second challenge for public organisations is to define tangible and measurable performance targets to be achieved. Most of these organisations are under legal obligation to consider public values such as equality, environment and culture. The embedded ambiguity in determining goals and indicators for public organisations allow politicians to 'defer and displace political conflict so that its costs can be better managed later. In addition, they permit politicians to preserve flexibility in the face of technical uncertainty by delegating the resolution of technical questions to others more expert in the specific problems at hand' (Jos and Tompkins, 2004, p 270). Lane (1997, p 1-10) similarly points out that the new public management imposing result-oriented public policies on public institutions is challenging traditional public administration models.

There is little doubt that the infusion of new managerial public policy instruments to public administration changes both administrative culture and administrative values. The shift to performance-based public policies seeking to encourage public managers to take risks may have the opposite effect (Terry, 1998). March and Olsen (1995, p 146) observed that accountability can increase responsiveness to external standards, but it can also 'lead to procrastination and excessive consideration of possibilities, reduce risk taking, make decision-makers cautious about change and about risking mistakes that might become public, and dispose them to persistence in courses of action that appear to have failed.'

This short account about the internal weakness of strategic planning and performance auditing demonstrates that implementation problems are not specific to Turkey. Incompatibility of policy tools between the public and private sector is itself a factor that prevents the successful implementation of these tools in many administrative systems including Turkey. Nonetheless, the problem of implementation becomes more acute in countries like Turkey, where the traditional administrative culture and structure negatively influences the nature and outcome of public policy formulation and evaluation tools such as strategic planning and performance auditing (Celenk, 2009, p 43).

The administrative culture argument leads us to our third argument. Strategic planning as policy formulation and performance audit as a policy evaluation tool became fashionable mainly due to the dominance of the new public management approach in Western countries. Referring to our metaphor, the boomerang was created by Australian aborigines to hunt animals like kangaroos. It is not possible to hunt kangaroos in a land other than Australia, as this species is indigenous – if the boomerang had been given to Eskimos, it would obviously not have any meaning for them, as it would not be useful for their hunting needs. Strategic plans and performance audits are policy tools that emerged in the early 1980s in response to the needs of Anglo-Saxon countries in particular. Therefore their usefulness should be assessed in their success to address these needs.

Perhaps there is limit in drawing an analogy between the boomerang and strategic plan/performance audits considering the fact that there are some common factors that led Western countries and Turkey to choose the path to new public management. Nonetheless, the AKP government temporarily and pragmatically opted out of transferring public policy tools associated with new public management since it required the financial assistance of international organisations for overcoming its economic crisis. Although there was a long ongoing discussion among public administration scholars and the top figures of Turkish bureaucracy, policy tools such as strategic plans, performance budgeting, regulatory impact analysis, and so on were never issues of priority. The AKP government, unlike the governments of most Western countries, has not asked for any assistance from universities, think tanks or leading scholars during the process of formulation and introduction of these policy tools. The Institute of Economic Affairs and Centre for Policy Studies in the UK, the University of Chicago and scholars such as David Osborne and Ted Gaebler in the US were quite influential during the reform process. On the other hand, in Turkey neither the Public Administration Institute for Turkey and the Middle East (that prepared two significant reform proposals in 1963 and in 1991) nor leading universities in public administration were consulted during the reform process. Thus, public policy tools such as strategic planning and performance auditing have been pragmatically transferred to Turkey without any domestic contribution, as their implementation was a requirement for gaining financial assistance from international organisations and the EU.

The fourth argument, then, is the strong relationship with the motive and reward of keeping up with the reform. The end of the stand-by agreement with the IMF in 2008 and the deteriorating relationship with the EU ended up with the deceleration of momentum in administrative reform. The government decided not to push hard for the implementation and enforcement of the public policy formulation and evaluation tools that it assertively legislated for a few years ago. Although the AKP government has repeatedly declared that 'it remains committed to the EU reform track, EU officials have become increasingly critical of the deceleration in pace, urging it, through formal and informal channels, to stick to its reform commitments' (Patton, 2007, p 340). Some optimistic views express that Turkey needs time for the norms, values and practices embedded in the reforms to be internalised (Kubicek, 2005). On the other hand, according to Tocci (2005), the inducement to keep up the pace of reform has diminished because the entry of Turkey to the EU is uncertain.

No matter what the reasons for the AKP to slow down the reform process, most reforms were direct transfers from OECD countries. The views, opinions and critiques of the opposition parties, NGOs and universities were not taken into consideration. Foreign experts designed the formulation and implementation of strategic planning and performance auditing (Övgün, 2010, p 146). These policy tools have been transferred as technical instruments without any consideration to the Turkish administrative culture. They emerged in Western democracies with deep-seated, risk-averse managerial cultures (Christoph, 1992). On the other hand, several studies in Turkey defined collectivism, solidarity and harmony as the leading traits of the Turkish administrative culture. These characteristics do not provide a suitable administrative culture for the dissemination of strategic planning and performance auditing, which primarily aim to increase the accountability and openness of bureaucracy. If the performances of public organisations could have been audited in Turkey, administrators of public organisations would not only be accountable for the legality of their actions, but also for their technical and economic competence. They would be required to present factual predicates for action and reasoned explanations of decisions rather than claiming the legality of their actions. So policy tools that increase the accountability of public administrators are more likely to meet with resistance.

Conclusion

It is possible to argue that the use of new public policy tools such as strategic plans and performance budgeting may eventually lead to a change in administrative culture. Although this argument seems plausible, it assumes that the government in power would use its authority to enforce the implementation of such policy tools. Nonetheless, the AKP government, instead of taking measures to support the implementation of these policy tools, actually disregarded poorly prepared strategic plans and attempted to prevent performance auditing mainly due to the 'boomerang effect'.

Given the fact that international organisations and the EU do not have the leverage power that they once enjoyed, and the lack of the government's desire to push for implementing public policy, the demand from citizens could legitimate and disseminate the use of modern policy tools in Turkey. As Nietzsche (1969, p 84, quoted in Butler, 2005, p 11) indicated, we give an account only when it is requested, and only when that request is backed up by power. Most Turkish citizens were negatively affected by the lack of necessary public policy formulation, implementation and evaluation techniques and tools during the financial crisis at the beginning of the 2000s. AKP came to power with the promise of consolidating Turkish democracy and creating the conditions for a sustainable economy. However, apart from a few liberal circles (TEPAV, TUSIAD),[7] there was no specific demand from large sections of the society for the government to give value for money for their tax payments. Accountability of government expenditure seems to be a request of international organisations and the EU rather than Turkish citizens.

Some Turkish scholars explain the inertia of Turkish citizens on the basis of elitist theory, claiming that the legalistic tradition of the decision-making of Turkish bureaucrats led to the exclusion of the masses from political decision-making (Heper, 1991, p 17). However, the AKP government came to power targeting the entrenched interests of bureaucratic and military elites. It has repeatedly claimed to yield the power enjoyed by Kemalist elites to the people and to use public revenues to people's benefit. During the 14 years of its rule, there were many allegations of corruption and misuse of public revenue against the AKP government, but the party not only managed to survive but also to strengthen its power base by increasing its votes from 34 per cent in 2002 to 49 per cent in 2015. So, it would be naive to expect the AKP to introduce public policy formulation and evaluation tools that may risk exposing the negative outcomes of its policies, unless it meets strong demand from different sections of society. Ironically, Turkish electors brought the party in to formulate and implement sound and effective public policies to respond to the economic crisis. A possible crisis in current public policies or demand from various social groups may again trigger demand for using policy analysis methods and tools.

Notes

1. The Ministry of Development was established to assume the duties and responsibilities of the SPO in 2011.
2. *Results-oriented government: A guide to strategic planning and performance measurement in the public sector* (Government of Alberta), *Performance indicator: A practical guide* (Victoria), *Key performance indicator* (New South Wales) and *Performance information for management and accountability purposes* (Tasmania) were among the documents translated by the Court of Accounts.
3. *The coordination of infrastructure activities in metropolitan municipalities, Activities to prevent traffic accidents, Struggle with hospital infections, Refuse management in Turkey: National regulations and evaluation of implementation results, Planning and control of seashores, Public sector websites in transition to e-government, Activities conducted in the context of Turkey's e-transition* – these were among the performance audit reports prepared during this time. These reports, which were deposited on the website of the Court of Accounts about a year ago, are no longer accessible.
4. The amount paid to local governments by the people or organisations using public areas such as the beaches, lakes, streets, and so on.
5. 'The state allows plundering of seashores for money', 'Turkey's shores are left to God's protection', 'The state is itself a plunderer' – these were some of the newspaper titles.
6. Sayıştay Kanunu'nda Değişiklik yapılması Hakkında Kanun Teklifi [Law proposal amending the law on the Turkish Court of Accounts], 18 April 2013 (www.hukukihaber.net/mevzuat/sayistay-kanununda-degisiklik-teklifi-h32634.html).
7. TEPAV, Economic Policy Research Foundation for Turkey; TUSIAD, Turkish Industry and Business Association.

References

Akdoğan, Y. (2003) *Muhafazakar demokrasi*, Ankara: AKP.
Butler, J. (2005) *Giving account of oneself*, New York: Fordham University Press.
Byrne, S. and Hart, P.S. (2009) 'The boomerang effect: A synthesis of findings and a preliminary theoretical framework', in S.C. Beck (ed) *Communication yearbook 33*, New York: Routledge, pp 3-33.
Celenk, A.A. (2009) 'Europeanization and administrative reform: The case of Turkey', *Mediterranean Politics*, vol 14, no 1, pp 41-60.
Christoph, J.B. (1992) 'The remaking of British administrative culture: Why Whitehall can't go home again', *Administration and Society*, vol 24, no 2, pp 163-81.
Court of Accounts (2006) *The planning and control of seashores*, Performance Audit Report, The Presidency of Court of Accounts, Ankara, June.
Güler, B.A. (2003) 'İkinci dalga: Siyasal ve yönetsel liberalizasyon: Kamu yönetimi temel kanunu', *AÜ SBF GETA Tartışma Metinler*, no 59, Special Issue, pp 1-34.
Hedley, T.P. (1998) 'Measuring public sector effectiveness using private sector methods', *Public Productivity and Management Review*, vol 21, no 3, pp 251-8.
Heper, M. (1991) 'The state and interest groups with special reference to Turke', in M. Heper (ed) *Strong state and economic interest groups: The post-1980 Turkish experience*, Berlin and New York: De Gruyter, pp 3-24.

Hughes, O.E. (2003) *Public management and administration: An introduction*, Basingstoke: Palgrave Macmillan.

Jos, P.H. and Tompkins, M.E. (2004) 'The accountability paradox in an age of reinvention: The perennial problem of preserving character and judgment', *Administration and Society*, vol 36, no 3, pp 255-81.

Karacan, E. (2010) *Performans esaslı bütçeleme sistemi ve Türkiye uygulaması*, DPT Uzmanlık Tezi, Ankara: Koza Yayıncılık.

Koçak, S.Y. (2010) 'Legislative reforms in Turkey: The case of public administration', *Petroleum – Gas University of Ploiesti Bulletin, Law & Social Science*, vol LXII, no 1, pp 9-18.

Köseoğlu, O. and Şen, M.L. (2004) 'Kamu sektöründe performans yönetimi: politikalar, uygulamalar ve sorunlar', *Akademik İncelemeler Dergisi*, vol 9, no 2, pp 113-36.

Kubicek, P. (2005) 'The European Union and grassroots democratization in Turkey', *Turkish Studies*, vol 6, no 3, pp 361-77.

Lane, J.E. (1997) 'Introduction – Public sector reform: Only deregulation, privatization and marketization?', in J.E. Lane (ed) *Public sector reform: Rationale, trends and problems*, London: Sage Publications, pp 1-16.

March, J.G. and Olsen, J.P. (1995) *Democratic governance*, New York: Free Press.

Mashaw, J.L. (2009) 'Bureaucracy, democracy and judicial review: The uneasy coexistence of legal, managerial and political accountability', *Public Law and Legal Theory Research Paper Series*, no 194, Yale Law School (http://papers.ssrn.com/abstract #1431601).

Ministry of Development (2013) *Boşluk değerlendirme raporu*, Stratejik Yönetimde Kapasite Geliştirme Projesi (www.sp.gov.tr/tr/html/54/Stratejik+Yonetimde+Kapasite+Gelistirme+Projesi).

Mulgan, R. (2000) '"Accountability": An ever-expanding concept?', *Public Administration*, vol 78, no 3, pp 555-73.

Nietzsche, F. (1969) *On the genealogy of morals*, translated by Walter Kaufmann, New York: Random House.

Övgün, B. (2010) *Devlet ve planlama*, Ankara: Siyasal Kitabevi.

Papadopoulos, Y. (2003) 'Cooperative forms of problems of democratic accountability in complex environments', *European Journal of Political Research*, vol 42, pp 473-501.

Patton, M.J. (2007) 'AKP reform fatigue in Turkey: What has happened to the EU process?', *Mediterranean Politics*, vol 12, no 3, pp 339-58.

Romzek, B.S. (2000) 'Dynamics of public sector accountability in an era of reform', *International Review of Administrative Sciences*, vol 66, pp 21-44.

Şener, H.E. (2009) *Administrative reform as an opportunity: The EU accession process in Hungary and Turkey*, Ankara: Phoenix.

Songür, N. (2008) 'Belediyelerin stratejik planlama sürecindeki gereklilikleri yerine getirme durumları üzerine bir araştırma', *Çağdaş Yerel Yönetimler*, vol 17, no 4, pp 63-86.

Terry, L.D. (1998) 'Administrative leadership, neomanagerialism, and the public management movement', *Public Administration Review*, vol 58, pp 194-200.

Tocci, N. (2005) 'Europeanization in Turkey: Trigger or anchor for reform?', *South European Society and Politics*, vol 10, no 1, pp 73-83.

TODAİE (1991) *Kamu yönetimi araştırması genel rapor*, No 238, Ankara: TODAİE Yayınları.

TÜSİAD (2002) *Kamu reformu araştırması*, Yayın No TÜSİAD/T 2002-12/335, İstanbul.

FOUR

Methods of policy analysis: the US and Turkish cases

Hüseyin Gül and Muhittin Acar

Introduction

Policy sciences, public policy studies and policy analysis are relatively new subjects to Turkish academia, even though there have been several studies on public policies in different disciplines ranging from political science and public administration to economics, from law to sociology, and from public finance to business administration. Yet these studies often lack any policy science and/or policy analysis perspective. There is also not much research examining and classifying the types of issues covered or policy research and analysis methods (quantitative or qualitative) used in those studies. Despite some encouraging developments, especially since the 2000s, regarding public policy studies and an increasing number of courses and textbooks on public policy in Turkey, the literature on public policy research and analysis is still quite limited. In fact, no methodology books are exclusively dedicated to policy research in the Turkish literature other than a few methodology books that include direct reference to the policy sciences (Baydar et al, 2008; Keser Ashenberger, 2015; Sert, 2015) and some general research textbooks covering some examples of qualitative research techniques applicable to policy studies and analysis (Yıldırım and Şimşek, 2000; Kuş, 2012; Aziz, 2014).

This chapter is dedicated to discussing the current status of policy analysis and research in general, in both the US and in Turkey. Such a discussion is closely dependent on the definition of policy analysis as well as the differences between the two cases. A broader definition of policy analysis would lead to a consideration of a large number of policy issues, policy analysis and research techniques. If policy analysis is defined as 'applied social and scientific research pursued by government officials, non-governmental organisations, specialists or academics', and 'usually directed at designing, implementing, and evaluating existing policies, programs, and other specific courses of action adopted or contemplated by states or governments' (Howlett and Ramesh, 2003, cited in Geva-May and Maslove, 2006, p 433), then a broader approach to policy research and analysis methods and techniques must be taken. However, if policy analysis is defined as 'the use of reason and evidence to choose the best policy among a number of alternatives' (MacRae and Wilde, 1985, p 12), then policy analysis and research would be more about either the cost-benefit or input-output analysis of policy choices available in a specific context or sector, about the estimation of the possible outcomes of a policy adopted or about the measurement of the impact of a policy implemented. The analysis provided in this chapter takes the broader approach to policy research and analysis.

This chapter provides a review of the methods and techniques of policy analysis and research methods and techniques commonly used in national and international policy studies, analysis and education. It first investigates the positivist and post-positivist or interpretivist approaches to policy analysis and research. Second, it reviews what types of policy research and analysis methods and techniques are commonly used in public policy studies and research courses, particularly in the US. Third, it provides the findings of a survey on the types of policy research techniques and methods commonly used in public policy studies in Turkey based on content analysis of a sample of articles, courses and textbooks. Finally, it ends with a summary of the findings, comparing and contrasting the types of methods and techniques used in public policy studies and courses in both the US and in Turkey.

Trends in policy analysis and research

A recent study conducted by Morçöl and Ivanova (2010, p 269) on courses offered in public policy and public affairs programmes at universities and colleges in the US and the methodological preferences of policy professionals shows that there is still a dominance of quantitative methods in policy analysis education and research. Yet discussions on social science methodology have moved beyond a simple conflict of positivist and interpretivist (post-positivist or constructionist) views, and the use of mixed methodologies has become common in public policy analysis and in many other fields of social sciences in recent decades. For the purposes of discussion and analysis, a comparison of positivist and interpretivist approaches to social science inquiry and policy sciences is provided below. It also helps clarify the analytical method employed in this chapter by underlining the characteristics and differences of these two basic competing and intertwined approaches.

Positivist tradition

Positivist analysis is grounded in quantitative (numerical) techniques, microeconomics, rationality and objectivity, and in 'the realist notion that there is a world independent of our observations of it' (Kolaf et al, 2008, p 19). A positivist approach claims that quantitative methods provide 'the tools for applying a natural science model to the social sciences' (Manicas, 2007, p 9). In the positivist approach, socioeconomic and political issues are considered as technical questions, and numbers are applied to capture and understand these issues and problems. It is also believed that empirical evidence is an efficient indicator of knowledge and learning, and thus scientific inquiry is often an attempt to demonstrate facts by collecting more data. In this attempt, individuals may be the primary units of analysis as a convenient metric, or 'measured as voting statistics, rational persons and utility aggregators, or as demographic entities' (deLeon, 1997, pp 80-1). Moreover, research conducted under the influence of the dominant positivist methodology is often extremely reductive in character, and tends to oversimplify reality in order to make it operational and measurable (Miller and Salkind, 2002).

The positivist social science tradition has deeply influenced policy analysis, especially in the US, as Morçöl and Ivanova (2010, p 255) note that the widespread use of quantitative methods in the areas of policy research and education indicates the ongoing dominance of the positivist approach and its methodology and techniques. In the positivist approach, 'valid', 'reliable' or 'accurate' inquiry can only 'follow faithful adherence to scientific method' (Brewer and deLeon, 1983, p 100). 'In this tradition, data are collected by conducting surveys in which everyone is asked the same set of questions, or by making use of the numbers collected by government or by other organizations, or by otherwise gathering information in a form that allows what is observed to be captured by numbers' (Kolaf et al, 2008, pp 34-5). It was assumed that collecting data about social problems and their causes as well as the effectiveness of policies to solve these problems would help correct the direction of public policy. Besides, it was also believed that 'once the society knew, *really knew*, the facts and figures of social disorganization, corrective action would inevitably follow.... All that was needed in the way of research was documentation of the extent and distribution of the problem' (Weiss, 1983, p 214; original emphasis). Accordingly, positivist policy analysis has, it is argued, promoted the goals of improving performance orientation, efficiency and objectivity, of providing better, more complete information, and faith in rational decision-making and normative economic models (deLeon, 1997, p 121; Geva-May and Maslove, 2006, pp 417-18). In such an understanding, policy research has been considered to have its merit in adding a measure of rationality to the policy-making process by providing objective, valid and non-political data, conclusions and recommendations, and by helping to overcome the irrational or non-rational and political excesses of the policy-making process.

It could be argued that the main goal of policy analysis and research is to meet the demand for knowledge by policy-makers and related or interested others about socioeconomic problems or issues, possible policy alternatives to these problems or issues, and the impact of policy implementation and responses by target groups. Policy analysts and specialists, think tanks and other related or interested parties produce, compile and analyse information not only about the aforementioned aspects but also about the various aspects and stages of the policy-making process and involved actors and their roles in this process. And as argued by Brewer and deLeon (1983, pp 100-1), policy analysts and researchers must also be prepared to develop new methods and techniques as they face new challenges posed by constant change and specific problems and issues.

Post-positivist (interpretivist) approaches in policy analysis and research

The methods of inquiry to produce data may vary for different reasons, and there are other factors beyond objective, technical and systematic analysis at the level of policy research and methodology. 'One can trace the source of these debates back to the social constructionist critique of the 1960s and 1970s, or farther back to the phenomenological and hermeneutic critiques of the over-quantification of human sciences in the 19th century' (Morçöl and Ivanova, 2010, p 256). Morçöl and Ivanova (2010, p 256) maintain that, as one of the earliest critiques of quantitative methods, Lasswell (1971) viewed the knowledge of public policy as 'contextual and temporal and therefore difficult to quantify and generalize.' In addition, Denhardt (1981, p 63) points out that 'By limiting ourselves to the examination of "measurable (or countable) facts" of public policies or the "manifest behaviour" of organisational actions, we implicitly endorse the social conditions that have created those facts and those behaviors' (cited in deLeon, 1997, p 94). In other words, only observing and reporting the actions or outcomes in numbers, without questioning and exploring what really lies behind these observations and numbers, may lead policy analysts to accept the face value of their observations and established societal norms and practices. Moreover, it is often really difficult or impossible to produce 'accurate', 'timely' and 'valid' data of reality.

Thus, what policy analysts and their analyses produce are very often a representation of a simplified, abstracted, incomplete and inadequate view of the world because analysts and policy-makers with their own values and positions ignore complexities, conditions and interests involved in a policy matter, take shortcuts and use simple routines (Morçöl, 2012, p 8). Accordingly, Foster et al (2010, p 521) argue that studying public policy and conducting policy research require all analysts, regardless of their positivist or post-positivist orientation, to take normative values, subjective positions and political context into account. In Mead's view, policy research requires skills in policy analysis, political analysis and the business of government (Mead, 2013, p 399), and necessitates laying hands on the institutions through such realistic and robust techniques as documentary research or field interviewing, even if these techniques lack the precision and rigour possible with statistical models (Mead, 2005).

In post positivist approaches, the methods of natural sciences are seen to be unfit in human (social, cultural) sciences, 'because human beings were meaning-making and interpreting entities, and the meanings they make and their actions could be understood only in their own contexts' (Morçöl and Ivanova, 2010, p 256). Interpretivists (post-positivists or constructionists) criticise the positivist policy research paradigm because it is 'too restricted in philosophy', 'too limited in its scope', 'too disciplined in its approach', so much 'empirical in its application' and 'too mechanical in its interpretation' (deLeon, 1997, pp 75, 80-1). Accordingly, positivist methodology and rational or utilitarian approaches are seen to be inadequate for understanding the social world because they tend to overlook individual values and positions, and to oversimplify socioeconomic and political phenomena (Morçöl, 2012, p 8; deLeon, 1997, pp 83-95). The empirical attributes of socioeconomic and political phenomena often cannot be observed directly (Frankfort-Nachmias and Nachmias, 1992, p 31). In such cases, the only way to produce data (empirical evidence) about the phenomenon in question may be to make inferences or to take the representations (parameters, operational definitions etc) of reality as the 'truth' or 'fact'. In addition, it is often ignored that socioeconomic and political issues have normative, subjective and conflict-ridden aspects, and that policy-making is political in its nature.

Durning (1993), writing on the interpretivist perspective or, more specifically, hermeneutics approaches, asserts that 'All reject positivism; view phenomenology or a variation of it, as a better way to interpret the nature of knowledge; and accept an interpretative or hermeneutic paradigm of it' (cited in deLeon, 1997, p 111). 'Facts' are considered to be interpreted and reinterpreted as a function of time, place, conditions, positions, values, meanings and other variables that are beyond the scientific bounds and control of positivist techniques. In fact, the insight from the hermeneutic school is that 'there is a wide variety of possibly important interpretations (personal, consensual, symbolic, "factual", etc) that can be particular utility in the policy process' (deLeon, 1997, pp 93-4). Hermeneutics seeks for 'clarity and understanding', while positivist methodology searches for 'certainty'. Similarly, critical theory insists on a more democratic discourse and 'multiple and equally respected perspectives in both fact and value' since 'there are multiple perspectives and purposes to a problem ... that needs to be simultaneously coexamined' in order to identify and distinguish plural, common and emergent interests and positions by allowing the genuinely communicative participation of citizens (deLeon, 1997, pp 94, 87). Habermas suggests that a highly rational, technical and functionalist-oriented perspective 'omits much in the nature of a person's value structure, omissions that can frequently and seriously skew the results' (Habermas, 1987, cited in deLeon, 1997, p 87). In a full democracy, the goal is not simply to reconcile conflicting interests, 'but to design institutions that encourage discourse, which, in turn, is necessary to identify and distinguish plural, common, and emergent issues' (Warren, 1992, p 12, cited in deLeon, 1997, p 90).

Thus, post-positivist or interpretivist policy analysis is grounded more in flexible qualitative techniques, politics, power, language, subjectivity, positions, meaningful citizen participation and in the constructionist notion that the things we know are the social constructions of the real world (Kolaf et al, 2008, p 19; Foster et al, 2010, pp 519-21). DeLeon (1997, p 71) argues that interpretivist approaches (post-positivist approach, constructionist perspective, hermeneutics, critical theory, complexity theory etc) make a valuable contribution to the discussion on policy research and analysis by calling for the utilisation of a multidisciplinary approach, and of a broader range of methodology and research techniques in policy analysis. There are many contemporary models of policy inquiry that are 'all equally legitimated as a function of problem under investigation: all are necessary, none is sufficient. Qualitative methods such as field research, participatory action research, and even grounded theory can be just as demanding as strictly quantitative models' (deLeon, 1997, p 71). The interpretivist perspectives particularly promote the use of images, words, texts, photographs, sound recordings, participative observation, in-depth interviews and so on rather than numbers and mere questionnaires (Yanow, 2007, p 406; Kolaf et al, 2008, p 35). The call for the use of numerous research models and multidisciplinary approaches also stems from the complexities of socioeconomic and political life as well as a multifaceted policy puzzle.

There are also several other factors that limit the capacity of public policies to solve problems, such as limits to the power of governments and human capacity, varying positions, interests, actors and values involved in the policy-making process, biased or distorted interpretations of the conditions and issues, and the complexity of human behaviour (Brewer and deLeon, 1983, p 89; Weiss, 1983; Dye, 2002, pp 15-17).

According to Brewer and deLeon (1983):

> For example, value preferences or conflicts and confusion about what a program's real purposes are nearly always confound the evaluator and must be treated.... (p 351)

> [Besides the] choice of topics, the organization of the problem, the application of the method, and the formulation of the results all eventually hinge on the judgment, knowledge, and skill of the analyst in carrying out each of these tasks. (p 135)

This is why 'public policy problems in their natural setting almost never subscribe to a single disciplinary position' (deLeon, 1997, pp 74-5). Thus, the methods and techniques of inquiry to produce data may vary in public policy analysis and research.

Common research and analysis methods in the field of public policy

A combined use of positivist and interpretivist policy analysis and research methods and techniques in public policy teaching and inquiry is now widespread. One of the main reasons for this is that socioeconomic problems and issues and policies dealing with them have become more complex and multifaceted, requiring the effective and coordinated use of combined research and analysis methods and techniques (Patton, 1987, pp 60-5). Another reason is that the boundaries between policy analysis and management have become increasingly fuzzier. A further reason is that the need for knowledge has increased due to globalization and the demand for faster and better policy decisions. Last, but not least, many changes have taken place in political and administrative systems that have had an impact on the policy-making process (Radin, 2013, p 17), such as the development of new public management and governance approaches, policy convergence and evidence-based decision-making. In fact, some multinational organisations such as the Organisation for Economic Co-operation and Development (OECD) and The World Bank have promoted the use of governance approaches, market-based mechanisms and evidence-based policy-making in their own work and for their member or client nations (OECD, 2007). These developments have led to shifts in the role and functioning of government agencies in society and the economy by introducing performance measures, new ways of service production and delivery (outsourcing, contracting out, policy transfer etc), flexibility and competition into policy-making and administrative systems. Therefore, this chapter is based on a perspective that combines positivist (quantitative, numerical), post-positivist and interpretivist (qualitative, nominal) methods and techniques.[1]

A review of the literature in the US

Morçöl and Ivanova (2010, p 260) provide a list of methods and techniques used in social inquiry and policy analysis and teaching, as seen in Table 4.1. Their list is based on the contents of well-known policy analysis textbooks, literature with critical assessments of mainstream policy analysis methods and the general social science methods literature in the US (Morçöl and Ivanova, 2010, p 259). It serves as a reference for evaluating the types of research and analysis methods used in policy studies and taught in the areas of public policy, political science and public administration.

Studies conducted since the 1980s on the methods taught in educational programmes on public policy and political science and public administration indicate that quantitative methods have been prevalent (Morçöl and Ivanova, 2010, p 262). However, a review of the literature also suggests that the use of qualitative and combined methods (methodological pluralism) have also increased in recent decades, partly because of the increased complexity of policy issues and problems as well as contributions by post-positivist critiques. Kolaf et al (2008, p 35) point out that, 'Some questions more readily call for qualitative methods, some for quantitative. But most research areas benefit from a mix of methods. It is believed that both qualitative and quantitative methods have a great deal to contribute to our understanding of the social world.'

Morçöl and Ivanova (2010, p 262) themselves conducted research focusing on Masters in public policy programmes and programmes with similar names, such as the Master's in Public Administration and Policy, the Master's in Public Affairs, the Master's of Science (MS) in Public Policy and Management Programme along with programmes that specialised in policy areas such as the environment, health, education and urban affairs, planning or policy. The findings of their research showed that quantitative courses constituted large majorities of methods courses taught in both the Master's programmes (88 per cent) and PhD programmes (79 per cent). This study by Morçöl and Ivanova (2010, pp 266-7) displayed that quantitative methods were mentioned more times than qualitative methods in the titles and descriptions of the research courses. Most commonly used methods included statistical analyses, surveys, regression analysis and cost-benefit analysis, and experimental and quasi-experimental studies. Ethical analysis was found to have the highest frequency count among the qualitative methods, followed by case studies, interviews, focus groups, legal analysis and participant observation.

Table 4.1: A classified list of methods of social inquiry and policy research

Quantitative (numerical)		Qualitative (nominal)	
Design methods			
Cross-sectional	Quasi-experimental	Comparative design	
Longitudinal	Panel studies	Case study design	
Experimental	Repeated measures	Systems design	
Data collection methods			
Data-mining		Conference call	Qualitative (long, in-depth,
Secondary data		Focus group	structure, semi-structured)
Survey		Observation	interview
			Participant observation
			Screening conference
Statistical data analysis methods			
Correlation analysis		Computer-assisted qualitative analysis	
Linear or log-linear regression analysis			
Statistical analysis			
Time-series analysis			
Combined methods			
Cost-benefit analysis		Action (policy) research	Historical method
Cost-effectiveness analysis		Appreciative inquiry	(historiography, life history,
Decision analysis tree		Archival research	oral history, biographic
(Dynamic) systems analysis (modelling)		Assumptional analysis	analysis, genealogy)
Game theory		Brainstorming	Judgemental forecasting
Geographic information system		Category analysis	Grounded theory
Input-output analysis		Case study	Hermeneutics
Linear programming		Collaborative (participatory)	Legal analysis
Meta-analysis		inquiry	Metaphor analysis
Mixed methods		Conversational analysis	Myth analysis
PERT-CPM		Content analysis	Narrative analysis
Simulation (optimisation, computer modelling)		Critical theoretical analysis	Nominal groups
(Social) network analysis		Deconstruction	Oral history study
Sociometry		Deliberative inquiry	PEST (political, economic,
Time-series forecasting		Discourse analysis	social, technologic) analysis
		Documentary research	Phenomenological methods
		Delphi technique	Policy evaluation research
		Dramaturgical interviewing	Policy process analysis
		and analysis	Political feasibility analysis
		Ethical analysis	Post-structural analysis
		Ethno-methodology	Semiotics
		Ethnographic semantics	Social constructivist analysis
		Ethnography	Socio-drama
		Feminist analysis	Space analysis
		Frame (reflective) analysis	Storytelling analysis

Source: This table is largely based on the classification by Morçöl and Ivanova (2010, p 260) and partly on a study by Gül (2015, pp 15-29)

A final study to review here is a survey conducted among policy professionals in 1998. This study by Morçöl (published in 2001) indicated a remarkable consistency with the findings of the abovementioned research on the methods taught in educational programmes for public policy and political science and public administration. The findings showed that the most common quantitative methods used by policy professionals were, in sequence, surveys, regression analysis, cost-benefit analysis, quasi-experiments, simulations and time-series analysis, whereas the most common qualitative analysis methods included brainstorming, political feasibility analysis, Delphi technique and assumptional analysis. However, some qualitative methods (brainstorming and assumptional analysis), and both qualitative and quantitative methods (political feasibility analysis and Delphi) commonly used by policy professionals were not taught in any of the sample educational programmes (Morçöl and Ivanova, 2010, pp 265, 266, 268).

Methods of policy analysis in Turkey

Methodology and data sources

As mentioned above, public policy research and analysis as well as policy studies are relatively new in Turkey. Thus, there is very limited research on the subject and there are limited sources, not only in terms of textbooks, but also with regard to scholarly articles or publications on public policy and/or policy research and analysis. In order to provide a review of the studies and courses on public policy or policy studies in general in Turkey, an internet survey was conducted. In the survey, the terms 'public policy' and 'public policy analysis' were searched using the Google search engine,[2] and the first 350 hits were reviewed. Among them only 51 articles that related to 'public policy' and 'public policy analysis' were found to meet the criteria and selected for analysis. The criteria included the year of publication to be 2000 or after, and the type of publication to be a scientific journal article in addition to their subject being related to 'public policy' or 'public policy analysis'. The rest of the reviewed internet material did not meet these criteria and was not included in the sample. The excluded studies were Master's theses, professional theses, doctoral dissertations, book chapters, symposium proceedings, policy notes or reports, short commentaries, textbook materials and so on. The contents of the 51 articles were analysed in order to determine their year of publication, their subject or field, specialisation of the authors, methodology and type of analysis used.

Findings

The results of the content analysis of the 51 articles included in the sample indicate that 20 per cent of them are about education and health with 25 per cent about urban regeneration, regional development, environmental problems and violence against women. The rest are about such issues as gender equality, migration, employment, e-government, governance, rent control, security development, intellectual property rights and social policy, among others. In addition, the specialisations of the authors are in political science and public administration (19 cases), public administration (6 cases), economics (3 cases), labour economics (2 cases), social work (2 cases), city and regional planning (2 cases), public finance (2 cases), education (2), business administration (2 cases), police academy (2 cases), and social policy, health administration, agricultural economics, law, medicine, nursing, engineering and public bureaucracy (2 cases for each of these fields). These findings show that almost half of the 51 reviewed articles were authored by academicians in the field of either political science and public administration or just public administration.

The findings of the research also reveal that the methodology of the study is clearly stated in only 15.7 per cent of the articles analysed and 9.9 per cent include only the goal of the study; 74.5 per cent do not include anything regarding the methodology or goal of study, and 4 per cent do not even have a summary. These findings suggest that the issue of research methods and techniques is yet to get fair attention in journal articles on public policy in Turkey.

Table 4.2 shows the methods and techniques of policy research and analysis used in the 51 articles analysed in this study. The results reveal that a literature review is the most common method/technique for policy research and analysis used in scientific journal articles published in Turkey. Literature analysis is adopted in 51 per cent of the journal articles reviewed (26 cases) whereas another 15.8 per cent (8 cases) utilised literature review and analysis together with a review of laws and regulations. Other policy analysis and research methods and techniques include policy process/cycle analysis in three cases out of a total of 51 (5.9 per cent), content analysis in another three cases (5.9 per cent) and case studies in one (2 per cent).

Simple counts of frequency distribution and average amounts to a mere 7.9 per cent, but they represent the most common combined use of quantitative and qualitative research and analysis techniques in the articles on policy analysis. The other combined uses of research and analysis methods and techniques include PEST analysis, secondary data analysis and literature review and analysis, frequency distribution

Table 4.2: Methods and techniques of policy research in Turkey

Variable	Number	%
Literature review and analysis	26	51.0
Review of literature and laws and regulations	7	13.8
Simple frequency distribution and average	4	7.9
Policy process/cycle analysis	3	5.9
Content analysis	3	5.9
Secondary data analysis and literature review	2	3.9
Review of laws and regulations	1	2.0
Frequency distribution, literature review	1	2.0
Case study	1	2.0
Secondary data analysis and cross-tabulation	1	2.0
PEST analysis	1	2.0
Regression and t test	1	2.0
Total	51	100

and literature review and analysis, each of which was used in only one case (three cases in total, or 5.9 per cent).

The results presented in Table 4.2 also display that there are only two cases (3.9 per cent) where directly quantitative research techniques are applied. One of the two articles on environmental economy and public policies in the field of economics employs secondary data analysis and cross-tabulation, and another one on marketing conducted in the field of business management utilises regression and t test techniques.

Table 4.3: Methods of policy analysis in Turkey

Variable	Number	%
Quantitative analysis	6	11.8
Qualitative-quantitative analysis	2	3.9
Qualitative-quantitative compilation/review	5	9.8
Qualitative analysis	2	3.9
Qualitative compilation/review	36	70.6
Total	51	100

Table 4.3 shows the general research methods used in the policy research and analysis in Turkey. The data presented in Table 4.3 are also in support of the more detailed account of the research and analysis methods and techniques presented in Table 4.2. A total of 74.5 per cent of the policy research techniques (38 cases) used in the sample articles are classified under qualitative methods of analysis, whereas only 11.8 per cent (six cases) are classified under quantitative methods of analysis. The rest (13.7 per cent) are combined methods of analysis.

The internet search also reveals that 16 departments or programmes offer courses on public policy or public policy analysis. Yet the number of courses is much higher since some departments or programmes[3] offer courses on public policy or public policy analysis at undergraduate and graduate levels. An analysis of the course titles reveals that a great majority of them are titled as 'public policy analysis', although these courses are, in general, basic public policy courses, covering public policy concepts, models, process/cycle and actors, and some case studies of specific public policy implementations. Generally speaking, the word 'analysis' is used to refer either to the analysis of public policy cycle or process and the models of public policy/decision-making, or, in a couple of cases, to programme evaluation.

The internet search gave us no hits on any courses directly related to policy research methods and techniques. Similarly, no textbooks on policy research methods are published in Turkish. The only book including chapters on policy research methods is edited by Nevra Seggie and Bayyurt (2015). In this edited book there are two chapters on policy research methods. One is titled 'Qualitative policy analysis' ('Nitel politika analizi') by Keser Ashenberger (2015), and the other is titled 'Evaluation research' ('Değerlendirme analizi') by Sert (2015). Another research methodology book including sections on policy/action research and evaluation research is by Baydar, Gül and Akçil (2008, pp 124–5). Other books are general qualitative or quantitative research books with no specific reference to policy research analysis and methods, such as by Yıldırım and Şimşek (2000), Kuş (2012) and Aziz (2014).

The search results further show that the number of books or textbooks on public policy and public policy analysis is also limited. The latest and most well-known contribution to the field is an edited book titled *Public policy: Theory and practice* (*Kamu politikası: Kuram ve uygulama*) by Yıldız and Sobacı (2013). It should also be mentioned here that the first book with translated chapters directly on public policy in Turkey is an edited book by Saybaşılı, titled *Basic approaches in political science* (*Siyaset biliminde temel yaklaşımlar*) published in 1985. It is also important to note that the *Journal of Legislation* (*Yasama Dergisi*) dedicated two of its 2015 issues to public policies and public policy analysis (although published in 2016) under the editorship of C. Babaoğlu. This could be seen as a sign of increasing attention given to public policy studies in Turkey. Other major books and/or textbooks on public policy and public policy analysis include, but are not limited to, books by Çevik and Demirci ([2008] 2015), Kartal (2011), Kaptı (2011) and Özel (2015), and an encyclopaedia edited by Altınok and Gedikkaya (2016). There are also several general public administration books with specific chapters on public policy. The publication dates of all of these works date to the late 2000s and after.

Last, since the edited book by Yıldız and Sobacı (2013) is the best available source on public policy in Turkey, it is worthwhile analysing its contents. It is divided into two parts including 26 chapters, as well as an introduction and conclusion. The first part covers theoretical and analytical discussions on public policy and public policy analysis, and the second part is made up of some case studies or reviews of different public policies. The topics of the chapters range from urban regeneration to health reform, from immigration policy to disaster management, and from education policy to environmental policy, among others. An analysis of the chapters displays that literature review and analysis is the most common research and analysis technique used (in 12 cases). The other common techniques include secondary data analysis (5 cases), analysis of documents and reports (5 cases), qualitative analysis of in-depth interview data (3 cases), analysis of law and regulations (3 cases), and the policy cycle/process analysis (2 cases). Other methods and techniques of research and analysis include qualitative analysis, comparative qualitative analysis, policy implementation model, storytelling methods and discourse analysis, each of which is used once in separate chapters. There is one chapter in the book worth mentioning that is directly related to public policy research and analysis methods, titled 'Interpretative approaches to public policy' ('Kamu politikasına yorumlamacı yaklaşımlar') by Orhan (2013).

Another major textbook has been written by Çevik and Demirci (2012), which mainly offers a literature review of concepts, theories, actors and the process/cycle of public policy, and decision-making and policy analysis models. The content of public policy open course material by Yıldız (2011) is also akin to the contents of these two books. What is common to all of these books is that they lack a chapter introducing commonly used methods and techniques of policy research and analysis and their application in the practice of policy research.

Conclusion

The number of studies regarding public policy in Turkey has increased in recent years, although there is much ground still to cover. Many of the early studies lacked any policy science and/or policy analysis perspectives, with little research done on public policy research and analysis. Our study aimed to try to close this gap.

According to the results of this study, qualitative methods and techniques are dominant in policy research and analysis in Turkey, making up three-quarters of the methods and techniques used. Combined research and analysis methods make up 13.7 per cent, whereas quantitative analysis is only 11.8 per cent of the total. Similarly, content analysis of courses on public policy or public policy analysis reveals that many of the courses titled 'public policy analysis' are generally basic public policy courses, and only a couple refer to programme evaluation or policy research. There are no courses or textbooks directly related to policy research methods and techniques in Turkish other than general qualitative or quantitative research books with no specific reference to policy research analysis and methods. Public policy textbooks also lack any chapters introducing the widely used methods and techniques of policy research and analysis, and their application.

The findings from this study could be briefly compared with those reported by Morçöl and Ivanova (2010, p 262). The methods and techniques commonly used in public policy studies or courses in Turkey are qualitative in general in contrast to the widespread use of quantitative methods and techniques in the US. The list of the most common quantitative methods used by policy professionals in the US, provided by Morçöl (2001), includes quantitative (surveys, regression analysis, cost-benefit analysis, quasi-experiments, simulations and time-series analysis) and qualitative analysis methods and techniques (brainstorming, political feasibility analysis, Delphi technique and assumptional analysis). In contrast, the results of this study reveal that the qualitative methods and techniques such as literature reviews, review of laws and regulations, policy process/cycle analysis, content analysis and case studies are dominant in Turkey. Other qualitative techniques are combined research and analysis methods, such as frequency distribution, average, PEST analysis and secondary data analysis, and quantitative analysis techniques, such as cross-tabulation, and regression and t tests.

In short, the variances in the application of research and analysis methods utilized in the US and Turkey could mostly be attributed the differences in the historical development of policy studies and the development level of policy studies and research in these two countries. The US has a long tradition of positivist scientific research, the roots of which can be traced back to the 19th century, whereas Turkey lacks such a long tradition. Despite several early examples of public policy reports and studies from the 1950s and onwards, the adaption of a public policy perspective and the use of policy research methods and techniques in such studies are new in Turkey. Other reasons for this difference include, but are not limited to, competency and transparency in the application of these methods, the availability and accessibility of data for policy research and analysis, and variations in policy issues and orientations. For instance, if researchers do not have access to data sets on the outcomes of public policies, they may be forced to make use of qualitative analysis techniques such as reading and analysing legal documents or reviewing and analysing the literature. Of course, research skills would also play a role here, particularly by increasing the reliability, transparency, precision and trustworthiness of policy research. Research conducted properly, skilfully and transparently makes it easier for others to learn how such studies are carried out, and to see how properly established research standards, procedures and principles are applied.

The recent growth in the use of qualitative methods and techniques in the US and their widespread use in Turkey can be seen as a sign of a general trend away from the use of positivist methodology and its quantitative techniques towards the increased application of post-positivist (interpretivist) qualitative methods and techniques. It could be argued that this trend toward an increased use of qualitative research methods or a mix of qualitative and quantitative research methods and techniques is required by the growing complexities of socioeconomic and political life, and the proliferating use of a multidisciplinary approach.

Notes

[1] We need to be precise in the meaning and scope of the term 'method' here. 'Research method' may refer to the rules and tools of empirical inquiry, and policy research and analysis. 'Method' involves design, sampling, data collection and data analysis techniques and steps, and so on, separately or all together within the framework of scientific ethics, rules and procedures (Baydar et al, 2008, p 104; Morçöl and Ivanova, 2010, pp 259-61).

[2] The use of the internet as a source may be seen as questionable since it may cause a selection bias due to the existence of some related journals without internet access. The other option was to select a few sample journals with internet access (such as those published by the Public Administration Institute for Turkey and the Middle East, TODAİE, or those published by the faculties of political sciences or economics and administrative sciences, or graduate schools), and draw a sample of articles for analysis from them according to the established criteria. However, the internet survey option was used since it covers and reaches more journals. Our search provided a rich and diverse source of articles on the subject, as many journals are now accessible on the internet and can be browsed by search engines.

[3] These departments or programmes are: Department of Political Science and Public Administration at Pamukkale University, Department of Political Science and Public Administration at Bandırma 17 Eylül University, Department of Political Science and Public Administration at Ankara University, Department of Political Science and Public Administration at Süleyman Demirel University, Department of Political Science and Public Administration at Hacettepe University, and the Programme of Public Policy and Management at Nevşehir Hacı Bektaş Veli University, among others.

References

Altınok, H. and Gedikkaya, F.G. (2016) *Kamu politikası ansiklopedisi*, Ankara: Nobel.

Aziz, A. (2014) *Sosyal bilimlerde araştırma yöntemleri ve teknikleri* (9th edn), Ankara: Nobel.

Baydar, M.L., Gül, H. and Akçil, A. (2008) *Bilimsel araştırmanın temel İlkeleri*, Yayın No 79, Isparta: Süleyman Demirel Üniversitesi Yayınları.

Brewer, G.D. and deLeon, P. (1983) *The foundations of policy analysis*, Homewood, IL: The Dorsey Press.

Çevik, H.Ç. and Demirci, S. ([2008] 2015) *Kamu politikası: Kavramlar, aktörler, süreç, modeller, analiz, karar verme*, Ankara: Seçkin.

deLeon, P. (1997) *Democracy and the policy sciences*, Albany, NY: State University of New York Press.

Denhardt, R.B. (1981) 'Towards a critical theory of public organizations', *Public Administration Review*, vol 41, no 6 (November-December), pp 628-35.

Durning, D. (1993) 'Participatory policy analysis in a social service agency: A case study', *Journal of Policy Analysis and Management*, vol 12, no 2 (Spring), pp 231-57.

Dye, T. (2002) *Understanding public policy*, Upper Saddle River, NJ: Prentice Hall.

Foster, R.H., McBeth, M.K. and Clemons, R.S. (2010) 'Public policy pedagogy: Mixing methodologies using cases', *Journal of Public Affairs Education*, vol 16, no 4 (Fall), pp 517-40.

Frankfort-Nachmias, C. and Nachmias, D. (1992) *Research methods in the social sciences*, New York: St Martin's Press.

Geva-May, I. and Maslove, A. (2006) 'Canadian public policy analysis and public policy programs: A comparative perspective', *Journal of Public Affairs Education*, vol 12, no 4 (Fall), pp 413-38.

Gül, H. (2015) 'Kamu politikası analizi, yöntemleri ve teknikleri', *Yasama Dergisi*, vol 29 (Ocak-Nisan), pp 1-31.

Habermas, J. (1987) *The theory of communicative action: Lifeworld and system: A critique of functionalist reason*, vol 2 (translated by T. McCarthy), Boston, MA: Beacon.

Howlett, M. and Ramesh, M. (2003) *Studying public policy: Policy cycles and policy subsystems* (2nd edn), Toronto: Oxford University Press.

Kaptı, A. (2011) *Kamu politikası süreci*, Ankara: Seçkin.

Kartal, F. (ed) (2011) *Türkiye'de kamu yönetimi ve kamu politikaları*, Ankara: TODAİE.

Keser Ashenberger, F. (2015) 'Nitel politika analizi', in F. Nevra Seggie and Y. Bayyurt (eds) *Nitel araştırma: Yöntem, teknik, analiz ve yaklaşımları*, Ankara: Anı, pp 323-42.

Kolaf, L., Dan, A. and Dietz, T. (2008) *Essentials of social research*, Maidenhead: Open University Press.

Kuş, E. (2012) *Nicel-nitel araştırma teknikleri* (4th edn), Ankara: Anı.

Lasswell, H. (1971) *A preview of policy sciences*, New York: Elsevier Publishing Company.

MacRae, D., Jr and Wilde, J.A. (1985) *Policy analysis for public decisions*, Lanham, MD: University Press of America.

Manicas, P. (2007) 'The social sciences since world war II: The rise and fall of scientism', in W. Outhwaite and S.P. Turner (ed) *The Sage handbook of social science methodology*, Los Angeles, CA: Sage, pp 7-32.

Mead, L.M. (2005) 'Policy research: The field dimension', *Policy Studies Journal*, vol 33, no 4, pp 35-57.

Mead, L.M. (2013) 'Teaching public policy: Linking policy and politics', *Journal of Public Affairs Education*, vol 19, no 3, pp 389-403.

Miller, D.C. and Salkind, N.J. (2002) *Handbook of research design and social measurement* (6th edn), Thousand Oaks, CA: Sage.

Morçöl, G. (2001) 'Positivist beliefs among policy professionals: An empirical investigation', *Policy Sciences*, vol 34, pp 381-401.

Morçöl, G. (2012) *A complexity theory for public policy*, New York and London: Routledge.

Morçöl, G. and Ivanova N.P. (2010) 'Methods taught in public policy programs: Are quantitative methods still prevalent?', *Journal of Public Affairs Education*, vol 16, no 2, pp 255-77.

Nevra Seggie, F. and Bayyurt, Y. (eds) (2015) *Nitel araştırma: Yöntem, teknik, analiz ve yaklaşımları*, Ankara: Anı.

OECD (Organisation for Economic Co-operation and Development) CERI (Centre for Educational Research and Innovation) (2007) *Evidence in education: Linking research and policy*, Paris: OECD (http://hdl.voced.edu.au/10707/161992).

Orhan, G. (2013) 'Kamu politikasina yorumlamacı yaklaşımlar', in M. Yıldız and M.Z. Sobacı (eds) *Kamu politikası: Kuram ve uygulama*, Ankara: Adres Yayınları, pp 72-93.

Özel, M. (2015) *Yerel yönetimlerde yerel kamu politikası yaklaşımları*, Konya: Çizgi.

Patton, M.Q. (1987) *How to use qualitative methods in evaluation*, Newbury Park, CA, London and New Delhi: Sage.

Radin, B.A. (2013) 'Policy analysis reaches midlife', *Central European Journal of Public Policy*, vol 7, no 1 (June), pp 8-27.

Saybaşılı, K. (1985) *Siyaset biliminde temel yaklaşımlar*, Istanbul: Birey Toplum.

Sert, G. (2015) 'Değerlendirme analizi', in F. Nevra Seggie and Y. Bayyurt (eds) *Nitel araştırma: Yöntem, teknik, analiz ve yaklaşımları*, Ankara: Anı, pp 162-71.

Warren, M. (1992) 'Democratic theory and self-determination', *American Political Science Review*, vol 86, no 1 (March), pp 8-23.

Weiss, C.H. (1983) 'Ideology, interests and information: The bases of policy positions', in D. Callahan and B. Jennings (eds) *Ethics, social sciences and policy analysis*, New York and London: Plenum Press, pp 213-47.

Yıldırım, A. and Şimşek, H. (2000) *Sosyal bilimlerde nitel araştırma yöntemleri* (2nd edn), Ankara: Seçkin.

Yanow, D. (2007) 'Qualitative-interpretive methods in policy research', in F. Fischer, G.J. Miller and M.S. Sidney (eds) *Handbook of public policy analysis: Theory, politics, and methods*, Boca Raton, FL: CRC Press, Taylor & Francis, pp 405-15.

Yıldız, M. (2011) *Kamu politikası ders notları*, Ankara: TÜBA ((http://www.acikders.org.tr/course/view.php?id=66)).

Yıldız, M. and Sobacı, M.Z. (eds) (2013) *Kamu politikası: Kuram ve uygulama*, Ankara: Adres Yayınları.

Part Two
Policy analysis by governments

FIVE

Policy analysis in Turkey's central government: current practices and future challenges

Uğur Sadioğlu

Introduction

This chapter focuses on recent developments and institutional transformations in the Turkish central government's administrative system, and analyses prominent policy-making actors.

A detailed discussion of current practices and future challenges in policy analysis in Turkey's central government would be incomplete, however, without a brief historical overview.

During the founding of the Republic in Turkey, a modern political-administrative system was shaped based on a unitary state and parliamentary political regime, with the Assembly and the 'parliamentary government' system playing a dominant role. The 1924 Constitution, from which the current constitutional regime originates, instituted a classical parliamentary regime, and the President of the Republic and Council of Ministers were defined as the executive bodies of the political-administrative system (Eroğul, 2000, p 257), with principal executive powers. Turkey adopted a multi-party system in 1950 and a new constitution in 1961 (Sabuncu, 2002, p 31).

In the 1950s, the Democratic Party had tried to reduce the privileges of the bureaucratic class, to remove bureaucratic channels, to reduce the economic status of the bureaucracy, to limit the state's intervention in the social structure and to strengthen the private sector (Berkman and Heper, 2002, p 151). In this period, the international organisations' technical assistance to the developing countries affected the public administration. During the last years of the 1940s and the 1950s, reports of foreign experts and commissions – (Neumark, Conk and Savun, Barker Mission, Martin and Cush, Leimgruber, UN Working Group, Chaileux Dantel) (see Yayman, 2016, pp136-156) – made to the Turkish public administration focused on organizational structure, managerial processes and personnel management. However, the application was limited and priority was given to depoliticization in order to make the bureaucracy efficient and effective (Berkman and Heper, 2002, pp 152-154).

Although the 1961 Constitution did not amend the governmental and central executive organs in general terms, it added some major players such as the

Constitutional Court, State Planning Organisation (SPO) and State Personnel Department (SPD) to the policy-making process (Heper, 1994, pp 667-8; Polatoğlu, 2000, pp 89-90). Initiated in the 1950s following reports by foreign experts, discussions on the re-organization of Turkey's public administration yielded some results at the project and report levels in the 1960s due to studies by the Public Administration Institute for Turkey and the Middle East (TODAİE), the Ministry of Internal Affairs and SPO (Berkman and Heper, 2002, pp 154-6; see Tanör, 1995).

Due to the nature of its economic policies, the Economic Stability Decisions of 24 January 1980 changed Turkey's economic perspective and the 1982 Constitution re-defined the players Turkey's central government. The 1982 Constitution relies on the executive organ, with its political responsibility defined through a classical parliamentary regime, the Prime Minister and Council of Ministers. It also defined a stronger President for the Republic, with more roles to play. The fundamental ceremonial authorities of the presidency were not amended, but its powers and duties concerning legislation, execution and jurisdiction were strengthened (see Gözler, 2013). The President was vested with the power to chair the National Security Council, which orients general strategic and security policies; he/she can preside over the Council of the Ministers whenever he/she deems it necessary; and the Council of Ministers is authorised to issue decrees, having the force of the law during extra-ordinary administration procedures. Such regulations included in this Constitution turned the President of the Republic into a crucial actor in the policy-making process (Polatoğlu, 2000, pp 84-6; Sabuncu, 2000, p 108; Özbudun, 2014, p 66; Gözler, 2015, p 55).

At the same time, the role and power of the Prime Minister and prime ministry also increased in central government, with Prime Ministers also acting as leaders of political parties, and a political culture adopted in which the Prime Minister plays an indisputable role in the decision-making process. The 1982 Constitution also vested more power in the Prime Minister in terms of selecting, authorising and firing other ministers. As the Prime Minister's position was strengthened, the number of public institutions and organisations affiliated with the prime ministry also increased (Sabuncu, 2002, p 219). Important institutions such as the Undersecretariat of the Treasury, SPO, Undersecretariat of Foreign Trade, Undersecretariat of Customs, Turkish Statistical Institute, Supreme Economic Councils, Housing Development Administration (TOKİ), General Staff of the Turkish Armed Forces, Regional Development Administration of the Southeastern Anatolia Project and the National Intelligence Organization were all organised under the prime ministry (Polatoğlu, 2000, pp 87-9; Gözübüyük, 2013, p 120).

New policy players emerged during the mid-1980s as the free market economy gained strength, the role of the state in social welfare was reduced, definitions and targets of development policies changed, and the functions and significance of the SPO diminished in accordance with a neoclassical development approach, necessitating a new economic-political organisation (see Kepenek and Yentürk,

2005; Şahin, 2006; Karluk, 2009). This neo-liberal policy adopted by the Turkish governments was followed through the departments and authorities that were established under the prime ministry before and after the 24 January 1980 Decisions, which were a critical juncture in economic policies. The Economy Coordination Board and the Money Credit Board are two examples representing the new governance style, and demonstrate how political actors in central government, particularly the Prime Minister, became the most influential in economic policies. Economic administration has been under the control and directive of the Prime Minister since 1984 (Heper, 1994, pp 669-71; Berkman and Heper, 2002, p 159), with the SPO becoming an executive unit instead of a policy and plan preparing center (Dik, 2017, pp 149-55). A similar case emerged for the administration of the economy in this period, with a discussion regarding managing and directing the Ministry of Finance, Ministry of Customs and Trade, SPO and the Central Bank of the Republic of Turkey (CBRT) through a central authority (see Bakır, 2012).

New public sector actors came into prominence as the importance of regulatory organisations in policy-making and implementation processes increased. New public management (NPM) and governance paradigms contributed significantly to the legitimacy and structure of these regulatory authorities (Sezen, 2003, pp 112-13; Güler, 2010, pp 323-4). The Capital Markets Board of Turkey (CMB) was first established in 1982 and other regulatory organisations (for example, the Competition Regulatory Authority [Rekabet Kurumu, or RK]), Banking Regulation and Supervision Agency [BDDK] and Energy Market Regulatory Authority [EMRA, or Enerji Piyasası Düzenleme Kurumu, EPDK]) were established in the 1990s and 2000s (Acar, 2004, pp 97-8; Leblebici et al, 2012, pp 83-4). There are nine regulatory and supervisory authorities in accordance with Central Government Budget Law no 6767 of 2016 for the year 2017. Regulatory organisations, however, have been moved away from governance ideals and practice after 10 years of reform (see Ayhan and Üstüner, 2015). Regulatory organisations have begun to lose their independent qualifications in the administrative reform process in recent years. From a hierarchical perspective, they have been under the direct responsibility and the indirect supervision of the Ministries since 2011.

Furthermore, privatisation of public economic enterprises is also related to changes in the policy means and implementation of central government. Since the mid-1990s, policies aimed at harmonisation with the European Union (EU) have also initiated institutional transformation at central government level. Although the Europeanisation process did not require conformance with a template for public administration organisation, it referred to a governance understanding based on rule of law, democratic principles, rights and freedoms, and led to serious institutional transformations, requiring, for example, the establishment of the Secretariat-General for EU Affairs in order to carry out negotiations with the EU at central government level (Ömürgönülşen and Öktem, 2007, pp 20-1).

During the early 2000s, a new institutional transformation and policy-making understanding shaped by the EU integration process started to be adopted in Turkey. In this period, the NPM approach was the dominant factor for public administration reform. Through the Public Financial Management and Control Law no 5018 of 2003, most of the essential components of the NPM reforms (strategic planning, performance-based budgeting and internal inspection processes) started to be applied to public administration, and were also accompanied by a decentralisation process. In 2011, a major transformation in central government and all public administration systems took place. Decrees having the force of law were enacted in this year, important new ministries were established at central government level, other essential central government institutions (such as the SPO, Secretariat-General for EU Affairs, Undersecretariat of Foreign Trade, Undersecretariat of Customs, Undersecretariat of Maritime Affairs, etc) were transformed into ministries, and new institutions and organisations emerged that brought significant changes to the ministries. This comprehensive transformation can also be regarded as a *re-centralisation* process.

These major institutional transformations were also accompanied by attempts to realise a new political-administrative system through the presidency of the Republic. Discussions set forth a comprehensive political-administrative system and proposals to change the government system. In particular, a referendum in 2007 adopted an election procedure to the Constitution in which citizens would directly elect the President of the Republic. This situation, combined with the strong powers of the President of the Republic, furthered discussions on instituting a presidential system. A decade later, as a result of the referendum held in April 2017, Turkey adopted a presidential government system. In this system, which will take effect in 2019, the government will be separate from Parliament, the Prime Minister and Council of Ministers will be abolished, and the elected President will be authorised to establish government and appoint ministers. This transformation into a presidential government system will further contribute to re-centralisation at ministerial level, and deeply affect the policy-makers, processes and implementations of public policies in Turkey.

This chapter is organised as follows. The next section analyses the policy actors and dynamics that have been influential in the post-1990 period at central government level in Turkey. In particular, a new institutional transformation – policy-making shaped by the EU integration process and the centralisation of the prime ministry during the 2000s – is examined. This is followed by analysis of the recent constitutional changes in Turkey through a discussion of the presidential system, followed by an evaluation of the transformation of policy-making actors in central government.

Centralisation of the prime ministry in the 2000s

In Turkey, the 1990s are considered 'lost' years. Political turmoil, maladministration of the economy, chronic problems of public administration, increasing terrorist incidents, destruction created by the earthquake in Gölcük in 1999, a pervasive informal economy, inefficiency of the private sector and the fragile structure of the finance sector are considered to have contributed to the subsequent 2001 financial crisis (see Yeldan, 2012). Political, bureaucratic and institutional frameworks that had not complied with the liberal economy came under pressure for reform. Following the crisis, the policy entrepreneurship of Kemal Derviş played a pivotal role in micro-institutional reform guided by international intergovernmental organisations (Bakır, 2009). Some of the key changes since 2001 that relate to central government can be summarised as follows: (1) re-organisation of the state and certain private banks under the Savings Deposit Insurance Fund (TMSF); (2) transformation of state banks from a public economic enterprise to a joint stock company and their privatisation; (3) ensuring the autonomy of the CBRT; (4) ensuring public finance discipline; (5) ensuring transparency, accountability, flexibility and efficiency in public administration; and (6) sustaining economic policies based on export, foreign investment and real economic growth policies.

In accordance with the policy recommendations of Strengthening The Turkish Economy – Turkey's Transition Program (STEP), fundamental regulations such as a budget law, code of obligations, law of expropriation, public procurement law, law on the central bank, law on banks, law on the economic and social council, and a law on natural monopoly were included in the STEP programme (Sadioğlu and Öktem, 2011, pp 55-6). According to Taşar (2010, pp 77-8, 81-2), the GEGP experience in Turkey is a good example of a stability programme at local, regional and international level, global economic policies and the 'regulatory state' approach. As a result of the financial crisis, Turkey was more anchored to the International Monetary Fund (IMF) and EU, which increased their influence in Turkey's national policies, and the democratic regime was strengthened by EU admission reforms. Membership negotiations for Turkey included chapters on the 'customs union, free movement of capital, environment, consumer and health protection, competition policy, common agriculture policy, transport policy, public procurement, financial control, financial and budgetary provisions, taxation' (Bilici, 2013). Since 2006, eight additional chapters have not been open for negotiation for the accession negotiations between Turkey and EU Commission. Turkey–EU relations are strategic as they cover issues of mutual interest, from energy to security, democracy to culture and economic administration (Bilici, 2013, pp 107, 113-16). The subsequent transformation of the Secretariat-General of EU Affairs to the Ministry of EU Affairs in 2001 is important since it shows how dedicated Turkey is to the EU membership process (Saylam and Ömürgönülsen, 2013, p 186). Instrument independence of the CBRT in monetary and exchange rate policies was ensured, regulatory and supervisory authorities in tobacco, sugar and telecommunication sectors were established, and TEKEL (Monopoly on Tobacco and Alcoholic Products) was transformed from a public economic enterprise to a state-owned corporation.

The Abdullah Gül Government (58th government), which was established when the Justice and Development Party (Adalet ve Kalkınma Partisi, AKP) came to power in 2002, put comprehensive public administration reform on the agenda, starting from the prime ministry, while adopting the economic targets and steps of the GEGP. Attaching affiliated institutions of the prime ministry to the line ministries, bringing economic administration under a single umbrella, implementing comprehensive reforms after discussing every aspect of the ministries, and sustaining the functions of regulatory and supervisory institutions on the condition that the government reserved the right to determine macro policies were all included in the government programme (Dik, 2017, pp 173-4). The 59th government, established by Recep Tayyip Erdoğan, Prime Minister, maintained this programme for 10 years. Parliament first approved the Law on the Fundamental Principles and Restructuring of Public Administration, Law no 5227, although it did not actually come into force since the President did not ratify it in 2004. This law was prepared according to NPM and governance perspectives, and adopted the principles of efficiency, effectiveness, transparency, participation and accountability in public administration. Taking the reason why it has been adopted, its content, purposes and means of application into consideration, this law is very much in line with the NPM approach.

The most radical institutional change envisaged by this law was to shift authority, duties, resources and policy-making powers from central to local governments, transferring the provincial organisations of almost all ministries, excluding the Ministries of Defence, Justice and Foreign Affairs, to special provincial administrations. Indeed, this was the most important point of criticism about the law. It also aimed to strengthen the Ministry of Economy, making it the only authority in economic administration, merge some of the line ministries and reduce their numbers, introduce vice-ministers, transfer the Prime Ministry Higher Audit Board to the Turkish Court of Accounts, and simplify the hierarchy of the ministries. Although these reforms could not be realised in 2003, most of them – except the transfer of provincial organisations – were later fulfilled through various laws enacted between 2003 and 2011 (see Güler, 2010).

The Public Financial Management and Control Law no 5018 of 2003 is one of the most significant reforms in terms of policy-making, planning and budget management. It is based on fiscal transparency (Article 7), accountability (Article 8), and strategic planning and performance-based budgeting (Article 9). The new budget system establishes a significant inspection–monitoring mechanism between the policy-making, planning and budgeting processes of all public institutions and organisations, from small municipalities to ministerial level. Criteria such as strategic planning, performance-based budgeting and performance management, which are among the most essential instruments of NPM, were incorporated into the Turkish public administration system. The purpose of this law is defined as the economic and efficient collection and utilisation of public resources, ensuring accountability and fiscal transparency in public fiscal management in line with the politics and objectives covered in the development plans and programmes (Article 1). With this law, 'Preparing government policies, development plans, annual programs, strategic plans and budgets; negotiating them with the authorised bodies; implementing them and making the implementation results and the relevant reports available and accessible to the public' (Article 7) were made compulsory. The goal was to enhance transparency in policy-making, implementation and evaluation at all administration levels, including central government. Again, in accordance with development plans and programmes, strategic plans through participation became mandatory for all public administration organisations. Public administration units are obliged to base their budgets and expenditures on their strategic plans and performance indicators (Article 9). Public administration units within central government, local governments and social security institutions are covered under this law, although there are some exceptions for regulatory and supervisory authorities (Article 2). The Ministry of Finance is responsible for monitoring fiscal policy whereas the Ministry of Development is in charge of defining the procedures and principles to associate the strategic planning process, its calendar, development plan and programme with the strategic plan. The Ministry of Finance is authorised to define the procedures concerning the compatibility of public administration with performance indicators stated in the strategic plans and issues concerning performance-based budgeting (Article 9). In accordance with this, the Ministry of Finance is authorised to prepare a Budget Call and Budget Preparation Guide; the Ministry of Development is authorised to prepare the Investment Circular and Investment Programme Preparation Guide in order to guide the preparation process of the budget proposals and investment programmes of the public administrations (Article 16). So the Ministry of Finance and Ministry of Development have gained more authority in terms of planning and budgeting. On the other hand, according to Biçer and Yılmaz (2009, pp 64, 76), Law no 5018 allowed Parliament to use its budgetary rights more efficiently. The Grand National Assembly of Turkey (Türkiye Büyük Millet Meclisi, TBMM) is expected to ensure that public authorities in particular fulfil their liabilities for accountability together with reviewing the authority's activity results reports, evaluation reports by the Court of Accounts and general eligibility declarations (Article 41). However, it is necessary to discuss to what extent Parliament, the executive branch or bureaucracy successfully implements these changes in practice (Biçer and Yılmaz, 2009, p 78).

Although the initial effects of the global financial crisis of 2008 were not seen in Turkey, the aftershocks have become apparent over time, as Turkey has faced fundamental institutional transformations. The reform discourses, changes in economic policies and terrorist attacks that Turkey has experienced in recent years have triggered serious institutional transformation. Examining the changes in the ministry system from the front would be useful for a holistic analysis.

In 2011 the government issued 35 decree laws; new ministries were established, current ministries were either merged or divided, and Law no 3046 on the organisation of the ministries was considerably amended. The new ministries that were established were the Ministry of Family and Social Policies, Ministry of EU Affairs, Ministry of Economy, Ministry of Youth and Sports and the Ministry of Development – the SPO had become the Ministry of Development, the Secretariat-General for EU Affairs became the Ministry of EU Affairs, and some units of the Undersecretariat of Customs and Trade, Undersecretariat of the Treasury and Undersecretariat of Foreign Trade became part of the Ministry of Economy. Some ministries were merged or divided, including the Ministry of Science, Industry and Technology, Ministry of Food, Agriculture and Livestock, Ministry of Environment and Urban Planning, Ministry of Forest and Water Management and Ministry of Customs and Trade. These changes in the ministerial system reflect a new centralisation model based on political power of the central government (Övgün and Özçağlar Eroğlu, 2016, p 382; see also Keleş, 2016). In particular, the strengthening of the powers of the Ministry of Environment and Urban Planning in urban planning, dwelling products and tutelage of city planning by local governments are some of the best examples of the 're-centralisation' wave.

In addition to these changes, (ministry without portfolio) state ministries were abolished and a 'vice-minister' was established as the highest executive in the ministry hierarchy after the minister. Vice-ministers are positioned between the elected minister and appointed undersecretary, and are appointed as public servants rather than Members of Parliament. The vice-minister assists the minister and ministry to fulfil the tasks assigned. The term of the vice-minister is limited to the term of government (3046, Article 21/A-Annex 3/6/2011-Decree Law no 643, Article 3).

Finally, the position of deputy prime minister was strengthened to play a central role in economic administration. Deputy prime ministers are nominated by the Prime Minister and appointed by the President of the Republic from among the ministers. At most, five deputy prime ministers can be appointed. They coordinate with the Board of Ministers on behalf of the Prime Minister, are consulted for special and essential issues, and assist with the composition of government and execution of general policies (amended on 3/6/2011, Decree Law no 643/Article 1, 3046, Article 4). Essential organisations were attached to deputy prime ministers, such as the BDDK, SPK and Undersecretariat of the Treasury. Strong organisations in central government were transformed into ministries and the prime ministry was strengthened through these reforms, which led to a 'prime ministerial government system' (Dik, 2017, pp 179-82).

Changes in 2011 limited the autonomy of independent regulatory authorities. Although they continue to carry out their activities with their own budgets and decision-making mechanisms, the government now assigns their boards, and a board/authority cannot be regarded as independent and carry out its activities independently as long as it is affiliated or associated with a ministry. Politicisation, centralisation, nepotism and bureau-pathologic problems are an ongoing issue in these organisations (Leblebici et al, 2012, p 104). The inclusion of political supervision may further these problems.

Institutions such as the SPO, Treasury, Foreign Trade, Customs and the Secretariat-General for EU Affairs, which were regarded as relatively autonomous, were transformed into ministries with the 2011 reforms, which then rendered them open to political influence, and deputy prime ministers put forward political

Figure 5.1: Hierarchy of a prime ministerial government system

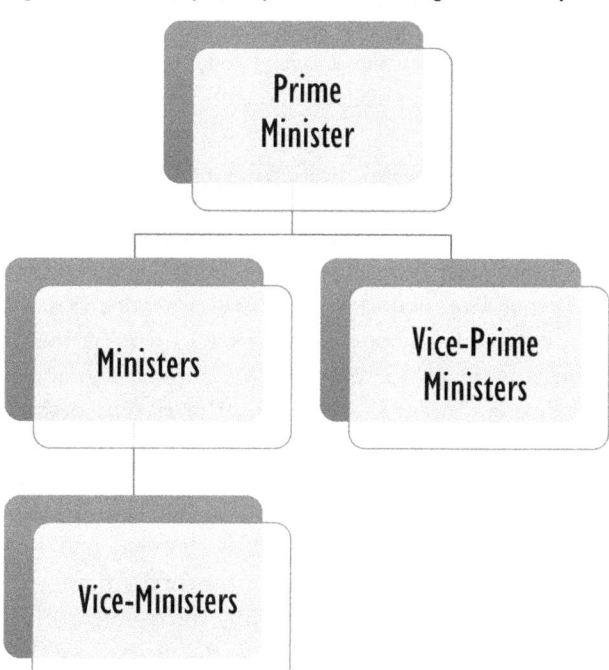

actors for roles in economic administration. A team consisting of the Prime Minister, deputy prime ministers, ministers and vice-ministers in general was given a central role in the policy-making process. The ministerial organisation even lost its significance, and coordination boards under the prime ministry (Economy Coordination Board, Financial Stability Committee, Interest-Free Finance Coordination Board, Coordination Council for the Improvement of Investment Environment and the Reform Coordination and Monitoring Board) came to the forefront. Policy-making under the prime ministry is one of the factors weakening the parliamentary government system. In the parliamentary system, relations between Parliament and bureaucracy arise because the ministers are deputies and each ministry has an independent public service area. In a system where the Prime Minister is institutionally strengthened, the influence of Parliament on the ministries diminishes.

Centralisation through presidency, a new period

Following the constitutional amendment adopted by the referendum held on 21 October 2007, the President of the Republic is chosen via public elections. This then brought into question the type of government system in Turkey. As the 1982 Constitution gives more powers to the President of the Republic that conflict with the parliamentary government system and by the combination of these authorities with the President of the Republic, who is elected by the public, these are considered to be a shift to a semi-presidential system. These changes led to uncertainties, and many considered them as steps towards a presidential system (Güler, 2010, p 136). According to Sevinç (2013, p 281), the election of the President of the Republic directly by the public could only be considered a 'quarter presidency'.

However, it should also be kept in mind that although the election of the President by the public was adopted in 2007, disparities in the nature of the government system only emerged after the President of the Republic, elected by the public for the first time, came into office on 28 August 2014. According to Gözler (2015, pp 248-55), before that date (from 1982 to 2014), the government system in Turkey was purely parliamentary. There was no issue of the President having too much power as these powers were subject to the 'counter signature rule' in the parliamentary government system. Therefore, the system before 2014 could not be labelled as a 'semi-presidential system'. However, after the 12th President of the Republic, Recep Tayyip Erdoğan, took office, the system was no longer purely parliamentary. Even though all the characteristics of the parliamentary system remain, only the election procedure has changed.

In order to describe the system as a presidential system, the issues of the President acting as the real head of the executive body and 'determining the overall policy of the country' are now discussed. For instance, in the case of the election of the leader of a political party that holds the majority in Parliament as the President of the Republic, he/she may attempt to determine the overall policy of the country. In such a case, the system would operate like a 'de facto presidential system', although legally it is not. Duverger (1980) defines systems where the public elect the President of the Republic as 'semi-presidential systems'. It might be argued that after 2014, the government system in Turkey became a 'semi-presidential government system', although this does not clearly explain the case of Turkey, because the determination of the country's policy by the President of the Republic depends only on gaining approval of the political party or parties holding the majority in the TBMM.

From 28 August 2014 to 7 June 2015, the period between the election of the President of the Republic by the public and the first general election thereafter, Turkey became a de facto presidential system (Gözler, 2015, pp 255-6). On 7 June 2015, a single party government could not be established since the AKP lost its majority in the TBMM, coalition negotiations between the AKP and Republican People's Party (Cumhuriyet Halk Partisi, CHP) yielded no result, and the President of the Republic decided for the first time to call for a new election. Thereupon, the 63rd government, officiating from 25 August 2015 to 24 November 2015 during the new election process, was established as an ad hoc Council of Ministers. This constitutional method was employed for the first time in the history of the Republic. As a result of the election held on 1 November 2015, AKP won a majority in the TMBB and was able to establish a government alone. Yet the government of Prime Minister Ahmet Davutoğlu (64th government) stayed in power from 25 November 2015 to 24 May 2016, at which point Davutoğlu had to step down as Prime Minister. This demonstrates that the President of the Republic and the Prime Minister may have political conflict although they are from the same political party. After the coup attempt on 15 July 2016, Turkey entered a new political process and the 'presidential government system' entered the political agenda.

According to Yayman (2016, p 290), well before the President of the Republic Tayyip Erdoğan, political leaders such as Necmettin Erbakan, Alparslan Türkeş, Süleyman Demirel and Turgut Özal had criticised the parliamentary system. It is claimed that these leaders who took office at the top of government had similar favourable opinions towards the presidential system. Supporters of the presidential system argued that there was a need for a dynamic government system in an environment where Turkey's national and foreign policy were intertwined, such as after the 1 November 2015 election. It seemed impossible to solve the chronic problems of Turkey through the 'fusty and worn-out structure' of the parliamentary system, and it was argued that in order to become a 'super state', the governing structure and decision-making mechanisms should be redesigned (Yayman, 2016, p 293). A new constitution and presidential system were suggested, and it was deemed that through complementary comprehensive public administration (state) reform, these problems would be solved and Turkey would leap forward. Furthermore, due to Turkey's effective role in regional matters, the presidential system was put forward as a bulwark against internal and external pressures aiming to create a chaotic atmosphere (Yayman, 2016, pp 293-7). However, there is a significant difference between the presidential system defined by Yayman and the presidential government system adopted in Turkey. According to Yayman, in presidential systems 'legislative and executive bodies are independent. Both are established by a separate election' (2016, p 298). In the system adopted in Turkey, elections of the TBMM and President of the Republic are held on the same day, the term of office of both is the same and the President of the Republic, who could also be the leader of a political party, can designate MPs. The issue appears again, because the 'president is not allowed to abolish the parliament' (Yayman, 2016, p 298). The most important feature of the presidential system is that the two bodies cannot put an end to each other's existence. However, in the new system, the President may decide to call for new parliamentary elections, if there is political instability.

As Eroğul (2000, p 351) stressed years ago, there is a constitutional issue in Turkey, and a new constitution will always be on the political agenda as an urgent problem of the Republic. Moreover, as none of the new constitution-making processes have so far observed principles of democratic participation (the constitutions or amendments to them have been drafted by political or bureaucratic elites), this has led to a weakening of the democratic constitutional system. Of course, the constitution in itself will not be sufficient to provide solutions to political, social and economic problems. However, the channels it will open and the democratic institutions and mechanisms that it will introduce may facilitate solutions to these problems (Yazıcı, 2016, pp 265-7). The functionality of new arrangements established by the new constitution appears to depend on whether the 'new state elites' and 'new politicians' will get on, as well as their ability to cope with the problems in Turkey's political life (Heper, 2006, pp 256-7).

The presidential government system and its evaluation

Law no 6771 on the amendment of the constitution, which was supported by the AKP and Nationalist Movement Party (*Milliyetçi Hareket Partisi,* MHP) was adopted on 21 January 2017. Due to the fact that a parliamentary majority could not be ensured to directly adopt the amendment, the law was presented to the public via a referendum on 16 April 2017. Voter participation in the referendum was 85.43 per cent; the rate of 'yes' votes to valid votes was identified as 51.41 per cent and that of 'no' votes was 48.89 per cent (YSK, 2017, p 1). Hence, the bill regulating the presidential government system, as well as critical amendments to the legislative and executive bodies, was adopted.

With this amendment, the term of office of the TBMM, which was reduced to four years by constitutional amendment in 2010, was increased back to five years. Elections of the TBMM and President of the Republic will be held on the same day every five years (Article 77). The TBMM may decide to call for new elections based on the votes of three-fifths (360) of the members. The President of the Republic may decide unilaterally to call for new elections. In such cases, the parliamentary and presidential elections shall be held together. If Parliament takes this decision in the second term of the President of the Republic, he/she may become a candidate one more time (Article 116). Another important amendment is that the number of members of the TBMM was increased from 550 to 600 (Article 75). The powers of the TBMM regarding legislation and the budget are preserved in general (Article 87). The TBMM will also exercise its knowledge acquisition and supervisory powers by means of 'parliamentary investigation, general debate, parliamentary inquiry and written question.' Among these, the most effective is that the parliamentary inquiry could be utilised regarding vice-presidents and ministers (Article 98). None of these supervisory tools directly relate to the President of the Republic.

According to the amendment, the term of office of the President of the Republic shall be five years, and a person may be elected as President for a maximum of two terms. Candidates for the presidency may be nominated by political party groups that gain a minimum of 5 per cent of the valid votes alone or in sum in the latest general elections, and that have at least 100,000 voters. Finally, the elected President shall no longer be a member of the TBMM (Article 101).

In this presidential government system, the President of the Republic is Head of State and the only person exercising executive power. The duties and powers vested in the President, as Head of State, are maintained by the 1982 Constitution (Article 104). The President appoints and dismisses vice-presidents and ministers. He/she appoints senior public executives, dismisses them, and regulates the procedures and principles of their appointment by presidential decree. The President may issue a 'presidential decree' on issues related to executive power. These must be in compliance with the law – it is stipulated that they may not contradict the laws or the Constitution, and if the TBMM issues a law on the same topic, the presidential decree shall become obsolete (Article 104).

Unlike the constitutional tradition maintained so far, the 2017 amendments define the 'general criminal responsibility' of the President. Accordingly, the initiation of an investigation of the President on allegations of a crime can be requested by an absolute majority (301) of the members of the TBMM. The TBMM may decide to open an investigation with three-fifths (360) of the total number of members of the TBMM. The report of the TBMM Investigation Committee shall be considered at the General Assembly and the TBMM may decide to send the President to the Supreme Court with two-thirds (400) of its members' votes. If it is decided to open an investigation of the President, he/she cannot decide to call for a new parliamentary election. The term of office of the President ends if he/she is sentenced by the Supreme Court to a crime that conflicts with the presidential eligibility criteria (Article 105).

After being elected, the President may appoint one or more 'vice-presidents'. The vice-president shall serve as the acting president and exercise the powers of the President in the event of vacancy of the presidential post for any reason, until a new President of the Republic is elected (45 days), or in the case of a temporary absence of the President (Article 106). Vice-presidents and ministers are appointed from among those eligible to be deputies and may be dismissed by the President (Article 106).

The establishment and abolishment of the ministries, their duties and authorities and the establishment of central and provincial organisations is regulated by 'presidential decree' (Article 106). One of the most important amendments regarding the Turkish public administration and policy-making process is included in this Article. All the regulatory processes, duties, authorities and organisational structures of the ministries that, pursuant to the 1982 Constitution, used to be established by law, are now left to the discretion of the President. Turkey is entering a period that is more dynamic and flexible regarding the future of the ministries and their decision-making processes.

In the new government system, the President only has the power of legislative proposal regarding the budget. The President presents the bill to the TBMM before the new financial year. If the budget law cannot come into force in time, the budget of the previous year is increased in line with the reappraisal rate and implemented until the new budget law is adopted (Article 161).

Apart from these fundamental amendments, words such as 'Prime Minister', 'Council of Ministers', 'ministers' and 'enactment' that are mentioned in the provisions of the 1982 Constitution are entirely amended in accordance with the presidential government system. The most radical amendments in the history of the Republic in terms of the government system were introduced with the 2017 constitutional amendments. The President of the Republic has been assigned as the most determinant actor at central government level, as Head of State and sole representative of the executive body. The granting of regulatory powers through the mechanism of presidential decree has completed this transformation process. The President holds decisive authority, not only at central government level, but also over all provincial organisations, local governments and other entities and institutions through the power of issuing decrees for the executive branch. Therefore, the President will become the principal actor in policy-making and implementation processes at all levels.

Could the Turkish presidential government system be deemed a pure presidential system? Presidential systems and parliamentary systems can be differentiated based on three basic differences. First, legislative and executive powers cannot dismiss each other in a presidential system, whereas reciprocal dismissal is possible in the parliamentary system. Accordingly, the Turkish 'presidential government system' does not comport itself according to the presidential system in that it grants authorisation to both powers for dismissal (albeit with conditions) in this respect. Although it is close to the parliamentary system in this regard, the abolition of the Prime Minister and Council of Ministers has changed the parliamentary system. Similarly, the conditionality for the dismissal of the President by the TBMM on the renewal of elections and the requirement for a three-fifths majority do not comport with the parliamentary system (Gözler, 2017, pp 15-16). According to Gözler (2017, pp 16-20), this amendment to the presidential system has introduced a 'strange parliamentary government system' and is based on the unity of powers. It is alleged that the current regulations would put the TBMM under the control of the President. However, in the presidential system there is a strict separation of powers. Secondly, the judiciary is assumed to be independent regardless of system. This has been another matter of criticism towards the new system, and it is asserted that the appointment of members of the Supreme Council of Judges and Public Prosecutors and the Constitutional Court has 'paved the way for the loss of independence for the judicial system against the President and the judicial branch has also been brought under the control of the President' (Gözler, 2017, p 20). It is indicated that the concept of 'abusive constitutionalism' developed by David Landau (2013) best describes the recent constitutional amendments in Turkey (see Gözler, 2017, p 20).

Thirdly, 'the balance and control mechanisms for the relations between the President and the legislative, executive and judiciary bodies are not regulated. The powers of the President, such as calling for new elections and appointing vice-presidents, ministers, senior government executives and members of the Supreme Council of Judges and Prosecutors, are granted without being subject to any control. Examples of such authorisation cannot be found in contemporary democracies' (Gözler, 2017, pp 21-2).

Turkey will go through a comprehensive legal-institutional preparation process between 2017 and 2019. In this period, balancing the criticisms of the presidential government system, election law, law on political parties and new constitutional amendments may be attempted. It will make the TBMM and all political parties responsible for making complementary arrangements for the new system. In addition, public administration reform, being on the agenda since 2000, will maintain its vitality. In this context, NPM-centred reform initiatives with neoliberal content are in need of input contributed by the neo-Weberian state and fed by democratic theory. In this way, devising a new government system in general, and policy-making in particular, could be adopted by the wider masses in terms of input and output legitimacy. After such an administrative reform, increasing reliance on the state and policy-making process will then positively influence social, political, economic, cultural and foreign relations with a multiplier effect.

Conclusion

There is no direct relationship between the type of governmental systems and strength of democracy; strong democracies may be observed in parliamentary, presidential or semi-presidential systems. In a presidential system, the president and parliament cannot dismiss each other. This allows for political stability and limits the political instability that may be caused by the regime. On the other hand, if the majority that elect the President and the majority that is dominant in Congress have different political orientations, then the system might become deadlocked. In parliamentary systems, both organs have mechanisms to dismiss each other. This fact yields different results based on the country, political structure, traditions and party system. In a semi-presidential system, the most ideal case is that the government has an absolute majority in Parliament and good relations with the President in order to work in harmony. In this system, there is always a risk of governmental instability and interruption of democracy. Among these, semi-presidential systems are regarded as risky systems of balance with various advantages and disadvantages. Therefore, a semi-presidential system did not meet the needs of Turkey, as political stability is one of the main concerns. A presidential system seems to be the best option to create a stable government in Turkey. However, providing stability for the government also has the potential to create threats that may break down the regime. Therefore, another option to ensure the stability of government and create a sound environment for democracy would be improving the parliamentary system. However, it should be kept in mind that constitutional engineering alone will not be enough to strengthen democracy. Apart from the constitution and law, there are other determining factors such as the level of economic development, equality in income distribution, population density and structure, political culture, political party system, election system, role of political actors and ability of different social groups to negotiate and compromise (Yazıcı, 2017, pp 185-7). These indicate that the transition from a prime ministerial to a presidential government system will have a limited impact on surmounting all political-economic problems.

Having analysed the organisation of Turkey's central government, it is seen that the expectation of the reform process was not a system with a tradition of centralisation and bureaucratic habits. The organisations and functions envisaged in Law no 3046 cannot meet the challenges of a rapidly changing economic, social, technological, political and cultural world. Hierarchical policy-making structures, slow bureaucracy and habits of intervention do not meet the definition of an efficient government. If the public policies, public services and public expenditures-investments are not in line with the needs and expectations of the people, trust in the government diminishes (see Saygılıoğlu and Arı, 2002). The executive characteristics of the prime ministry in the current situation and the presidency after 2019 should be re-organised in order to strengthen the policy-making role. The prime ministry, together with its affiliated, associated and related organisations, seems to focus on producing services rather than defining policies. Nevertheless, it is also possible to recommend bringing policy-making and public organisations that have similar characteristics and complete each other under a single umbrella. Policy areas, policy functions and authorities of public organisations must be clearly defined. Fundamental issues such as transfer of authorities, institutional flexibility, accountability and administrative transparency should be on the agenda of reform (Aydın, 2007, pp 170-4).

A presidential system is the final state of a system's transformation in which policy-making mechanisms are transferred from the prime ministry to the presidency. However, the new model not only brings a new institutional design to policy-making but also changes the models of policy-making with significant changes to the authority of actors in the policy process.

To conclude, there is still time for the new system's characteristics to take shape (post-2019), and comprehensive legislation-focused policy studies are needed in order to harmonise the presidential system's existing institutional structures and to define the new model entirely.

References
Acar, M. (2004) 'Düzenleyici reform ve kurullar', in M. Acar and H. Özgür (eds) *Çağdaş kamu yönetimi 2*, Ankara: Nobel Yayın, pp 90-112.
Aydın, A.H. (2007) *Türk kamu yönetimi* (2nd edn), Ankara: Seçkin Yayıncılık.
Ayhan, B. and Üstüner, Y. (2015) 'Governance in public procurement: The reform of Turkey's public procurement system', *International Review of Administrative Sciences*, vol 81, no 3, pp 640-62.
Bakır, C. (2009) 'Policy entrepreneurship and institutional change: Multilevel governance of central banking reform', *Governance*, vol 22, no 4, pp 571-98.
Bakır, C. (2012) 'Organizational change in economic bureaucracy in Turkey, 1980-2010: Interactions with national and global dynamics', Ankara: TUBITAK Project No 108K511, Unpublished report.
Berkman, A.Ü. and Heper, M. (2002) 'Political dynamics and administrative reform in Turkey', in A. Farazmand (ed) *Administrative reform in developing nations*, Westport, CT: Praeger, pp 151-62.

Biçer, M. and Yılmaz, H. (2009) 'Parlamentonun kamu politikası oluşturma ve planlama sürecindeki konumunun yeni kamu mali yönetim sistemi çerçevesinde değerlendirilmesi', *Yasama Dergisi*, vol 13, pp 45-84.

Bilici, N. (2013) *Avrupa birliği ve Türkiye* (6th edn), Ankara: Seçkin Yayıncılık.

Dik, E. (2017) *Türkiye'de bakanlık sisteminin geleceği*, Ankara: İmge Kitabevi.

Duverger, M. (1980) 'A new political system model: Semi-presidential government', *European Journal of Political Research*, vol 8, no 2, pp 165-87.

Eroğul, C. (2000) *Anatüzaye giriş (Anayasa hukukuna giriş)* (6th edn), Ankara: İmaj Yayınevi.

Gözler, K. (2013) 'Türkiye'de bir bilinmeyen: Isdar', in *Prof. Dr. Erdal Onar'a Armağan*, Ankara: Ankara Üniversitesi Hukuk Fakültesi Yayınları, vol II, pp 897-950.

Gözler, K. (2015) *Türk anayasa hukukuna giriş* (10th edn), Bursa: Ekin Basım Yayın Dağıtım.

Gözler, K. (2017) *Elveda anayasa – 16 Nisan 2017'de oylayacağımız anayasa değişikliği hakkında eleştiriler*, Bursa: Ekin Basım Yayın Dağıtım.

Gözübüyük, A.Ş. (2013) *Türkiye'nin yönetim yapısı* (12 bası), Ankara: Turhan Kitabevi.

Güler, B.A. (2010) *Türkiye'nin yönetimi – Yapı-* (2nd edn), Ankara: İmge Kitabevi.

Heper, M. (1994) 'Bureaucracy in the Ottoman-Turkish polity', in A. Farazmand (ed) *Handbook of bureaucracy*, New York: MarcelDekker, pp 659-74.

Heper, M. (2006) *Türkiye'de devlet geleneği* (2nd edn), Ankara: DOĞUBATI.

Karluk, R. (2009) *Cumhuriyetin İlanından günümüze Türkiye ekonomisinde yapısal dönüşüm*, İstanbul: Beta Yayınları.

Keleş, R. (2016) *Yerinden yönetim ve siyaset* (10th edn), İstanbul: Cem Yayınevi.

Kepenek, Y. and Yentürk, N. (2005) *Türkiye ekonomisi*, İstanbul: Remzi Kitabevi.

Landau, D. (2013) 'Abusive constitutionalism', *University of California Davis Law Review*, vol 47, no 1, pp 189-260.

Leblebici, D.N., Kurban, A. and Sadioğlu, U. (2012) 'Türk yönetim sisteminde bağımsız düzenleyici kurullar üzerine kuramsal tartışmalar', *Hacettepe Üniversitesi İktisadi ve İdari Bilimler Fakültesi Dergisi*, vol 30, no 2, pp 81-109.

Ömürgönülşen, U. and Öktem, M.K. (2007) *Avrupa birliği'ne üyelik sürecinde Türk kamu yönetimi*, Ankara: İmaj Yayınevi.

Övgün, B. and Özçağlar Eroğlu, H. (2016) 'Kamu yönetiminde yeniden merkezileşme eğilimi: Avrupa birliği bakanlığı üzerinden bir İnceleme', in Ş. Özkan Erdoğan and O. Zengin (eds) *Prof. Dr. Oğuz Onaran'a Armağan*, Ankara: Ankara Üniversitesi SBF Kamu Yönetimi Araştırma ve Uygulama Merkezi, pp 381-96.

Özbudun, E. (2014) *Türk anayasa hukuku* (15th edn), Ankara: Yetkin.

Polatoğlu, A. (2000) *Introduction to public administration: The case of Turkey*, Ankara: Middle East Technical University.

Sabuncu, Y. (2002) *Anayasaya giriş – EK: 1982 ANAYASASI* (8 bası), Ankara: İmaj Yayınevi.

Sadioğlu, U. and Öktem, M.K. (2011) 'Ulusal kalkınma sorunsalı açısından Türkiye'de kamu yönetiminin rolü ve önemi', *Sosyo Ekonomi*, vol 7, no 16, pp 41-67.

Saygılıoğlu, N. and Arı, S. (2002) *Etkin devlet – Kurumsal bir tasarı ve politika önerisi*, İstanbul: Sabancı Üniversitesi.

Saylam, A. and Ömürgönülşen, U. (2013) 'Avrupa birliği genel sekreterliğinden Avrupa birliği Bakanlığı'na: Türk kamu yönetiminde yeni bir bakanlık teşkilatlanması', *Akdeniz Üniversitesi İİBF Dergisi*, Avrupa Birliği ve Kamu Yönetimi Özel Sayısı, vol 13, no 25, pp 178-96.

Sevinç, M. (2013) *Anayasa yazıları* (3rd edn), Ankara: İmaj Yayınevi.

Sezen, S. (2003) *Türk kamu yönetiminde kurullar: Geleneksel yapılanmadan kopuş*, Ankara: TODAİE.

Şahin, H. (2006) *Türkiye ekonomisi, tarihsel gelişim ve bugünkü durum*, Bursa: Ezgi Kitabevi.

Tanör, B. (1995) *Osmanlı-Türk anayasal gelişmeleri: 1789-1980*, İstanbul: Der Yayınları.

Taşar, M.O. (2010) 'Türkiye'nin güçlü ekonomiye geçiş programı ve makro ekonomik etkilerin analizi', *Niğde Üniversitesi İİBF Dergisi*, vol 3, no 1, pp 76-97.

Yayman, H. (2016) *Türkiye'de devlet reformu ve başkanlık sistemi*, İstanbul: Doğan Kitap.

Yazıcı, S. (2016) *Yeni bir anayasa hazırlığı ve Türkiye – Seçkincilikten toplum sözleşmesine* (3rd edn), İstanbul: İstanbul Bilgi Üniversitesi Yayınları.

Yazıcı, S. (2017) *Başkanlık ve yarı-başkanlık sistemleri* (4th edn), İstanbul: İstanbul Bilgi Üniversitesi Yayınları.

Yeldan, E. (2012) *Küreselleşme sürecinde Türkiye ekonomisi: Bölüşüm, birikim ve büyüme*, İstanbul: İletişim Yayınları.

YSK (2017) *663 sayılı ve 27 Nisan 2017 tarihli Yüksek Seçim Kurulu Kararı*, T.C. Resmi Gazete, Sayı: 30050.

SIX

Territorial policy-making and administrative reform in Turkey

Can Umut Çiner

Introduction

From a scholarly point of view, Turkey cannot be easily understood or discussed by using a conceptual model, because Turkish political and administrative structures are complex and under contradictory influences. Furthermore, this context is overcomplicated for local or state mechanisms such as public administration, which is already a complex system by nature.

After the 1980s, Turkey, a mostly capital-dependent country that displays economic progress, reformed its state structure significantly as a result of the liberalisation process. Within this context, deregulation and privatisation policies and their implementation are also attached to the liberalisation process in particular. Substantially, the implementation of these policies, with the effects of foreign actors such as the International Monetary Fund (IMF) and The World Bank as well as the prospect of membership to the European Union (EU), constitute the crucial dynamics of the reform or reconstruction process. This process, which began in the 1980s, has altered the characteristics of the relationships between central and local administrations within the unitary state structure. This alteration has been further impacted by the Europeanisation of public policies. In today's Turkey, even though the EU can no longer be regarded as an important actor influencing the administrative reform agenda via public opinion, it should be emphasised that it is still a critical actor in the evaluation of policies such as decentralisation and territorialisation, together with the influence of other international institutions. Of course, the motivation for EU compliance was not only economic for the ruling party. Europeanisation was considered a pragmatic tool to achieve the government's political agenda of eliminating internal pressure on the government, in terms of state reform agendas, and in the name of democratic standards and reputation promotion in international relations.

There are five crucial areas of state/governmental reform in Turkey's recent political history. These relate both to the main elements of state reform and also to the public policies that delineate the phases of the reconstruction process of the government in Turkey. The first area is public finance management reform, which was initiated in the 1990s. The second is local administrations reform. Third is public administration reform. The fourth, public personnel management reform, appears as a focus for many years, but remains an unrealised objective

(Güler, 2003). The fifth reform of the governmental system, more specifically the significant ongoing process of transition to a presidential system, is proceeding. Transformation in these five areas constitutes a radical and dramatic shift in the state structure in Turkey. In governmental discourse, the aim of these radical transformations is 'to make the state a servant for its society', and the whole process has been called a 'silent revolution' (KDGM, 2014).[1] The public finance management reform was realised in the first phase, actualised with the Public Finance Management Credit borrowed from The World Bank in 1995. This was followed by the subsequent enactment of the Public Financial Management and Control Law no 5018 in 2003 (Kamu Mali Yönetimi ve Kontrol Kanunu). This law mainly constitutes the transition from a programme budgeting system to a strategic planning and performance budgeting system. It also secures uniformity of accounting in public finance management and the divergence of political and administrative responsibilities (Güler, 2003).

In 2002, immediately after the Justice and Development Party (Adalet ve Kalkınma Partisi, AKP) came to power, public administration reform, via Draft Law no 5227, on the Fundamental Principles and Restructuring of Public Administration (Kamu Yönetiminin Temel İlkeleri ve Yeniden Yapılandırılması Hakkında Kanun, 2004) was on the governmental agenda. It primarily arose from the aforementioned public finance management reform. Due to the social and political opposition that arose against this extensive reform package, it was not passed.[2] As a result, the ruling party chose to implement a strategy of legalising the regulations related to local administrations step by step. Law no 5216 on Metropolitan Municipalities (Büyükşehir Belediyesi Kanunu, 2004), Municipality Law no 5393 (Belediye Kanunu, 2005), Law no 5302 on Special Provincial Administration (İl Özel İdaresi Kanunu, 2005) and Law no 5449 on the Establishment, Coordination and Duties of Development Agencies (Kalkınma Ajanslarının Kuruluşu, Koordinasyonu ve Görevleri Hakkında Kanun, 2006) were thus enacted. These legal instruments aim to redistribute authority between local and central administration. In brief, a structure that provides the basis for decentralisation and territorialisation policies, which exclusively changes the scale of public administration.

Public administration reform could be characterised as the third phase of reconstruction. This can be understood as both the general state reform and the activities that serve to alter the organisational structure of the state. It is best considered as the general title of realised reforms related to the central administration. Central organisation of government consists of the structure of the ministries, related and affiliated institutions of the ministries, regulatory and supervisory bodies and changes regarding the central administration's provincial and district branches. In this context, decree laws that were issued in 2011 brought renewal to the state's organisational structure.[3] Additionally, some provisions of decree laws that were issued in 2016 could also be considered public administration reform.[4] Public personnel management reform, the fourth phase, has been ongoing since the mid-1990s, with some aspects being realised. However, reform procedures of Law no 657 on Civil Servants (Devlet Memurları Kanunu, 1965) are ongoing. The final phase, with an amendment to the constitution in 2007 (Law no 5678), which states that the President of the Republic should be elected by the public, has crucially transformed the parliamentary system in Turkey. This phase completed in 2017 when a law was proposed for additional constitutional amendments (Law no 6771) and accepted via a referendum in April 2017. Turkish people approved the presidential system.

These main pillars demonstrate the elements of state reforms and should also be considered as public policies that outline the reconstruction processes of the government in Turkey. In this context, when we examine the related literature, it is clear that the liberalisation polices put in place after the 1980s are the result of interactions between prior public policies aimed at government restructuring. The argument that these dimensions of reform policies are shaped by international dynamics is also mostly agreed on within the related literature (Güler, 2003, 2004; Bayramoğlu, 2005). The sustained reform process, proceeding to the level of dysfunction, could be considered a result of underdevelopment and generally shaped according to the depth of capitalism. This is compounded by the hypothesis of inefficacy of governmental bodies or the ideological assumption of the government as a problematic area.

The problem of formation and reformation of a state's territory is inevitably related to public policies at different levels.[5] This also constitutes a reflection of the political economy and institutional preferences of the government. From this point of view, the subject of this chapter is territorial policies, which cannot be understood without the context of the reconfiguration of the state structure in Turkey. These can be understood as part of the alterations that the country has experienced. They can be identified as a cluster of policies in the context of state reform in Turkey. In order to explain this issue, the chapter follows two paths. First, under the structure of the central administration, various public polices related to local administrations are analysed. There are some basic public policies behind the radical transformation of the organisation of the administration that has taken place in Turkey; these have basically transformed territory and territorial policy-making, such as annexation and metropolisation. Second, the effects of local administrations on the national public policy-making process are examined. The chapter focuses on various examples of how territorial-based policies were determined at central level. However, in order to achieve all of this, there is a need for some basic information regarding the structure and functioning of the central and local administrations in Turkey.

Background: Turkish administrative system

The Republic of Turkey is a unitary state. According to the 3rd chapter of the 1982 Constitution, 'the state constitutes a whole with its territory and nation.' Due to historical and sociological reasons, it has been legislated that the state's sovereignty should not be separated on the basis of territorial merits. It is stated in the Constitution that the state's territory is indivisible and the people living within this territory should not be separated based on language, religion or ethnicity. Therefore, Turkey is both administered by central and local administrations, according to the Napoleonic state tradition. The central administration is composed of organisations at the capital (ministries, the National Security Council, Council of State, etc) and provincial/territorial administration across the country. Local administrations also compromise territorial and functional administrations. The Turkish administrative system is built on the principles of both centralisation and decentralisation. According to the 123rd Article of the Constitution, the Turkish state has a unitary character; this means that in terms of organisation and functions, the central agencies and geographically and functionally decentralised agencies and institutions form a whole. In addition to this, the 126th Article lays down the essentials of the provincial or territorial branch of the central administration. According to this Article, the administration of the provinces is based on the principle of deconcentration. The 127th Article regulates the local administrations (Polatoğlu, 2000; Çiner, 2016b).

The integral unity of the administration, based on the principles of the 'unitary state' and the 'rule of law', is the fundamental principle that characterises the formation and functioning of the public administrations. The integral unity of the administration is based on three legal principles: they include the hierarchy principle that functions within the central administration's own organisations, the decentralisation principle, and the central administration's power of administrative tutelage over the acts and organs of the decentralised administrations.

There are four types of local administrations in Turkey in spite of the fact that the 1982 Constitution indicates three. These include the special provincial administration (*il özel idaresi*), municipality (*belediye*) and village (*köy*).[6] Metropolitan municipalities form the fourth type of local administration (Marcou, 2006). The number of metropolitan municipalities was increased from 16 to 30 with the 2012 reform, which is considered almost a revolution in the state tradition in place since the late Ottoman period. The government today has committed to increasing the number of metropolitan municipalities. As noted above, during the AKP rule, which began in 2002, special provincial administrations, municipalities and metropolitan municipalities' laws have been amended. Yet villages are still regulated by the Village Law no 442 that dates back to 1924 (Köy Kanunu).

Turkey aims to develop and needs to improve public service quality, as the most important function for public administration is the provision of public services. Because of this, the creation and implementation of public policies relate mostly to the provision of public services at a local level. Despite the fact that the administrative organisation is based on the centralisation principle in the 1982 Constitution, the implementation of all public services by the central administration is not indicated therein, while the central and local administrations' integral unity is.

In Turkey, the basic criterion for identifying the duties and responsibilities of central and local administrations is the qualification of local services, which is usually reduced to the law-making mechanisms. In other words, the law defines the role of the local administrations. The evolution of the sui generis local administration system originates in governmental traditions from the Ottoman Empire, wherein some services are regarded as central while others are considered local. For example, judicial and security services are considered areas of the central administration, whereas transportation and reconstruction services are considered the responsibility of municipalities. However, the distribution of duties is not always as clear as this. For example, social policies, social programmes such as aid, social services, culture and art policies are the responsibility of both the central and local administrations. The service-providing mechanism of these public policies is both very complicated and deprived of a division of labour perspective. The duality of the central and local administrations regarding these kinds of public services is the result of various administrations' desire to control certain types of public services due to election concerns.

In Turkey, the central and local administrations are based mostly on a centralist character (Ersoy, 1989). From this aspect, the absence of a legal framework for the division of labour, authority, duties and responsibilities between the central and local administrations is problematic. Indeed, this should be identified as one of the major problems in Turkish public administration and policy-making.[7] Briefly, there are no common principles or standards that regulate the relations between central and local administrations. The central administration implements the services that are mostly shaped by politics. From the executive's perspective, the goal of providing quality public services remains an issue that concerns the central administration. On the other hand, the rapidly growing local administrations are able to provide public services on their own, and are not subject to regulation over their responsibilities under the law or secondary legislation.

One of the most crucial elements of analysis of the policy-making process relates to the relationship between the central and local administrations. This is difficult because the central and local administrations' duties and responsibilities are not very clear. The difficulty of making policy analysis in this area is further exacerbated by their ambiguous relationship. However, it is clear that the central and local administrations have different roles during the process of public policy-making. While the central administration states the general principles and standards, the local administrations implement the duties decreed by law. Therefore, examples of the impact of local administrations on the central administration during certain

Table 6.1: Local administrations

Metropolitan municipalities	Metropolitan district municipalities	City municipalities	District municipalities	Town municipalities	Special provincial administrations	Villages	Local administration unions
30	519	51	400	397	51	18,329	787

Source: İçişleri Bakanlığı (2016)

territorial policy-making processes is limited. This should be considered a result of being a unitary state. The increase in centralisation tendencies is a natural outgrowth of Kurdish regional separatism and the effects of the civil wars in Iraq and Syria.

Towards a territorialisation of public policies in Turkey?

In Turkey, public policies are mostly territorialised as part of the local administrations' reforms. This territorialisation, the relationship between historical processes and reforms regarding local administrations, is substantially related to the efficiency and effectiveness of public policies at a local level. In terms of the policy-making process, territorialised factors have emerged because of the efficiency of politics by the extension of the central administration. Thus, in this part of the chapter we discuss the central administration's policy on local administrations in chronological order based on territorial reforms. In other words, this part is a policy analysis of local administrations. When we consider the related literature, it should be noted that there are a high number of academic studies with a similar approach (Ben-Elia, 2016).

As soon as the AKP came into power, it enacted a policy to close down small local administrations. This was due to (1) the financial inefficiency of local administrations, and (2) problems with urban planning and land development plans. The main objective of this policy was to change local administrations' fragmented structure to a more consolidated one as a consequence of the central administration's policy preference regarding the scale challenge. In other words, the ruling party reconfigured local administrations and the territorial policy-making process using a gradual strategy. In this context, they implemented a strategy to close down small local administrations that were located near municipalities in cities that were outside the scope of the metropolitan municipality. Afterwards, municipalities in the cities not defined as a metropolitan municipality were then defined and listed as a 'village' with a law that was based on population criteria. All of these policies also have an impact on the metropolitan municipalities. Moreover, the ruling party initiated a metropolisation policy, and there are indications that this policy will be maintained (Çınar et al, 2009; Zengin, 2014b).

The closing down policy

The closing down policy was implemented for small municipalities and villages located near city municipalities. The first reform attempt was related to Denizli, a medium-sized city. Denizli is a leading example of post-Fordism productivity relations and global commodity chains that have changed the city through a growing economic and commercial structure. Law no 5026 on the Annexation of Municipalities and Villages to Denizli Municipality (Bazı Belediye ve Köylerin Denizli Belediyesine Katılmasına İlişkin Kanun) in 2003 noted that 22 municipalities and 25 villages that are within the Denizli Municipality boundaries were administratively annexed to the Denizli City Municipality. However, this reform attempt was vetoed by then-President Ahmet Necdet Sezer in 2003, on the grounds that there may be challenges in the maintenance of public services and that local elections may be affected (Çınar et al, 2009, pp 65-71; Zengin, 2014b).

The AKP, after being unable to pass a more extensive reform law (no 5227), chose to implement a strategy of piecemeal legalisation of public administration-related reforms. Municipality Law no 5393 of 2005 was then issued. With the 8th Article of the Law (no 5393), under the title of 'Consolidation and annexation', the voluntary consolidation and annexation of smaller municipalities and villages were regulated. In addition to this, with the 11th Article of the Law on Metropolitan Municipalities, under the article titled 'Termination of the legal entity', the extension of boundaries and annexation policy were implemented in various cities with various joint decree laws. According to this Article, unless there is a conflict with the city development plan and fundamental infrastructure services, municipalities or villages that are closer than five kilometres to a municipality that has a population of over 50,000 should be consolidated with the larger municipality (Çınar et al, 2013; Zengin, 2014b).[8]

The policy of converting municipalities to villages[9]

Another public policy that directly affects local administrations is the definition of municipalities with a population of less than 2,000 as villages, and terminating the legal entity utilising a listing method mentioned in Law no 5025 (Bazı Belediyelerin Kaldırılması Hakkında Kanun).

First, we should note that this law was not enacted like Law no 5019 on the Administration of Metropolitan Municipalities (Büyük Şehir Belediyelerinin Yönetimi Hakkında Kanun Hükmünde Kararnamenin Değiştirilerek Kabulü Hakkında Kanunda Değişiklik Yapılmasına İlişkin Kanun) and Law no 5026 on the Annexation of Municipalities and Villages to Denizli Municipality. According to commissioners who are in favour of this law, in Europe the local administration echelon has shown a tendency to grow from the 1950s, smaller municipalities are inadequate for the maintenance of public services, the financial income is insufficient for the outcomes and they could not be administered rationally (Çınar, 2013, p 132). In 2008, Law no 5747 furthered the closing down policy. This Law reversed the two-tier structure that had previously been implemented with Law no 5747, which defined metropolitan municipalities and metropolitan district municipalities. In this context, first-tier municipalities were closed. After the elections following the Law, 240 town municipalities that were within the boundaries of the 16 metropolitan municipalities were transformed into or defined as neighbourhood units (Zengin, 2016).

With the Law, 862 town municipalities with populations of less than 2,000 were redefined as villages and closed down. After an appeal by the Republican People's Party (Cumhuriyet Halk Partisi, CHP), the Constitutional Court created an exception for the termination of affected municipalities. After the legal process between the Supreme Court and the Supreme Committee of Elections, the Ministry of Internal Affairs decreed that the 836 municipalities that had brought suit within the legal timeframe were able to avoid being defined as villages and remained municipalities in the elections (Çınar et al, 2009, pp 113-37; Zengin, 2014b). Thus, Law no 5025 was not implemented, Law no 5747 was limited, and therefore the attempt by the ruling party to consolidate smaller municipalities was not fully realised.

The policy of redefining municipalities as villages was partly achieved due to the legal process against Law no 5747. Reform law no 6360 regarding metropolitan municipalities, which was issued in 2012, was partly successful. However, it is important to remember that metropolitan municipalities numbered 16 until the Law was issued in 2012. After Law no 6360 was passed, the number of metropolitan municipalities has increased to 30. These legal administrative reforms require further exploration of the metropolisation process.

Metropolisation

Metropolisation is probably the most important territorial policy brought on by global economic relations. Capitalism makes metropolises more likely from an economic perspective as the growth of cities is related to subnational and supranational dynamics. In this context, metropolisation is a paradigm that fundamentally evaluates cities based on the effects of internal and external dynamics (Ghorra-Gobin, 2010, p 25).

In Turkey, as in Europe generally, cities demonstrate growth and development beyond the administrative and political boundaries. Since the days of the Ottoman Empire, Europe has constituted a crucial model of urbanism for Turkey. According to Marcou (2012, pp 107-8), the boundaries of local administrations and their organisations increase not to overcome the challenges of rapid urbanism, but to achieve control of the area through central administration and management of local relations. However, this assessment is only partly true for Turkey. On the one hand, with the development of capitalism the process of economic integration of the cities with the dynamic nature of globalisation is maintained. Furthermore, the transformation of rural areas as the boundaries of cities run over urban areas, and dynamics of urban transformation of old city centres, are other important issues. Because of these reasons the issue of 'urban land rent' formulation, which is a consensus for all political parties, became a popular word in Turkish.

In Turkey, with Law no 5216, dated 2004, metropolitan municipalities have become the most prominent actors of the local administration system. The most important element of the law is the policy of extension of boundaries; in other words, the 'compass regulation' (*pergel düzenlemesi*) of the 2nd provisional Article of the Law. We should underline that this policy was previously attempted with Law no 5019, although it did not come into force because of unintended consequences during the process of implementation.

With the compass regulation, metropolitan municipalities' boundaries were extended by drawing circles with a specific radius according to their population. Due to this regulation, the metropolitan municipalities' boundaries coincide with the cities' boundaries, both in Istanbul and Kocaeli. Metropolitan municipalities that had a population of up to 1,000,000 also had their boundaries extended up to 20km, those with a population between 1,000,000 and 2,000,000 had boundaries extended up to 30km and those with a population of over 2,000,000 had boundaries extended up to 50km (Çınar et al, 2009; Zengin, 2014a, 2016). The most important aspect of this regulation is reflected in the territorial policy-making process. According to monitoring following the law, the extension of the boundaries has directly affected the policy-making process of mayors during this period. From this perspective, we can assume that the reform reflects one substantial benefit of the territorial-based policy-making process.

According to Law no 6360, dated 2012, 14 city municipalities were defined as metropolitan municipalities. These metropolitan municipalities, whose boundaries were extended to conform to city boundaries, increased to 30 in number. Likewise, metropolitan municipality boundaries were matched to the boundaries of district municipalities. In the 30 metropolitan municipalities, special provincial administrations were abolished. Instead of these, Investment Monitoring and Coordination Presidencies were established with a legal entity and affiliation to the prefect. A total of 1,076 town municipalities and 16,480 villages that were within the boundaries of the metropolitan municipalities have lost their legal entities and been transformed into neighbourhood units. Additionally, the policy of defining municipalities as villages proceeded with Law no 6360. According to this Law, 559 municipalities that had populations of less than 2,000 were redefined as villages (Zengin, 2016).

In Turkey, we should look for both economic and social factors in addition to political reasons to understand the essence of existing metropolisation dynamics. We may assume that the metropolises are structures in which investors may act more comfortably. It can also be seen as a solution mechanism for the Kurdish problem without the political aspects of the Turkish administration needing to use an ethnicity-based approach. A clear solution to this problem can emerge as a regional administration's mechanism, either through language or ethnicity-based representation, which may be established as part of the local or central administrations. In this sense it can be seen as politically neutral; from the economic perspective with globalisation in mind, establishing attractive sites through metropolitan area administration is preferred instead of regional administration during the policy-making process (Çiner, 2014a). In the local administration organisation, which was created under the provisions of Law no 6360, it is well known that there are various problems related to representation in the metropolises with regard to the provision and delivery of justice and maintenance and organisation of public services. During the preparation for this chapter there were ongoing reform discussions and the establishment of new metropolises continued (İçişleri Bakanlığı, 2017; Sözcü, 2017). From an administrative point of view, if we look at the regulations that the Law puts forward, this Law establishes regionalisation and centralisation at a local scale. Also, in Turkey after this law, a dual structure emerges either with or without a metropolitan municipality. In metropolises, special provincial administrations were maintained, public services in rural areas were abolished and special provincial administrations still exist in areas without metropolises.

Another example of the mayors' influence in the policy-making process is Law no 6360.[10] It is well known that mayors had a crucial influence during the formulation of this law. According to the press, we can see a strong advocacy coalition from metropolitan mayors.

However, we need to take examine the parliamentary minutes for a detailed analysis regarding the background of this formulation. In addition, during the law and policy-making process it is possible to encounter a significant number of policy transfer components. The EU-funded Support to the Further Implementation of Local Administration Reform in Turkey (LAR 2) project helped the policy learning process in 2010-11. In this context, we need to emphasise that the German local administrative system *kreis-frei stadt* was largely imitated (Heinelt, 2011).

The dialectical relations between central and local administrations

In Turkey, the local administrations' policy-making powers are limited. The local authorities and their responsibilities are regulated clearly with related laws. Turkey also placed a reservation on Articles 4/6 and 9/6 provisions of the European Council's European Charter of Local Self-Government. According to this, there is a reservation on provisions about consulting with local administrations during resource allocation and local administrations' participation in the policy-making processes on issues that are self-governing.

From this point of view we can provide various examples for the effects of the local administrations on central administration such as special provincial administrations and municipalities on the territorial policy-making process. However, in practice, it should be highlighted that the villages have no effect at all.

Historically, the specific circumstance of the local administrations' responsibilities, authorities and assignments weakens the connection between the central administration and municipalities, which is already weak. With the growing strength of municipalities or the boost of municipalisation in Turkey, this strengthened, because the municipalities' (specifically the metropolitan municipalities') authorities and responsibilities are clearly identified. In particular, the metropolitan municipalities have begun to undertake almost every kind of responsibility in recent years. This may be seen as somewhat paradoxical; municipalities may be seen as squeezed into a more restricted and defined area in terms of their authorities and responsibilities due to being part a unitary state, yet they undertake almost every service aside from foreign policy or defence. In this context, we can rank all territorial policies among the responsibilities of metropolitan municipalities. For example, there is no obstacle for metropolitan municipalities to build schools.

The role of special provincial administrations

Special provincial administrations are the most crucial local administration unit for identifying and designing policies. With the amendment of Law no 5302 in 2005, special provincial administrations are formulated as a subsidiary mechanism that is out of reach of the central administration. As previously mentioned, following Law no 6360, special provincial administrations are abolished in metropolises. Currently, special provincial administrations have been maintained in areas where metropolises do not exist. Due to the fact that in Law no 5302 the special provincial administrations' responsibilities are ambiguously defined, they undertake some important roles in the implementation of various public policies.

Resources transferred from the ministries constitute a large part of the budget of special provincial administrations. Thus, like social and cultural services, both the central and local administrations have a significant impact on the territorial policy-making process. Similarly, for other public policies, provincial branches of the ministries are supported. For related public policies, it is clear that the ministries' provincial directorates are responsible for policy formulation. The role of special provincial administrations, in general, emerges in the sources of finance. This issue can be easily explained with the dual role of the prefect. Due to the fact that prefects are the heads of the special provincial administrations, they consider the relationship between the central administration and local administrations instead of the local dynamics of decision-making and implementation. The logic of the special provincial administrations is the representation of the state's interest rather than that of a local administration. The existence of the prefect is a kind of guarantee to avoid recurrent expenditures to investments that may create an obstacle for the politicisation of special provincial administrations. The existence of the prefect in the system ensures the priority of the central administration and the requirements of public services.

Within this framework, special provincial administrations constitute a more effective mechanism for issues related to the central administration than municipalities. Investment programmes of special provincial administrations regarding issues such as building hospitals, irrigation facilities and land use can be achieved with a decision from the provincial assembly. Thus, the central administration is able to work mutually with local administrations. The provincial assemblies are very effective in various kinds of policy-making processes, such as school construction.

Investment Monitoring and Coordination Presidencies

After the metropolitan municipality reform, in order to fill in the gaps that emerged due to the abolishment of special provincial administrations in metropolises, the

Investment Monitoring and Coordination Presidencies (IMCP, Yatırım İzleme ve Koordinasyon Başkanlığı) were established. IMCPs took over the duties of special provincial administrations that did not transfer to municipalities.

With the IMCPs, in order to execute investments and services under the control of the central administration, a unit was formed under the leadership of the prefect. These units had no legal entities when they were first established, but have grown stronger with recently obtained legal entities (decree with the force of Law no 674, 2016).

Therefore this unit, which is different from special provincial administrations, can be considered an important policy-making entity that may contribute to the territorial policy-making process of the prefects. Substantially, project-based IMCP activities that directly affect central and local relations may be considered another limited example.

Because their operation was not established with the law, we can possibly identify some important examples of policy-making for local administrations when we consider the dialectics of the central and local administrations in Turkey. The agents of the central administration maintain interactions between the central and local administrations by prefects in the provinces, and by sub-prefects in district sub-provinces.

City planning and coordination directorates

We should mention an important mediation function of the provincial branch of the central administration, an interaction that occurs between the central and local administrations by means of policy formulation. In order to mitigate problems that occur due to the central administration, provincial-level coordination mechanisms have been established: City Planning and Coordination Directorates (İl Planlama ve Koordinasyon Müdürlükleri). The secretary of this Directorate is the Ministry of Development (Kalkınma Bakanlığı) that pursues national-level planning activities. The purpose of these organisations is to transfer local administrations' problems to the state and to make them effective; in other words, to resolve them through the policy-making process. In particular, provincial investment inventories are to be shared via this mechanism, which is aimed at creating coordination between investments. If there is an important problem in realising the investments, for example, an interaction should be created between the municipalities and the General Directorate of State Hydraulic Works (Devlet Su İşleri) or General Directorates of Highways (Karayolları Genel Müdürlüğü).[11] This structure is based on solving coordination problems at the provincial level.

Within the annual programme, decisions are to be taken about the implementation of coordination and monitoring of the programme. In this context, the provincial coordination councils are to consider provincial investments and socioeconomic developments by means of local and regional development perspectives. The provincial coordination council (İl Koordinasyon Kurulları) comes together four times each year, in January, April, July and October, in order to solve problems, appraise the potential investments and allow for the interaction of these establishments. In these meetings, they monitor the investments and socioeconomic developments that constitute the basis of the public policy process and evaluate investment proposals for the upcoming year. Professional organisations with a public institution status that are identified by the prefect, such as the chambers of industry and commerce, associations, foundations and other non-governmental organisations, are invited to these meetings. It is also stated that the Ministry of Development and Development Agencies (Kalkınma Ajansları) is to be invited to meetings. The opinions shared in the council are to be reported to the central organisations by the provincial public institutions and regional directorates as an attachment of the investment proposals. The transference of the prefectorate opinions to the system is to be realised by the provincial planning and coordination directorates.

Other policy interaction mechanisms

We can provide different examples for organisations structured as a board. Likewise, in cities some councils that come together with the presence of the prefect could be considered as structures that have indirect effects on the policy-making process of local administrations and as the meeting of central and local administrations. Among these, the provincial community health council and the farmers' goods protection councils, regarding animal husbandry policies, are important.

If we concentrate on transportation policy, transportation coordination centres (Ulaşım Koordinasyon Merkezi, UKOME) in the metropolises (Law no 5216) and provincial traffic commissions (il trafik komisyonları) in 51 other cities can be assumed to be a considerable co-deciding mechanism. Also, in practice, the Social Assistance and Solidarity Foundations (Sosyal Yardımlaşma ve Dayanışma Vakıfları),[12] which ensure that the effects of the municipalities can be monitored transparently, should be added to this list.

Additionally, we also need to remember the Village Infrastructure Support Project (Köylerin Altyapısının Desteklenmesi, KÖYDES).[13] The functioning of the KÖYDES Allowance Commissions (KOYDES Tahsisat Komisyonları) can be considered an example of territorial policy-making, because the representatives of special provincial administrations (the Secretary-General and President of the provincial council) participate in the process with diverse actors from the central administration, such as prefects and sub-prefects. Another mechanism regarding energy policy that should be mentioned is Energy Support Commissions (Enerji Destek Komsiyonları). Their task is to provide energy support for enterprises. Commission members are mostly territorial administration representatives, and the main task is to revitalise the territorial economy.

Last in this context we can mention regional development agencies. The development agencies' law was enacted in 2006, and they began their activities in 2009. At a national level they are a structure in the framework of the governance mechanism that gathers public sector, private sector and non-governmental organisations within the coordination of the Ministry of Development. There are 26 development agencies working as coordinators and executors of regional development policies at regional level (Kalkınma Bakanlığı, 2016). The development agencies are administered with a project and governance-based approach in order to lead up economic and regional development in Turkey. The Development Councils (Kalkınma Kurulları) can be seen as one of the limited mutual territorial policy producer mechanisms.[14]

Conclusion

This chapter has reviewed the main reform trajectories, paying special attention to territorial policy-making issues since 2002. It has shown that the reforms were mostly determined and affected by the central administration. As a unitary state, centralisation in Turkey refers to uniformity in executing sovereignty over all of the state's territory, as well as in legalisation and practice of the rules. This also means that both the decision-making and monopoly of the right to use force is centralised. In this structure, the role of decentralisation is not to create an alternative but rather a subsidiary to the central administration. For this reason, it is not possible for local administrations to exist without the central administration. Thus, for the reason that the local/territorial is a category that can be determined according to the centre, the territorial policy-making process itself is within the sphere of the central administration. From the perspective of policy-making and implementation, the process that occurs between the central and local administrations favours the political preferences of the state. The context of this preference should be sought in historical, economic and sociological relations and the position of the sovereign class (Çiner, 2016a). Also, in Turkey, the broad definition of the central and local administrations' relationships creates a space for the local administrations through the assistance of the central administration.

The resolution of territorial-based policies in Turkey can only be achieved through the realisation of the relationships between central and local administrations. From this perspective, this chapter's main argument is that in Turkey, a significant portion of territorial-based policies can be realised through the central administration's determination. On the other hand, while it is limited, local administrations do have an indirect impact on public policies related to the central administration at various levels. Aside from this, there is no problem regarding the fulfilment of all the duties that are assigned by the central administration to the local administrations, or, if we put it in a more explicit way, fulfilment of all the duties aside from the ones that are enacted in the law. The important issue here is the definition of the policy-making mechanisms that are emerging from the interactions between the central and local administrations.

There is scarcely any literature on the relationship between the central and local administrations regarding the territorial-based policy-making process that is discussed here. For this reason, this chapter may be considered an important and innovative contribution to the examination of the relationship between the central and local administrations that provides a perspective that is unavailable in the Turkish, English and French literature.

From this perspective, the state reform changes the rules of the game between the central and local administrations as well as affecting the territorial echelons such as metropolisation. However, like every political and administrative reality, there are levels and qualifications that need to be explained. In the context of state reform, the results of territorial policies may be seen as decentralisation in some instances, but may also ensure centralisation in others.

The most important element of territorial policy-making, within the processes that were directly identified by the central administration, is the participation in the policy process of local administrators through cooperating with the ruling party as long as the national policy intertwines.

In addition to this, there are limited examples for cases in which local administrations affected the central administration; it should be expressed that the most important mechanism for this is the special provincial administrations. Moreover, the provincial coordination mechanisms should be considered one of the most important tools of the territorial policy-making process.

Notes

[1] This report can be qualified as a list of reforms about democratisation, human rights, political and economic liberalism and public administration.

[2] For a comprehensive summary of the public administration reform, see Dinçer (2015, pp 209-39).

[3] For a comprehensive evaluation of decrees with the force of law in 2011, see Akdoğan (2012).

[4] For example, decree laws no 674 and 678 (2016) reformed municipality law, specifically chapters 45 (Procedures in case of vacancy in a mayor's office), 57 (Failure in services), and 75 (Relations with other organisations).

[5] For the concept of territory, see Smith (2011); the public administration reform in France could be useful for this discussion. Also for territorialisation, see Duran (2011) and Chiasson (2012).

[6] Article 127, 'Local administrations are public legal personalities established to meet the common local needs of the inhabitants of provinces, municipalities and villages, whose principles of constitution and decision-making organs elected by the electorate are determined by law....'

[7] There are two unachieved reform initiatives related to this division of labour that can be stated in this chapter. One is the decree with the force of law in 2000 (Alada, 2001) and the other one is the 2003 Public Administration Main Law no 5227.

[8] For a complete list of cities whose municipalities and villages' legal entities were abolished according to the 11th Article of the Municipality Law no 5393, see Çınar et al (2013, pp 148-51).

[9] We should underline that this is not the same as the villagisation policy that we saw in Africa.

[10] For the role of the prefects after the metropolitan reform, see Çiner (2014b).

[11] Regulation on the Establishment and Functions of the City Planning and Coordination Directorates (İl Planlama ve Koordinasyon Müdürlükleri Kuruluş Görev ve Çalışma Yönetmeliği, 1988).

[12] The social aid mechanism is administered at national level by the Social Assistance Directorate-General (SADG) under the Ministry of Family and Social Policies (MoFSP), and is implemented in provincial (prefect) and sub-provincial (sub-prefect) levels by the Social Assistance and Solidarity Foundations (SASFs).

13 The project was started in 2005 through a government initiative and administered by Ministry of Internal Affairs to solve underdevelopment problems in villages, such as drinkable water and road construction.

14 Article 8 of Law no 5449 determines the development councils: a development council shall be composed of a maximum of 100 members – representatives from public administration, private sector and non-governmental organisations' representatives in the provinces.

References

Akdoğan, A. (ed) (2012) *Kanun hükmünde kararnamelerle yönetmek'*, Ankara: Alter Yayıncılık, pp 71-96.

Alada, A.B. (2001) 'Bir kanun hükmünde kararname tasarısı üzerine...', *İÜ Siyasal Bilgiler Fakültesi Dergisi*, vol 24, pp 35-46.

Bayramoğlu, Sonay (2005) *Yönetişim Zihniyeti Türkiye'de Üst Kurullar ve Siyasal İktidarın Dönüşümü*, Ankara: İletişim Yayınları.

Ben-Elia, N. (2016) 'Local government and the challenge of policy analysis', in G. Menahem and A. Zehavi (eds) *Policy analysis in Israel*, Bristol: Policy Press, pp 71-92.

Chiasson, G., with the collaboration of V. Nterizembo (2012) 'Territorialization', in L. Côté and J.-F. Savard (eds) *Encyclopedic dictionary of public administration* (www.dictionnaire.enap.ca).

Çınar, T., Çiner, C.U. and Zengin, O. (2009) *Büyükşehir yönetimi: Bütünleştirme süreci*, Ankara: Türkiye ve Orta Doğu Amme İdaresi Enstitüsü.

Çınar, T., Duru, B., Çiner, C. U. and Zengin, O. (2013) *Belediyenin sınırları*, Ankara: Türkiye ve Orta Doğu Amme İdaresi Enstitüsü.

Çiner, C.U. (2014a) 'La réforme métropolitaine en Turquie: Les discussions autour de la ville unifiée', *La Revue Administrative*, vol 402, pp 85-95.

Çiner, C.U. (2014b) 'Reconsidering the role of the prefects in Turkey: Public policies and metropolisation', *International Journal of Public Administration*, vol 37, no 8, pp 445-55.

Çiner, C.U. (2016a) 'Centralization and decentralization', in A. Farazmand (ed) *Global encyclopedia of public administration, public policy and governance*, Springer International Publishing, pp 1-6.

Çiner, C.U. (2016b) 'Turkish administrative structure', Unpublished course notes, Ankara: METU.

Dinçer, O. (2015) *Türkiye'de değişim yapmak neden bu kadar zor?*, İstanbul: Alfa.

Duran, P. (2011) 'Territorialisation', in R. Pasquier, S. Guigner and A. Cole (eds) *Dictionnaire des politiques publiques*, Paris: Presses de Sciences Po, pp 475-82.

Ersoy, M. (1989) 'Tarihsel perspektif içinde Türkiye'de merkezi yönetim-yerel yönetim ilişkileri', *ODTU MFD*, vol 9, no 1, pp 45-66.

Ghorra-Gobin, C. (2010) 'De la métropolisation: Un nouveau paradigme', *Quaderni*, vol 73, no 3, pp 25-33.

Güler, B.A. (2003) *Devlette reform*, Ankara: Mimarlık Dergisi.

Güler, B.A. (2004) 'Kamu yönetimi temel kanunu üzerine', *Hukuk ve Adalet Eleştirel Hukuk Dergisi*, vol 1, no 2.

Heinelt, H. (2011) 'Yerel *yönetim* reformuna ilişkin strateji belgesi: Yerel *yönetim* reformu alanındaki AB iyi uygulamaları', LAR 2 Unpublished Expert Report, Ankara.

İçişleri Bakanlığı (2016) *2015 yılı Mahalli* İdareler *Faaliyet Raporu*, Ankara.

İçişleri Bakanlığı (2017) *2017 performans programı*, Ankara.

Kalkınma Bakanlığı Bölgesel Gelişme ve Yapısal Uyum Genel Müdürlüğü (2016) *Kalkınma ajansları 2015 yılı genel faaliyet raporu*, Ankara.

KDGM (Kamu Düzeni ve Güvenliği Müsteşarlığı) (2014) *Sessiz devrim: Türkiye'nin demokratik değişim ve dönüşüm envanteri 2002-2014* (4th edn), Ankara: KDGM Yayınları.

Marcou, G. (2006) 'Local administration reform in Turkey: A legal appraisal based on European principles and standards', LAR 1, Unpublished Expert Report, Ankara.

Marcou, G. (2012) 'Villes et agglomérations: Les solutions mises en œuvre par les pouvoirs publics', *Annuaire Européen d'Administration Publique 2011*, Marseille: Presses de l'Université d'Aix-Marseille, pp 107-38.

Polatoğlu, A. (2000) *Introduction to public administration: The case of Turkey*, Ankara: METU.

Smith, A. (2011) 'Territoires', in R. Pasquier, S. Guigner and A. Cole (eds) *Dictionnaire des politiques publiques*, Paris: Presses de Sciences Po, pp 469-74.

Sözcü (2017) '21 yeni büyükşehir belediyesi geliyor' (www.sozcu.com.tr/2017/gundem/21-yeni-buyuksehir-belediyesi-geliyor-1662161/).

Zengin, O. (2014a) 'Büyükşehir belediyesi sisteminin dönüşümü: Son on yılın değerlendirmesi', *Ankara Barosu Dergisi*, vol 72, no 2, pp 92-116.

Zengin, O. (2014b) 'Yakın dönem büyükşehir belediyesi reformu ve orman köyleri meselesi', in D. İşçioğlu (ed) *Türk* dünyasında *yerel* yönetimlerin *sorunları*, Ankara: Nobel, pp 383-408.

Zengin, O. (2016) 'The transformation of rural areas through metropolitan municipality reform in Turkey', Paper presented at XIV World Congress of Rural Sociology, Canada: Ryerson University.

SEVEN

Policy-making at local level: an analysis of Turkish municipalities

Ulaş Bayraktar

Introduction

Turkish local governments have undergone a radical transformation since the 1980s under the guise of decentralising and democratising reforms. At the heart of such important waves of legal reforms lay the municipalities as the main service provider in urban settings. In the framework of this chapter, I present a general overview of the state of policy analysis in Turkish municipalities. I argue that municipalities governed by very strong executives prioritise populist services delivered through sub-contracts and controlled weakly by political and civil actors and arbitrarily by central government.

I develop this analysis of municipal policies by following the stages of the policy cycle. Introduced originally by Harold Lasswell in the 1950s and then developed by Gary Brewer in the early 1970s, the policy cycle approach distinguishes different phases of a policy from its emergence to termination (Howlett and Ramesh, 1995, pp 10-11). The model widely acknowledged and taught since the 1980s is based on five main stages. In the first stage, the problem is identified and the agenda is set with regards to this problem. If the problem appears in the agenda of public actors, a course of action is created, identified or borrowed to deal with it. The adoption of every formulated policy cannot be taken for granted as decision-makers may act with different motivations and thus alter the formulated course of action. Therefore, the decision-making deserves a closer examination. Similarly, the adopted policy may alter during its implementation due to the executers' practices, to the unexpected reaction of stakeholders and/ or to the unintended outcomes of the adopted policy. Finally, an eventual stage of evaluation is indispensable to be able to see the actual impact of the policy so that public actors can decide whether it will be sustained, modified or ended (Anderson, 1984, pp 36-8).

I develop my discussion on Turkish policy-making at the local level through these stages of the policy cycle approach. The stages of policy formulation and decision are combined as the hegemonic position of mayors is valid simultaneously for both stages. For this purpose, I first argue that populist, spectacular investments in the built environment predominate agendas of municipal policies. The reason behind this populist agenda, I argue, is the over-empowerment of mayors dominating local policy formulation and decision-making procedures. Since mayors appear as undisputable patrons of local politics, implementation of policies also develop in harmony with managerial maxims that prioritise the speed and efficiency of policies rather than public interest or democratic accountability. Last but not the least, I argue that adequate means of evaluation and supervision lack significantly in local policy-making. But before launching this discussion, I briefly describe the local governmental context in Turkey.

A brief note on Turkish local government

Very much inspired by the French model, Turkish public administration has been marked by a centralism that has traditionally eclipsed local governments. The 1982 Constitution defines them as 'public corporate bodies established to meet the common local needs of the inhabitants of provinces, municipal districts and villages, whose principles of constitution and decision-making organs elected by the electorate are determined by law.' As the Article of the Constitution reveals, the system is based on three layers: villages, provinces and municipalities. With the introduction of metropolitan governments, first in the three largest cities, İstanbul, Ankara and İzmir in 1984, another local layer was added to this scheme. At the very bottom of these levels we find rural villages that function rather like administrative bodies with neither significant political nor financial power.

The municipality is the governmental body of urban settlements. The initial Law of 1930 that remained in force for 75 years with numerous amendments stated 76 different duties of municipalities in areas such as urban infrastructure, basic urban services, town planning etc. Instead of enumerating the responsibilities one by one, the law in force now identifies broad areas of activity such as water, urban transport, hygiene, etc.

The metropolitan governments introduced in 1984 have strategic and operational responsibility in their territories for urban planning, transport, construction of facilities (social-educational, cultural, sports) and environmental protection. Besides these direct service delivery responsibilities, they act as an office of supervision and coordination over district municipalities by, for example, controlling and validating construction plans and approving their budgets. Although metropolitan mayors are directly elected, metropolitan councils consist of a proportion of district municipal councillors of the metropolitan area.

The governmental body responsible for delivering public services to the whole province, but especially to the rural settlements and areas, is the special provincial administration, which is presided by a centrally appointed governor over a general provincial council consisting of directly elected councillors. The abolition of the Villages Services Department and the transfer of its staff and equipment to provincial governments had enhanced their service delivery scope and capacity in 2004, but with the legal amendment that increased the number of metropolitan municipalities from 16 to 30 by enlarging municipal territorial jurisdiction to provincial borders, provincial governments in these areas were abolished.

The abolition of provincial governments, the abolition of rights of administrative tutelage of governors over municipalities as well as the empowerment of metropolitan mayors do not actually mean the absolute weakening of the appointed governors. In fact, they continue to enjoy a powerful status in local politics, not only as the local representatives of the empowered central agencies, but also thanks to the new domains of influence that emerged through governance bodies such as social solidarity funds and/or regional development agencies (Bayraktar and Yıldızcan, 2016).

It is generally acknowledged that Turkish municipalities have been financially and administratively strengthened since the 1980s. But it is not so easy to claim that this enhancement of resources and powers has contributed to the democratisation of local policy-making. On the contrary, the withdrawal of centralist pressures from the local political scene was accompanied by the multiplication of capitalist pressures since cities have meanwhile become a valuable focus of investment and ground rent. New local practices such as drafting urban plans at the local level, privatising municipal services and large-scale public investment rendered cities attractive centres for private investment. Since no attention was paid to guaranteeing public transparency and accountability in municipal decisions and investments, stories of corruption multiplied throughout the country (Bayraktar, 2014, pp 336-7).

Finally, despite the general rhetoric of decentralisation since the 1980s, the government has changed track to political centralisation since 2011 (Övgün, 2016). This new policy orientation has driven some central institutions forward such as the Housing Development Agency that has then de facto become the Ministry of Environment and Urbanism. Through the urban transformation projects, these central agencies spread their activities all across the country and have emerged as a central actor omnipresent in the urban and social transformation of localities. Moreover, competencies with regards to planning and construction also seemed to be gradually moved back to central institutions (Penbecioğlu, 2011).

Having put these broad lines of the Turkish local governmental system, we can now proceed with examining it more closely along with the stages of the policy cycle approach.

Local agendas dominated by mega-projects

Abovementioned changes of the local governmental system reveal the efforts to improve the service delivery capacity of municipalities. Borrowing one of the main approaches of the French school of public policies, I have discussed this trend under the 'referential of service delivery' indicating an emergence of new values, norms, algorithms and symbols that all shape the new structure and functioning of local governments (Bayraktar, 2013, 2016a).

According to this referential of service delivery, municipalities are expected to provide urban services in an efficient, effective and economical way. For instance, when the municipal councillors are asked about their mission, the response is unanimously 'service to their city' and what is implied by 'service' is mainly investment in public sector works, transportation and recreation (Aksu, 2015, p 119). The sine qua non of such a capacity of service delivery is that they function in a managerial style, just as found in private companies prioritising profit rather than public interest. The mayor becomes the CEO of the municipal organisation of which the borders must be enlarged in harmony with the principles of economies of scale. The increase in the number and extension of the borders of metropolitan municipalities reflect the pursuit of scale economy representing the algorithm of the suggested referential.

Such a fundamental change in the conception of local governments actually requires a new source of legitimation. So-called conventional services such as the delivery of basic urban services like public hygiene, simple infrastructure and ordinary recreational facilities would not be enough to justify the transformation of the major principles of municipal bodies. As the new referential imposes a unique way of delivering services based on managerial principles, the main source of differentiation among contenders of political power cannot be 'how', but 'what' services are to be delivered. Electors are believed to be expecting original and impressive concrete projects when making their minds on whom to support at the ballot box.

Restricted by the blurring of political distinctions on norms and values predetermined by the managerial rhetoric, candidates tend to attract the attention and support of electors through striking electoral campaigns in which populist policies and mega-projects, such as spectacular monuments, splendid landscaping and/or pretentious built environments, have become the most popular items. Electoral campaigns as well as the activity reports have become a catalogue of projects of construction, landscaping and entrepreneurship.

Sema Erder and Nihal İncioğlu (2013, pp 5-6) point to the year 1984 as the origin of project-based municipalism championed first by Bedrettin Dalan in Istanbul. His understanding of municipal politics imposed the replacement of traditional municipalism identified by daily tasks such as rubbish collection, tarification or licensing with a project-oriented municipalism undertaking large infrastructural investments. Since then, all actors from all political parties and ideologies adapted their programmes and activities in line with the project-focused perspective.

It is no surprise that public relation activities gain importance as urban investments start representing the major domain of municipal activities. The image of the municipality as a running, hardworking, productive institution should be communicated by all means: billboards, signboards, public screens, posters, newsletters, social media messages and web pages present images of municipal services. '(Metropolitan) Municipality is working' has become a nationwide motto used to accompany these images of operational municipalities.

The problem is that the catalogues start gradually looking alike, as what can be rationally conceived in an urban setting has technical and financial limits. Yet, candidates as well as elected officials need to distinguish themselves in order to justify their positions and/or aspirations. Projects thus become grander and more spectacular to mark the originality and mastery to such an extent that they are labelled as 'crazy-projects', implying the extraordinary imagination and courage of their promisers. Electoral campaigning then adopts an 'Olympic' motivation while seeking the *citrus, altius, fortius* of projects, paving the way to a gigantonomia destined to impress the public by grandeur (Bora, 2011). Bent Flyvbjerg (2005) prefers to call the object of this new political agenda 'mega-projects', and to relate it to Machiavelli who had argued that princes cunningly delude the public thanks to impressive investments launched with under-estimated costs and exaggerated outcomes.

The most illustrative example of such crazy projects is no doubt the Istanbul Canal that is planned to be 30 miles long, 25 metres deep and 150 metres wide between the Black and Marmara Seas (Jones and Agencies, 2011). Despite all opposition and warnings from urban planners, ecologists and activists, the President of the Republic insists that it is expected to cost about US$13 billion.[1]

The capital of Turkey, Ankara, is another outstanding case to refer to when crazy projects are the issue. Apart from many large and small ideas here and there, such as the statues of dinosaurs, auto-robots, cats, *seikbans*, soccer players, urban gates and so on, his most remarkable investment is the immense theme park that is spread over 1.2 million square metres on which 1,217 different activities are planned to attract annually at least 10 million visitors.[2] In an internet forum on theme parks, *gerstlaueringvar* summarises well the project: 'It's like they have plenty of money and plenty of land, and they have zero idea what to buy or how to make the park look better.'[3]

Such projects do not only belong to mayors of the governing Justice and Development Party (Adalet ve Kalkınma Partisi, AKP), as it is not rare to find similar ideas in cities governed by social democrats. We can refer to Ataturk's relief in Buca/İzmir. With it is size of 42 metres, it is the 10th largest relief in the world. The construction that continued for three years had cost 4.2 million liras.[4]

Flourishing of a gigantonomia based on such mega/crazy projects is not linked to a discursive change in politics which, indeed, coincides to a neoliberal shift in economy politics, facilitating what David Harvey (1985, 1989) calls the second circuit of capital identified with investments in the urban built environment. Deindustrialisation triggered by the opportunities of globalisation that enabled the displacement of industrial plants to the developing world, capitalists have become more enthusiastic in investing in urban settings that represented a very rich and easy source of rent. Legal frameworks fast adapted to the requirement of such investments further enhanced the interest in urban settings.

New reading of service delivery combined with the new economy politics focused on urban settings led to a project-based understanding of municipal politics orchestrated indispensably by a strong patron in the personality of mayors. So now let's have a closer look at this one man show on the municipal scene.

Mayors as one-and-only decision-makers

Since the 1990s, local political leadership has gained importance even in a Europe traditionally identifying with more collective and consensual forms of local government. A strong mayoral model expected to provide an accountable, executive and strategic leadership has become prominent in quite a number of European countries where strong, visionary and charismatic leaders are sought and praised (Borraz and John, 2004; Steyvers et al, 2008).

Through a redefinition of tasks between the councils and the executive wing that has strengthened the latter, local government has gained a dualist structure (Daeman, 2012, pp 38-9). One of the main conditions of this dualism was the introduction of the direct election of mayors. In addition to cases like Portugal and some of the German Länder where direct election of mayors goes back several decades, the 1990s have witnessed its introduction or generalisation in a variety of countries such as Germany, Italy, Poland, Hungary and England, and discussed in many more.

Until 1963, municipal councils elected Turkish mayors, although in the early days of the Republic, the appointed prefect had also assumed the mayoralty besides the presidency of the local branch of the single party. Direct election of mayors was introduced in 1963, but their emergence as influential and political actors took place a decade later, with the rise of social democrats to power in most of major cities, whereas central government was still controlled by the conservatives. Suffering significantly from political and financial restrictions and the pressures of central government, these social democrat mayors had developed an original and collective approach to local governments that would later be labelled 'new municipalism' (Tekeli, 1992, pp 88-91).

Mayors like Vedat Dalokay and Ali Dinçer in Ankara, Ahmet İsvan in İstanbul and Erol Köse in İzmit had become phenomenal figures of local politics and thus brought seats of mayoralty into prominence (Ceyhun, 1977; Dalokay, 1977; İsvan, 2002; Gürer, 2009). But the actual empowerment of mayors took place in the 1980s during which time local governments had gained important political and financial powers.

Apart from being the head of the executive wing of the municipal organisation, mayors also chair local decisive bodies, municipal councils and municipal committees. Consequently, the decision-making of municipal public policies has been marked by the omnipresence of mayors. Particularly in metropolitan settings, mayors appear as the one-and-only decision-makers with great powers, both in their parties and municipal organisations. An analysis of the decisive stage in the policy cycle will help us to elaborate the growing role of mayors in Turkish local governments.

Formally, the municipal council is the decisive body of Turkish local government deliberating and approving important issues such as the budget, annual financial report, municipal activity plans, urban plan changes, debts and use of municipal properties. However, in reality it remains a voting milieu where actual deliberations rarely occur, for a couple reasons. First, mayors act also as presidents of the council, inducing the system to a monist structure. As a matter of fact, it is the mayor who determines the agenda of the council and supervises the monthly meeting sessions. The great part of the agenda of municipal councils is based on propositions formulated and transferred by bureaucratic units of the municipality that are under the direct influence and supervision of the mayor. Moreover, in case of parity in a decision, it is the preference of the mayor that counts. In any case, the mayor disposes a right of veto to the decisions of the council on juridical pretexts (Bayraktar, 2007).

Second, deliberations on agenda items actually take place in specialised committees rather than assemblies of municipal councils. These committees comprise of at least three, at most five persons to be selected among its members in proportion of the weight of parties and independent members in the council. The agenda items transferred to committees by the council should be elaborated and reported back to the council in five or ten days to be directly put on the agenda by the chair of the council. Meetings of committees are open to representatives of public institutions, professional chambers, labour unions and related associations, albeit without disposing a right to vote. Empirical studies reveal that the determining power of councillors on committee decisions can be only limited as elaborated issues are usually either technically too complex or geographically widespread for councillors to be able to comment on (Aksu, 2015, pp 124-6; Arıknoğa, 2015, pp 66-9). Some councillors may even be unaware of the committee's agenda (Demiroğlu and Okutan, 2015, p 208).

Moreover, the council share its decisive power with the executive commission that is formally responsible for the implementation of council resolutions. Yet the latter enjoys significant powers of decision-making such as reviewing the municipality's strategic plan, annual work programme, budget and revenues and expenditures of the previous year to be submitted to the municipal council as well as adopting decisions of expropriation. The executive commission that meets at least once a week is a mixed commission with half of the members councillors elected by the municipal council, the other half municipal administrators selected by the mayor (one must be the fiscal administrator of the municipality). With the presence of mayors, the administrative wing of the municipality prevails over the elected wing, thus strengthens furthermore the hegemonic status of the mayor.

Mayors owe their overwhelming position not only to the operational structure of local governments, but also to political relationships along which candidates are determined. Candidacy and then election of mayors can only be possible with enormous economical resources as pre-candidacy, pre-electoral and electoral campaigns require huge expenses for activities of propaganda such as publicity, media appearances, meetings etc. All these have to be financed by candidates themselves as the support of political parties to candidates is negligible (Bayraktar and Altan, 2012). Consequently, those who are elected as mayors or even managed to be qualified as party candidates and to carry out an electoral campaign have to possess a significant wealth thanks to which they also enjoy an undeniable influence within their political parties and thus over other councillors and candidates. How mayors or mayoral candidates determine the electoral lists of councillors is no secret (Suğur, 2015, p 170).

In light of these observations, we can easily argue that mayors actually appear as the main decision-makers of Turkish local government thanks to the structural, political and personal powers they enjoy. No matter how councillors are the actors of the formal decision-making process, mayors exercise de jure and de facto pressures on the former so that their choices and preferences are reflected in council resolutions.

Faster and faster implementation of policies

Strengthening of the local executives is not peculiar to Turkey as new public management (NPM) principles prescribe a new governmental rational that is more concerned about 'getting things done as quickly, cheaply, effectively as possible -and usually about getting things done through other people' (Pollitt and Bouckaert, 2004, p 9). Hence, traditional values of the public sector such as democracy, accountability, equity and probity seem to be gradually replaced by private sector sermons of effectiveness, efficiency, economy and rapidity that are realised by re-scaling municipal organisations and privatisation of service delivery.

This new orientation at the expense of democratic values can be clearly seen in the booklet published by the governing AKP with the objective of presenting the justifications of the highly controversial amendment on metropolitan governments that enlarge their territories to provincial borders and abolish provincial governments, small municipalities and villages. The Party states very clearly that the main concern of the legal change is to enhance the capacity of service delivery in these territories. In the 54 pages of the booklet, the word 'service' (*hizmet* in Turkish) is mentioned twice a page 107 times whereas 'politics' appears five times, four of which are accompanied with 'service' in the form of 'politics of service' (*hizmet siyaseti*). The objective of politics of service is also explicitly formulated: 'to ensure the unity of the most efficient, fastest and best delivery of services required by the contemporary municipalism' (AKParti, 2012).

What is seen as democratically valuable as deliberation, consultation or planning is henceforth just a loss of time in the name of politics of service. Resolutions shaped and taken by watertight patronage of mayors ought to be implemented in the same manner as fast as possible. As Aytac Durak, mayor of Adana for more than two decades, states: 'Municipality should be governed just like a private company' (Durak, 2015, pp 266-7). According to Durak, privatisation of service delivery corresponds to the rationalisation of public administration by bringing the dynamism of the private sector into it (Durak, 2015).

Durak is not alone in this opinion, as by the 1980s, the delivery of public services by the private sector was put into practice (Karahanoğullar, 2004, p 323) in harmony with neoliberal maxims that became hegemonic all around the world. Since then, local public services can be either privatised, outsourced or delivered in partnership with private companies or by municipal companies. It should be noted that the presence of the private sector in the implementation of municipal policies is not a possibility but often a requirement as the legal framework not only encourages but also even indirectly urges the privatisation of services. Municipalities are banned from spending more than 30 per cent (40 per cent for those with populations less than 10,000) of their budget incomes for personnel costs (Article 43 of Law no 5393 on municipalities). Due to such restrictions, in-house delivery of services become quite troublesome, even impossible for municipalities that have no chance but to outsource the delivery of services as costs of outsourcing bypass the restrictions on personnel expenses.

Municipal executives express no reluctance in outsourcing services as this form of service delivery also represents quite a number of advantages for them. First of all, each outsourcing means a tender in which unwritten conditions always play important roles. Apart from personal corruptions that have been no secret for anyone in Turkey, municipalities may unofficially burden the financing or delivery of some other services unrelated with the content of the tender on the subcontractor. Moreover, municipalities de facto keep their say on the recruitment of personnel for the outsourced services. The influence of municipalities is much more extended with regards to companies founded by themselves. These municipal economic corporations are among the private law entities with which municipalities may contract for the provision of public services. Therefore, outsourcing to municipal or private corporations represents a window of opportunity for municipalities to carry out services and implement policies in a more flexible and faster way by bypassing the legal framework through subcontracts.

In addition to outsourcing the simple delivery of services, municipalities can or often ought to establish large-scale and long-term partnerships with the private sector. Since the 1980s, different schemes of public–private partnerships have been launched. Local authorities can actually transfer the building and operation (*yap-işlet*) of establishments destined for public service provision to the private sector (for example, thermal power plants), whether or not they retain the ownership of the infrastructure (*yap-işlet-devret*). Both these sectors can also develop joint projects – particularly in the housing sector – based on the principle of sharing revenues or income (Bayraktar and Massicard, 2012).

Until the constitutional amendment of 1999, such public–private partnerships in the delivery of public services had been subjected to administrative law in the form of either administrative agreements (the most common type being 'concession agreements') or unilateral authorisation of the administration. Since then, public services have been delivered through private law contracts and through arbitration for discrepancies arising from concession agreements (Bayraktar and Tansug, 2016, p 220).

Resolutions taken mainly by mayors are thus implemented in a managerial way aiming at the fastest and most efficient delivery of services. It should be surprising for no one that such a policy process could be hardly supervised, that policy outcomes could not be democratically evaluated. To verify this hypothesis, in the final section of the chapter I discuss the evaluation phase of the Turkish local policy cycle.

Non-evaluation of policies

Evaluation of implemented policies is the final stage of the policy cycle at which the outcomes, impacts, deficiencies and dysfunctions are to be assessed. Actors involved in or concerned about policy are expected to make an evaluation about whether the course of action is a success or failure by examining its impact and outcomes. This evaluation can be juridical, political or civic. In this final part of the chapter I discuss how such policy evaluations take place at local level.

The first dimension of the evaluation would be juridical supervision with the objective of verifying the legality of municipal policies. The activity report that is presented by the mayor and presented in April to the council for approval is the main instrument of internal supervision of municipalities. If the report is rejected by the three-quarters of the council, the mayor is considered insufficient, and with the Council of State's approval, the mayor is dismissed from his/her functions. Yet, this legal mechanism of control is hardly used and there has been almost no example of such a dismissal of a mayor by the council's vote (Azaklı and Özgür, 2005, p 311). To understand the ineffectiveness of supervision of annual activities, it would be enough to recall the supremacy of mayors over councillors noted above.

The ex-mayor of Çanakkale, a mid-sized city in the southern Marmara region, İsmail Özay (2002) admits very frankly this strengthened position of mayors:

> I have been a mayor for 13 years that means I am a democratic professional.... In fact, being a local executive in Turkey is being a democratic sultan. If you do not control yourself, you enjoy extraordinary powers. The principles of control are defined by the mayor himself. Of course, there are means of control, but those are tools of tutelage. There is no serious control in local governments. I believe that the present system of local governments resembles rather to a system of democratic sultanate.

The reign of mayors may only be true for municipalities enjoying the support and tolerance of central bureaucracy, but for others it would be unjust to ignore the pressures exercised by central government through two different channels. In addition to the internal supervision carried out by the council, the Court of Accounts externally audits municipal expenses on behalf of the Grand Assembly. As a second instrument of supervision, the Ministry of Interior controls municipalities through its civil inspectors. In case of identification of an irregularity or deficiency in the delivery of service, the municipal administration can be sued or the prefect can take over the delivery of service and encash expenses from the municipality's financial resources. Last but not least, mayors or councillors who are subjected to investigation or prosecution due to an occupational offence may be suspended from office as a precautionary measure until the rendition of the final judgment. However, a recent decree in the framework of the state of emergency declared after the failed coup of 15 July 2016 has introduced the suspension of deputy mayors or councillors accused of supporting terrorist organisations and the appointment of new mayors. Until now, councils had elected new mayors from among themselves to substitute suspended ones. Currently, more than two dozen mayors have been appointed by this practice replacing mayors elected from the pro-Kurdish party.

There is no room for doubt that the abovementioned mechanisms of external supervision exercised by central government are widely open to political instrumentalisation in order to punish or repress the opposition. When this manipulated means of external audit is combined with the ineffective supervision of the subordinated council, it is obvious that evaluation of municipal policies has not actually been carried out, technically or politically.

Yet it would be unjust to think that evaluation of public policies is only a matter of institutional supervision, as service providers are also veritable actors of the policy process. After all, local governments are elected organs that are theoretically accountable to the public in general at least from election to election. Yet, the centralised and non-democratic structure and functioning of political parties do not allow electors to take part in the candidate determination process. As noted above, in general, those who dispose and can mobilise large economic resources manage to be qualified as mayoral candidates. Given the highly fragmented and conflictual political life, electors often content themselves with the candidate of the party to which they feel the closest. Therefore, elections do not actually represent an evaluation of policies implemented by a mayoral mandate.

Democratic evaluation of local policies is not restricted to elections since citizens can theoretically express their opinions by other means such as pressure groups, associations and ad hoc gatherings. Activities of professional chambers should be highlighted in the first place because in particular, chambers of doctors, jurists and engineers have been very active advocates of public interest since the 1970s (Batuman, 2013). They have managed to improve, change or abolish countless policies by appealing to the administrative justice and organising campaigns. Yet, as the administrative proceedings become much more expensive and troublesome due to pressures on the justice exercised by central government and the activities of the chambers are restricted, their capacity with regards to conducting public evaluation and supervision has been very much reduced.

Civic activism could not fill the lacuna that emerged due to the ineffectiveness of chambers since the state coup of September 1980, which brought about a devastated civil sphere. Even the flourishing of civil societal bodies since the late 1990s could not actually overcome the generalised apathy towards political initiatives, and remained in a narrow project-oriented perspective. Such NGO projects aimed primarily at delivering services in domains where public institutions fall short technically and politically thus play complementary rather than supervisory roles. Adoption of such a project-based civil activism prioritised fundraising activities, thus neglecting to a great extent initiatives of collective mobilisation (Toprak, 1996; Groc, 1998; Navaro-Yashin, 1998).

The absence of civic mobilisations with the objective of supervising public policy-making does not indicate a total absence of social organisations. As a matter of fact, since the early stages of Turkish urbanisation, first newcomers and then the public in general have been inclined to be involved in informal solidarity networks structured along ethnic, religious or geographical identities. Mainly functioning within clientelist relationships, these social gatherings brought about and then maintained the reproduction of patronage politics, both at national and local levels (Erder, 1996; Işık and Pınarcıoğlu, 2000; Kurtoğlu, 2003). Public evaluation of policies has thus become a matter of 'where' and 'for whom' rather than 'how' and 'why', focusing on their eventual beneficiaries.

The predominance of patronage politics has hindered the democratic and civic functioning of participatory mechanisms introduced in the aftermath of the interest that emerged after the organisation of the HABITAT-II Summit in Istanbul in 1996. Becoming compulsory with the municipal reform of 2004-05, city councils, for instance, have been either co-opted by the political elite or instrumentalised on behalf of the personal or organisational interests of political or even civil actors. Far from engendering channels of policy evaluation and supervision, these so-called participatory platforms were far from going beyond participatory tokens (Bayraktar, 2016b).

Finally, the state of media should be noted, as an adequate evaluation of public policies requires access to objective information. While mainstream media suffers significantly from political and economic pressures, it has mainly focused on national politics or on the agenda of grand metropoles, among which Istanbul appears as the main subject of interest by far, where the local press remains weak and ineffective due to its economic and political bottlenecks. Consequently, citizens are deprived of objective and up-to-date information about policies that are adopted and implemented in their localities, and are thus prevented from taking action towards getting involved in public policy processes.

In short, evaluation of local public policies seems to be exempted from effective supervision, not only by institutional actors, but also from civil bodies. Mayors' supremacy in agenda-setting and decision-making has been coupled by a lack of adequate mechanisms for evaluating and supervising, contributing to the maintenance of the one-man-show within local government.

Conclusion

In this chapter I have discussed the state of policy-making at a local level in Turkey, concentrating mainly on municipalities as the primary local bodies. In order to examine the nature of their policy-making, I followed the stages of the policy cycle, identifying the main characteristics of each stage.

To start with, I argued that conventional urban services have been eclipsed by flamboyant projects of construction and recreation in municipal agendas, since political competition among local power contenders has become a contest of concrete projects. Political values, perspectives and ideologies thus lose ground as different competitors' project proposals do not reveal themselves to be significantly different, politically. It is personalities and not the political standing that is in electoral question.

Mayors are obviously the spearheads of this project-based agenda-making, as they enjoy a personal omnipresence on all institutional, political and personal levels. Accordingly, they also appear as the main actors of local decision-making processes, eclipsing, to a great extent, the formal decision-makers, namely, the councillors.

The supremacy of mayors in decision-making is also reproduced in the implementation of policies as the weight of privatisation, partnership and outsourcing in public services has significantly increased. With the growing involvement of the private sector, the execution of public policies has adopted a managerial style, meaning that the status of mayors resembles that of CEOs.

Finally, public policies determined, decided and executed mainly by mayors seem to be relatively immunised from public supervision if they go along with central government. The limits of internal institutional supervision, the obsolescence of professional chambers, the cultural weakness of civil society as well as the ineffectiveness of the local press all represent poor assessment of public policies, thus bringing mayors a relative immunity in public policy evaluation.

In short, Turkish municipal policies seem to be highly marked by populist-driven agendas propagated by strong mayors and executed in a managerial style, without being effectively evaluated by institutional or civic bodies.

Notes

[1] See www.borsamatik.com.tr/haber-detay/kanal-istanbulun-maliyeti-13-milyar-dolar/72062/
[2] See www.melihgokcek.com/proje-detay/anka-park-25.html
[3] See www.themeparkreview.com/forum/viewtopic.php?f=2&t=67415&sid=5be42701dfdd51b18e29a5737e2cf25b&start=100
[4] See www.gazetevatan.com/buca-da-ataturk-dagi-258839-gundem

References

Aksu, Ç. (2015) 'Büyükşehir belediye meclisinin yapısı, işleyişi ve yerel demokrasi: Adana örneği' in P.U. Semerci (ed) *Yerel demokrasi sorunsalı*, Istanbul: İstanbul Bilgi Üniversitesi Yayınları, pp 111-32.

AKParti (2012) 'Sorular ve cevaplarla yeni büyükşehir belediye yasası' (https://goo.gl/drSq3Y).

Anderson, J.E. (1984) *Public policymaking: An introduction* (2nd edn), Boston, MA: Houghton Mifflin Company.

Arıknoğa, E. (2015) 'Türkiye'de dönüşen büyükşehir ve yerel siyaset', in P.U. Semerci (ed) *Yerel demokrasi sorunsal*, Istanbul: İstanbul Bilgi Üniversitesi Yayınları, pp 49-71.

Azaklı, S. and Özgür, H. (2005) 'Belediye Organları ve Organlar Arası İlişkiler: Başkan, Meclis ve Encümen', in H. Özgür, M. Hüseyin ve Kösecik Muhammet, *Yerel Yönetimler Üzerine Güncel Yazılar-1*, Ankara: Nobel Yayın Dağıtım, pp 297-319.

Batuman, B. (2013) '70'ler: Siyasetin Odağındaki kent, kentin odağındaki Siyaset', *Toplum ve Bilim*, vol 127, pp 68-87.

Bayraktar, U. (2007) 'Turkish municipalities: Reconsidering local democracy beyond administrative autonomy', *European Journal of Turkish Studies* (http://ejts.revues.org/index1103.html).

Bayraktar, U. (2013) 'Özgün bir siyasal bilimi geliştirmek adına bir ilham kaynağı olarak fransız kamu politikası analizi yazını', in M. Yıldız and Z. Sobacı (eds) *Kamu politikası: Kuram ve uygulama*, Ankara: Adres, pp 114-29.

Bayraktar, U. (2014) 'Decentralisation, poly-centralisation and re-centralisation of Turkish politics', in K. Göymen and O. Sazak (eds) *Centralisation decentralisation debate revisited*, Istanbul: İstanbul Politikalar Merkezi, pp 321-46.

Bayraktar, U. (2016a) 'Türkiye kent siyasetinin post-politik halleri', *Modus Operandi*, vol 4, pp 19-49.

Bayraktar, U. (2016b) *Sustainable Cities e-participation for a politics of local commons*, Istanbul: TESEV (http://tesev.org.tr/wp-content/uploads/2016/12/SK.Rapor_.ENG_.pdf).

Bayraktar, U. and Altan, C. (2012) 'Explaining Turkish party centralism: Traditions and trends in the exclusion of local party offices in Mersin and Beyond', in N. Watts and E. Massicard (eds) *Negotiating political power in Turkey: Breaking up the party*, New York: Routledge, pp 17-36.

Bayraktar, U. and Massicard, E. (2012) *Decentralisation in Turkey*, Paris: Agence Française de Développement.

Bayraktar, U. and Tansug, C. (2016) 'Local service delivery in Turkey', in H. Wollmann, I. Koprić and G. Marcou (eds) *Public and social services in Europe: From public and municipal to private sector provision*, London: Palgrave Macmillan, pp 217-32.

Bayraktar, U. and Yıldızcan, C. (2016) 'Governors as new agents of governance in Turkey', Paper presented at the International Workshop 'Non-Public Actors In Turkish Policy-Making', 8 March, Istanbul.

Bora, T. (2011) 'Büyük olsun, bizim olsun', *Birikim*, vol 270, pp 15-18.

Borraz, O. and John, P. (2004) 'The transformation of urban political leadership in Western Europe,' *International Journal of Urban and Regional Research*, 28 (March), pp 107-20.

Ceyhun, D. (1977) *Bir yeni dev: Çağımızın trajiği*, Istanbul: Tekin.

Daeman, H. (2012) 'Revitalising representative democracy', in L. Schaap and H. Daeman (eds) *Renewal in European local democracies: Puzzles, dilemmas and options*, Berlin: Springer, pp 27-54.

Dalokay, V. (1977) *Yelkenimizdeki rüzgarı çaldılar! Yılmadık*, Çağlar Matbaası.
Demiroğlu, E.T. and Okutan, M.E. (2015) 'Büyükşehir belediye meclisinin yapısı, işleyişi ve yerel demokrasi: İstanbul örneği', in P.U. Semerci (ed) *Yerel demokrasi sorunsalı*, Istanbul: İstanbul Bilgi Üniversitesi Yayınları, pp 205-21.
Durak, A. (2015) *Söyleyeceklerim var*, Ankara: Bilgi.
Erder, S. (1996) *Istanbul'a bir kent kondu: Umraniye*, Istanbul: Iletisim.
Erder, S. and İncioğlu, N. (2013) *Türkiye'de yerel politikanın yükselişi*, Istanbul: İstanbul Bilgi Üniversitesi Yayınları.
Flyvbjerg, B. (2005) 'Machiavellian megaprojects', *Antipode*, vol 37, no 1, pp 18-22.
Gürer, G. (2009) 'Gözde Gürer'le Haftanın Sohbeti: Selahattin tonguç' (http://gozdegurer.blogspot.com/2009/06/selahattin-tonguc.html).
Groc, G. (1998) 'La "société civile" turque entre politique et individu', *CEMOTI*, vol 26, pp 43-74.
Harvey, D. (1985) *Urbanisation of capital*, Oxford: Blackwell.
Harvey, D. (1989) *The urban experience*, Baltimore, MD: Johns Hopkins University Press.
Howlett, M. and Ramesh, M. (1995) *Studying public policy*, Oxford: Oxford University Press.
Isık, O. and Pınarcıoglu, M. (2000) *Nöbetleşe yoksulluk*, Istanbul: Iletişim.
İsvan, A. (2002) *Başkent gölgesinde İstanbul*, Istanbul: Iletişim.
Jones, S. and Agencies (2011) 'Istanbul's new Bosphorus canal "to surpass Suez or Panama"', *The Guardian*, 27 April (www.theguardian.com/world/2011/apr/27/istanbul-new-bosphorus-canal).
Karahanoğulları, O. (2004) *Kamu Hizmeti*, Ankara: Turhan.
Kurtoğlu, A. (2003) *Hemşehrilik ve şehirde siyaset*, Istanbul: Iletişim.
Navaro-Yashin, Y. (1998) 'Uses and abuses of "state and civil society" in contemporary Turkey', *New Perspectives on Turkey*, vol 18, pp 1-22.
Övgün, B. (2016) 'Kamu yönetimi reformunda bir açmaz: yerelleşme mi, merkezileşme mi?", *Mulkiye*, vol 40, no 3, pp 159-80.
Özay, İ. (2002) 'XI. Sivil Toplum kuruluşları sempozyumu sunumu', in Sivil Toplum Kuruluşları, *Yerelleşme ve yerel yönetimler*, Istanbul: Tarih Vakfı Yurt Yayınları, pp 67-74.
Penbecioğlu, M. (2011) 'Kapitalist kentleşme dinamiklerinin Türkiye'deki son 10 yılı: Yapılı çevre üretimi, devlet ve büyük ölçekli kentsel projeler', *Birikim*, vol 270, pp 62-73.
Pollitt, C. and Bouckaert, G. (2004) *Public management reform: A comparative analysis*, Oxford: Oxford University Press.
Steyvers, K., Bergström, T., Bäck, H., Boogers, M., Ruano de la Fuente, J.M. and Schaap, L. (2008) 'From princeps to president? Comparing local political leadership transformation', *Local Government Studies*, vol 34, no 2, pp 131-46 (http://dx.doi.org/10.1080/03003930701852179).

Suğur, N. (2015) 'Büyükşehir belediye meclisinin yapısı, işleyişi ve yerel demokrasi: Eskişehir örneği' in P.U. Semerci (ed) *Yerel demokrasi sorunsalı*, Istanbul: İstanbul Bilgi Üniversitesi Yayınları, pp 165-83.

Tekeli, İ. (1992) *Belediyecilik yazıları*, Istanbul: IULA-EMME.

Toprak, B. (1996) 'Civil society In Turkey', in A.R. Norton (ed) *Civil society in the Middle East*, Leiden: E.J. Brill, pp 87-118.

Part Three
Experts, international actors and public opinion

EIGHT

Beyond developmentalism: the role of experts and expertise in Turkey's environmental policy disputes

Gökhan Orhan

Introduction

The exact role of experts in policy analysis is an under-investigated area in Turkey, because there has been a limited use of policy analysis techniques in policy-making and implementation. Although experts do play a certain role in giving policy advice to policy-makers, it is rather challenging to generalise the patterns of policy advice in Turkey. The character of expert involvement varies according to the policy area under investigation and also differs from case to case. Instead of making a general analysis, focusing on a complex policy area like environmental policy, in which experts play a pivotal role due to the complexity of the problems, may shed some light on the role of experts in the policy process in Turkey.

Drawing from previous research on environmental policy disputes, this chapter aims to investigate uses of policy analysis techniques and the role of experts in the environmental policy process. Top-down, centrally imposed developmental projects rely heavily on developmentalist discourses. Certain experts advocate these projects as indisputable elements of a country's development trajectory as well as solutions to various problems, such as energy supply and balance of payments problems. However, there is substantial opposition to these projects on the basis of their negative social, economic and environmental consequences. Although authorities snub opposition claims on the basis of ignorance (or for being ideological), the only dilemma about expertise in environmental policy is not the one between the experts and (lay)people. Different groups of experts inform both policy-makers and other groups that challenge the official policy process in highly contested environmental policy disputes in Turkey. There are competing discourse coalitions that draw from experts from a variety of levels (either individual or corporate) with potentially different values and interests, perceptions of the situation and policy preferences, and there is an ongoing struggle to determine policy outcomes. This chapter aims to identify the role of experts and the way they use their expertise in articulating certain policy positions and support interests advocated in their respective discourse coalitions. If problems and solutions are socially constructed, and deeply held values on issues influence the rest of the process, including experts, the impartiality of experts should be open to scrutiny and discussion for a more transparent policy process.

In the following section, the evolution of the role of experts in the policy process is analysed and their role in environmental policy disputes detailed. After setting the context, the role of experts in policy processes in Turkey and policy discourses on environmental policy disputes is discussed. The chapter concludes with an assessment of the contextual factors that influence the role of experts in the policy process in Turkey.

Role of experts and expertise in the policy process

Experts and expertise occupy a vital role in contemporary societies. From health to energy and transport to communications, we trust and rely on experts in almost all spheres of life. Experts define problems and propose solutions for complex policy problems. Paradoxically, however, their position is under more scrutiny these days. In conjunction with the postmodern condition and 'post-truth' discussions, the roles of science, scientists and experts have recently been challenged and are starting to lose their distinguished place in contemporary societies.

In this section, the evolution of the role of experts in the policy process is summarised with reference to the changes that have taken place since the second half of the 20th century. Laying out historical developments is particularly important in understanding the current status of experts and the criticisms they face, since they have failed to meet some of the promises they undertook in the second half of the 20th century.

Public policies are about '... what governments choose to do or not to do' (Dye, 1992, p 2). They are about the decisions and non-decisions of governments on a specific policy field within a particular period of time. Public policies also regulate the public realm and allocation of values in a society. Policy analysis, on the other hand, is about the study of policies, and could be defined as 'a process of multidisciplinary inquiry designed to create, critically assess and communicate information that is useful in understanding and improving policies' (Dunn, 2008, p 1).

For mainstream accounts, policy analysis is an interdisciplinary field of study and practice that aims to solve the problems of modern societies. Policy analysis draws profoundly from evidence. As underlined by Harold Lasswell (1965), there is a crucial role for expert knowledge in this process, and policy analysis expected to benefit from the findings of various disciplines of the social and natural sciences and expertise accumulated throughout history (Lasswell, 1965), from fact finding to problem definition and proposing alternatives to implementation. Experts and expertise are indisputably involved in almost all phases of policy-making and implementation.

Although the undisputed authority of science and expertise in the policy process dates back to the Enlightenment's ideals and rationalism advocated in modernity, developments during and after the Second World War have played a definite role in postwar developments. New methods developed in economics, psychology and operations research were utilised during the war and employed in civilian life in the aftermath of war. The rise of behaviouralism also contributed to the supremacy of quantitative techniques over others. In Lasswell's words, 'the battle for method is won' (Lasswell, 1965, p 7).

In this context, boundary organisations linked the scientific community and other players in the policy process. Evidence-based policy analysis contributed to the authority of science through the incorporation of rigorous research evidence into public policy debates and internal public sector processes for policy evaluation and programme improvement, as well as improving the reliability of advice concerning the efficiency and effectiveness of policy settings and possible alternatives (Head, 2009). Evidence-based policy analysis became rather widespread, and has been influential in many circles, including in the UK White Papers (Cabinet Office, 1999).

Overall, we cannot speak of any problem regarding the authority of science and scientists during the 1950s and 1960s. This is what Collins and Evans called the 'first wave' of science studies (Collins and Evans, 2002, p 239). In this period, science and scientists enjoyed a special authority.

According to Collins and Evans, in this period,

> ... a good scientific training was seen to put a person in a position to speak with authority and decisiveness in their own field, and often in other fields.... Because the sciences were thought of esoteric and authoritative, it was inconceivable that decision-making in matters that involved science and technology could travel in any other direction than from the top down. (Collins and Evans, 2002, p 239)

There was faith in the straightforward link between the authority of science and the policy process, independent of social practices.

However, the role and nature of expert involvement in the policy process has varied over time, and the undisputed position of science, scientists and experts did not last long. From the 1970s onwards the authority of experts was questioned from a constructivist angle. Interpretive approaches to policy analysis challenged certain assumptions of mainstream approaches to policy analysis, such as the possibility of top-down, neutral and value-free policy analysis, and brought different perspectives and alternative methods to the sphere of policy analysis.

Interpretive methods in policy analysis are based on assumptions such as 'possibilities of multiple interpretations' and the impossibility of 'brute data whose meaning is beyond dispute' (Yanow, 2000, p 5). According to Dwora Yanow, it is not possible for an analyst to stand outside of the policy issue free of its values and meanings as well as his/her own values and beliefs. The argument acquired through interpretation is subjective and reflects the past experience of the analyst, including their education, experience, training, familial and communal ties (Yanow, 2000, p 6). If problems and solutions are socially constructed, deeply held values on issues influence the rest of the process – that is, scientists and experts cannot act independent of the social processes and institutions surrounding them. 'As living requires sensemaking and sensemaking entails interpretation', Yanow argues, 'so does policy analysis' (Yanow, 2000, p 5).

There are a number of occasions where social processes are embedded in both scientific inquiry and the policy domain. Drawing from the BSE crisis in the UK, Irwin and Wynne point to the intrinsically social character of science in framing the public debate. Although statements from the Department of Health and prominent academics referred to tiny risks of catching BSE from eating beef, public reaction manifested itself in sudden drops in meat consumption, in the face of uncertainties and scientists' inability to secure public trust. For Irwin and Wynne,

> Science offers a framework which is unavoidably social as well as technical since in public domains scientific knowledge embodies implicit models or assumptions about the social world. In addition, as an intervention in public life, scientific knowledge involves rhetorical claims to the superiority of the scientific worldview but it also builds upon social processes of trust and credibility. Whilst claiming to stand apart from the rest of society, science will reflect social interests and social assumptions. (Irwin and Wynne, 1996, pp 2-3)

In this context, scientists, regulators and industry's initial and misleading claims on BSE both reflected the socially embedded nature of scientific claims and contributed to a public distrust on the basis of their statements.

This is what Collins and Evans called the 'second wave' of science studies, and in this wave the social character of scientific research was highlighted and the neutral image of scientists and experts questioned (Collins and Evans, 2002). In parallel to the conventional wisdom of the era, the governance paradigm's policy proposals, such as 'participation of stakeholders' and 'democratisation of the policy process', were offered as viable alternatives to solve the policy problems of modern societies (Orhan, 2014). Thus, extending public participation in both politics and science emerged as a solution to the problem of technocracy, scientism and a top-down policy style in the second wave of science and technology studies. Leaving aside other critical issues concerning the difficulty of participation (Orhan, 2014), the levelling of experts and people were criticised in the 'third wave' of science and technology studies, and in a number of cases, problems stemming from laypeople's ignorance or exaggeration were highlighted to display problems of the second wave of science and technology studies.

The third wave of science and technology studies was introduced by Collins and Evans (2002) and later developed by Collins, Evans and Weinel (Collins et al, 2010). In their first article published in 2002, Collins and Evans dealt with what they called 'the problem of extension'. According to Collins and Evans,

> the need to extend the domain of technical decision-making beyond the technically qualified elite to enhance political legitimacy replaced the 'Problem of Legitimacy' with the 'Problem of Extension' in which there is a tendency towards dissolving the boundary between experts and the public and there are no longer any grounds for limiting the indefinite extension of technical decision-making rights. (Collins and Evans, 2002, p 235)

In this context, they recognise problems concerning the first wave; yet again, they do not completely discard arguments of the second wave, but would like to reinstate the role of the expert in the policy process. They criticise notions of the lay expert, stand against technological populism, and argue that demands for increased public participation in science have the tendency to lead to a 'levelling of the epistemological playing field' and to a collapse of the concept of expertise (Collins et al, 2010, p 186).

Collins et al also refer to Miller, who argues about the knowledge deficit between scientific researchers and members of the general public, and the inevitability of a gap between them (Miller, 2001, p 118). For Miller, 'scientists and lay people are not on the same footing where scientific information is concerned, and knowledge, hard won by hours of research, and tried and tested over the years and decades, deserves respect' (Miller, 2001, p 118).

Collins et al aim to recreate a role for science in policy and to reproduce the central role of science and scientists, to develop a new understanding of expertise, and to concentrate their efforts in reclaiming the status of experts, and they try to do so without disregarding the political nature of scientific enterprise on the one hand, and the importance of local knowledge on the other. Yet again, they keep these hierarchical relations intact.

Overall, human societies face a number of new and complex problems, such as global warming, food security and immigration, and there is a well-developed literature on the impact of experts, either as part of policy communities or global policy networks and epistemic communities (Orhan, 2015). The practice of public policy-making and implementation has been shaped by growing relations of governance, involving a number of players from various levels. This characteristic of public policy-making makes it a complex process where a large number of factors interact with each other in various ways. As Sabatier pointed out, the policy process is an extremely complex process in which a number of diverse players are involved, and interest groups and governmental agencies and legislatures at different levels of government, researchers and journalists are engaged in one or more aspects of the process (Sabatier, 1999, p 3).

There is an ongoing debate about the role of the scientific community and experts in the policy process. This is also about the role of values and ideologies in the policy process and the role of scientists and experts is not unquestioned, which is especially the case in environmental policy, where the policy process necessarily depends on experts and scientists for almost all stages.

The role of experts and expertise in environmental policy disputes

Environmental policy is a relatively new, nonetheless highly sophisticated, policy area. Environmental policies are interrelated with a number of other policy areas, and environmental problems are highly complex, with their solutions necessitating environmental policy integration, coordination and stakeholder participation. Experts have a significant role to play. They get involved in fact finding, measuring the scale of the problem, devising appropriate solutions for pollution, for example, pollution prevention and developing comprehensive strategies to reconcile the demands of environmental policy and other policy areas. As the interdependent character and complex nature of environmental problems makes it more prone to expert knowledge, a number of disciplines in both the natural and social sciences are needed to measure and determine the scale of the problem, or to define the problem and propose alternatives to solve and prevent further damage to the environment.

In this context, there is almost a consensus on the very central role of experts from a variety of disciplines, both in the social and natural sciences, as well as engineering. Furthermore, first-generation approaches to environmental policy display a faith in science and technology to solve environmental problems through their expertise in the field. However, interpretive approaches, and in particular, discursive policy analysis, challenge the notion of nature as an external entity and the role of experts and scientists in apprehending this entity. For example, Latour challenges the notion of 'nature as an independent entity obeying its own laws and the privileged authority of scientists and experts to represent this entity' (cited in Hajer and Versteeg, 2005, p 178). As outlined in Hajer and Versteeg, Latour claims that

> ... the presentation of nature as an external object, understandable only for the experts has served as a dogma, ... limiting the options for human action ... facts and values, morality and reality, science and politics should be seen as inseparable. Nature would then become an essentially negotiable concept that can be represented not only by scientists but also by poets, architects, farmers and laymen. (cited in Hajer and Versteeg, 2005, p 178)

If nature becomes an essentially negotiable and contested concept, the role of experts is also under scrutiny concerning their authority in defining the problem and offering alternative solutions. Indeed, we are not in a position to accept experts' position as a given, and recognise the political nature of their relationships with others, in advocacy or discourse coalitions, policy networks and other forms of alliances. In sum, policy processes as a whole cannot be evaluated and studied independent of the values and ideologies attached to experts and expertise throughout the whole process.

The contested nature of environmental problems and environmental policy has also been witnessed in a number of environmental disputes, among which global climate change has been the major example. This has been a controversial issue for global environmental politics since it was discovered by natural scientists. Although scientific findings on climate change provided a solid base and established the terms of discussion (Cook et al, 2013), a number of political and ideological differences separated countries and industries in their response to climate change. Indeed, a number of factors, ranging from domestic industries to the energy regime of a country, influence their response to climate change and the international regimes established to mitigate climate change. Ideological differences on the policy impact of scientific findings further exacerbated the problem because certain actors questioned the cost of mitigation efforts compared to improvements in expected climate change (Lomborg, 2007). Overall, there has been an ongoing struggle concerning the existence and seriousness of global climate change, and the role of carbon fuel lobbies are well documented in spreading environmental scepticism (Jacques et al, 2008). It is not only global warming as such; there are a number of other areas related to environmental policy and public health, such as DDT use, the hole in the ozone layer and acid rain, as well as tobacco and second-hand smoking in which a group of respected scientists led effective campaigns to mislead the public and deny well-established scientific knowledge and consensus on these issues (Oreskes and Conway, 2011).

It is as if we are moving toward a new phase in the science–society interface. After all, the policy process is not a gentleman's business, and there is always selective use of evidence to defend a particular policy position or particular interest. Sometimes scientific evidence is used solely to support political arguments and to legitimise a course of action; it is frequently disregarded, sidelined or even discredited if it challenges established practices and vested interests (Orhan, 2012). However, in this new era it is not only these methods, but we could also speak of concerted action by 'deniers', 'sceptics', 'doubters' or 'contrarians'. Furthermore, the year 2016 witnessed the rising popularity of a new term, 'post-truth', the Oxford Dictionaries Word of the Year in 2016, defined as 'relating to or denoting circumstances in which objective facts are less influential in shaping public opinion than appeals to emotion and personal belief' (Oxford Dictionaries, 2016).

This is what we have observed in the rest of the world, and in Turkey the role of experts and expertise has changed and been challenged on the basis of beliefs and emotions; there is a new type of expert in the policy process with rather different priorities, whom we could call the *embedded expert*, and in the following section the emergence of this new type of expert is discussed in more detail.

The role of experts in the policy process in Turkey

As summarised earlier in Chapter Two (this volume), the Turkish Ottoman history has a rich tradition and experience in utilising expert knowledge. In a similar vein, 19th-century modernisation efforts enjoyed the considerable contribution of foreign experts, not only in the military, engineering and medicine, but also in other areas including music (Kaya, 2002). The young Turkish Republic also resorted to experts in its modernisation efforts in areas ranging from forestry to education and infrastructure to health. The rise of public policy analysis in the US during the postwar era also had a number of repercussions on Turkish politics and policy processes such as the establishment of the State Planning Organization (SPO), and its implications on the policy process have been well documented. Although several opportunities existed on the part of Turkish bureaucracy to develop a policy framework along the lines of the new methods developed by public policy analysis, the reluctance of politicians in handing power over to the bureaucrats and technocrats, say the experts, made it difficult to attain.

The 1980s witnessed a breakthrough concerning the state tradition. For some commentators, post-1980 developments paved the way for using experts in a number of domains. In the post-1983 period in particular, Turgut Özal's governments resorted to experts to reorganise the state through more technical and rational lines. In this process politics was shaped around a discourse of 'rational principles and techniques' in parallel to Özal's developmentalist and pragmatic ideas. A new breed of experts with expertise in domains, ranging from academia to media, had started to gain power in the political realm (Şahan, 2013, pp 130-1). As detailed in Chapter Two (this volume), the 1980s and 1990s witnessed the introduction of a new type of experts employed in newly established agencies to bypass traditional bureaucracy and inform the policy process. A number of other regulations and reforms in the public sector were also introduced in the early 2000s as part of austerity measures imposed by donors and the European Union (EU) accession process, including strategic planning and regulatory impact assessments.

For some other commentators, a number of other factors also contributed to the rise of experts and expertise in the policy process in Turkey. For Keskin, a number of other factors such as the qualitative and quantitative changes in mass communications, the development of international cooperation and partnerships and the rise of new social movements generated a demand and contributed to a rise in the number of experts and use of expertise. Proliferation of media outlets contributed to the rise of a new breed of investigative journalism; independent research and consultancy firms increased their customer portfolios; and professional election campaigns also required a new type of experts and expertise. Furthermore, a number of players in the political arena started to look for expert knowledge in their respective domains. For instance, left and liberal political movements, their foundation and associations, civil society organisations (CSOs), professional chambers, trade unions, pressure groups, international/ transnational organisations and corporations and new social movements such as feminist and environmentalist movements have all sought and resorted to expert knowledge in their respective areas of activity (Keskin, 2002, pp 146-7, cited in Şahan, 2013, p 130, endnote 6).

Although there is an increasing appeal for experts, and a number of players from all levels of government resorted to experts, a limited appeal for the use of expert knowledge in the policy process has been well documented in a number of studies. A rare study on the relationship between scientific research and public policy was commissioned by the Turkish Academy of Sciences (TÜBA) in 2005. Findings of this study were published in a report titled *Scientific research and policy interface (Bilimsel araştırma ve politika ilişkisi)*. The report identified a number of obstacles that hinder the relationship between disseminating scientific research and making it available to policy-makers. Among others, insufficiency of funds and resources allocated to scientific research has been identified as a major problem. Yet again, the reluctance of academics in establishing cooperation with politicians and bureaucrats has also been underlined as a problem area, and it has been argued that political parties are not in the habit of using research when shaping policy, with politicians and bureaucrats rarely feeling the need to consult scientific studies and therefore, policies are not usually based on scientific research. Limited transparency on the part of public authorities and problems in the freedom of expression are also cited as a problem area (TÜBA, 2005).

The report offers some recommendations to overcome problems in disseminating scientific research and making it available to policy-makers. Consequently, the major conclusion from the report is that political parties and/or politicians should pay more heed to scientific research, while academics should stay closer to politics, and both should make further efforts to develop a mutual collaboration. The facilities provided to academics should also be improved, and academicians should be encouraged to do research and make efforts to ensure that it reaches policy-makers. The report also highlights the necessity for increasing the number of freelance researchers in Turkey and the need for more research focused on implementation and local problems, appointing qualified people in bureaucracy who attach importance to research and are able to utilise it. It recommends NGOs and the media fund policy-related research, publicise their research and put pressure on policy-makers and politicians to utilise research findings. It further recommends a social research centre, both as a depository for practical research undertaken in the country, and as a platform where politicians and researchers can meet (TÜBA, 2005).

The findings and recommendations from the report highlight a number of problems concerning the role of experts in the policy process. Yet again, this issue is an under-investigated area of inquiry. Although there is a rich literature on the impact and role of bureaucrats and technocrats in the Turkish state tradition throughout the 19th and 20th centuries, there are few studies on recent developments and trends concerning the changing role of experts and expertise in the policy process. Even in recent pieces on decision-making in Turkey, authors refer to already existing claims on the role of bureaucrats and technocrats. Conventional wisdom about the 'top-down state tradition in Turkey which refers to the autonomy of experts in defining what is good for the country and implementing those decisions in a straightforward and top-down manner' (Çevik, 2004, p 174) needs verification given the substantial changes that have taken place in the past two decades – there has been a massive overhaul of bureaucratic and political positions in the past 15 years, including expert positions.

Indeed, there is a complex process in the field, and we need a closer look at the relationship between experts and policy-makers. For instance, the role of policy advisers and their performance is also controversial in Turkey. As documented in a number of studies, policy advisers at various levels of Turkish public administration have not been very influential in shaping the policy process. As illustrated by Abakay, a journalist employed as an adviser to a number of state ministers for 11 years, a policy adviser informing the policy process with its intellectual traits has been a rare occurrence, the exception rather than the rule (Abakay, 2008), and resembling a personal secretary. In a similar vein, policy advisers at several levels of Turkish public administration do not have clear-cut job definitions and a well-defined status. Although they inform policy-makers to a certain extent, through providing alternatives about policy options, the final decision lies with their superiors. In the final analysis, already existing discourses of economic development, economic growth and modernisation prevail over other forms of rationalities.

In this context, the proliferation of think tanks in Turkey also deserves attention. They are increasingly visible in Turkey compared to the past, and have proliferated in numbers and in their areas of expertise (Yıldız et al, 2013). Yet again, their effectiveness in shaping policy outputs is an issue that needs attention. According to Bağcı and Aydın, there is not a well-developed think tank culture in Turkey for a number of reasons, including insufficiency of sustainable domestic funds, problems in human resources (qualified staff) and research quality and reluctance of public authorities to take advice from external sources (Bağcı and Aydın, 2009, p 123). Despite the problems they face in their operations, certain think tanks with close ties to governments enjoy a privileged position (Yıldız et al, 2013, pp 196-7; Gül and Yemen, 2016, p 679), and could be labelled as *partisan* think tanks.

More traditional ways of policy-making and implementation have also been bypassed on a number of occasions. The impact of the scientific community has not changed much in the past 10 years, and the trajectory of events following the publication of the TÜBA report has not deviated from the already existing path.

To cut a long story short, the link between experts and policy-makers has a rather unique character in the past 10 years. Although governments pay tribute to governance principles, policies devised for major reforms were made in small and closed groups of experts/bureaucrats attached directly to political authority without following the formal legislative processes involving participation, consultation, deliberation and transparency, not to mention reliable data. For instance, there is an illustrative legislative process, thoroughly analysed by Şahin on urban renewal in historical sites, where some mayors and their advisers had the upper hand in drafting legislation through bypassing experts from relevant professional organisations, such as the Chamber of Architects, and government agencies, such as the Ministries of Culture and Tourism and Public Works and Settlements. As a result, the municipalities' authority on declaring and implementing urban renewal in historical sites has been strengthened, mostly based on the lobbying efforts of these influential mayors throughout the legislative process (Şahin, no date).

A similar pattern was followed in education reforms, popularly named '4+4+4' reforms, in which the compulsory education system was radically reformed. Under normal conditions, the policy process is supposed to proceed through the involvement of experts representing a variety of stakeholders, from academia and unions through Education Council meetings. In reality, a highly top-down policy process was followed with the involvement of a rather small number of *embedded experts* representing political authority, without allowing a proper deliberation on the nature and future of education policy and proposed reforms. Ironically, even the Secretary of Education was not informed about the reform process initiated by the leadership of his own party.

Another vivid example of a top-down policy change and administrative reform was the legal changes concerning metropolitan municipalities. The new Law on Metropolitan Municipalities was prepared by a small group of *embedded experts* based in the Ministry of Interior without much consultation with the public and in a secretive manner, in parallel to the political rationale dictated by the government. Even though it has a very pretentious introduction detailing the benefits of a participatory, democratic and transparent administration, a form of local centralisation was established through shutting down smaller municipalities and village administrations by transferring authorities to metropolitan municipalities, even in the rural areas (Orhan, 2014, p 283).

Vested interests and other political priorities play a major role in this process, and sometimes ideological priorities and values, and the economic priorities of the accumulation regime determine policy discourses along the lines of dominant players surrounding the policy process. There is no straightforward link between data, which may not be available anyway, and policy change. This issue has been highlighted in a number of policy areas such as education and innovation (Şirin, 2016) and air pollution (Orhan, 2012). Şirin highlights a very important issue: 'other countries take decisions on the basis of data, meanwhile in Turkey priorities are determined on the basis of ideological concerns instead of data' (Şirin, 2016). Nowadays, the role of ideologies and values in determining public policies is underlined more often in Turkey. According to Belge (2016), 'there is a clash of values rather than a clash of policies.' Indeed, it is impossible to speak of a policy process independent of values and ideologies and, of course, there will be losers and winners in the policy process. Yet again, use of data in legitimising certain policy choices as well as sharing policy objectives and criteria is expected to be an indispensible part of the policy process. In this case, 'clash/disagreement is not only about policies themselves, but rather the values they represent' (Belge, 2016).

The recent trend in Turkish politics and policy concerning the role of experts represents both a continuity and departure from the first wave of science studies. Generally speaking, the modernisation tradition of the country, through economic development and prioritisation of economic development and growth concerns over others, has sustained itself in the past two decades. Meanwhile, instead of validating and defending policy positions on the basis of expert knowledge based on science and technology, values, ideologies and certain political preferences started to have the upper hand in justifying policy choices. Participation and all forms of access has been granted to licensed non-governmental organisations (NGOs), think tanks and *embedded experts* in the policy process, and other NGOs and critical professional organisations have been rather sidelined.

In the following section, the changing character of expertise is discussed with reference to environmental policy disputes in Turkey, because Turkey's new accumulation regime has intensified the assault on the environment and deepened the developmentalist attitude of previous governments. In this process, the status of experts and expertise has been sidelined and a new type of expertise has prevailed over other forms.

Experts and environmental policy disputes in Turkey

The development of environmental policy in Turkey has been rather late with a number of contradictions embedded in it. Although Turkey faces a number of environmental challenges and needs certain solutions, environmental policies are rather ad hoc, reactive and piecemeal, with a number of issues concerning implementation and monitoring. First of all, the existing development paradigm of an institutionalised tradition of state-led, positivistic economic development shapes the predominant discourse of policy. This idea of development is an important element of Turkey's Westernisation project, and is institutionalised in various ways. This paradigm poses considerable challenges to the implementation of environmental policies, and we could find traces of this behind problems faced during the institutionalisation of environmental policy in Turkey (Orhan, 2007, p 56).

In this context, we should remind ourselves of the original appeal of policy analysis – an interdisciplinary inquiry for the solution of public problems. The interdisciplinary character of policy analysis stems from the interrelatedness and complexity of contemporary societies' policy problems. Globalisation contributes to the repertoire of policy problems with the involvement of an ever-increasing number of players from all levels. At the end of the day, there is an increasing demand for policy coordination, participation and cooperation at all levels of analysis for a sound policy process, including environmental policies.

As suggested elsewhere, the centralised Turkish political and administrative system does not bring cooperation, coordination and integration in all circumstances due to the very fragmented nature of Turkish bureaucracy. There is a centralised but fragmented and disjointed bureaucracy, units of which act independent of each other, and cooperation depends on personal relations on an ad hoc basis. Among several problems concerning the implementation of existing environmental legislation, problems stemming from bureaucratic fragmentation stand out. Most key actors complain about the fragmentation and lack of cooperation in Turkish bureaucracy in general and environmental policy in particular. This means that problems with environmental policy integration are widespread, and despite several provisions concerning the integration of environmental concerns into other policy areas, policy integration has not been institutionalised and is yet to become part of standard operating procedures. In sum, Turkey fails to cooperate in environmental problem-solving and does not present a bright picture in terms of integration and coordination of policies. Other organisations are yet to integrate environmental concerns into their decision-making processes (Orhan, 2007, pp 56-7). In fact, it is quite the opposite – we can speak of a reverse (economic) policy integration, in which all other policy domains are subordinated to economic policy priorities and capital accumulation.

Although the increasing influence of environmentalist discourse and the environmentalist challenge have provided some prospects for opening up the environmental policy process, the predominant exclusionary style of politics is still dominant. There are few avenues for participation, and these were not effectively operationalised (Orhan, 2007, p 57). This issue of experts and publics has manifested itself in a number of other occasions in Turkey. It is especially the case where decisions are taken in a top-down manner without stakeholder involvement. Given the limited avenues for participation in Turkey, there are quite a few examples of confrontations on these matters, and in particular the environmental consequences of developmental projects, such as dams, energy installations, large-scale mining projects, the conversion of urban green spaces and new industrial zones have been major issues of contestation in Turkey. On these occasions regarding these contestations we cannot speak of a major role played by relevant experts and scientists in the planning stage. Rather, centrally planned developments were implemented in a top-down manner with political and economic concerns and authorities resorting to discourses on expertise, science, rationality and economic development and progress in legitimising their policy choices. Those groups that stood against governments' policies are easily labelled as 'irrational and emotional' if not 'traitor and agents of foreign powers' or 'ideological, short-sided and biased'. We cannot speak of a rational speech situation where parties take their turn in voicing their concerns over the issues under consideration (Orhan, 2015).

In such a centralised policy-making and implementation process, a genuine 'participation' of people and involvement of experts and scientists has the potential to make a serious contribution to the quality of policies. Even those so-called 'emotional and irrational' environmental movements resort to experts in bringing their case to the forefront of public discussions. On some other occasions, representatives of certain NGOs were invited for consultation, but yet again, they are handpicked from pro-government or pro-industry groups. Governments' failure on being transparent and consulting widely, as well as relying solely on organised industrial interests, results in scepticism towards certain experts and authorities. This attitude, in turn, negatively affects the role of experts in our societies (Orhan, 2015).

The Bergama Gold Mine dispute, concerning the use of a cyanide-leaching method in extraction, represents a major crack in the top-down, centrally planned developmentalist approach in Turkey. In this case, an environmental movement and the mining interests and governmental bodies have their own discourse concerning the risks involved. Competing discourse coalitions formed on this issue, and scientists were divided, and informed both coalitions in different ways with their own conception of risk. Experts supporting the mining coalition favoured the mine project and another group of experts supporting the environmentalist coalition, including professional organisations, stood against it. However, consecutive governments favoured the mining coalition despite warnings from experts from a variety of disciplines and court orders on the cessation of mining activity on the basis of risks involved and irregularities in the policy process. Although the environmental movement had defended its environmental rights through direct action and judicial mechanisms, a major struggle took place in the realm of discourse. The mining interests diverted attention from the existing risks to the exploitation and utilisation of natural resources for the economic development of the country, and even accused the environmental movement of being agents of foreign countries that aimed to block Turkey's economic development. The tradition of state-led economic development that shapes the predominant discourse of policy and is institutionalised in various ways in Turkey prevailed over the concerns of environmental and health risks, and the Turkish government's eagerness to attract foreign direct investment and its fear of international arbitration also contributed to overruling high court judgments on this gold mine in Bergama (Orhan, 2006).

On top of this, the use of new policy discourses derived from the governance paradigm such as policy integration, the participation of stakeholders, reorganisation and empowerment of environmental bureaucracy, introduction of independent regulatory boards and sometimes discourses on sustainability have been used as instruments to sideline environmental concerns in Turkey. There is a certain mismatch between the words and deeds of authorities in Turkey (Orhan, 2014, p 284). As Dryzek argued '... perhaps more often than simply resisting environmental values, recalcitrant actors will try to cloak themselves in the language of environmentalism ... and can sponsor other discourses of environmental concern more conducive to their own interests' (Dryzek, 1997, p 11). In Turkey there are a number of occasions in which authorities employed the language of environmentalism in a selective manner on the one hand, and the governance paradigm on the other, to further their agenda in a much more centralised and coordinated manner for economic expansion, with detrimental effects on environmental quality and sustainability. Here one can speak about the performative dimension of politics and policy-making. Indeed, Turkish authorities have crossed boundaries and employed their opponents' discourse in enhancing their own positions (Orhan, 2014, pp 284-5).

For instance, soon after environmentalists and local people started to criticise some water development projects, the then Prime Minister Erdoğan and the then Secretary of the Environment and Forestry, Eroğlu, challenged the environmentalist groups on the basis of their environmentalism. The Prime Minister even classified environmentalists as 'real' and 'fake (pseudo)' – those who don't object to projects with a potential to destroy the environment were seen as 'real' environmentalists. Prime Minister Erdoğan accused environmentalists of being 'spare time (pastime)' environmentalists, and criticised them for doing nothing. He claimed himself as the 'real environmentalist (environmentalist by heart)', and referred to the water development projects and forestation projects he completed when he was mayor of İstanbul Metropolitan municipality.[1] Secretary of the Environment and Forestry Eroğlu, addressing a ceremony in a hydro-power plant that is going to be constructed on the Sakarya River, also argued that: 'This hydro-power station will produce 49 to 50 million kilowatt hour energy every year. We are not environmentalists by words but by essence, this is our difference. When we say environmentalism now, we are the ones who know environmentalism.'[2]

While some features of developmentalism have been kept intact, a number of new environmental policy ideas were employed in defending their position. Environmental discourses employed for the legitimisation of development policies could easily be clustered under five categories: institutional restructuring for the sake of policy integration; utilisation of 'national' natural resources to eliminate Turkey's energy dependency; criticising "water flows, Turks just stare" mentality, implying the unused water flow is wasteful; promotion of renewable energy sources compared to finite resources; and the protection of biological diversity (Orhan, 2011, p 5).

Scientists also face a number of problems in conducting research and explaining their opinion on controversial issues. For instance, Professor Dr Onur Hamzaoğlu faced a number of charges for disseminating his research findings on industrial pollution and its detrimental health effects in Dilovası region. In parallel to these developments, governments and industrial interests took decisive steps in limiting the influence of environmental opposition: intimidation, threats and the stigmatisation of environmental movements; limiting the options of environmental movements through rising trial and expert fees; further centralisation of authorities; making alterations in the legal and institutional framework; use of emergency expropriation/confiscation to accelerate the investment process; and arbitrariness (Orhan, 2016).

Based on the detrimental effects on environmental quality and economic infeasibility, environmentalist groups and professional organisations have challenged a number of new developmental projects in the past few years, such as the third airport for İstanbul, the third bridge in Bosphorus, and a number of associated highway projects. Professional organisations have played a major role in the Bergama case and other areas of contestation through informing the public about the alternatives, risks involved in mega-projects and especially the environmental consequences of developmental projects. Professional organisations have also brought a number of contested issues to the courtroom. Although there exist some court decisions for a stay of execution, public authorities continued their business as usual, and some of those projects have even finished and are in service. This is about arbitrariness and the further centralisation of authority without paying attention to experts' opinions. Furthermore, there are efforts on the part of governments to limit the authority and functions of professional organisations.

At the time of writing this chapter, policy practice in Turkey faces a major problem, in addition to the problems created by the long political and bureaucratic traditions in the country. Turkish politics and policy-making is in complete turmoil, following the failed coup attempt in July 2016. The country is governed by statutory decrees in a top-down and reactive manner, with ad hoc solutions to existing problems. The Turkish Parliament adopted a new law on 20 August 2016, and the 80th article of the law bypasses several existing checks and balances in the administrative system, authorising the Cabinet to make investments and land-use decisions in the case of legal conflicts. These kinds of changes signify further centralisation. If this trend continues, the country will move further away from interdisciplinary, participatory/deliberative policy-making and implementation and policy integration. Despite calls for democratisation and decentralisation in the early 2000s, there is a re-centralisation concerning policy processes in general and environmental policy processes in particular.

Conclusion

Policy analysis is an interdisciplinary and knowledge-based process of inquiry in which experts and expertise occupy a central place. The role of experts, however, has passed through a number of phases, and at the moment it is much contested. The distinguished position of experts in the policy process faces a new challenge these days, and sometimes laypeople and sometimes a new breed of embedded experts take a number of policy positions, in favour of dominant interests and their policy choices. In post-truth situations, it is not expertise as such but the way one articulates its position that matters. The re-centralisation of policy processes and the predominance of certain economic interests in policy processes sidelines experts who are supposed to enlighten the process in the name of the common good.

What we have seen in the Turkish case is the continual sidelining of expert opinions, including that of professional chambers, and the predominance of developmentalist discourses in environmental policy processes. At the end of the day, experts from a variety of public authorities are bypassed to enable environmentally risky development projects, ranging from power plants to mining projects and major infrastructure projects such as bridges, airports and highways. These projects are undertaken without much deliberation, despite experts' opposition on the grounds of the environmental, ecological, economical and social infeasibility of the projects. Yet again, embedded experts have been available for most of the occasions, and the use of environmental discourses has been a common feature of the legitimisation process.

Notes
1. See www.hurriyet.com.tr/gundem/9728287.asp and www.haberler.com/erdogan-in-cevrecinin-daniskasiyim-dedigi-gun-haberi/
2. See http://uygarozesmi.blogspot.com/2011/01/struggles-to-stop-small-scale.html

References

Abakay, A. (2008) *Bakan danışmanının not defteri*, Ankara: İmge.

Bağcı, H. and Aydın, A. (2009) 'Dünyada ve Türkiye'de düşünce kuruluşu kültürü', in H. Kanbolat and H.A. Karasar (eds) *Türkiye'de stratejik düşünce kültürü ve stratejik Araştırma Merkezleri: Başlangıcından bugüne Türk düşünce kuruluşları*, Ankara: Nobel, pp 57-123.

Belge, M. (2016) 'Değerler dünyası', *T24* (http://t24.com.tr/yazarlar/murat-belge/degerler-dunyasi,15679).

Cabinet Office (1999) *Modernising government White Paper*, London: The Stationery Office (https://ntouk.files.wordpress.com/2015/06/modgov.pdf).

Collins, H.M. and Evans, R.J. (2002) 'The third wave of science studies: Studies of expertise and experience', *Social Studies of Science*, vol 32, no 2, pp 235-96.

Collins, H.M., Weinel, M. and Evans, R.J. (2010) 'The politics and policy of the third wave: New technologies and society', *Critical Policy Studies*, vol 4, no 2, pp 185-201.

Cook, J., Nuccitelli, D., Green, S.A., Richardson, M., Winkler, B., Painting, R., et al (2013) 'Quantifying the consensus on anthropogenic global warming in the scientific literature', *Environmental Research Letters*, vol 8, no 2 (http://iopscience.iop.org/1748-9326/8/2/024024/pdf/1748-9326_8_2_024024.pdf).

Dryzek, J.S. (1997) *The politics of the earth: Environmental discourses*, Oxford and New York: Oxford University Press.

Dunn, W.N. (2008) *Public policy analysis: An introduction* (4th edn), Englewood Cliffs, NJ: Prentice Hall.

Dye, T.R. (1992) *Understanding public policy* (7th edn), Englewood Cliffs, NJ: Prentice Hall.

Gül, H. and Yemen, A. (2016) 'Türkiye'de düşünce kuruluşlarının kamu politikası süreçlerindeki rolü ve etkisi', in M.A. Çukurçayır et al, *Kamu yönetiminde değişimin yönü ve etkileri (KAYFOR 13 Bildiriler Kitabı)*, Konya, pp 656-82.

Hajer, M. and Versteeg, W. (2005) 'A decade of discourse analysis of environmental politics: Achievements, challenges, perspectives', *Journal of Environmental Policy and Planning*, vol 7, no 3, pp 175-84.

Head, B. (2009) 'Evidence-based policy: principles and requirements', in 'Strengthening Evidence-based Policy in the Australian Federation: Roundtable Proceedings' (http://www.pc.gov.au/research/supporting/strengthening-evidence/03-chapter2.pdf).

Irwin, A. and Wynne, B. (eds) (1996) *Misunderstanding science? The public reconstruction of science and technology*, Cambridge: Cambridge University Press.

Jacques, P.J., Dunlap, R.E. and Freeman, M. (2008) 'The organisation of denial: Conservative think tanks and environmental scepticism', *Environmental Politics*, vol 17, no 3, pp 349-85.

Kaya, C. (2002) *Osmanlı Devleti hizmetinde üç yabancı danışman: Charles Ambraise, Bernard-Helmuth van Moltke, Guiseppe Donizetti*, Yayınlanmamış Yüksek Lisans Tezi, Anadolu Üniversitesi Sosyal Bilimler Enstitüsü, Eskişehir.

Keskin, F. (2002) *Demokratik toplumlarda yeni siyasal seçkinlerin konumu: 1980 sonrası Türkiye'de kamuoyu araştırmacıları ve siyasal danışmanlar*, Yayınlanmamış Doktora Tezi, Ankara Üniversitesi Sosyal Bilimler Enstitüsü, Ankara.

Lasswell, H.D. (1965) 'The policy orientation', in D. Lerner and H.D. Lasswell (eds) *The policy sciences*, Stanford, CA: Stanford University Press, pp 3-15.

Lomborg, B. (2007) 'Changing the climate debate', *Prospect Magazine*, 25 November (www.prospectmagazine.co.uk/magazine/changingtheclimatedebate/#.UcF3Mvl7JrU).

Miller, S. (2001) 'Public understanding of science at the crossroads', *Public Understanding of Science*, vol 10 no 1, pp 115–120.

Oreskes, N. and Conway, E.M. (2011) *Merchants of doubt: How a handful of scientists obscured the truth on issues from tobacco smoke to global warming*, New York: Bloomsbury Press.

Orhan, G. (2006) 'The politics of risk perception in Turkey: Discourse coalitions in the case of Bergama Gold Mine dispute', *Policy & Politics*, vol 34, no 4, pp 691-710.

Orhan, G. (2007) 'Institutions and Ideas in the Institutionalisation of Turkish Environmental Policy', *Critical Policy Analysis*, vol 1, no 1, pp 42-61.

Orhan, G. (2011) 'Institutions and ideas revisited: The role of new environmental policy ideas in de-institutionalisation of Turkish environmental policy', Paper presented at IPA-2011 6th International Conference in 'Interpretive Policy Analysis: Discursive Spaces. Politics, Practices and Power', 23-25 June, Cardiff University.

Orhan, G. (2012) 'Lack of evidence as evidence: The case of air pollution in Turkey', 2012 Berlin Conference 'Evidence for Sustainable Development', 5-6 October, Freie Universität Berlin, Germany.

Orhan, G. (2014) 'Public participation as a depoliticisation process: The case of environmental policy', in K. Göymen and O. Sazak (eds) *Centralisation decentralisation debate revisited*, Istanbul: Sabancı University IPC and Fredrich Neumann Stiftung, pp 262-91.

Orhan, G. (2015) 'Dilemmas of democratisation in the policy process: The role of experts and people revisited', in K. Göymen and R. Lewis (eds) *Public policymaking in a globalised world*, Istanbul: Sabancı University IPC and Fredrich Neumann Stiftung, pp 86-105.

Orhan, G. (2016) 'Barriers to environmental movements in Turkey: Strategies of investors and public authorities in bypassing environmental resistance in Turkey', International Conference on 'Political Ecology, Environmentalism and Greens in the Centre and East of Europe: Past, Present', Université libre de Bruxelles, 2-3 June, Brussels.

Oxford Dictionaries (2016) 'Word of the Year 2016 is….' (https://en.oxforddictionaries.com/word-of-the-year/word-of-the-year-2016).

Sabatier, P.A. (1999) 'The need for better theories', in P.A. Sabatier (ed) *Theories of the policy process*, Boulder, CO: Westview, pp 3-17.

Şahan, S. (2013) *Seçim kampanyalarında profesyonelleşme: Türkiye'de seçim kampanya uzmanları ve lider danışmanları*, Yayınlanmamış yüksek lisans tezi, Ankara Üniversitesi Sosyal Bilimler Enstitüsü Halkla İlişkiler ve Tanıtım Anabilim Dalı, Ankara.

Şahin, S.Z. (no date) 'The third face of local government reform from below: The case of urban renewal policy in Turkey', Unpublished manuscript.

Şirin, S. (2016) 'Dünya, verilerle karar veriyor, biz ideolojiyle', AJ Türk (http://aljazeera.com.tr/al-jazeera-ozel/dunya-verilerle-karar-veriyor-biz-ideolojiyle).

TÜBA (Türkiye Bilimler Akademisi) (2005) *Bilimsel araştırma ve politika ilişkisi* [*Scientific research and politics relations*], Ankara: TÜBA Yayınları.

Yanow, D. (2000) *Conducting interpretive policy analysis*, Thousand Oaks, CA: Sage.

Yıldız, M.,Çelik, D., Arslan, N., Çiftçi, L., Eldemir, S. and S. Sinangil (2013) 'Kamu politikalarında düşünce üretim kuruluşlarının rolü', in M. Yıldız and M.Z. Sobacı (eds) *Kamu politikası: Kuram ve uygulama*, Ankara: Adres, pp 188-208.

NINE

Europeanisation of policy-making in Turkey and its limits[1]

H. Tolga Bölükbaşı, Ebru Ertugal and Saime Özçürümez

Introduction

Domestic policy-making processes are exposed to external influences and/or pressures in a world of increasing globalisation. One extreme form of influence and/or pressure stems from Turkey's process of accession to the European Union (EU). As the long(est) standing candidate for EU accession for more than half a century, Turkey was declared a formal candidate for accession with the Helsinki European Council of 1999. While the impact of the EU has been a continuous feature of domestic policy-making, the EU's influence peaked especially in the early 2000s. As this collective volume shows, given the legacy of the 'heavy' state tradition characterising Southern Europe, including Turkey (Diamondourous et al, 2006, p 5), the development of systematic evidence-based policy analysis and evaluation in policy-making remains at an early stage.

In the absence of feedback mechanisms as such, policy cycles have been typically deprived of systematic policy learning, understood as 'updating beliefs about key components of policy' (Radaelli, 2009, pp 1146-7). Moreover, due, in part, to these institutional features, public policy-making has not fostered home-grown policy ideas. A characteristic of developing countries, this feature of the policy process has exposed Turkey to international influences and pressures stemming from international actors. Although it is difficult to empirically disentangle the relative roles of international organisations and the EU, this chapter aims to show the variegated role of the EU in changing Turkey's domestic policy-making and governance. While it is difficult to dissect the policy process into policy-making (constituted of processes of agenda-setting, policy formulation and decision-making) and implementation, we aim to focus on the former, delimiting our study to analysing changes in policy outputs. Since our aim is not to study implementation processes, changes in policy outcomes reflected in behavioural changes (and their impact) remain largely outside the remit of this chapter.

As widely argued in the public policy literature, policy change should be measured on the basis of policy outputs rather than policy outcomes (Bauer and Knill, 2014, p 32). This is because policy outcomes are affected by a number of intervening and extraneous factors and are, at best, only indirectly related to the causal influence of the EU. This chapter draws on empirical evidence on policy-making processes and policy outputs in three key policy areas: macroeconomic policies, regional development policies and immigration and asylum policies.

The chapter addresses two research questions: How much change has there been in the macroeconomic, regional development and immigration policies and governance in Turkey during the 2000s? And to what extent do these changes represent instances of Europeanisation, whereby the EU constitutes the 'prime focus of change' (Featherstone and Kazamias, 2000, p 3) in interaction with, or as opposed to, other key international actors? In addressing the first question, this chapter traces significant changes in the principles, objectives, procedures and instruments of these key policy sectors following the 'policy structure approach'.[2] It also shows that these changes resulted in stronger government policy commitment in these sectors measured through increased 'policy intensity' and 'policy density'.[3] All of these changes led to an ever-larger 'policy capacity' in the Turkish state.[4] In addressing the second question, the chapter concludes that while it is difficult to disentangle the exclusive, net causal impact of the EU on domestic policies, the 'transformative power' of the EU in shaping policy structures, expanding both the density and intensity of these policies and enhancing the policy capacity, is overwhelmingly large in Turkey.[5]

Empirical evidence in each policy sector is collected through comparative historical case study methods that involve a review of programming and legislative documents, and semi-structured qualitative interviews as well as a survey of print media. The interviews, which were conducted between 2009 and 2013, included key policy-makers in the Central Bank of the Republic of Turkey (CBRT), Undersecretariat of Treasury, Ministry of Development (formerly, the State Planning Organization, SPO), Ministry for EU Affairs, State Ministry for Economic Affairs, Ministry of Interior, Development Agencies in different regions, representatives of big business (TUSIAD), and officials from the EU Delegation to Turkey, Organisation for Economic Co-operation and Development (OECD), International Monetary Fund (IMF), The World Bank, United Nations Refugee Agency (UNHCR) and International Organization for Migration (IOM).

The chapter is structured as follows. We first unpack the changes in the policy structure in macroeconomic, regional development and immigration policies by analytically dissecting the sector in terms of the dominant principles, objectives, procedures and instruments. Second, we explore the extent to which these changes can be attributed to the transformative power of the EU in each policy sector. The chapter concludes with a discussion of the main findings in all three policy sectors.

Unpacking changes in macroeconomic policies and governance

Changing macroeconomic regime from the 1990s to the 2000s

Macroeconomic policy-making and governance had already gone through changes starting with a new economic programme introduced in 1980 after the economic crises of the late 1970s. The new regime aimed at building an outward-oriented economy based on free market principles. While single-party governments implemented tighter macroeconomic policies during the 1980s, the 1990s saw populist cycles of easy macroeconomic policies with the return of coalition governments. The policy regime was still characterised by fiscal dominance. Under the Treasury's dominance, the CBRT was largely accommodating successive governments' expansionary fiscal policies (Bakır, 2007, p 26). The economic crisis hitting in 1994 led to an amendment in the CBRT's law, bringing upper limits on advances to the Treasury. The restructured Treasury emerged as the main centralised executive arm of the government, and the 1990s saw initiatives towards securing fiscal consolidation through World Bank projects. Excessive borrowing, however, continued, and by the end of the 1990s, even analysing, let alone controlling, public finances became virtually impossible. It was in this context that technocratic preparations had already started through World Bank projects. A Special Expert Commission was convened to draw up a background report as part of preparations for the 8th Development Plan. Although the Commission had completed its roadmap for overhauling fiscal institutions in 2000 before the crisis hit, no legislative reform had been passed. It was the economic crisis in 2001 that proved, in the words of key policy-makers, an 'inflection point', leading to a 'new policy regime', 'a cultural change' or 'a revolution' in macroeconomic policy and governance. The government immediately enlisted the help of Dr Kemal Dervis, then Vice President of The World Bank. Dr Dervis designed the 'Strengthening the Turkish Economy' Programme (STEP), a comprehensive package foreseeing the legal and institutional reorganisation of macroeconomic as well as microeconomic policies and governance. Items in the package were urgently passed by Parliament.

As part of STEP, in monetary policy, the CBRT became politically independent (Law no 4651 on the Central Bank of the Republic of Turkey, 2001). The new law redefined CBRT's primary objective as price stability, and prohibited the Bank from granting advances and extending credits to the Treasury. In order to bring down chronic inflation, the Bank pursued an implicit inflation-targeting strategy that was then followed by an explicit inflation-targeting regime. In fiscal policy, STEP aimed at achieving fiscal consolidation through hefty primary surpluses. It introduced radical institutional changes aimed at reorganising debt management and rationalising public expenditure (Law no 4749 on Regulating Public Finance and Debt Management, LRPFDM, 2002 and Public Financial Management and Control Law, PFMCL, no 5018, 2003).

Changes in the structure of macroeconomic policies

Changing principles: 'stability culture'

Interviews and documents reviewed show that a broad consensus emerged around the main principles of mainstream approaches to macroeconomic theory (new classical macroeconomics and new Keynesianism): (1) a resolute commitment to price stability as the principal objective of macroeconomic policy through an entirely de-politicised (*read*, independent) central bank; (2) installation of monetary dominance by bringing an end to fiscal dominance; and (3) stable finances allowing the CBRT to pursue its primary objective of price stability (Arestis, 2009). In the new fiscal regime, for example, the ubiquity of the concepts of 'fiscal discipline', 'fiscal control' and 'fiscal stability' in the letter of new legislations reveals their spirit. Interviews with high-ranking bureaucrats corroborate the observation that the fundamental principle guiding these reforms was 'stable public finances'. The institutionalisation of the principle of 'stability culture' and its attendant norm of 'sound money' also characterised the monetary policy regime. A review of the legislative process shows that this principle was virtually written into law in Parliament without much debate. Interviews with high-ranking bureaucrats, regular reports of the CBRT and speeches by CBRT governors repeatedly feature 'credibility of policies' and 'reputation of the monetary authority' – all of which are the hallmarks of a previously alien, newly imported 'stability culture'.

Changing objectives: 'balanced budgets' and 'price stability'

In fiscal policy, STEP aims to 'strengthen the balance of public finances in a way that will prevent deterioration in the future', (Treasury, 2001, pp 14, 30) and declares that 'discipline will be applied to public expenditures to achieve maximum savings.' In line with the new objectives as announced by STEP, the LRPFDM aims to maintain the 'confidence and stability of markets and macroeconomic balances' (Article 1). With a view to 'maintaining fiscal discipline', the PFMCL declares that fiscal policies should aim at securing 'macroeconomic stability' (Article 13a). It also states that 'it is essential to ensure revenue and expenditure balance in budgets' (Article 13h). Policy-makers interviewed unanimously expressed that the primary objective of budgetary policies should be 'balanced budgets'. The emphasis on 'balancing the budget' was also very clear in the budget speeches of the Ministers of Finance all throughout the 2000s. In fact, post-crisis governments went even further than maintaining a balance; they aimed to secure sizable primary surpluses. In monetary policy, the new CBRT law re-defined its objective as '[t]he primary objective of the Bank shall be to achieve and maintain price stability.' Minister Dervis declared time and again that with the new law, the Bank would 'pursue price stability without allowing inflation'. As interviews show, all actors 'knew' that the exclusive objective of monetary policy had now become price stability.

Changing procedures: independent Central Bank and the 'Super Ministry'

In terms of procedures, the monetary policy regime experienced a complete reversal during the early 2000s. With the CBRT gaining independence, the institutional arrangements allowing for fiscal dominance were dismantled. There was a clear change in the fundamental powers of the CBRT: '[t]he Bank shall be the ultimate body authorized and responsible to implement the monetary policy' (Article 4(b)). Additionally, in parallel to European countries where national treasuries were institutionally strengthened in the run-up to Economic and Monetary Union in the 1990s, the Turkish Treasury increasingly gained control in determining the conduct of fiscal policies. This was the case especially after the 2000-01 crises, when Minister Dervis became responsible for the Treasury. Due, in part, to Dr Dervis' technocratic credentials and his supra-political identity (Bakır, 2009), the Treasury turned into a 'Super Ministry', assuming the coordination role of STEP through his 'institutional entrepreneurship'.[6] Crowding out the SPO and Ministry of Finance, the Treasury emerged as the centre of gravity. Such reorganisation in policy-making processes, in the words of IMF officials of the time, enhanced the reputation of institutions and the credibility of policies. STEP led to a different mode of coordination between the Treasury and the CBRT. The institutional prerogatives of fiscal dominance had been terminated, and there emerged a need for establishing the transparency and credibility of the institutions vis-à-vis each other. The CBRT's Law emphasised the centrality of the Bank's communication policy and envisaged a transparent monetary policy. The institutional arrangements ensuring fiscal transparency were to be put into place for the CBRT to carry out its duties for ensuring price stability. STEP had foreseen that a new public borrowing law be passed by Parliament aiming 'to bring transparency and accountability to the state', defining borrowing 'limits with clarity and transparency' (Treasury, 2001, p 21). The texts of the LRPFDM and PFMCL ubiquitously reflect the centrality of transparency in the implementation of fiscal policies.

Changing strategic instruments: fiscal rules, multi-annual programming, inflation targeting and the Monetary Policy Committee

Efforts at adopting a rule-based macroeconomic policy regime during the 1990s proved unsuccessful due to wavering political commitment. It was only with the introduction of fiscal rules as strategic instruments implemented under STEP that runaway spending was controlled. The government followed a fiscal rule regime, the 'backbone' of which was the IMF-imposed deficit rule alongside expenditure, revenue, debt and borrowing rules (Kaya and Yilar, 2011, p 66). These IMF conditions served as 'de facto fiscal rules' (Kraan et al, 2007, p 20). After a decade under IMF programming, however, the government decided not to continue with another IMF programme in 2008. There was an initiative to introduce a law on fiscal rules in 2010, but it was quickly shelved. The government introduced multi-annual programming instruments with the implementation of the PFMCL in 2006. The Medium-Term Fiscal Plan, drawn in accordance with the Medium-Term Programme, were, thus, new strategic instruments. In the area of monetary policy, the CBRT switched to a new strategic instrument of inflation targeting in 2002 after decades of nominal targeting of monetary aggregates and the exchange rate. In the meantime, the new law had instituted the highly technical core policy-making instrument, the Monetary Policy Committee (MPC), taking the Bank's key monetary policy decisions. With the introduction of the formal inflation-targeting regime, the MPC became the key decision-maker in determining interest rates and identifying (jointly with the government) and announcing the inflation target. All of these instruments helped ensure the implementation of macroeconomic policies in line with the overarching principle of stability culture and the objectives of balanced budgets and price stability.

Transformative role of the EU

The early 2000s saw significant changes in all dimensions of the structure of macroeconomic policies. The extent of change during this period had been extensive – all policy objectives, principles, procedures and instruments saw a series of transformations. These dimensions reflect those in the EU's models, frameworks, structures, policies and instruments. However, it was primarily as a result of IMF officials working in close cooperation with qualified technocrats in the Turkish bureaucracy that these changes were engineered. In this transformation process, Turkey was 'under the double "vincoli esterni" (external constraints) of the IMF and the EU' (Bolukbasi, 2012, p 348), with both actors pointing to the identical direction and content of policy change. As the EU-anchored political reform, it delegated its supervisory role to the IMF. The role of the EU was, in this respect, more indirect. International financial markets began rewarding the government's reform efforts toward EU accession, which resulted in the lowering of borrowing costs and the extension of loan terms. Existing research also shows that rising levels of capital inflows, which were instrumental in ensuing growth in the 2000s, were also made possible by Turkey's accession prospects (Bolukbasi, 2012, p 348). While the declared principles and objectives remained largely intact, the period towards the end of the 2000s had seen some loosening up in the operation of procedures, such as the waning of the CBRT's de facto independence (Gürkaynak et al, 2015), and the shelving of the bill on fiscal rule. The timing of the changes in the policy structure correspond to an increasingly adverse international macroeconomic context and waning of the credibility of the EU anchor itself, due in large part to rising anti-Turkish accession rhetoric in leading member states (Bolukbasi and Ozcurumez, 2011).

Unpacking changes in regional development policies and governance

Regional development policy in flux: from the 1990s to the 2000s

The process that started with the official declaration of Turkey's EU candidacy in 1999 marked a turning point in Turkey's regional development policy. Previously characterised by continuity, Turkey's regional policy started to undergo noticeable changes throughout the 2000s as a response to the accession partnerships and progress reports of the EU, and especially the requirements of the EU's pre-accession financial assistance. EU conditionality and pre-accession financial assistance programmes promoted the removal of the '*exclusive* right' of the central state to define the means and goals of regional development, not through formal constitutional changes, but through 'the setting of the rules and principles of the disbursement' of the pre-accession funds (Bruszt, 2008, p 614). Just how much Turkey's regional policy has changed is a matter of debate. However, analysis of change through the policy structure approach can yield fruitful insights. It could be argued that whereas regional policy existed all but in name in the pre-2000 period, it acquired a fully-fledged policy structure in the 2000s.

Changes in the structure of regional development policies

Changing objectives: regional convergence versus regional competitiveness

The officially defined aim of regional policy in Turkey, as in five-year national development plans, until the 2000s was the balancing of interregional differences or reducing regional disparities. In practice, however, this objective always remained secondary to the primary aim of national development. In the 2000s the regional economic competitiveness of every region was added as an objective and even superseded the older one in practice, according to interviews. This shift came first with the Preliminary National Development Plan (PNDP) (SPO, 2003), formulated at the instigation of the EU, which contained both objectives. Later, the 9th and 10th Development Plans (SPO, 2006; MoD, 2013), as well as the National Strategy of Regional Development (NSRD) (MoD, 2014), emphasised regional competitiveness as the policy objective. The difference between the old and new objectives is that instead of reducing regional disparities through re-distribution by a central authority, the new objective forces regions to self-rely on endogenous potentials, and to exploit the possibilities that are perceived to exist for innovation and flexible specialisation in order to increase regional competitiveness. This reflects the EU's approach, whereby 'competitiveness' gained 'ascendancy over solidarity or equity considerations' (Begg, 2010, p 80), as evidenced in the Lisbonisation of the EU's regional policy.

Changing principles: strategic planning, programming, partnership

Even though regional policy and planning were the responsibility of the then State Planning Organization (SPO, re-named the Ministry of Development [MoD] in 2011) since 1960, neither the principles of regional planning nor the concept of 'region' were defined in the pre-2000 period. Instead, sectoral planning dominated the distribution of public investments in national planning, whereby spatial considerations were ignored. The national planning approach advocated that first, national economic growth should be achieved based on efficiency and only after that should resources be allocated for regional development (Tekeli, 2008, pp 267-72). Only a few regional plans were formulated in this period in a piecemeal and ad hoc fashion.

In the 2000s several principles were introduced as a result of EU conditionality and the implementation of financial assistance. One was the shift from sectoral to strategic planning including the principle of programming. This involves a focus on basic aims and objectives and prioritisation of issues as well as an holistic approach to development that builds horizontal links between policies, as illustrated by the PNDP, the 9th and 10th Development Plans and the NSRD. Programming in regional planning has led to a shift from individual project support to programme financing, with plans covering multi-annual periods. According to the interviews, programming fulfilled a void in policy formulation by facilitating the link between plans and budgetary allocations.

Another principle introduced into regional policy-making is partnership, which follows the EU's practice of 'close consultations between the Commission, the Member State concerned and the competent authorities designated by the latter at national, regional or local level' (CEC, 1988, article 4), as well as economic and social partners. Turkish law establishing regional Development Agencies (DAs) stipulates that regional plans should be prepared in accordance with the principle of partnership, and requires that local stakeholders participate in the formulation of strategic regional plans (OJ, 2006). Moreover, the 9th and 10th National Plans as well as NSRD officially declare that 'subsidiarity' (MoD, 2013, p 135; 2014, p 2; SPO, 2006, p 91), 'partnership' and 'multi-level governance' (MoD, 2014, p 2) form the core principles of development policy. The principle of regionalisation has also been introduced with the decision of the Council of Ministers in 2002 to form 26 statistical planning regions in Turkey in accordance with the EU's Nomenclature of Territorial Units for Statistics classification.

Changing procedures

Two important procedural features characterised regional policy in the pre-2000 period. First, decision-making was excessively centralised so that regional policy and plans were devoid of sub-national institutional structures for implementation. Second, lack of horizontal coordination mechanisms among central institutions was endemic. In the 2000s, two key developments sought to change the procedural features of regional policy. First is the law establishing regional DAs in 2006 (OJ, 2006) as requested by the EU in its successive progress reports in the early 2000s. Accordingly, regional plans would be formulated by DAs at regional level through participatory processes rather than the old method of deciding them at the centre. Second, a Regional Development High Board composed of ministers (such as for industry, technology, labour and social security, agriculture, transport, tourism, environment and urbanisation, and forestry) and a Regional Development Committee composed of undersecretaries was formed to coordinate sectoral policies for the purpose of regional development.

These procedural changes aim to reproduce the EU's multi-level governance in the Turkish context, and hence envisage shared decision-making, cooperation and negotiation, rather than hierarchy, across territorial levels (Marks et al, 1996; Hooghe and Marks, 2001). The interviews indicate, however, that in practice, the procedural changes are far from encouraging a bottom-up approach to regional policy design and implementation, noting, in particular, the requirement for regional plans to be approved by the Regional Development High Board as well as the continuing excessive interventions of the Ministry of Development in the work of the DAs. Hence, as confirmed by the burgeoning literature on the functioning of DAs in Turkey (Ertugal, 2017), the principles of subsidiarity, partnership and multi-level governance introduced in official national programming documents, as noted above, are not being implemented in practice.

Changing instruments

In the pre-2000 period, regional policy instruments were ambiguous, ranging from Priority Development Areas (KÖYs) to ad hoc regional projects. Even though the large-scale Southeast Anatolia Project started in 1988, this was essentially a public works project devised for the special circumstances of this region (Tekeli, 2008). In the 2000s, with the establishment of DAs in 26 NUTS II regions and their associated budgets, regional policy acquired its own permanent institutional and financial (although meagre) instruments for the first time. The grant schemes that the DAs are operating for distributing financial resources, involving calls for project proposals, have largely been copied from the practices of the EU's disbursement of financial assistance. Interviews indicate that in practice the new institutional and financial instruments have not produced their intended effect. The grant schemes have largely failed to mobilise regional partnerships among the public, private and civil society actors, while the amount of financial resources distributed are completely inadequate to address development needs.

The transformative role of the EU

EU conditionality has played two important roles in the policy-making process of regional development policy. First, the EU unleashed a process of change across all components of the policy structure throughout the 2000s. The extent of change has been higher with respect to policy objectives and principles, which are a function of formal and legal changes through policy and programming documents and a new law. These components of change are also the ones that bureaucrats have internalised most, according to the interviews. Due to an implementation deficit, the extent of change with respect to policy procedures and instruments has been less, tempered with vested interests (of politicians and local elites) in implementation, according to the interviews.

Second, EU conditionality has left in its aftermath a place for other international organisations, in particular the OECD, to influence domestic policy. Even though accession negotiations on Chapter 22 of the Acquis on regional policy and structural instruments started in 2013, the gradual waning of EU credibility, both in general and specifically in this policy field (see Ertugal, 2011), has left room for other international actors to exert influence. Given the high degree of overlap between the EU's regional policy approach and the regional development policy framework promoted by the OECD, the changes in the 2000s converged the mind-sets of Turkish bureaucrats to that of their counterparts in the OECD, where Turkey is a full member and where technical knowledge and sheer data play more important roles than the highly politicised EU process. The domestic influence of the OECD, in contrast, is much more diffuse, less intense and less dense than EU conditionality. The OECD's influence on domestic regional development policy is readily apparent in the NSRD (2014) and in the interview responses.

Unpacking changes in immigration policies and governance

Immigration policy in flux: from the 1990s to the 2000s

Set against a background of the post-Cold War period, when Turkey's experience was diversifying from one of a country of emigration to a country of destination (including circular and temporary) and transit for a variety of source countries from Newly Independent States (NIS), Moldova, Sub-Saharan Africa, Afghanistan, Iran and Iraq, there was substantial need for a change in Turkey's immigration policy. Law no 6458 on Foreigners and International Protection (LFIP) in Turkey was approved in April 2013. With the promulgation of this law, Turkey has a centralised piece of legislation governing the area, with the General Directorate on Immigration and Asylum under the Ministry of Interior overseeing the whole policy area. Before this law, the policy field was governed by dispersed agencies and legislation. Passport Law no 5682 and Law no 5683 on Residence and Travel of Foreigners in Turkey, which are important in terms of immigration policy, can be traced back to the 1950s. In the post-1990 period, when Turkey experienced the Iraq crisis with mass movements and also increasing arrivals of people from the post-Soviet Republics (circular, temporary and permanent), the principle of control of these movements still dominated the legal texts and policy-maker claims. Until the 2000s, with Law no 4817 on Work Permits for Foreigners, there was no major change on legislation on foreigners. The post-2011 mass influx of Syrians has challenged the system in different ways to introduce governance structures for international protection in the face of forced migration as a consequence of the humanitarian crisis.

Changes in the structure of immigration policies

Changing principles: control of movement, public security and human rights

Review of the policy-making process, initiatives by various ministries, EU progress reports for Turkey (with a focus on Chapter 24) and agencies as well as the legal framework itself reveals that competition among the paradigms of public safety and security vis-à-vis control is a consistent and multi-faceted one in Turkish immigration policy. Moreover, Turkey proceeded with the signing of the readmission agreement in 2013 while linking it more to the debate on visa liberalisation for Turkish citizens travelling to the EU rather than a detailed debate on the costs of a readmission agreement for Turkey. Additionally, in response to the 2011 Syrian crisis, Turkey aimed to advocate an open border policy presenting Syrian refugees as 'guests' (and therefore to be treated not as threats to public safety and security but to be welcomed along the lines of Turkey's commitment to the international human rights regime, principles of no return and temporary protection), only to end up since late 2013 with a debate on whether some of these individuals are engaging in the conflict in Syria, committing petty crime in urban centres in Turkey or upsetting public order and safety as illegal urban immigrants.

Changing objectives: needs-based governance to legal framework and institutions

The laws governing the status of foreigners in Turkey had been separated into three sub-categories prior to the introduction of the new law in 2013. These categories for rules governing foreigners were 'public law on foreigners, private law on foreigners and laws on foreigners with special status'. These included the European Convention on Human Rights, the Turkish Constitution, Passport Law no 5682, Law no 5683 on Residence and Travel of Foreigners, and Law no 4817 on Work Permits for Foreigners (added in 2003). While the law on Work Permits centralised the work permit procedure in the Ministry of Labour and Social Security, there has, as yet, been no single institution that would implement the laws on foreigners. The LFIP introduced the Directorate General for Migration Management (DGMM) to centralise procedures for foreigners. This institution is expected to coordinate all the other institutions that act as part of the governance of immigration and asylum, and to act as an 'expert institution' for these policy fields. It is expected to support efforts for establishing the necessary institutional and administrative infrastructure for governing migration, to coordinate efforts to harmonise Turkey's legislation with that of the EU in the fields of immigration and asylum by comparing existing legislation with that of the EU in accordance with the needs of both, and to follow the projects funded by the EU in the field of immigration and asylum, and inform the Ministry of Interior of efforts made.

The National Programme of 2003 includes an Action Plan for Asylum and Immigration, which envisions a common effort to harmonise Turkey's immigration and asylum legislation, infrastructure, legal and administrative capacity with that of the EU, and to implement projects to this end. The LFIP has transformed the institutional structure for governing immigration policy in Turkey toward a civilian administrative body. In the post-2003 period, various regulations, directives and laws have been introduced to combat irregular migration and the unregistered employment of foreigners. For example, Turkish Citizenship Law no 403 also aimed at preventing fake marriages by regulating citizenship acquisition by allowing foreigners to be eligible to apply for Turkish citizenship three years after the registration of the marriage. At the same time, the LFIP upholds public safety and security while combating irregular migration and organised crime, promoting the co-existence of foreigners and natives in harmony towards social cohesion. Domestic policy makers introduced changes to these laws in the context of the EU accession process in accordance with their own policy preferences.

Changing procedures in immigration and asylum policy

The most significant change in terms of the governance of migration and asylum concerns the procedures in the policy process in drafting and implementing the LFIP, which became inclusive and transparent, and this experience was unmatched and unprecedented, according to some scholars, for this particular policy field. Such a process has been characterised by some scholars as the formation of an 'epistemic community' around the immigration and asylum policy process (Ozcurumez and Turkay, 2011). There have been a series of workshops, meetings and seminars to exchange ideas and provide opportunities for communicating and input into the process, and the drafting of legislation. In all of these meetings, academics, civil society organisations (CSOs) and international organisations have discussed the shortcomings of existing practices, international and EU legislation, best practices around the world and the roles different stakeholders would aim to see themselves play once the legislation is adapted. The participants contributed to discussions on how principles of security, sovereignty and international human rights norms would be part of the new legislation. With the mass influx of Syrians, the introduction of a Temporary Protection Directive for Syrians also revised the kinds of services that would be provided to Syrians in contrast to people of other nationalities seeking international protection in Turkey. While the UNHCR and IOM played major roles in the governing of international protection and irregular migration, the Directorate General for Disaster Management and NGOs also became active in the governance of international protection and immigration, along with other line ministries.

Changing instruments

One major challenge in the introduction of new administrative structures has been the requirement to remove the gendarmerie and police forces from the borders, replacing them with civilian officers. This has been repeated since 2001 when the National Programme had been prepared, and re-examined in 2003 and 2008. In order to meet the requirements for a civilian authority, a Border Management Bureau was established in 2008, and a draft law on the Organisation and Duties of the Border Security Directorate General has been prepared, which would govern all control on land and sea borders, to ensure public order at the border gates, and to control passengers' entry and exit. There have been various projects to improve the legal, administrative and technical capacity of Turkey, and to harmonise its legislation with that of the EU on migration and asylum. Among these projects are the TR02-JH-03 Asylum-Migration Twinning Project as part of the 2002 EU Financial Cooperation, which has resulted in proposals leading to the introduction of the Task Force on Migration and Asylum Action Plan, which began its work in November and December 2004. Since the summer of 2015, the EU–Turkey Deal has placed the debates on the role of the EU in the governance of international protection in Turkey.

The transformative role of the EU

In 1999, a major shift occurred with Turkey's candidacy status being confirmed and the start of accession negotiations. Chapter 24 of the accession negotiations began with a full screening of the immigration policy process. Interview data suggests that the very first project to change immigration policy had begun with a project *fiche* from 2002 originating from the Secretariat General for EU Affairs at the time. The domestic policy change does not necessarily 'mimic' the EU template as a whole, but points to 'cognitive transformation', as noted by an interviewee, and a change in 'perceptions' among the policy-makers concerning immigration policy. This 'cognitive transformation' is identified as a shift from the exclusively security-concerned paradigm to multiple ways and means through which to address the migration policy, including the human rights perspective, and through international collaboration. The objectives of the policy have shifted toward harmonisation with the EU Acquis (transition to civilian border management, readmission agreements and combating irregular migration, and a single law that governs migration policy). The procedures have also shifted toward the establishment of a new administrative structure and an inclusive policy process. The tools to be used for this purpose have also been identified as further collaboration with the EU through projects, information and expertise exchange.

Comparative conclusions

In addressing our first research question of how much change there has been in the macroeconomic, regional development and immigration policies and governance in Turkey during the 2000s, this chapter shows that there have been significant changes in the policy structures of these policies. These changes were more pronounced in the principles, objectives and instruments than in the procedures. The reason for this is that whereas the former (principles, objectives and instruments) mainly relate to the policy-making stage involving the more straightforward transposition of legislative and organisational changes, the latter (procedures) mainly relate to the implementation stage, which is partly a function of political-level capacities (see below). Implementation challenges, the exploration of which is beyond the scope of this chapter, in turn, tend to undermine the institutionalisation of changes in policy-making. Notwithstanding, the changes registered in the policy structures of the three policy areas under investigation reflect increases in the government's commitment in these policy structures measured in their policy density and intensity (Bauer and Knill, 2014).

In terms of policy density, the narratives above show that the breadth and differentiation of legislative and administrative intervention by the government had increased. Accordingly, the number of policies (that is, policy item density) has increased in all policy sectors. For example, macroeconomic policies during the 2000s aimed at sustaining price stability and balanced budgets, the regional development policy aimed to tackle both regional disparities and regional competitiveness, and the immigration policy to control cross-border movement and balance public security with human rights. At the same time, instrument density has also increased in all three policy sectors with more instruments in each policy sector: fiscal rules, multi-annual programming, inflation targeting and the MPC in macroeconomic policies; multi-annual programming, regional DAs, the grant scheme, and institutions for coordination such as the Regional Development High Board in regional development policy, and the instruction of a new administrative structure, the DGMM, with its local representatives, its own policy coordination strategies with NGOs, international organisations and line ministries working in immigration policy.

In parallel, the policy intensity of these interventions has increased. This period saw increasing numbers and degrees of changes in instrument settings (that is, substantive intensity), resulting in an expanded scope of the government's intervention. For example, targeting inflation directly (rather than following intermediate targets of monetary aggregates) and setting hard fiscal rules such as sizable primary balances are among the examples of increased intensity in macroeconomic policies. In regional development policy, examples include the distribution of financial resources through the grant scheme at regional level and the widening of the policy scope to include every region (not only underdeveloped regions). In immigration policy, many new projects on training and knowledge transfer plans for comparative development of immigration and asylum governance, widening the recruitment of new central and local personnel for specialised governing of immigration and asylum, are examples of increased substantive intensity. The period also saw, although to a lesser extent than other dimensions of policy change, expansions in the administrative and procedural changes (that is, formal intensity) that affect the probability of implementation. In macroeconomic policies, the politically independent CBRT, with a powerful MPC and the Super Ministry under Dr Dervis, were among significant sources of formal intensity. In regional development policy, participatory processes in the formulation of regional plans were introduced in the institutional design of DAs coupled with the recruitment of new, highly-qualified personnel in the regions, and these increased the probability of the implementation of new policies. In immigration policy, again, participatory processes of policy-making and implementation constitute examples of increasing formal intensity in this sector.

All of these changes in the policy structures as well as policy outputs, as the above narratives show, point to the increased 'policy capacities' of the Turkish government as conceptualised by Wu, Ramesh and Howlett (2015, pp 167-8) and Howlett and Ramesh (2015, p 303). We should note that policy output dimensions (policy density and intensity) and dimensions of policy capacity are not necessarily mutually exclusive categories. First, the bureaucracy's *analytical-level capacities*, which ensure that policy actions are 'technically sound' and contribute to the 'attainment of policy goals' after having investigated policy alternatives, increased during the early 2000s, and have remained at a relatively higher level in comparison to the 2000s thereafter. In all three policy sectors under study, the increasing ability to determine the strategic components of interventions in policy programming is a good example of increasing analytical-level capacity in the 2000s.

Second, *operational-level capacities*, which foster the 'alignment of resources with policy actions so that they can be implemented in practice', have also increased during the 2000s. Linking budgetary allocations to strategic priorities in the financial components of policy programming is an example of increasing operational-level capacity.

Finally, *political-level capacities* affording 'policy-makers and managers the room to manoeuvre and the support required to develop and implement their ideas, programmes, and plans', increased during the early 2000s. The sheer ability to introduce unwelcome innovations such as rendering the CBRT politically independent against the will of politicians, pushing through severe austerity measures targeting a hefty primary balance under crisis conditions, establishing regional DAs in a highly centralised unitary state, a completely new structure of governing migration and asylum all attest to the high political-level capacities in the 2000s. With the exception of immigration policies, whose issue salience increased with the Syrian conflict, political-level capacities in macroeconomic and regional development policies have been declining since the late 2000s. In macroeconomic policies, loosening of post-2001 crisis constraints and exiting from IMF programming in 2008, which exposed the bureaucracy to political pressure, have led to the weakening of political-level capacities in the late 2000s. In regional development policies, the relative decrease in domestic issue salience, when it became clear that the new regional DAs would not act as managing authorities for EU funds as originally hoped by politicians and bureaucrats alike, has led to a decrease in political-level capacities in the late 2000s. The overall pattern of increase in policy capacities in the 2000s and relative stability since then is at odds with the declining prospects of Turkey's EU accession. In fact, an excessive focus on EU–Turkey diplomatic relations conceals under-the-radar, ongoing intensification and densification of public policies in Turkey in the pre-accession process.

The answer to our second research question, to what extent these changes represent instances of Europeanisation whereby the EU constitutes the 'prime focus of change', is more mixed. The narratives on the three policy areas attest to the overwhelming cumulative transformative effect of the EU and other international actors. The earlier stages of the policy cycle, starting with the agenda-setting stage and continuing with the policy formulation and policy adoption stages, all bear the imprint of the EU. The transformative impact of the EU in informing the different dimensions of the policy structures leading to increases in both the density and intensity of these policies is tremendous. Regardless of whether international actors serve as triggers or anchors, the episodes of transformation we have focused on show that the direction of domestic change remains the same. In almost all of these episodes of change, international actors categorically reinforced the EU's instruments and mechanisms of transformative impact. It is, therefore, empirically difficult to isolate the independent, exclusive, causal links by revealing the mechanisms of domestic policy change as a result of the EU. Nonetheless, just like in the Southern European countries starting with the 1980s and countries in Central and Eastern Europe and Western Balkans starting with the 1990s, the EU has indeed been the 'prime focus of change'. This is not surprising given the density and intensity embedded in the EU's models, frameworks, principles, objectives, procedures, instruments, agendas, rules and policies aiming at wholesale transformation, which we now call 'Europeanisation'.

In studying changes in policy-making in Turkey we focused on the EU's impact on policy outputs. To do so, we analysed the agenda-setting, policy formulation and decision-making stages of policy processes in three policy sectors. We thus excluded the implementation stage of policy processes from our analysis. We observe that when it comes to understanding the EU's impact in implementation and hence, outcomes, the overwhelming transformative impact fades. Existing research on other policy areas in Turkey provides limited clues as to how domestic interests shape the direction, content and magnitude of the EU's impact on policy outcomes. This research shows that domestic institutions, too, filter these effects, producing unintended outcomes (Bolukbasi and Ertugal, 2013). We therefore need further empirical research focusing on the implementation stages of policy processes in all policy sectors – only then, we believe, can we have a complete picture of the EU's impact on policy outcomes.

Notes

1. This chapter presents the findings of a multi-annual collaborative research project funded by TUBITAK (Project No 109K443) on 'Transformations in Policy and Governance in Turkey: The Case of Three Policy Areas'. We would like to thank Caner Bakır and an anonymous reviewer for their incisive comments and insightful suggestions.
2. The 'policy structure approach' aims to unpack the key features of a given policy by focusing on *principles* governing the policy, policy *objectives*, *procedures* in policy-making and governance, and *instruments* at the disposal of the policy (Bolukbasi and Ertugal, 2013 based on Hall, 1993 and Graziano, 2011).
3. In the public policy literature, 'policy intensity' refers to the intensity of intervention in a given policy area measured in 'the level and scope of governmental intervention' ('substantive intensity') and 'administrative capacities' (including 'financial, personnel and organisational resources') and 'administrative procedures' ('formal intensity'). 'Policy density' refers to the 'extent to which a certain policy area is addressed by 'governmental activities' measured in 'the number of policies' ('policy density') and 'the number of policy instruments' that are used ('instrument density') (Bauer and Knill, 2014, pp 33-4).
4. The public policy literature differentiates between three levels in conceptualising 'policy capacity': (1) 'analytical-level capacities' (the extent to which policy actions are 'technically sound' and the degree to which they contribute to the 'attainment of policy goals' after having investigated policy alternatives); (2) 'operational-level capacities' (whether the administration fosters the 'alignment of resources with policy actions so that they can be implemented in practice'); and (3) 'political-level capacities' (which afford 'policymakers and managers the room to manoeuvre and the support required to develop and implement their [autonomous] ideas, programs, and plans') (Howlett and Ramesh, 2015, p 303; Wu et al, 2015, pp 167-8).
5. The EU's 'transformative power' is generally conceptualised as 'successful, top-down Europeanization of member states and attempts at external governance transfer toward third countries' impacting domestic change in policy-making, governance and policies themselves (van Huellen and Boerzel, 2013, p 5).
6. 'Institutional entrepreneurs', as conceptualised in the public policy literature, refers to an 'individual who mobilizes ideas, resolves conflicts, and steers their implementation for … institutional changes' (Bakır, 2009, p 272). Dr Dervis emerged as an institutional entrepreneur as he has led a series of institutional changes in macroeconomic policies and governance. These changes have gone beyond changes in policy outputs (through administrative, legal and organisational change), giving way to behavioural changes of key actors. These were reflected in changes in policy outcomes with the implementation of the new policy regime.

References

Arestis, P. (2009) *New consensus macroeconomics: A critical approach*, Working Paper, no 564, The Levy Economic Institute of Bard College (www.levyinstitute.org/pubs/wp_564.pdf).

Bakır, C. (2007) *Merkezdeki Banka*, Istanbul: İstanbul Bilgi Üniversitesi Yayınları.

Bakır, C. (2009) 'Policy entrepreneurship and institutional change: Multi-level governance of central banking reform', *Governance*, vol 22, no 4, pp 571-98.

Bauer, M. W. and Knill, C. (2014) 'A conceptual framework for the comparative analysis of policy change: Measurement, explanation and strategies of policy dismantling', *Journal of Comparative Policy Analysis: Research and Practice*, vol 16, no 1, pp 28-44.

Begg I. (2010) 'Cohesion or confusion: a policy searching for objectives', *Journal of European Integration*, vol 32, no 1, pp 77-96.

Bolukbasi, H.T. (2012) 'Political economy', in M. Heper and S. Sayari (eds) *Routledge handbook of modern Turkey*, London: Routledge, pp 341-52.

Bolukbasi, H.T. and Ertugal, E. (2013) 'Europeanisation of employment policy in Turkey: Tracing domestic change through institutions, ideas and interests', *South European Society and Politics*, vol 18, no 2, pp 237-57.

Bolukbasi, H.T. and Ozcurumez, S. (2011) 'Of context, interaction and temporality: Historical institutionalism and Turkey's approach to the ENP and the UfM', *Comparative European Politics*, vol 9, no 4-5, pp 543-61.

Bruszt, L. (2008) 'Multi-level governance – the eastern versions: Emerging patterns of regional developmental governance in the new member states', *Regional & Federal Studies*, vol 18, no 5, pp 607-27.

CEC (Commission of the European Communities) (1988) Council Regulation EEC No 2052/88 of 24.03.88, in *Official Journal of the European Communities*, No L 185; 15.07.88, Brussels: CEC.

Diamondourous, P.N., Gunther, R., Sotiropoulos, D. and Malefakis, E. (2006) 'Introduction: Democracy and the state in the new Southern Europe', in F. Gunther, P. Nikiforos and D.A. Sotiropoulos (eds) *Democracy and the state in the new Southern Europe*, Oxford: Oxford University Press, pp 1-41.

Ertugal, E. (2011) 'Europeanization and institutional change: Explaining regional policy reforms in Turkey', *Policy & Politics*, vol 39, no 2, pp 257-73.

Ertugal, E. (2017) 'Challenges for regional governance in Turkey: The role of development agencies', *METU Journal of Architecture*, vol 32, no 2, pp 203–24.

Featherstone, K. and Kazamias, G. (2000) 'Introduction: Southern Europe and the process of "Europeanisation"', *South European Society and Politics*, vol 5, no 2, pp 1-24.

Graziano, P. (2011) 'Europeanization and domestic employment policy change: Conceptual and methodological background', *Governance*, vol 24, no 3, pp 583-605.

Gürkaynak, R., Kantur, Z., Tas, M. and Yildirim, S. (2015) *Monetary policy in Turkey after Central Bank independence*, London: Centre for Economic Policy Research (www.cepr.org/active/publications/discussion_papers/dp.php?dpno=10904).

Hall, P.A. (1993) 'Policy paradigms, social learning, and the state: The case of economic policymaking in Britain', *Comparative Politics*, vol 25, no 3, pp 275-96.

Hooghe, L. and Marks, G. (2001) *Multi-level governance and European integration*, New York and London: Rowman & Littlefield.

Howlett, M. and Ramesh, M. (2015) 'Achilles heel of governance: Critical capacity deficits and their role in governance failures', *Regulation and Governance*, vol 10, pp 301-13.

Kaya, F. and Yilar, S. (2011) 'Fiscal transformation in Turkey over the last two decades', *OECD Journal of Budgeting*, no 1, pp 59-74.

Kraan, D.J., Bergvall, D. and Hawkesworth, I. (2007) 'Budgeting in Turkey', *OECD Journal on Budgeting*, vol 7, no 2, pp 7-58.

Marks, G., Hooghe, L. and Blank, K. (1996) 'European integration from the 1980s: State-centric v multi-level governance', *Journal of Common Market Studies*, vol 34, no 3, pp 341-78.

MoD (Ministry of Development) (2013) *Onuncu kalkınma planı 2014-2018* [*Tenth development plan 2014-2018*], Ankara: Kalkınma Bakanlığı (www.kalkinma.gov.tr/Lists/Kalknma%20Planlar/Attachments/12/Onuncu%20Kalkınma%20Planı.pdf).

MoD (2014) *Bölgesel gelişme ulusal stratejisi 2014-2023* [*National strategy for regional development 2014-2023*], Ankara: Kalkınma Bakanlığı (www.bgus.gov.tr/dokuman/BolgeselGelismeUlusalStratejisi(2014-2023).pdf).

OJ (Official Journal) (2006) 'Kalkınma ajanslarının kuruluşu, koordinasyonu ve görevleri hakkında kanun' ['Law on the establishment, coordination and tasks of development agencies'], *Official Journal*, 08/02/2006, no 26074.

Ozcurumez, S. and Turkay, S. (2011) 'Bir epistemik topluluk oluşurken: Türkiye'de iltica çalışmaları, politikası ve aktörleri' ['An epistemic community in the making: Asylum studies, policy and actors in Turkey], in Ö. Çelebi, S. Özçürümez and Ş. Türkay (eds) *İltica uluslararası göç ve vatansızlık: Kuram, kavram ve politika*, Ankara Office: UNHCR Publications, pp 28-48.

Radaelli, C.M. (2009) 'Measuring policy learning: Regulatory impact assessment in Europe', *Journal of European Public Policy*, vol 16, pp 1145-64.

SPO (State Planning Organization) (2003) *Preliminary national development plan 2004-2006*, Ankara: Republic of Turkey (www.mod.gov.tr/Lists/OtherPublications/Attachments/8/Preliminary%20National%20Development%20Plan%20(2004-2006).pdf).

SPO (2006) *Dokuzuncu kalkınma planı 2007-2013* [*Ninth development plan 2007-2013*], Ankara: Devlet Planlama Teşkilatı (www.metu.edu.tr/system/files/kalkinma.pdf).

Tekeli, İ. (2008) *Türkiye'de bölgesel eşitsizlik ve bölge planlama yazıları* [*Essays on regional inequality and regional planning in Turkey*], Istanbul: Tarih Vakfı Yurt Yayınları.

Treasury (2001) *Strengthening the Turkish economy: Turkey's transition program*, Ankara: Republic of Turkey Undersecretariat of Treasury (www.tcmb.gov.tr/wps/wcm/connect/9d473f48-f02c-4631-94e7-ee64593f250d/strengteningecon.pdf?MOD=AJPERES&CACHEID=9d473f48-f02c-4631-94e7-ee64593f250d).

van Huellen, V. and Boerzel, T.A. (2013) *The EU's governance transfer: From external promotion to internal protection?*, SFB-Governance Working Paper Series, no 56, Berlin: Collaborative Research Center (SFB) 700, June.

Wu, X., Ramesh, M. and Howlett, M. (2015) 'Policy capacity: A conceptual framework for understanding policy competences and capabilities', *Policy and Society*, vol 34, pp 165-71.

TEN

Public opinion and public policy in Turkey

Sedef Turper

Introduction

The link between public opinion and public policy has been fundamental for the study of public policy analysis, as the policy preferences of the electorate are considered central in policy-making in representative democracies (Powell, 2000). In such democracies, politicians are expected to be responsive toward citizens' wishes and demands, and to follow public preferences as they change (Wlezien and Soroka, 2009). Previous research exploring the relationship between public opinion and public policy has documented well that policy-makers are attentive to public opinion and respond to changes in public policy preferences. A vast amount of earlier research has illustrated that the voting behaviour of members of the Congress in the US is guided in part by the policy preferences of their constituency (Miller and Stokes, 1963; Kuklinski, 1977; Mayhew, 2004), the majority of policies introduced in representative democracies are congruent with the aggregate policy preferences of citizens (Monroe, 1979, 1998), and changes in public opinion are important drivers of policy change (Page and Shapiro, 1983). While these earlier studies established the link between public opinion and policy-making in representative democracies, they further focused on the circumstances under which public preferences play a larger role in shaping public policies.

A substantial body of previous research has highlighted the centrality of the issue of saliency in explaining the relationship between public policy preferences and policy responsiveness. Briefly defined as the importance that citizens attach to an issue, issue saliency is found to be mediating the opinion–policy link. Previous studies have demonstrated that citizens are more likely to pay attention to the political discussions and behaviours of politicians on those issues that they find important (Edwards et al, 1995; Lindaman and Haider-Markel, 2002), and politicians are more likely to be responsive towards citizens' demands when the issues at hand are salient to the public (Monroe, 1998; Hill and Hurley, 1999; Burnstein, 2003). Therefore, the public opinion and policy link is expected to be stronger for those salient issue domains when compared with issues that are not salient to the public.

This chapter focuses on the political attitudes and policy preferences of Turkish citizens in various salient policy domains. To this end, we make use of several public opinion surveys conducted in Turkey during the period between 1990 and 2015, and organise our findings in to two main sections. In the first section we introduce general attitudes towards politics in Turkey. We start our discussion with an overview of the level of political interest in Turkey, and explore how this varies across different sub-populations. Following a brief discussion on internal efficacy among the Turkish public, we conclude the first section with a survey of policy issues considered to be important by Turkish citizens over the last 10 years. In the second part we focus on Turkish public policy preferences in those salient policy domains, and present the public policy preferences of Turkish citizens in the fields of the economy, healthcare and education. The chapter concludes with a brief discussion on the link between public opinion and policy-making in the Turkish political context.

Overview of general attitudes towards politics in Turkey

The extent to which the general public is interested in politics is crucial for disentangling the relationship between public opinion and public policy, as political interest is found to be highly correlated with political engagement (Norris et al, 2004). To investigate the extent to which the Turkish public is interested in politics, we utilise data from five consecutive rounds of the World Values Survey (WVS) conducted between 1990 and 2011 (WVS, 2015). Table 10.1 presents the mean levels of political interest in Turkey on a scale ranging from 0 to 1, where higher values indicate higher levels of interest in politics.[1] As Table 10.1 illustrates, the level of political interest in Turkey varies considerably over time. While the overall level of political interest in Turkey ranged between 0.38 and 0.50 during the period between 1990 and 2011, the percentage of those respondents expressing no interest in politics at all is recorded as 29, 23, 34, 33 and 18 per cent in 1990, 1996, 2001, 2007 and 2011, respectively.

Further inspection of Table 10.1 reveals that men are significantly more interested in politics when compared to their female counterparts in Turkey. In line with the findings of previous research documenting gender differences in the levels of general interest in politics (Campbell and Winters, 2008; Coffé, 2013), male respondents are found to be approximately 0.12 points more interested on a 1-point political interest scale when compared to females. Further analysis of the data illustrates that those respondents who expressed being 'very' interested or 'somewhat' interested in politics on average constituted 56 per cent of the male population as opposed to only 39 per cent of the female population. In a similar vein, on average, 34 per cent of the female respondents indicated that they are not interested in politics at all as opposed to 21 per cent of the male respondents.

Inspection of Table 10.1 demonstrates that the level of political interest in Turkey also varies across educational groups, and the level of political interest increases as we move from low educational group to medium and high educational groups in all waves of the survey. To be more specific, those respondents who do not hold a secondary school diploma in the low educational group are found to be on average 0.09 points less interested in politics on a 1-point political interest scale when compared to their counterparts with a secondary school diploma in the medium educational group. Similarly, when compared to their highly educated counterparts with at least some university education, those respondents in the medium educational group are observed to be considerably less interested in politics. The differences in the mean levels of political interest between the low and high educational groups ranged between 0.10 and 0.28 points over the years, with a mean of 0.18 points. The difference between age groups in terms of their levels of interest in politics, however, is found not to be displaying a clear pattern.

Table 10.1: Political interest over time by gender, education and age (mean, SD)

	1990	1996	2001	2007	2011
Overall	0.429 (0.333)	0.500 (0.328)	0.382 (0.329)	0.379 (0.326)	0.476 (0.327)
Gender					
Male	0.490 (0.322)	0.552 (0.323)	0.450 (0.327)	0.444 (0.335)	0.533 (0.278)
Female	0.363 (0.318)	0.446 (0.325)	0.313 (0.329)	0.313 (0.302)	0.417 (0.297)
Education					
Low	0.411 (0.323)	0.460 (0.331)	0.342 (0.318)	0.350 (0.316)	0.451 (0.288)
Medium	0.511 (0.300)	0.591 (0.294)	0.439 (0.315)	0.409 (0.326)	0.510 (0.284)
High	0.643 (0.306)	0.660 (0.281)	0.621 (0.288)	0.460 (0.315)	0.551 (0.276)
Age					
15-29	0.435 (0.318)	0.468 (0.322)	0.388 (0.322)	0.359 (0.315)	0.493 (0.281)
30-49	0.441 (0.338)	0.515 (0.327)	0.384 (0.327)	0.390 (0.327)	0.485 (0.292)
50+	0.394 (0.346)	0.524 (0.342)	0.367 (0.347)	0.395 (0.326)	0.442 (0.306)

Data source: WVS (1990-2011)

As far as the feelings of internal efficacy among Turkish citizens are concerned, survey studies reveal that a considerable share of the Turkish population believes that politics is too complicated to understand, and often finds it difficult to articulate their policy preferences. According to European Social Survey (ESS) data from 2004 and 2008, those who regularly or frequently find politics too complicated to understand constituted approximately 45 per cent of the Turkish population.[2] Similarly, when asked to evaluate how easy they find it to make their mind up about political issues, those respondents stating that they find it either 'very difficult' or 'difficult' constituted 54.4 and 60.8 per cent of the Turkish population in 2004 and 2008, respectively.[3]

In order to better understand which policy preferences of Turkish citizens are likely to influence policy-making processes in Turkey, we further explore the issue of saliency in Turkey over the last 10 years by utilising data from the Eurobarometer Survey conducted in Turkey (2014-15). Table 10.2 presents the issues that are identified as one of the two most important problems that Turkey had been facing during the period between 2004 and 2015.[4] Inspection of Table 10.2 reveals that economic problems constituted the most salient issue in Turkey in all the years that the survey was conducted. While the majority of the Turkish population has identified economy-related problems as one of the foremost important problems that Turkey had been facing during the period between 2004 and 2013, the proportion of those Turkish citizens who mentioned economic problems as one of the two most important problems in Turkey decreased from 53.3 per cent in 2013 to approximately 44 per cent in 2014 and 2015.

As illustrated in Table 10.3, unemployment, economic crises, inflation and taxation are cited as the most important economic problems in Turkey. Unemployment has been singled out as the most important economic problem over the last 10 years. Approximately two out of every three Turkish citizens referred to unemployment as being one of the most important problems in Turkey in the 2000s. However, public concerns over unemployment have gradually decreased from 2010 onwards. While economic crises was the second most cited economic problem in Turkey during the period between 2004 and 2015, concerns over rising prices and inflation have significantly increased over the last few years. Furthermore, taxation in Turkey has been regularly identified as one of the most important economic problems that Turkey has been facing over the last 10 years.

Further inspection of Table 10.2 suggests that issues of terrorism, crime, quality of the educational system and healthcare services have also been identified as salient political issues in Turkey over the last 10 years, next to economic issues. While terrorism was identified as the second most salient issue for the Turkish public and had become highly salient from 2006 onwards, concerns over crime had been the third most referred problem that Turkey had been facing over the last 10 years. When compared to these policy domains, concerns over the quality of educational and healthcare services have been less frequently identified as one of the two most important problems in Turkey. However, a cautionary note needs to be introduced at this point. The survey questions utilised for analysing the issue salience in the current study require respondents to identify the most important problems that the country faces, and hence, necessitate a simultaneous evaluation of two different characteristics of issue salience; namely, the importance of the issue and the degree to which the issue is a problem (Wlezien, 2005). Therefore, our findings should be interpreted carefully. On the basis of our findings, it should not be concluded that educational and healthcare policy issues have not been important to the Turkish public over the last 10 years. Our analysis rather demonstrates that problems related to these issue domains have less frequently been considered as one of the two foremost pressing problems in Turkey when compared to problems related to the economy, crime and terrorism.

Table 10.2: Most important problems in Turkey (%)

	2004	2005	2006	2007	2008	2009	2010	2011	2012	2013	2014	2015	Average
Economic issues	70.4	59.3	57.6	53.4	55.0	59.8	59.7	54.1	50.4	53.3	44.4	44.2	55.1
Terrorism	9.3	17.2	26.0	24.9	27.5	21.5	25.0	28.9	32.9	21.9	16.1	18.3	22.5
Crime	3.3	6.7	5.7	9.9	3.8	4.0	3.9	3.1	3.6	8.1	4.2	6.1	5.2
Education	5.7	5.5	3.5	3.3	3.1	2.3	2.3	2.4	2.9	4.8	5.0	5.4	3.8
Healthcare and social security	4.7	3.3	2.6	2.8	2.1	1.8	1.6	1.3	1.3	2.1	1.4	2.2	2.3

Data source: Eurobarometer Survey (2004–15)

Table 10.3: Most important economic problems in Turkey (%)

	2004	2005	2006	2007	2008	2009	2010	2011	2012	2013	2014	2015
Unemployment	36.8	34.8	32.0	30.8	26.6	32.2	32.5	27.8	23.9	21.8	20.5	13.8
Economic crisis	23.4	16.8	17.1	14.0	17.1	18.3	16.4	13.2	12.9	15.2	7.0	11.8
Rising prices/inflation	7.3	4.8	5.7	4.5	7.8	5.8	6.6	7.9	7.7	6.6	8.9	11.6
Income inequality	2.3	1.8	1.5	1.4	0.8	1.6	2.4	2.3	2.6	5.2	2.0	2.5

Data source: Eurobarometer Survey (2004–15)

Policy preferences of the Turkish public

In this section we explore the Turkish public's policy preferences on three salient issue domains in Turkey, namely, economic, healthcare and educational policies. Although the issues of terrorism and crime were also identified as salient issues among the Turkish public, in the absence of adequate survey data, our analysis focuses solely on the previously mentioned three issue domains.

As discussed in the previous section, the economy has been one of the most salient political issues in Turkey over the last 10 years. A recent cross-sectional time series study conducted by the Centre for Turkish Studies at Kadir Has University demonstrates that approximately one-third of the Turkish population considers the government's recent economic policies to be successful (Kadir Has Üniversitesi Türkiye Çalışmaları Merkezi, 2015). According to the findings of this study, those Turkish citizens evaluating the economic policies carried out by the government as being successful constituted 34.5, 31.5, 33.5 and 34.8 per cent of the Turkish population in 2011, 2012, 2013 and 2014, respectively. However, a larger proportion of the Turkish population has been critical of the economic policies carried out by the government between 2011 and 2014. Those who assessed the economic policies of the government as being unsuccessful constituted 40.7 per cent of the Turkish population in 2011, and the proportion of those Turkish citizens who were critical of the government's economic policies are recorded as high as 42.0, 48.1 and 43.7 per cent in 2012, 2013 and 2014, respectively.

While only a small proportion of respondents mentioned income inequality when prompted by an open-ended question inquiring about their opinions on the most pressing economic problems that Turkey faces, when asked directly, a large majority of the respondents agreed to the statement that income inequality is a prominent problem in Turkey. A detailed survey of Turkish public perceptions regarding the economic problems in Turkey reveals that income inequality is considered to be a severe problem, and it is expected to be addressed by the economic policies implemented by the government. The analysis of data from the International Social Survey Programme (ISSP) conducted in Turkey in 2009 illustrates that a sizable majority of the Turkish population is concerned that income differences in Turkey are considerably large.[5] As illustrated in Table 10.4, those who agreed with the statement asserting that income differences between people with a high and low income in Turkey are too large constituted 94.7 per cent of the Turkish population. Furthermore, the differences between gender, age, education and income groups in evaluating income inequality in Turkey have also been found to be minor, pointing at the existence of an overarching consensus over the extent that income differences prevail in Turkey. An overriding majority of Turkish citizens further expressed a preference for affirmative action to be taken by the government to reduce income inequality in Turkey. While 92.3 per cent of the Turkish population agreed with the statement suggesting that it is the government's responsibility to reduce income differences between those with a high and low income, those who disagreed with the statement constituted only 2.1 per cent of the population.[6]

Table 10.4: Public evaluation of income inequality in Turkey (raw numbers, %)

	Strongly agree/ agree		Neither agree nor disagree		Strongly disagree/ disagree	
Income differences in Turkey are too large	1,444	(94.7)	59	(3.9)	22	(1.4)
It is the government's responsibility to reduce differences in income	1,409	(92.3)	86	(5.6)	32	(2.1)

Data source: ISSP (2009)

The tax regime in Turkey has been criticised for aggravating the income inequality problem in Turkey as it largely relies on indirect taxes (Tekin, 2010). Therefore, the need to introduce a tax reform that would remedy the income inequality problem in Turkey has long been a dominant theme in public discussions of the economic policies to be implemented in Turkey. With regards to the tax regime preferences of the Turkish public, survey studies demonstrate that a substantial majority of Turkish citizens support a progressive tax regime in which people with a higher income would contribute a larger share of their income as tax money. In

2009, 76.5 per cent of the Turkish population suggested that people with a higher income should pay a larger or much larger share of their income as tax when compared to people with lower levels of income (ISSP, 2009). Those Turkish citizens supporting a proportional tax regime in which people with a high and low income pay the same share of their income as tax constituted 17.1 per cent of the Turkish population, whereas those Turkish citizens expressing a preference for lower tax rates to be in place for people with a high income made up only 6.4 per cent of the population.[7] The comparison of the tax policy preferences of the 10 per cent of the Turkish population with the highest and lowest income further reveals that large majorities of the highest and lowest income groups alike support a progressive tax regime. With regards to existing tax policies for people with a high income that were in place in 2009, approximately a quarter of the Turkish population suggested that the tax rates are about right, whereas 57.5 per cent asserted that the tax rates for people with a high income are lower than what they would ideally like those tax rates to be. Those respondents who evaluated the tax rates for people with a high income as higher than what they ideally should be, however, constituted approximately 16 per cent of the Turkish population.[8]

Table 10.5: Public evaluation of tax policies in Turkey (raw numbers, %)

	Total population		Lowest income decile		Highest income decile	
People with a high income should pay ... of their income as tax						
a much larger/larger share	1,053	(76.5)	95	(78.5)	93	(73.2)
same share	236	(17.1)	17	(14.0)	29	(22.8)
a much smaller/smaller share	88	(6.4)	9	(7.4)	5	(3.9)
Taxes in Turkey today for those with a high income are ...						
much too low/too low	739	(57.5)	60	(56.6)	70	(56.9)
about right	342	(26.6)	25	(23.6)	35	(28.5)
much too high/too high	204	(15.9)	21	(19.8)	18	(14.6)

Data source: ISSP (2009)

Privatisation of state-owned businesses and industry had been another economic policy issue that marked public discussions in Turkey from the 1980s onwards, and a major privatisation programme has been carried out in Turkey in the aftermath of the 2001 economic crisis (Öniş, 2011). Survey studies demonstrate that public support for privatisation policies had gradually increased during the period between 1990 and 2001, and provided a solid public support base for the privatisation programme that was introduced by the Justice and Development Party (Adalet ve Kalkınma Partisi, AKP) government. As illustrated in Table 10.6, those Turkish citizens expressing that the private ownership of business and industry should be increased constituted 52.2 per cent of the Turkish population in 1990, rising to 55 per cent in 1996 and to 62 per cent in 2001. However, by 2007, public support for policies aiming at increasing the share of private ownership of businesses in the Turkish economy has significantly decreased. As Table 10.6 demonstrates, a majority of the Turkish public expressed a preference for an increase in the shares of state-owned businesses and industry in 2007 and in 2011. Further inspection of public preferences on government and private ownership of businesses and industry in 2011 reveals that women, people with at least some university education and people over 50 years of age are slightly more in favour of an increase in the private ownership of businesses and industry when compared to their male, less educated and younger counterparts, respectively.

Table 10.6: Public preferences for business ownership (raw numbers, %)

	1990		1996		2001		2007		2011	
Private ownership	516	(52.2)	1,027	(55.0)	2,092	(62.1)	557	(44.2)	709	(46.2)
State ownership	473	(47.8)	839	(45.0)	1276	(37.9)	704	(55.8)	825	(53.8)

Data source: WVS (1990-2011)

All in all, our findings from the analysis of Turkish public preferences for economic policies reveal that a large majority of the Turkish population considers income inequality as a crucial problem that needs to be addressed by government policies. The survey of public assessments of the existing tax regime in Turkey and public preferences for tax policies suggests that there exists a considerable level of potential support for a tax policy reform. Our findings hint that a substantial proportion of the Turkish population would support a tax reform aimed at reducing income differences between those with a higher and lower income by introducing higher tax rates for those with a higher income. With regards to debates over private and state ownership of business and industry, however, we observe no such overarching consensus over one of the alternative economic policies.

With regards to healthcare policies, it is important to note that the share of health expenditure in the state budget recently increased from 2.6 per cent in 2002 to 5.8 per cent in 2011, and the government's policies have led to a perceptible improvement in healthcare services provided in Turkey over the last 15 years (Başlevent and Kirmanoğlu, 2016). Survey studies illustrate that the increase in healthcare expenditure and the recently implemented healthcare policies have also led to an increase in levels of satisfaction with healthcare services among the Turkish population. Table 10.7 presents the overall satisfaction rates on a 1-point scale where lower values indicate lower levels of satisfaction whereas higher values represent greater satisfaction.[9] As Table 10.7 demonstrates, overall satisfaction with healthcare services in Turkey has significantly improved during the seven-year period between 2004 and 2011. Our findings demonstrate that the mean level of satisfaction with healthcare services increased from 0.563 in

2004 to 0.646 in 2011, and the mean level of satisfaction has improved across all gender, education and age groups.

Further inspection of Table 10.7 reveals that differences in the mean levels of satisfaction with healthcare services across educational and age groups have been reduced over the seven-year period. However, our findings demonstrate that there are still significant differences across educational and age groups in terms of their levels of satisfaction with healthcare services by 2011. We find that the level of satisfaction decreases as we move from the low education group to the medium and high education groups. More specifically, highly educated Turkish citizens with at least some university education are found to be 0.21 points less satisfied with healthcare services on a 1-point scale when compared to their less educated counterparts who do not hold a secondary school diploma in 2004. The differences in the mean levels of satisfaction between highly and less educated citizens are, however, found to decrease during the period between 2004 and 2011, recorded as 0.08 points in 2011. In a similar vein, Turkish citizens over 50 years of age are found to be significantly more satisfied with healthcare services compared to their younger counterparts. The differences in the mean levels of satisfaction with healthcare services between the lowest and highest age tertiles are recorded as 0.12 and 0.06 points on a 1-point scale in 2004 and in 2011, respectively.

Detailed analysis of data from the Health and Healthcare Module of the ISSP that was conducted in Turkey (2011) reveals that 36 per cent of Turkish citizens evaluate the Turkish healthcare system as being effective, whereas a larger proportion of the Turkish public (44.3 per cent) agrees with the statement suggesting that the healthcare system in Turkey is ineffective.[10] Furthermore, when asked whether the healthcare system in Turkey needs any changes, only 15.4 per cent of the Turkish population asserted that it needs no changes, and the remaining 84.6 per cent suggested that there is a need for change.[11] Approximately 43 per cent of the Turkish population suggested that a few changes are needed in the Turkish healthcare system, and those citizens indicating that the healthcare system in Turkey needs many changes or needs to be changed completely constituted 41.8 per cent of the Turkish population.

Although approximately 85 per cent of the Turkish population expressed that there exists a need for change in the Turkish healthcare system, only a small proportion expressed a willingness to pay higher taxes in order to improve the healthcare system in Turkey. As presented in Table 10.8, those citizens stating that they would be 'very' or 'fairly' willing to pay higher taxes to improve the Turkish healthcare system constituted only 23.8 per cent of the Turkish population. While approximately 22 per cent of the Turkish population remained neutral on the issue, the majority of the Turkish population (54.4 per cent) suggested that they would be 'fairly' or 'very' unwilling to pay higher taxes to improve the healthcare system.[12] The willingness to pay higher taxes to improve the healthcare system is found to be slightly higher among males, the highly educated and elderly when compared to their female, less educated and younger counterparts, respectively.

Taken as a whole, our findings from the examination of public preferences on the healthcare issue suggest that a healthcare reform that would address the shortcomings of the healthcare system in Turkey could consolidate public support, provided that proposed changes in the healthcare system can be attained without exerting an additional tax burden for Turkish citizens.

Table 10.7: Satisfaction with healthcare services by gender, education and age (mean, SD)

	2004	2008	2011
Overall	0.563 (0.330)	0.544 (0.300)	0.646 (0.231)
Gender			
Male	0.561 (0.327)	0.535 (0.305)	0.646 (0.239)
Female	0.565 (0.332)	0.551 (0.296)	0.646 (0.226)
Education			
Low	0.621 (0.330)	0.567 (0.308)	0.673 (0.242)
Medium	0.507 (0.317)	0.520 (0.291)	0.627 (0.230)
High	0.411 (0.289)	0.502 (0.282)	0.588 (0.252)
Age			
15-29	0.505 (0.332)	0.531 (0.287)	0.610 (0.242)
30-49	0.561 (0.330)	0.529 (0.300)	0.638 (0.230)
50+	0.630 (0.315)	0.571 (0.312)	0.675 (0.223)

Data source: ISSP (2011)

As far as educational policies are concerned, the share of education expenditure in the state budget substantially increased from 10 to 15 per cent during the period between 2004 and 2011 (Başlevent and Kirmanoğlu, 2016), and a series of curricular and structural reforms has taken place under the AKP government (Aksit, 2007; itim Reformu Girişimi, 2013). Survey studies illustrate that the proportion of those Turkish citizens who are dissatisfied with the educational system in Turkey has slightly decreased from 39.1 per cent in 2004 to 37.4 per cent in 2008 (ESS, 2004, 2008),[13] and as of 2011, those who express having 'very little' or 'no' confidence at all in the educational system in Turkey constituted 26.3 per cent of the Turkish population.[14] As presented in Table 10.8, almost half of the Turkish citizens indicated having a 'complete' or 'a great deal' of confidence in the educational system Turkey. While a majority of the female respondents and people over 50 years of age expressed having a 'complete' or 'a great deal' of confidence in the Turkish educational system, the percentage of those male and younger respondents expressing high levels of confidence in the educational system is found to be 8 and 11 percentage points lower, respectively. However, the most significant differences in the levels of confidence in the educational system in Turkey are observed between high and low educational groups. While

58.8 per cent of those less educated respondents without a secondary school diploma indicated having a 'complete' or 'a great deal' of confidence in the Turkish educational system, only 32.3 per cent of the highly educated Turkish citizens with at least some university education expressed having high levels of confidence in the educational system.

Table 10.8: Confidence in the educational system in Turkey (raw numbers, %)

	Complete/a great deal		Some		Very little/not at all	
Overall	718	(48.0)	385	(25.7)	394	(26.3)
Gender						
Male	265	(43.2)	170	(27.7)	178	(29.0)
Female	453	(51.2)	215	(24.3)	216	(24.4)
Education						
Low	449	(58.8)	174	(22.8)	141	(18.5)
Medium	163	(39.1)	127	(30.5)	127	(30.5)
High	71	(32.3)	56	(25.5)	93	(42.3)
Age						
15-29	155	(41.1)	105	(27.9)	117	(31.0)
30-49	259	(47.9)	138	(25.5)	144	(26.6)
50+	294	(52.0)	140	(24.8)	131	(23.2)

Data source: ISSP (2011)

While the education system that had been implemented in Turkey during the period between 1997 and 2012 was based on an eight-year uninterrupted compulsory primary education, the government proposed a major structural educational reform in early 2012. The proposed and later adopted educational reform has introduced a total of 12 years of compulsory education consisting of three four-year terms (4+4+4), with the options of enrolment in vocational schools and home education after fourth grade. Several education unions and non-governmental organisations (NGOs) have criticised the reform on the grounds that it will lead to a reduction in formal schooling, especially for girls living in rural areas, and will pave the way for child marriages as well as child labour (TÜSEV, 2012; Eğitim Reformu Girişimi, 2012). These discussions as well as instances of public demonstrations against the educational reform have also been extensively covered by the Turkish media (Ay, 2012; Hurriyetegitim.com, 2012; Mıhcı, 2012), and contributed to public discussions of the educational reform policies.

Survey studies reveal that the criticism against educational reform has also been reflected in public opinion regarding educational policies in Turkey. A recent survey study conducted during the last month of the years 2011, 2012 and 2013 demonstrates that prior to the proposal and adoption of educational reform in 2012, those Turkish citizens evaluating the educational policies carried out by the government as being unsuccessful constituted 39.6 per cent of the Turkish population (Kadir Has Üniversitesi Türkiye Çalışmaları Merkezi, 2015). As illustrated in Table 10.9, the percentage of those respondents evaluating the educational policies of the government as being unsuccessful, however, has dramatically increased to 48.8 per cent in 2012 and to 45.5 per cent in 2013 after the introduction of educational reform. The proportion of those Turkish citizens positively evaluating the educational policies of the government also gradually decreased from 39.8 per cent in 2011 to 34.5 per cent in 2012, and to 32.2 per cent in 2013. Our findings from the survey of the educational policy preferences of the Turkish public reveals that although a large majority expressed having confidence in the education system in Turkey in 2011, the structural reform introduced to the Turkish educational system in early 2012 seems to have led to a discontent with the government's educational policies.

Table 10.9: Public evaluation of the government's educational policies (%)

	December 2011	December 2012	December 2013
Successful	39.8	34.5	32.2
Neither successful nor unsuccessful	20.6	16.7	22.3
Unsuccessful	39.6	48.8	45.4

Data source: Compiled from Kadir Has Üniversitesi Türkiye Çalışmaları Merkezi (2015)

Conclusion

A substantial body of earlier research established the centrality of the issue of saliency in explaining the relationship between public policy preferences and policy responsiveness. Therefore, in this chapter, we started our analysis by surveying the issues that have been salient to the Turkish public over the course of 12 years, between 2004 and 2015, and our analysis pointed to the issues of the economy, terrorism, crime, healthcare services and education as being crucial for understanding Turkish public opinion and the policy nexus. Our findings illustrate that economic problems constituted the most salient issue in Turkey in all the years covered in our analysis. While terrorism has become highly salient, especially from 2006 onwards, concerns over crime and the quality of educational and healthcare services have consistently been identified as being among the five most salient issues for the Turkish public.

A vast amount of literature on public opinion and policy responsiveness asserts that political parties respond to public opinion, not only by adjusting their policy positions as a response to shifts in public opinion (Adams et al, 2004; Ezrow et al, 2011), but also by selectively emphasising the issues that citizens prioritise (Spoon and Klüver, 2014). In his recent study, Bulut analyses the issue attendance of political parties by utilising data from Turkish laws, parliamentary bills, oral questions and party manifestos issued between 2003 and 2013, and his findings suggest that the political parties in Turkey display issue responsiveness to a considerable extent (Bulut, 2016). His research illustrates that the bills drafted by the members of the governing party (AKP) and the main opposition party (Republican People's Party [Cumhuriyet Halk Partisi, CHP]) reflected the issue priorities of the Turkish public in their legislative agendas. Accordingly, while the economy, education and crime constituted three of the five mostly prioritised issues in the legislative agenda of the AKP, the bills drafted by members of the CHP prioritised all the salient issues in the public agenda with the only exception of the healthcare issue. Furthermore, Bulut's study illustrates that both the AKP and CHP responded to changes in public opinion by legislating more bills under the topics of economy and defence when these two issues became more salient to the Turkish public, especially after 2009, and hence, documents a directional correspondence between the public agenda, on the one hand, and the legislative agendas of the governing party and the main opposition party, on the other.

Our analysis of the policy preferences of the Turkish public on the issues of the economy, healthcare services and education further pointed at probable causes of discontent with certain public policies in Turkey as well as potential areas for policy change, where a substantial public support can be consolidated. To briefly summarise, our findings suggest that economic policies, especially those targeting income inequalities, are of central concern to the Turkish public, and there exists a considerable level of potential support for a tax policy reform that would aim at reducing income differences. Public support for the government's privatisation programmes, however, is found to have substantially decreased over the last few years. While our findings suggest that a healthcare reform would consolidate public support provided that proposed changes in the healthcare system be attained without exerting an additional tax burden on the Turkish citizens, the recent structural reform in the Turkish educational system is found to have led to a discontent with the government's educational policies.

Notes

[1] The question reads as, 'How interested would you say you are in politics?' The response options are listed as: (1) very interested; (2) somewhat interested; (3) not very interested; and (4) not interested at all. For the analysis, the responses are rescaled to range between 0 and 1, where higher values indicate higher levels of interest in politics.

[2] The full question wording reads as, 'How often does politics seem so complicated that you can't really understand what is going on?' The response options are listed as: (1) never; (2) seldom; (3) occasionally; (4) regularly; and (5) frequently.

[3] The question reads as, 'How difficult or easy do you find it to make your mind up about political issues?' The response options are listed as: (1) very difficult; (2) difficult; (3) neither difficult nor easy; (4) easy; and (5) very easy.

[4] For analysis of the most important problems, we utilised aggregated data for those years where multiple surveys were conducted. The full wording of the question reads as, 'What do you think are the two most important issues facing Turkey at the moment?' The response options provided

are listed as: (1) crime; (2) the economic situation in Turkey; (3) rising prices/inflation/cost of living; (4) taxation; (5) unemployment; (6) terrorism; (7) housing; (8) the financial situation of your household; (9) immigration; (10) health and social security: (11) the education system; (12) the environment, climate and energy issues; (13) pensions; (14) working conditions; (15) living conditions; and (16) other.

5 The question reads as, 'To what extent do you agree or disagree with the following statement: differences in income in Turkey are too large.' The respondents are asked to choose between the following response options: (1) strongly agree; (2) agree; (3) neither agree nor disagree; (4) disagree; and (5) strongly disagree.

6 The question reads as, 'To what extent do you agree or disagree with the following statement: it is the responsibility of the government to reduce differences in income between people with high incomes and those with low incomes.' The respondents are asked to choose between the following response options: (1) strongly agree; (2) agree; (3) neither agree nor disagree; (4) disagree; and (5) strongly disagree.

7 The full wording of the question reads as, 'Do you think people with high incomes should pay a larger share of their income in taxes than those with low incomes, the same share, or a smaller share?' And the respondents are asked to choose between the following response options: (1) much larger share; (2) larger share; (3) same share; (4) smaller share; and (5) much smaller share.

8 The question reads as, 'Generally, how would you describe taxes in Turkey today for those with high incomes?' The response options are provided as: (1) much too high; (2) too high; (3) about right; (4) too low; and (5) much too low.

9 The full wording of the question reads as, 'In general, how satisfied or dissatisfied are you with the healthcare system in Turkey?' The response options are listed as: (1) completely satisfied; (2) very satisfied; (3) fairly satisfied; (4) neither satisfied nor dissatisfied; (5) fairly dissatisfied; (6) very dissatisfied; and (7) completely dissatisfied. For the analysis, the responses are rescaled to range between 0 and 1, where higher values indicate higher levels of satisfaction with the healthcare system in Turkey.

10 The question reads as, 'How much do you agree or disagree with the following statement: the healthcare system in Turkey is inefficient.' Respondents are asked to choose between the response options of: (1) strongly agree; (2) agree; (3) neither agree nor disagree; (4) disagree; and (5) strongly disagree.

11 The question reads as, 'In general, would you say that the healthcare system in Turkey needs no changes, a few changes, many changes, or needs to be completely changed?', with the following response options: (1) needs no changes; (2) needs a few changes; (3) needs many changes; and (4) needs to be completely changed.

12 The question reads as, 'How willing would you be to pay higher taxes to improve the level of healthcare for all people in Turkey?' The response options are listed as: (1) very willing; (2) fairly willing; (3) neither willing nor unwilling; (4) fairly unwilling; and (5) very unwilling.

13 The full wording of the question reads as, 'Now, using this card, please say what you think overall about the state of education in Turkey nowadays?' The response options are presented in an 11-point response scale labelled at the lower end as 'extremely bad' and at the higher end as 'extremely good'.

14 The question reads as, 'In general, how much confidence do you have in the educational system in Turkey?' The response options are listed as: (1) complete confidence; (2) a great deal of confidence; (3) some confidence; (4) very little confidence; and (5) no confidence at all.

References

Adams, J., Clark, M., Ezrow, L., Glasgow, G., Adams, J., Clark, M., et al (2004) 'Understanding change and stability in party ideologies: Do parties respond to public opinion or to past election results?', *British Journal of Political Science*, vol 34, no 4, pp 589-610 (http://doi.org/10.1017/S0007123404000201).

Aksit, N. (2007) 'Educational reform in Turkey', *International Journal of Educational Development*, vol 27, no 2, pp 129-37 (http://doi.org/10.1016/j.ijedudev.2006.07.011).

Ay, H. (2012) '120 sivil toplum örgütü 4+4+4 eğitim sistemine destek çıktı' (www.sabah.com.tr/egitim/2012/03/28/120-sivil-toplum-orgutu-444-egitim-sistemine-destek-cikti).

Başlevent, C. and Kirmanoğlu, H. (2016) 'Economic voting in Turkey: Perceptions, expectations, and the party choice', *Research and Policy on Turkey*, vol 1, no 1, pp 88-101 (http://doi.org/10.1080/23760818.2015.1099784).

Bulut, A.T. (2016) 'Measuring political agenda setting and representation in Turkey', *Party Politics*, 1354068815625232 (http://doi.org/10.1177/1354068815625232).

Burnstein, P. (2003) 'The impact of public opinion on public policy: A review and an agenda', *Political Research Quarterly*, vol 56, no 1, pp 29-40 (http://doi.org/10.1177/106591290305600103).

Campbell, R. and Winters, K. (2008) 'Understanding men's and women's political interests: Evidence from a study of gendered political attitudes', *Journal of Elections, Public Opinion and Parties*, vol 18, no 1, pp 53-74 (http://doi.org/10.1080/17457280701858623).

Coffé, H. (2013) 'Women stay local, men go national and global? Gender differences in political interest', *Sex Roles*, vol 69, no 5-6, pp 323-38 (http://doi.org/10.1007/s11199-013-0308-x).

Edwards, G.C., Mitchell, W. and Welch, R. (1995) 'Explaining presidential approval: The significance of issue salience', *American Journal of Political Science*, vol 39, no 1, pp 108-34 (http://doi.org/10.2307/2111760).

Eğitim Reformu Girişimi (2012) *4+4<8 Kesintisiz Temel Eğitim Nedir?* (http://www.egitimreformugirisimi.org/wp-content/uploads/2017/03/444_Gerekce-Metni.pdf).

Eğitim Reformu Girişimi (2013) *Eğitim izleme raporu 2012* [*Education monitoring report 2012*].

ESS (European Social Survey) (2004) *Round 2 data file edition 3.4*, Norwegian Social Science Data Services, Norway – Data archive and distributor of ESS data for ESS ERIC.

ESS (2008) *Round 4 data file edition 4.3*, Norwegian Social Science Data Services, Norway – Data archive and distributor of ESS data for ESS ERIC.

Eurobarometer Survey (no date) *Standard Eurobarometer Survey Series data file*, GESIS Data Archive, Cologne.

Ezrow, L., de Vries, C., Steenbergen, M. and Edwards, E. (2011) 'Mean voter representation and partisan constituency representation: Do parties respond to the mean voter position or to their supporters?', *Party Politics*, vol 17, no 3, pp 275-301 (http://doi.org/10.1177/1354068810372100).

Hill, K.Q. and Hurley, P.A. (1999) 'Dyadic representation reappraised', *American Journal of Political Science*, vol 43, no 1, pp 109-37 (http://doi.org/10.2307/2991787).

Hürriyet (2012) 'Kadınlar 4+4+4'e karşı meclise yürüyor' (www.hurriyetegitim. com/haberler/26.03.2012/kadinlar-444-icin-meclise-yuruyor).

ISSP (International Social Survey Programme) (2009) *Module on social inequality – IV data file*, GESIS Data Archive, Cologne (http://doi.org/doi:10.4232/1.11506).

ISSP (2011) *Module on health and health care data file*, GESIS Data Archive, Cologne (http://doi.org/doi:10.4232/1.12252).

Kadir Has Üniversitesi Türkiye Çalışmaları Merkezi (2015) *Türkiye sosyal – Siyasal eğilimler araştırması kantitatif araştırma raporu* (www.khas.edu.tr/uploads/turkiye/tssea-2015.pdf).

Kuklinski, J. (1977) 'District competitiveness and legislative roll-call behavior: A reassessment of the marginality hypothesis', *American Journal of Political Science*, vol 21 (August), pp 627-38 (http://doi.org/10.2307/2110584).

Lindaman, K. and Haider-Markel, D.P. (2002) 'Issue evolution, political parties, and the culture wars', *Political Research Quarterly*, vol 55, no 1, pp 91-110 (http://doi.org/10.1177/106591290205500104).

Mayhew, D.R. (2004) *Congress: The electoral connection* (2nd edn), New Haven, CT: Yale University Press.

Mıhcı, H. (2012) *Neden 4+4+4?* (http://bianet.org/bianet/egitim/137299-neden-4-4-4).

Miller, W.E. and Stokes, D.E. (1963) 'Constituency influence in Congress', *American Political Science Review*, vol 57, no 1, pp 45-56 (http://doi.org/10.2307/1952717).

Monroe, A.D. (1979) 'Consistency between constituency preferences and national policy decisions', *American Politics Quarterly*, vol 7, no 1, pp 3-19.

Monroe, A.D. (1998) 'Public opinion and public policy, 1980-1993', *Public Opinion Quarterly*, vol 62, no 1, pp 6-28.

Norris, P., Lovenduski, J. and Campbell, R. (2004) *Gender and political participation*, London: The Electoral Commission.

Önis, Z. (2011) 'Power, interests and coalitions: The political economy of mass privatisation in Turkey', *Third World Quarterly*, vol 32, no 4, pp 707-24 (http://doi.org/10.1080/01436597.2011.567004).

Page, B.I. and Shapiro, R. (1983) 'Effects of public opinion on policy', *The American Political Science Review*, vol 77, no 1, pp 175-90.

Powell, B.G. (2000). *Elections as instruments of democracy: Majoritarian and proportional views*, New Haven, CT: Yale University Press.

Spoon, J. and Klüver, H. (2014) 'Do parties respond? How electoral context influences party responsiveness', *Electoral Studies*, vol 35, pp 48-60 (http://doi.org/10.1016/j.electstud.2014.04.014).

Tekin, A. (2010) 'OECD ülkelerinde yapılan vergi reformlarının değerlendirilmesi', *Dumlupınar Üniversitesi Sosyal Bilimler Dergisi*, no 26, pp 54-70.

TÜSEV (2012) *Eğitimde '4+4+4 yasası': Tasarı, yasalaşma ve uygulama süreçlerinde STK'ların katılımı. Vaka analizi* (www.tusev.org.tr/usrfiles/images/444YasasiVakaAnaliziTR.31.10.13.pdf).

Wlezien, C. (2005) 'On the salience of political issues: The problem with "most important problem"', *Electoral Studies*, vol 24, no 4, pp 555-79 (http://doi.org/10.1016/j.electstud.2005.01.009).

Wlezien, C. and Soroka, S.N. (2009) 'The relationship between public opinion and policy', in R.J. Dalton and H.-D. Klingemann (eds) *The Oxford handbook of political behavior*, New York: Oxford University Press, pp 799-817.

WVS (World Values Survey) (2015) 1981–2014 Longitudinal aggregate v.20150418 (www.worldvaluessurvey.org).

Part Four
Parties and civil society-based policy analysis

ELEVEN

Political parties and public policy in Turkey*

Selim Erdem Aytaç

Introduction

The prominent political theorist Robert A. Dahl (1971, p 1) emphasised 'the continuing responsiveness of the government to the preferences of its citizens' as a key characteristic of democratic governance. Simply put, a responsive government is a government that is attentive to, and influenced by, the voice of the people (Sartori, 1976). In the specific context of *policy* responsiveness, a government is responsive if there is a high level of congruence between the policy preferences and actions of the elected representatives and collective public attitudes towards policy issues (Hobolt and Klemmemsen, 2005). Evidence from Western democracies suggests that there is indeed a close correspondence between public opinion and policy behaviour of governments (Page and Shapiro, 1983, 1992; Stimson et al, 1995; Hobolt and Klemmemsen, 2005).

Political parties are considered to be significant actors in the realisation of this ideal of a responsive government. At the most fundamental level, political parties are supposed to transmit popular preferences into policy (Stokes, 1999). In Anthony Downs' (1957) classical framework of electoral competition, parties choose the vote-maximising position in the relevant policy space, and accordingly, just as economic competition leads firms to produce what consumers want, electoral competition induces parties 'to give voters what they want' (Stokes, 1999, p 251).

This view of electoral competition corresponds to what it is also called the 'mandate' view of elections (Manin et al, 1999). In this framework parties make policy proposals during campaigns and explain how these proposals would affect citizens' welfare, often outlined in the election campaign manifestos. In turn, citizens evaluate which of these proposals best serve their interests and choose the party whose proposals they want to see implemented – giving a 'mandate' to a party to carry out its promises. As such, elections serve to realise the selection and implementation of policies that best correspond to the public's demands.

---

* This chapter is a slightly modified version of an article originally published (in Turkish) as 'Türkiye'de Siyasi Partilerin Seçim Beyannamelerindeki Politika Öncelikleri, 2002-2015', *SİYASAL: Journal of Political Sciences*, vol 26, no 2, pp 7-26.

A first crucial step towards assessing the responsiveness of political parties in a country, then, is to look at what policy issues different parties emphasise. Which public policy categories are prioritised by the political parties? Is there a divergence in the prioritisation of different policy categories across political parties, or are there some policy areas that are emphasised by all major parties? Can we observe some trends over time? And finally, is there evidence that the policy categories prioritised by political parties corresponds to what the public considers as salient and important issues facing the country? In this chapter we address these questions in the Turkish political context from 2002 to 2015.

In order to analyse what policy categories Turkish parties emphasised during this period, we turn to election manifestos. Dating back to the 19th century in the UK, election manifestos are detailed policy documents prepared by parties ahead of elections, presenting the official declaration of a party's policy proposals (Quinn, 2014). In line with the 'mandate' view of elections, ideally the manifesto of the party that wins the election is supposed to be endorsed by the electorate. Thus the winning party has the right as well as the mandate to carry out the policies outlined in its election manifesto. There is evidence in the literature that voters pay attention to the campaign platforms of parties as outlined in their manifestos, and that they also update their perception of parties' policy preferences and positions accordingly (Fernandez-Vazquez, 2014).

In the following we first look briefly at the Turkish political landscape from 2002 to 2015. Next we describe our dataset for election manifestos, and then analyse the distribution of policy categories in the election manifestos of four major parties during this period. We conclude with a summary of the main patterns observed, and discuss how the policy categories prioritised by political parties match the Turkish electorate's concerns during this period.

Background on the Turkish political landscape, 2002–15

In the period from 2002 to 2015, four political parties dominated the Turkish political landscape. The Justice and Development Party (Adalet ve Kalkınma Partisi, AKP) is a conservative, right-wing party founded in 2001 by some leading members of the then existing conservative, pro-Islamist parties. Since its foundation, it has won pluralities in all of the five legislative elections held in 2002, 2007, 2011, June 2015 and November 2015. The party held a majority of seats in Parliament and was able to rule with a single-party government throughout this period, except for a brief interlude between the June 2015 and November 2015 elections.

The main opposition party during this period has been the Republican People's Party (Cumhuriyet Halk Partisi, CHP). Founded in 1919, CHP is the oldest political party in Turkey with a left-wing, social democratic, secular ideology. Another major opposition party is the Nationalist Movement Party (Milliyetçi Hareket Partisi, MHP). Founded in 1969, MHP has a right-wing, Turkish nationalistic and Eurosceptic ideological outlook.

The fourth major player in the Turkish political arena has been the Kurdish political movement, with a number of different political parties associated with it due to the banning of its parties by the Constitutional Court. In the legislative elections of 2002, the Democratic People's Party (Demokratik Halk Partisi, DEHAP) won 6.2 per cent of the popular vote but failed to gain any seats in Parliament due to not reaching the 10 per cent national threshold required for having representation. Candidates of the subsequent parties of the Kurdish political movement, the Democratic Society Party (Demokratik Toplum Partisi, DTP) and the Peace and Democracy Party (Barış ve Demokrasi Partisi, BDP) contested the 2007 and 2011 elections as independents to bypass the 10 per cent threshold. Finally, in the election of June 2015, the People's Democratic Party (Halkların Demokratik Partisi, HDP) fielded party candidates rather than independent ones, and the party managed to surpass the 10 per cent election threshold with about 13 per cent of the national vote. This was the first time for a party in the Kurdish political movement to directly win seats in Parliament. The HDP saw a decrease in support in the snap election of November 2015, but its vote share still remained at about the 10 per cent threshold.

The vote shares and number of seats in Parliament of the major political parties in Turkey during the period 2002 to 2015 are presented in Table 11.1.

Table 11.1: Vote shares and seats in Parliament of the major political parties in Turkey, 2002–15

	2002	2007	2011	June 2015	November 2015
AKP	34.3 (363)	46.6 (341)	49.8 (327)	40.9 (258)	49.5 (317)
CHP	19.4 (178)	20.9 (112)	26 (135)	25 (132)	25.3 (134)
MHP	8.4	14.3 (71)	13 (53)	16.3 (80)	11.9 (40)
DEHAP/DTP/BDP/HDP	6.2	5.2* (26)	6.6* (35)	13.1 (80)	10.7 (59)

Note: Vote shares of parties are reported outside the parentheses and the numbers in parentheses indicate the number of parliamentary seats (out of 550) gained by parties as a result of the election. MHP and DEHAP did not win any seats in Parliament in the 2002 election as they failed to pass the 10 per cent electoral threshold. In the 2007 and 2011 elections the parties associated with the Kurdish political movement (DTP and BDP, respectively) fielded independent candidates to bypass the 10 per cent national threshold, and the vote shares indicated in these elections for these parties (marked with *) refer to the total number of votes cast for independent candidates.

The policy-making processes of Turkish political parties, that is, how they develop the campaign platforms and manifestos, is rather opaque, and there is little systematic research in this area. In the parties' organisational charts it is possible to see research and development (R&D) departments led by a deputy chair. These departments are responsible for developing policies in line with the party's overall principles. Among the responsibilities of the R&D department of AKP, for example, are to field public opinion surveys and to establish think tank teams to develop policies. Analogous departments also exist in the organisational charts of CHP, MHP, and DTP/BDP/HDP. In this chapter our focus is not on the specifics of these policy-making procedures, but on the outcomes of these activities, as reflected in the campaign manifestos.

Election manifestos of major Turkish political parties: an overview

As election manifestos, or programmes, are political parties' authoritative policy statements, they are valuable resources to study parties' policy priorities and preferences. For this reason we turn to the Manifesto Project (CMP/MARPOR), a database of political parties' election manifestos, covering over 1,000 parties from 1945 until today, in more than 50 countries (Volkens et al, 2016).[1] The database relies on a standardised, comparative content analysis of parties' manifestos by quantifying the statements included in these manifestos with the support of coders from different countries. Using the dataset it is possible to study parties' policy positions and preferences with a common framework.

The coding unit in MARPOR is a quasi-sentence, which contains exactly one statement or 'message' delivered by the party manifesto. Once the quasi-sentences in a manifesto are identified, each of them is coded into one of the 56 standard categories of policy areas. These categories are constructed such that they are comparable between parties, countries, elections and across time, and can also be grouped under seven major policy domains: external relations, freedom and democracy, political system, economy, welfare and quality of life, fabric of society and social groups (see Table 11.2). It should be noted that many of the categories have positive and negative versions because parties can take opposite positions. For example, the category of protectionism within the economy domain has positive and negative versions, as a party could be in favour of or against pursuing protectionist policies.

Table 11.2: Seven major policy domains and categories in the Manifesto Project

External relations	Freedom and democracy	Political system	Economy
Foreign special relationships Anti-Imperialism Military Peace Internationalism European integration	Freedom and human rights Democracy Constitutionalism	Decentralisation/ centralisation Governmental and administrative efficiency Political corruption Political authority	Free enterprise Incentives Market regulation Economic planning Corporatism Protectionism Economic goals Keynesian demand management
Welfare and quality of life	Fabric of society	Social groups	
Environment Culture Equality Welfare state Education	National way of life Traditional morality Law and order Civic mindedness Multiculturalism	Labour groups Agriculture and farmers Middle class and professional groups Minority groups Non-economic demographic groups	Economic growth Technology and infrastructure Controlled economy Nationalisation Economic orthodoxy Marxist analysis Anti-growth economy

We start our analyses by focusing on the distribution of parties' statements across these seven major policy domains. Figure 11.1 presents the distribution of manifesto statements from AKP, CHP and MHP for the five elections between 2002 and 2015, and of DTP/BDP/HDP for the four elections between 2007 and 2015.[2] This aggregate analysis reveals that among the seven major policy domains identified by MARPOR, economy and welfare and quality of life stand out as the most frequently appearing, with a partial exception for DTP/BDP/HDP. This is especially true for AKP. Statements related to these two policy domains made up about 63 per cent of all statements in the latest election (November 2015) manifesto of AKP, compared to 56 per cent for CHP, 54 per cent for MHP and 40 per cent for DTP/BDP/HDP. Between the domains of economy and welfare and quality of life, AKP gave consistently more priority to economy. The frequencies of statements related to the each of the remaining five domains are tightly clustered and remain below 10 per cent of all statements. The domain of political system was a rather significant theme in the 2002 manifesto of AKP (13 per cent of all statements), the party's first election when it came to power, but in subsequent elections this theme was devoted much less space, ranking last

Figure 11.1: Distribution of manifesto statements across policy domains for AKP, CHP, MHP and DTP/BDP/HDP, 2002–15

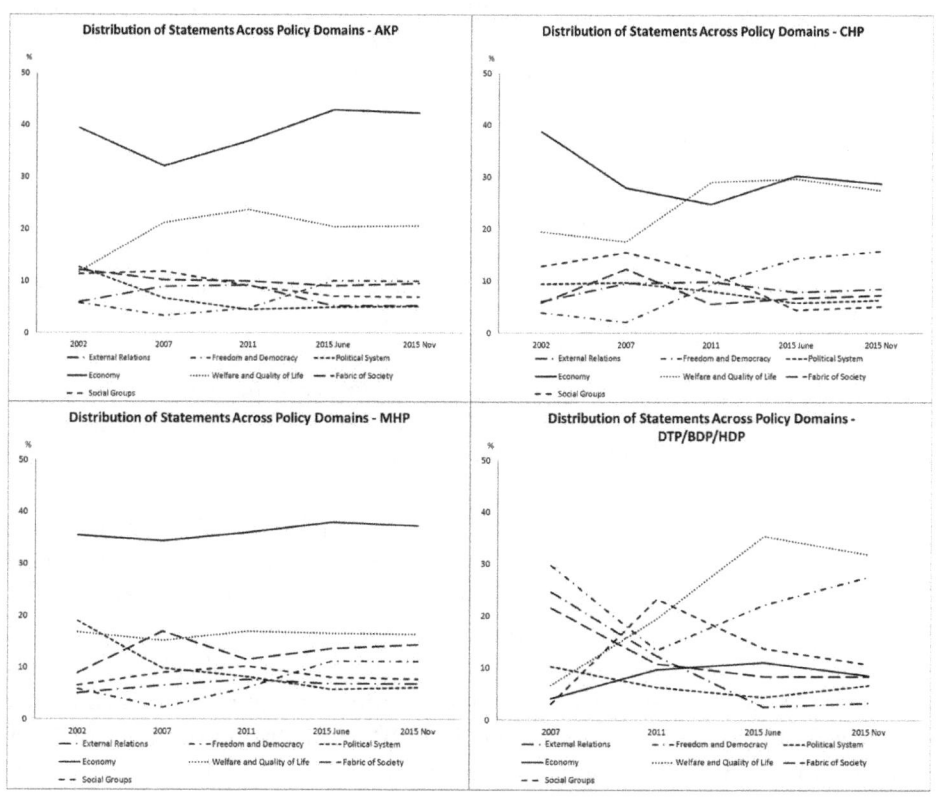

among the policy domains in the November 2015 election with a proportion of about 5 per cent of all statements.

The two policy domains of economy and welfare and quality of life are also prominent in the manifestos of CHP, the main opposition party during this period. Yet, while in AKP's manifestos we observed the economy being prioritised over welfare and quality of life, this is not the case in CHP's manifestos. In the June and November 2015 elections, policy statements related to welfare and quality of life found as much place as the economy in CHP's manifestos, and in 2011 welfare and quality of life was the most frequently appearing theme in CHP's manifesto (about 29 per cent of all statements). A third frequently appearing policy category in CHP's manifestos is freedom and democracy. This finds more space in the manifestos starting with the 2011 election, and particularly in the 2015 June and November elections.

Among the four parties considered, MHP seems to have the most consistent distribution of policy domains in its campaign manifestos over time, as there is little variance in the relative proportions of different domains across the elections. The domain of the economy stands out as the most frequently appearing theme (about more than a third of all statements on average), outdistancing the remaining six policy domains. The frequencies of statements related to the remaining domains are tightly clustered without a significant variation over time. The domains of welfare and quality of life and fabric of society are devoted more space than the other domains in this group, but the differences are quite small. As was the case in the manifestos of AKP, the domain of political system faded in importance from 2002 to 2015, declining from 19 per cent of all statements in 2002 to just 6 per cent in November 2015.

Moving to DTP/BDP/HDP, it can be seen that unlike the other three parties, there are no dominant policy domains throughout the period of interest. Nevertheless, the domains of welfare and quality of life and freedom and democracy could be considered as the most prevalent themes in the parties' manifestos, especially in the twin elections of 2015. In this respect, the manifestos of DTP/BDP/HDP are closer to those of CHP than AKP and MHP, although the difference in emphasis on freedom and democracy between DTP/BDP/HDP and CHP manifestos is still considerable. Perhaps the biggest divergence point between the manifestos of DTP/BDP/HDP and those of the other three parties is that DTP/BDP/HDP devotes significantly less space to the domain of the economy.

This aggregate analysis at the level of the major policy domains reveals that among the policy domains considered by MARPOR, the economy and welfare and quality of life dominate the election manifestos of the Turkish political parties over the period 2002-15. The domain of the economy is especially a major theme in the manifestos of the right-wing parties of AKP and MHP, while the domain of welfare and quality of life is also a prominent theme in the manifestos of the left-wing parties of CHP and DTP/BDP/HDP. In addition, in the 2015 elections the domain of freedom and democracy was also frequently referred to in the manifestos of these left-wing parties, especially those of DTP/BDP/HDP. The remaining policy domains of external relations, political system, fabric of society and social groups have consistently received relatively little attention by the parties, with statements related to each of these policy domains typically constituting about or less than 10 per cent of the total number of statements in the manifestos.[3]

Category-level analyses

As explained earlier, in the MARPOR dataset, each statement in a party manifesto is coded into one of the 56 standard categories of policy areas. In this section we analyse the distribution of these policy categories in the four parties' manifestos over time. To keep the analysis manageable and meaningful, instead of presenting the results related to all of the 56 categories, for each party we identify the most frequently mentioned 10 policy categories during the period 2002-15 (2007-15 for DTP/BDP/HDP), and track the distribution of statements related to these policy categories over time.

Figure 11.2 presents the distribution of manifesto statements across policy categories for AKP. The most frequently mentioned policy category in AKP's manifestos is 'technology and infrastructure: positive', by a considerable margin. The proportion of statements related to this category was rather modest in the 2002 manifesto, but gained prominence in the following elections. Statements in this category emphasise the importance of modernisation of industry and the transportation and communication infrastructure in the country. As such, it can be inferred that projects and calls for public spending on transportation infrastructure (for example, roads, bridges, tunnels, airports, ports) and communication infrastructure (for example, broadband internet) constitute important parts of AKP's election manifestos.

Another important policy category in AKP's manifestos, which somewhat declined in salience in the two 2015 elections, is 'welfare state expansion.' This category consists of policy statements that are in favour of introducing, maintaining or expanding public social services or social security schemes such as government funding of healthcare, child care, elder care and pensions, and social housing. The proportion of statements related to this category peaked in the 2011 election campaign manifesto, possibly to mitigate the negative effects of the 2009 global financial crisis. Other policy categories that consistently found a prominent place in AKP's manifestos over the period 2002-15 are 'economic planning: positive', 'economic growth', 'incentives: positive', 'education expansion', 'free enterprise: positive', 'law and order', 'democracy' and 'agriculture and farmers'.

In addition to these consistently salient policy categories, a significant trend we observe in AKP's manifestos concerns the space devoted to the category of 'free enterprise: positive'. This category was the second most frequently mentioned policy category in the party's 2002 manifesto, but received much less attention in subsequent elections. Statements in this category include favourable mentions of

Figure 11.2: Distribution of manifesto statements across policy categories for AKP, 2002–15

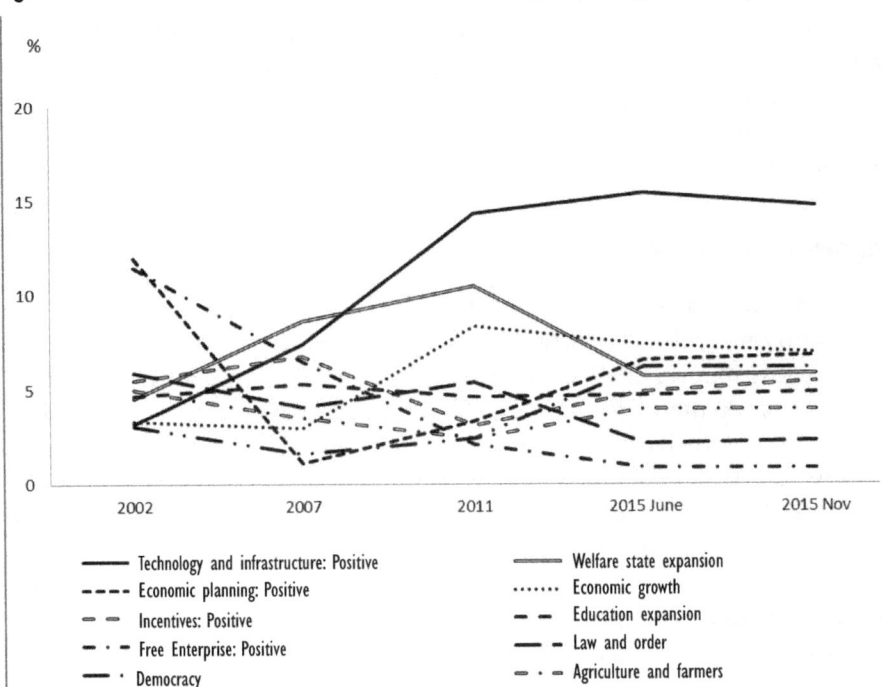

the free market, and emphasise a laissez-faire economy, superiority of individual enterprise over state systems, private property rights, and personal enterprise and initiative. As mentioned earlier, the 2002 election was AKP's first election, and in the aftermath of the 2001 economic crisis and corruption scandals, calls for economic efficiency and a bigger role for the private sector in the economy had considerable appeal. After coming to power in the 2002 election, AKP devoted less space to such calls in its election manifestos.[4]

Next we present the distribution of manifesto statements across policy categories for CHP during 2002-15 in Figure 11.3. The first thing to notice in CHP's manifestos is that there is not a single policy category dominating others, in contrast to what we had observed in AKP's manifestos. The space allocated to the most frequently mentioned 10 policy categories during the period of 2002-15 are quite close to each other. As was the case in AKP's manifestos, the category 'technology and infrastructure: positive' is the most frequently mentioned policy category in this period. It is closely followed by 'welfare state expansion', with a peak in the space allocated to statements in this category in the 2011 election manifesto. We had observed a similar peak in AKP's 2011 manifesto as well, suggesting that both parties tried to address the fall-out of the 2009 global crisis, which had affected the Turkish economy quite significantly. While in AKP's statements 'economic planning: positive' constituted the third most frequently mentioned policy category, the category of 'education expansion', emphasising the need to expand and improve educational provisions, came third in CHP's

Figure 11.3: Distribution of manifesto statements across policy categories for CHP, 2002–15

manifestos, with a consistently high presence. Other policy categories in CHP's manifestos over the period 2002-15, in decreasing order of space allocated, are 'economic growth', 'democracy', 'incentives: positive', 'agriculture and farmers', 'equality: positive', 'political corruption: negative' and 'culture: positive'.

It is possible to observe two trends in the distribution of statements across policy categories in CHP's manifestos. First, there is a significant increase in the space devoted to the category of 'democracy' over time, beginning particularly with the 2011 election manifesto. While statements related to the 'democracy' policy category constituted about 2 per cent of all statements in the 2002 manifesto, they increased more than fivefold to about 11 per cent in the November 2015 election manifesto, becoming the most frequently mentioned policy category in that document. The second trend is related to the categories of 'economic goals' and 'free enterprise: positive'. Statements related to these two categories constituted about 11 per cent of all statements in the 2002 manifesto of CHP, yet their total share dropped below 1 per cent in the November 2015 manifesto. We had observed a similar trend related to the 'free enterprise: positive' policy category in the case of AKP manifestos.

Figure 11.4 presents the distribution of manifesto statements across policy categories for MHP during 2002-15. As in the manifestos of AKP and CHP, the most frequently mentioned policy category in MHP's manifestos during this period is 'technology and infrastructure: positive'. The second most frequently mentioned policy category is 'national way of life: positive'. Statements in this category include favourable mentions of the country's nation and history as well as appeals to patriotism and nationalism. Given that MHP is a (Turkish) nationalist party, it is not surprising that a significant space is devoted to this category in the party's manifestos, and we see that statements in this category were especially prevalent in the 2007 election manifesto, constituting the second most frequently mentioned policy category by a small margin. MHP had remained outside Parliament as a result of failing to pass the 10 per cent national threshold in the 2002 election, thus it seems that the party heavily relied on nationalistic statements as its campaign strategy in 2007, and managed to get back to Parliament. Other policy categories in MHP's manifestos over the period 2002-15, in decreasing order of space allocated, are 'welfare state expansion', 'economic growth', 'economic planning: positive', 'agriculture and farmers', 'democracy', 'incentives: positive', 'education expansion' and 'governmental and administrative efficiency'.

Figure 11.4: Distribution of manifesto statements across policy categories for MHP, 2002–15

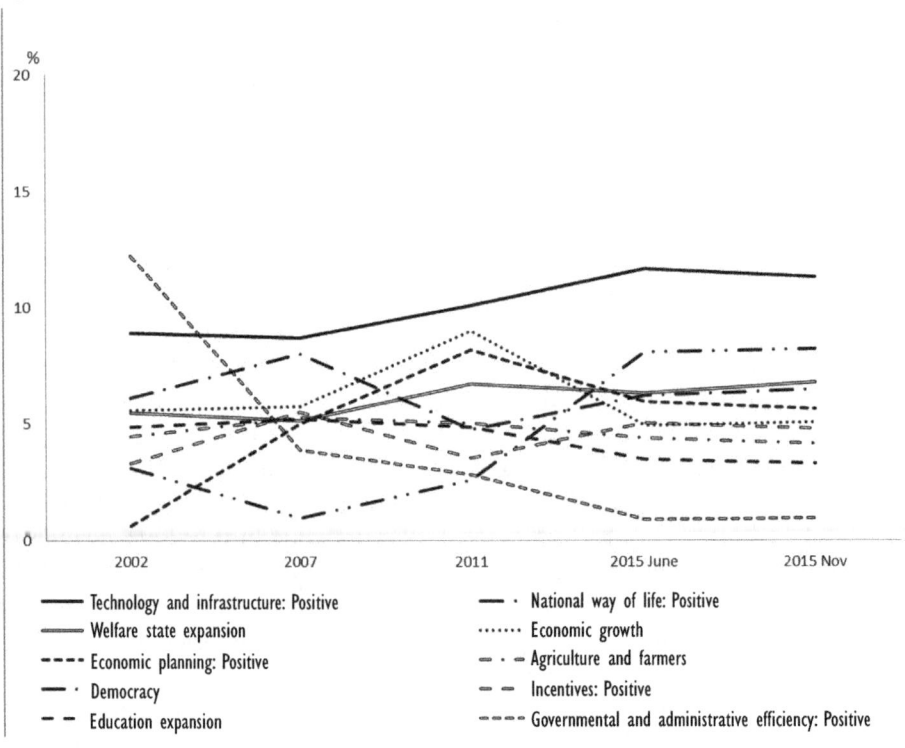

Two trends are noticeable in the manifestos of MHP during this period. First, there is a significant decline from 2002 to 2015 in the space allocated to statements in the category of 'governmental and administrative efficiency: positive'. Statements in this category constituted the most frequently mentioned policy category in the

Policy analysis in civil society organisations

party's 2002 election manifesto (about 12 per cent of all statements). Yet in 2015 the percentage of statements in this category barely reached 1 per cent. Statements in this category emphasise the need for efficiency and economy in government and administration, including calls for administration restructuring, cutting down on the civil service and improving bureaucratic procedures. As mentioned earlier, the 2002 election was conducted in the aftermath of the 2001 economic crisis and corruption scandals, and MHP was one of the coalition parties in power during this period. It is possible that the MHP leadership tried to contain the electoral damage due to its incumbency status in this period by emphasising efficiency in the administration and bureaucracy in its election campaign. This emphasis gradually declined in subsequent campaign manifestos. Second, the space devoted to the categories of 'economic planning: positive' and 'democracy' increased significantly from 2002 to 2015. Statements related to the category 'democracy' were especially frequent in manifestos of the twin elections of 2015.

Finally, the distribution of manifesto statements across policy categories for DTP/BDP/HDP during 2007-15 is presented in Figure 11.5. We see that this distribution of policy categories in DTP/BDP/HDP election manifestos is quite different from those of AKP, CHP and MHP. The most frequently mentioned policy category in the election manifestos of AKP, CHP and MHP, 'technology

Figure 11.5: Distribution of manifesto statements across policy categories for DTP/BDP/HDP, 2007–15

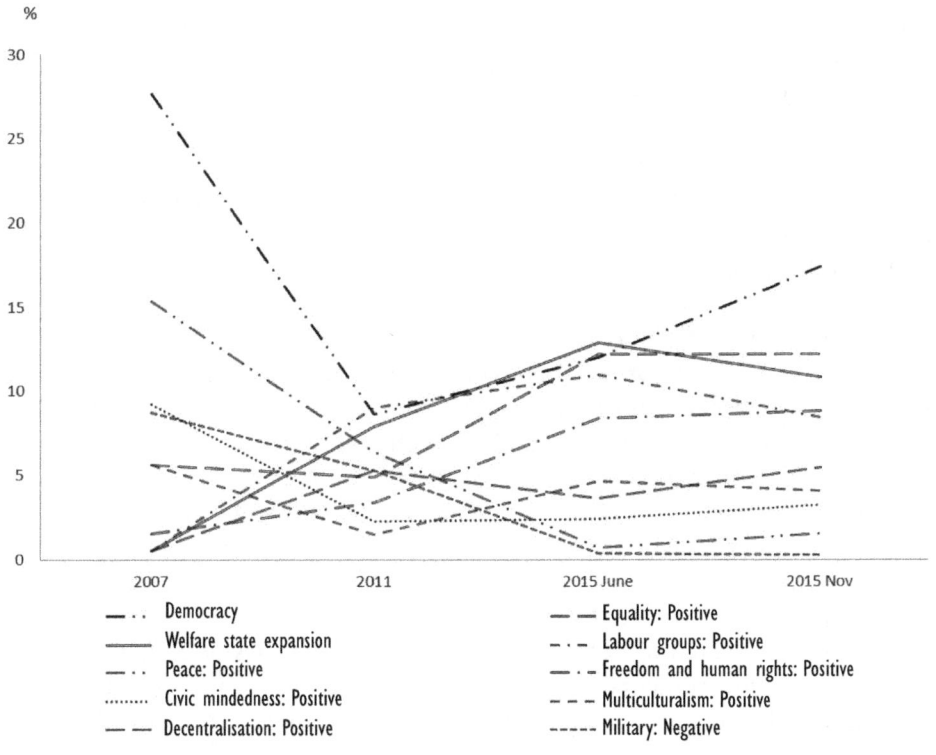

and infrastructure: positive', does not even make it to the top 10 most frequently mentioned policy categories in DTP/BDP/HDP manifestos. Instead, the most frequently mentioned policy category is 'democracy', which was especially dominant in the 2007 and November 2015 election manifestos. Statements related to this category emphasise favourable mentions of democracy as the 'only game in town', the need for the involvement of all citizens in political decision-making, and support for rule of law, division of powers, independence of courts, etc. It should be noted that the category of 'democracy' was not among the three most frequently mentioned policy categories in the manifestos of AKP, CHP and MHP in any election. Another important policy category in DTP/BDP/HDP manifestos is 'equality: positive', which gained prominence in the 2015 election manifestos. Other important policy categories in DTP/BDP/HDP's manifestos, in decreasing order of space allocated, are 'welfare state expansion', labour groups: positive', 'peace: positive', 'freedom and human rights: positive', 'civic mindedness: positive', 'multiculturalism: positive', 'decentralisation: positive' and 'military: negative'.

Conclusion

The analysis of the election manifestos of four major political parties in Turkey reveals clear patterns regarding the prioritisation of policy issues. Policy issues related to the domains of the economy and welfare and quality of life are the most important themes in the election manifestos. Parties especially emphasise policy proposals regarding technology and infrastructure investments as well as welfare state expansion. As policy proposals in these areas include calls for more public spending on infrastructure and expansion of social services and social security schemes, they could be seen as efforts to support economic growth as well as to address economic hardships experienced by citizens. The left-wing social democratic CHP also puts considerable emphasis on education expansion and democracy.

We should also mention that the election manifesto priorities of DTP/BDP/HDP diverge considerably from the other three parties. In particular, DTP/BDP/HDP put considerable emphasis on democracy and equality. Policy proposals in these categories call for special protection for underprivileged social groups, provisions to end discrimination, measures for the involvement of all citizens in political decision-making and an emphasis on the importance of human and civil rights. As the parties associated with the Kurdish political movement consider themselves as the voice of vulnerable minorities in Turkey, it is no surprise that these parties' manifestos put relatively more emphasis on issues such as equality and democracy.

An important trend that is observed in the manifestos of AKP and MHP is that the space devoted to policy proposals in the categories of 'free enterprise: positive' and 'governmental and administrative efficiency: positive' decreased substantially from 2002 to 2015. The 2002 election was conducted in the immediate aftermath of the 2001 economic crisis, and there was widespread popular dissatisfaction with the inefficiency and size of the bureaucracy as well as an allegation of corruption. It seems that the right-wing parties of AKP and MHP responded to the public's concerns in these areas at that time by devoting significant space in their election manifestos to policy proposals of restructuring and cutting down on the civil service, improving bureaucratic procedures and greater reliance on the private sector in the economy. As the memories of the crisis years faded away in the later elections, however, parties started to put much less emphasis on such policy proposals.

Given this analysis of the content of major Turkish political parties' election manifestos, can we say that they adequately reflect the public's policy concerns and priorities? In Chapter Ten (this volume), Turper presented an analysis of policy issues that are considered to be important by the Turkish public over the last 10 years. Specifically, analysing the Eurobarometer surveys conducted in Turkey annually between 2004 and 2015, she reports that economic problems, and specifically unemployment, constituted the most salient issue for Turkish citizens in all years that the survey was conducted. Moreover, she also highlights that in a survey conducted as part of the International Social Survey Programme (ISSP), about 95 per cent of the respondents 'agree' or 'strongly agree' that 'income differences in Turkey are too large', and about 92 per cent 'agree' or 'strongly agree' that 'it is the government's responsibility to reduce differences in income'. Thus, in addition to economic difficulties, income inequality seems to be a major concern for Turkish citizens, and they also expect primarily the government to act on reducing it.

These public opinion data suggest that there is a good correspondence between the public's concerns and election manifestos of major Turkish parties over the period 2002-15. As we have seen, policy issues related to the domains of the economy and welfare and quality of life are the most important themes in the parties' manifestos, and the economy is the most salient issue for Turkish citizens. Moreover, welfare state expansion, a major theme in parties' election manifestos, also corresponds well to the public's concern with income inequality. And given the different constituencies of major parties, it is perfectly understandable that while the right-wing parties AKP and MHP give more priority to economic growth and infrastructure investments, the more left-wing leaning parties of CHP and DTP/BDP/HDP prioritise more equality and democracy, as well as welfare state expansion.

For further research, more studies are needed to understand the policy-making process of the parties. This is a research area that is currently not well developed in the Turkish context. We have scant information as to how the parties prepare their campaign platforms and election manifestos – whether they use expert opinion, employ outside consultants or resort to public opinion surveys to identify and develop policy proposals. Systematic studies in this respect would significantly enhance our understanding of the link between political parties and public policy in Turkey.

Notes

1. See https://manifestoproject.wzb.eu/
2. The original dataset of the Manifesto Project includes data only for AKP and CHP in the 2002 election. We were able to obtain the coding of the MHP 2002 election manifesto from the Turkish team that coded the manifestos in the subsequent elections. Data are available on request.
3. One important exception in this respect is that the domain of external relations seems to constitute about 25 per cent of all statements in the 2007 election manifesto of DTP/BDP/HDP. Looking in more detail, the relevant policy categories listed under external relations for DTP/BDP/HDP are 'military: negative' and 'peace: positive'. The period around the 2007 election in Turkey was a period of intense armed conflict with respect to the Kurdish issue, so it is quite plausible that the party of the Kurdish political movement emphasised these policy categories in its election manifesto. The categorisation of these policy categories under the domain of external relations is somewhat misleading as they referred to domestic conflict.
4. A similar dynamic is observed in the policy category of 'political corruption: negative'. This category includes statements in favour of the need to eliminate corruption, abuses of bureaucratic power and clientelistic practices. This category was among those frequently appearing in AKP's 2002 election manifesto (4.7 per cent of all statements), yet in subsequent elections it faded in importance (constituting just 0.77 per cent of all statements in the 2015 November election manifesto, for example). This category is not included in the analyses here because it is not among the most frequently mentioned 10 policy categories in AKP's manifestos during the whole period 2002-15.

References

Dahl, R. (1971) *Polyarchy: Participation and opposition*, New Haven, CT: Yale University Press.

Downs, A. (1957) *An economic theory of democracy*, New York: Harper & Row.

Fernandez-Vazquez, P. (2014) 'And yet it moves: The effect of election platforms on party policy images', *Comparative Political Studies*, vol 47, no 14, pp 1919-44.

Hobolt, S.B. and Klemmemsen, R. (2005) 'Responsive government? Public opinion and government policy preferences in Britain and Denmark', *Political Studies*, vol 53, no 2, pp 379-402.

Manin, B., Przeworski, A. and Stokes, S.C. (1999) 'Elections and representation', in A. Przeworksi, S.C. Stokes and B. Manin (eds) *Democracy, accountability, and representation*, New York: Cambridge University Press, pp 29-54.

Page, B.I. and Shapiro, R.Y. (1983) 'Effects of public opinion on policy', *American Political Science Review*, vol 77, no 1, pp 175-90.

Page, B.I. and Shapiro, R.Y. (1992) *The rational public: Fifty years of trends in American policy preferences*, Chicago, IL: University of Chicago Press.

Quinn, T. (2014) *Mandates, manifestos, and coalitions: UK party politics after 2010*, London: The Constitution Society.

Sartori, G. (1976) *Parties and party systems: A framework for analysis*, New York: Cambridge University Press.

Stimson, J.A., MacKuen, M.B. and Erikson, R.S. (1995) 'Dynamic representation', *American Political Science Review*, vol 83, no 3, pp 543-65.

Stokes, S. C. (1999) 'Political parties and democracy', *Annual Review of Political Science,* vol 2, no 1, pp 243-67.

Volkens, A., Lehmann, P., Matthiess, T., Merz, N. and Regel, S. (2016) *The manifesto data collection*, Manifesto project (MRG/CMP/MARPOR), Version 2016b, Berlin: WZB (Wissenschaftszentrum Berlin für Sozialforschung).

TWELVE

Policy analysis in civil society organisations

Güneş Ertan

Introduction

Studies on policy analysis are traditionally confined to public organisations. However, as governance practices are deepening all around the world, more and more non-governmental actors are gaining direct or indirect powers to influence policy-making processes, or are becoming service providers in various policy issue areas that used to be considered the sole domain of public organisations (Salamon, 2002). Hence, policy analysis practices in civil society organisations (CSOs) are also becoming an important question for policy studies.

Despite certain set-backs in the last few years, since the early 1990s, CSOs in Turkey have become considerably more visible and powerful actors in the policy process (Keyman and Icduygu, 2005). Putting aside the effectiveness of Turkish CSOs in shaping policy processes or in carrying out governmental services,[1] this chapter is mainly concerned with providing a short synopsis of the state of civil society in Turkey, and an overview of CSOs' decision-making processes by combining data from various empirical studies. We start by discussing the roots of weak civil society in Turkey followed by an illustration of the current state of civil society. In the following sections we examine policy analysis practices in CSOs with a focus on prevalent decision-making structures and the role of external funds, as well as agenda-setting and evaluation processes. We conclude by arguing that CSOs in Turkey are yet to become effective implementers of policy analysis tools.

A short historical overview of civil society in Turkey

It is almost common knowledge that Turkey is characterised by a very strong, centralised state tradition and a weak civil society. Heper and Yıldırım (2011) consider pervasive populism, clientelism, opportunism and personalism coupled with scarcity of tolerance, altruism and pluralism as the main explanations for the weakness of civil society in Turkey.

The roots of its weak civil society can be traced back to the power of the state and the bureaucratic elite during the Ottoman era (Mardin, 1969). According to Mardin (1969), the Ottoman ruler elite was mainly concerned with keeping control of a religiously and ethnically heterogeneous empire that was spread over a vast amount of land. Consequently, there was not much tolerance for the emergence of different interest groups (Heper, 2000).

Moreover, all of the land under the control of the empire legally belonged to the Sultan. Having total control over economic life also significantly contributed to the suppression of any social group that could challenge the power and authority of the state elite (Mardin, 1969). As Mardin (1969, p 279) puts it:

> In Ottoman society there were no institutional political privileges and immunities, all Ottoman citizens stood in a direct rather than mediated relationship to the supreme authority. This missing link we call civil society. It could be expected that Turkey would encounter difficulties in the development of modern democracy to the extent that this depends on this missing link.

Overall, there was no room for the development of intermediary structures that could function independently from the state. According to Heper and Yıldırım, (2011) trade guilds, village councils and tribal organisations in the Ottoman era were the only organisations that distantly correspond to intermediary structures, since they were still closely monitored and controlled by state bureaucracy.[2]

The dominance of the omnipotent centralised state in all aspects of political, economic and social life did not change much with the birth of modern Turkey in 1923. The lack of basic intermediary structures between state and society continued to be one of the foundational characteristics of the new Republic (Heper and Yıldırım, 2011). Some of the idiosyncrasies of Turkey's extreme emphasis on the formation of a unitary state can be traced back to the dissolution of the Ottoman Empire. During the late 1800s and early 1900s, various non-Muslim minorities such as the Serbians and Greeks claimed their independence, almost always with the support of a foreign power. This dissolution process has mostly been perceived as an act of betrayal by the Turks, and developed as a sense of insecurity and fear towards the minorities that remained within the borders of modern Turkey. The series of Kurdish insurgencies in the 1920s and 1930s also fed the feelings of threat and anxiety of the Kemalist elite, and led to the emergence of a strict centralised state system that emphasised unity at the expense of diversity and pluralism (Baban, 2005).

Following the proclamation of the new Republic, the Turkish state actively promoted the formation of CSOs, but this top-down approach led to emergence of many CSOs that acted as extensions of the state, and failed to function as intermediaries between citizens and the state (Karaman and Aras, 2000).

According to Keyman and Icduygu (2005), since the late 1980s there have been important structural transformations in Turkish state and society. More specifically, these transformations occurred with regards to the four defining elements of the modern Turkish republic, which are (1) a strong state tradition through which the state acts as the privileged and sovereign power operating almost independently from society by an assumed capacity to transform society from above, and deciding which groups, in what ways, could legitimately participate in political life. (2) National developmentalism, as a corollary of the strong state tradition, where the state has been the dominant economic actor until the 1980s with an emphasis on planned, important substituting industrialisation. (3) An organic vision of society, as a way of defining state society relations on the basis of mutual duties and services instead of individual rights and freedoms. (4) The republican model of citizenship, through which the republican elite framed the notion of citizenship as a morally loaded category to achieve a unified national identity by emphasising national interest, individual duties and state sovereignty, instead of a more liberal approach emphasising individual autonomy, rights and freedoms. By the early 1980s, these four elements of Turkish modernity started to be challenged and transformed by the forces of economic and cultural globalisation (Keyman and Icduygu, 2005).

Acceleration of the European Union (EU) accession process by the end of the 1990s also contributed immensely to changes in civil society in Turkey. Following the 1999 Helsinki and 2002 Copenhagen decisions, in 2002, the conservative Justice and Development Party (Adalet ve Kalkınma Partisi, AKP) won the general election, and was able to set up a majority government without the need for coalition partners for the first time in more than 10 years. While the reform processes had already started in 2001, it was the AKP government that displayed a strong political will to implement extensive reforms to meet the Copenhagen political criteria (Kirisci, 2004; Muftuler-Bac 2005; Aydın-Duzgit and Keyman, 2007). These reforms were in the form of changes in the 1982 Constitution that was written by the junta regime, and legislation of new laws. By the end of 2004, nine reform packages had been passed by the Turkish National Assembly, TBMM (Kubicek, 2005). There is extensive research on these institutional reforms (see, for example, Rumford, 2001; Öniş, 2003; Schimmelfennig et al, 2003; Kubicek, 2005; Sarigil, 2007; Usul, 2010). These institutional changes had a significant impact on a variety of issues that are vital for a functioning democracy, such as minority rights, women's rights, restriction of military power and more importantly from a civil society perspective, there have been important improvements in the legal framework in which CSOs operate. For example, the 2004 Association Law removed various restrictions and requirements for establishing and managing associations, and has been considered an important step in liberalising the legal environment for CSOs.

In addition to institutional changes, Rumelili and Boşnak (2015) identify several other mechanisms through which the EU has been shaping civil society in Turkey. These include improving the autonomy and capacity of CSOs through financial assistance; incentivising building and expanding networks among CSOs in Turkey, as well as with European CSOs and Turkish public organisations; and legitimising CSOs' activities and agendas. In addition to these, EU programmes have also encouraged CSOs to design their social programmes using change models based on inputs, outputs and outcomes, and introduced policy analysis tools such as strategic planning and programme evaluation through their funding requirements. These EU programmes were also operational in transforming the opaque working styles of many CSOs into more transparent structures through strict and formal accountability requirements.

Overall the EU has contributed significantly to the strengthening of civil society in Turkey. However, at the organisational level, Rumelili and Boşnak (2015) indicate that the distribution of these benefits has been limited to a restricted group of CSOs that work in some issue areas and to the ones that have the human and material resources to acquire and manage EU funds. Rumelili and Boşnak (2015) also underline the increasing professionalisation of civil society fostered by the EU.

Regardless of these caveats, the EU has been the single most important external actor to have a significant and positive impact on civil society in Turkey in the last few decades, although in recent years it has started to lose its leverage as Turkey has turned its back to the West, becoming more and more aggressive in its foreign policy to become a regional power and a leader in the Middle East and North African (MENA) states. While Turkey is still a candidate country and EU funding for CSOs continues, the EU's power to legitimise civil society actors and their agendas, as well as its role in structuring the normative debates, is significantly eroding (Aydın-Duzgit and Kaliber, 2016). However, despite recent setbacks, EU guidelines and the Acquis continue to act as a template in many technical and less politicised policy issue areas.

Recent political events also had detrimental outcomes on Turkish civil society. The State of Emergency that has been in effect as a result of the July 2016 coup attempt has already led to the closing down of more than 2,000 organisations. Overall, the current picture of civil society is bleak, and it is currently hard to make judgements about the prospects of possible positive changes in the near future.

Mapping the current state of civil society in Turkey

This section aims to provide an overview of the current landscape of civil society in Turkey. Figure 12.1 displays the percentage of active members of CSOs in OECD countries based on World Values Survey (WVS) data. OECD countries that were not surveyed in the 6th wave of the WVS are not included. Specifically, Figure 12.1 displays membership rates for art, environmental, humanitarian, recreational, mutual aid and religious organisations in addition to labour unions, political parties and professional associations. Turkey ranks lowest in all types of CSOs with the exception of membership of political parties. The differences between Turkey and all other OECD countries included in the study are especially stark in recreational, religious and art-related organisations. This indicates that while membership in change-oriented organisations is also limited in non-Turkey OECD countries, membership in less politicised organisations is exceptionally lower in Turkey compared to other OECD members. In addition to this, when non-CSO member individuals were asked in a nation-wide representative study

Policy analysis in civil society organisations

if they would like to join a CSO in the future, 85 per cent of the respondents indicated that they were not considering such behaviour (YA DA, 2015) These findings suggest an overall weakness in civic participation in Turkey, with no expectation for significant progress in the near future.

Figure 12.1: Membership of CSOs, OECD vs Turkey

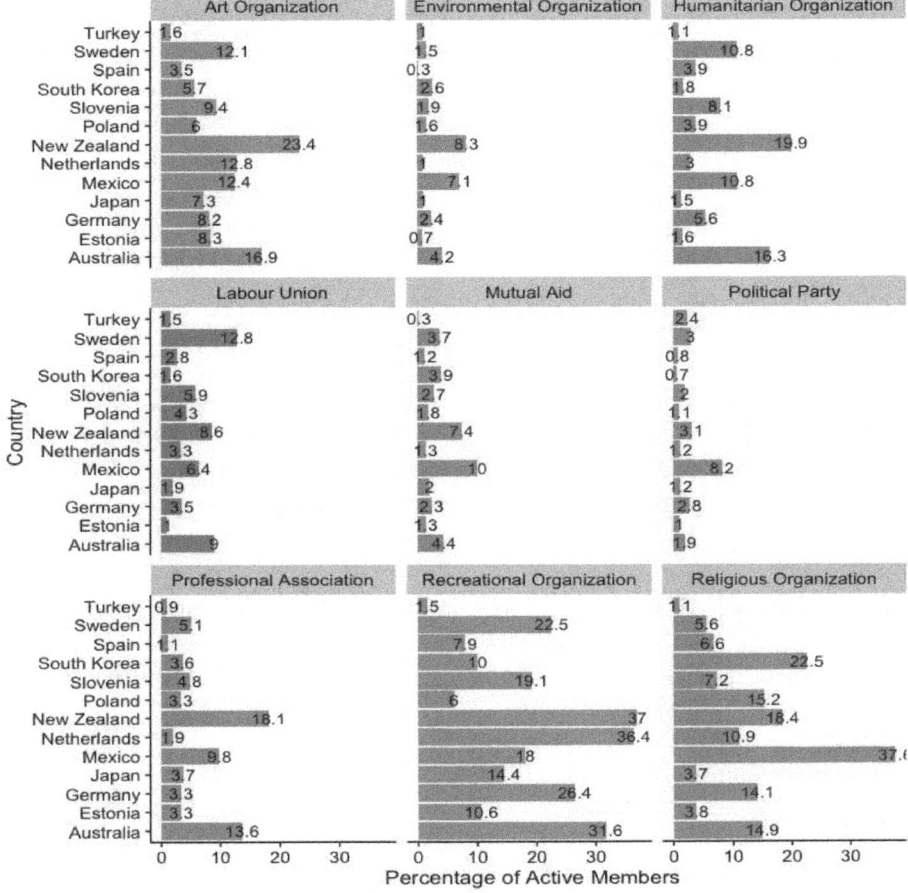

Source: World Values Survey, 6th wave, 2000-14, compiled from www.worldvaluessurvey.org/wvs.jsp

In addition to the macro-structural factors and historical processes mentioned in the previous section, low levels of membership of CSOs in Turkey can also be explained by extremely low levels of interpersonal social trust (Aytac et al, 2017) and confidence in CSOs. In Turkey primordial ties and religious loyalties still have primacy over horizontal ties established among autonomous actors, and dominance of these types of bonding ties hinders the flourishing of vibrant, autonomous and bridging CSOs (Kalaycıoglu, 2002). For example, while the OECD average percentage for people expressing a high level of trust is about 59 per cent, only 12 per cent of people interviewed in Turkey stated high levels of trust in others (OECD, 2011).

Lack of social trust in larger society is also manifested in the relations and networks of CSOs in Turkey. A high level of political polarisation among CSOs is one of the defining characteristics of the topography of civil society in Turkey. Most CSOs choose partners in line with their ideological preferences, and organisations that are inclusive of various political views are rare. Lack of organisations that can act as bridges (sometimes known as 'concord' organisations) among politically distant social groups further contributes to low levels of social trust (Nelson et al, 2007). The divided structure of the network of CSOs in Turkey also inhibits the collective action efforts of civil society towards generating a meaningful impact on society as well as CSOs' organised attempts for affecting public organisations and having a role in policy-making processes.

As Table 12.1 indicates, associations constitute the largest category among all CSOs in Turkey. The total number of CSOs is around 130,000, quite an increase considering that the number was around 70,000 in 2000 and 61,000 in 1994. However, when we assess these numbers in a comparative context, as displayed in Table 12.2, it is possible to see that the total number of CSOs is still substantially lower when compared with advanced democratic nations. There are 616 people per CSO in Turkey, and while this ratio is much better in comparison to some other MENA countries such as Egypt and Afghanistan, it substantially drops when we look at some advanced democracies such as France (49 people per CSO) and Germany (140 people per CSO).

Table 12.1: CSOs by legal status

Status	Frequency
Association	108,172
Foundation	4,968
Unions	221
Professional association	4,794
Cooperative	8,575
Total	126,730

Source: DERBIS (2015) Department of Associations, Ministry of Interior, Turkey. Adapted from YA DA (2015)

Table 12.2: Number of CSOs in select countries

Country name	Number of CSOs	Number of people per CSO
Turkey	126,629	616
India	3,300,000	397
USA	1,532,000	209
France	1,350,000	49
UK	900,000	72
Germany	580,298	140
Brazil	338,000	614
Italy	301,191	201
Russia	227,196	634
Canada	165,000	217
Hungary	70,000	140
Croatia	47,496	89
Egypt	40,000	2,287
Afghanistan	5,789	5,618

Source: Adapted from YA DA (2015)

Figure 12.2 demonstrates the percentage of Turkish CSOs by their number of members based on the findings of a study of 2,500 associations (YA DA, 2015). In Turkey the legal requirement to establish an association is to have about 20 members (ranges between 20 and 25). About 30 per cent of surveyed associations have 50 or fewer members, indicating that there are considerable number of organisations whose membership numbers barely exceed the minimum requirements (YA DA, 2015). The same study also shows that 90 per cent of associations have 25 or fewer founding members, suggesting that most associations were established based on the initiatives of a very small number of individuals, and do not denote formal structures reflecting or emerging on the basis of mass mobilisations (YA DA, 2015).

Figure 12.2: Associations by membership numbers

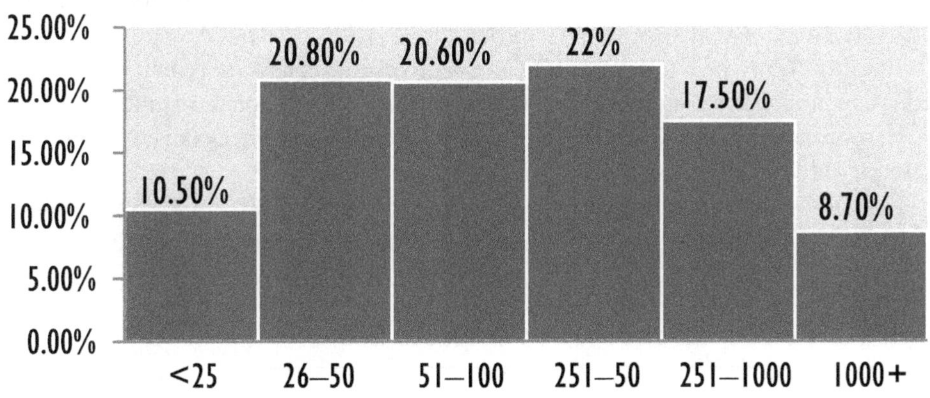

Range	Percentage
<25	10.50%
26–50	20.80%
51–100	20.60%
251–50	22%
251–1000	17.50%
1000+	8.70%

Source: YA DA (2015)

Moreover, the same study shows that only about 9 per cent of associations have more than 1,000 members. These numbers are also indicative in terms of revealing the scarcity of organisations that have a strong social base, or that have the capacity to mobilise large numbers of individuals for various collective action efforts. These overall low membership numbers among associations also raise questions about their representational limits.

Policy analysis in civil society organisations

Recent decades have witnessed an increasing reliance on civil society for governance practices. The theoretical underpinnings of these developments were based on an ambitious line of research that flourished during the early 1990s[3] after the fall of communist regimes in Eastern Europe in the late 1980s. These studies examined the causal mechanisms that linked strong civil society with democratic outcomes. Advocates of this positive relationship between civil society and democracy argued that civil society promotes democracy by acting as an intermediary between the state and society through five different mechanisms, by:

Policy analysis in Turkey

- representing the interests of different social groups in society
- bolstering democratic values such as trust and toleranceacting as schools of democracy through participation in decision-making processes within the CSOs themselves
- holding states accountable
- affecting policy-making processes based on the interests of the social groups they claim to represent.[4]

This section aims to highlight to what extent policy analysis practices within CSOs in Turkey are in line with some of these assumptions based on available data. We first look into prevalent decision-making structures.

Figure 12.3 demonstrates the profile of CSO executive board members in Turkey based on four demographic variables including age, gender, marital status and education, using data from a study that was carried out to reveal the characteristics of CSO executives in Turkey (YA DA, 2015). According to the study only about 14 per cent of CSO executives in Turkey are female and 8 per cent executives are younger than 30. Figure 12.3 was generated using multiple correspondence analyses (MCA), a technique for illuminating associations among categorical variables by visualising contingency tables.[5]

The elements that are highly clustered together in Figure 12.3 indicate a high tendency of these categories to co-exist among CSO executives in Turkey. In

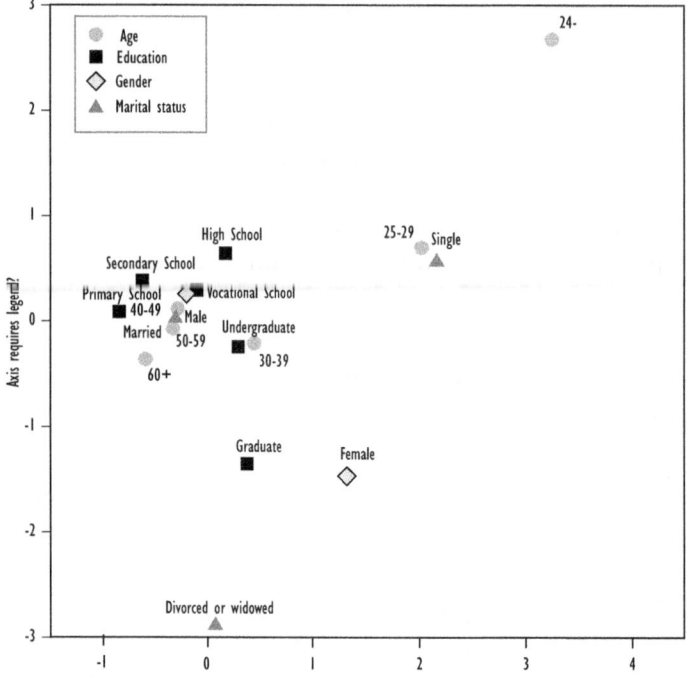

Figure 12.3: Profiles of CSO executive board members in Turkey

Source: Reproduced from YA DA (2015)

other words, married older males with various educational degrees tend to be a common characteristic of many of the executive board members.

This finding may suggest a lack of diversity and representativeness in the decision-making structures of many CSOs in Turkey since overall the data indicates that younger adults and females are under-represented on the executive boards of many CSOs.

In addition to lack of diversity at administrative levels, various studies show that decision-making processes in many CSOs in Turkey are far from being participatory, and membership rarely translates into increased levels of democratic values such as social trust and tolerance when compared with non-members. As displayed in Table 12.3, it is not possible to talk about a competitive process for the executive boards of a majority of the CSOs. About 70 per cent rely on a single list for elections.[6] According to another study of 217 CSOs in Denizli province, social trust and tolerance among members of CSOs and non-members were not significantly different (Decamoğlu, 2008). Moreover, the same study demonstrates that top-down and executive-dominated decision-making processes are common in most organisations (Decamoğlu, 2008). In other words, there is not much evidence for the Tocquevillian argument that CSOs act as schools of democracy within Turkey. Instead, CSOs seem to operate as microcosms of larger society in which hierarchical norms and principles dominate social relations as well as decision-making processes. In line with the overall population in Turkey, cosmopolitan and democratic values also seem to be considerably scant among CSO members.

Another important role of CSOs with regards to governance and democracy is to what extent they represent the interests of different social groups. This issue is very much related with the emergence of agendas at organisational level. How do CSOs decide to tackle certain policy problems but not others? We know that about 40 per cent of CSOs in Turkey rely on grants for their operations (YA DA, 2015), and according to various studies, especially for professionalised CSOs, the emergence of their agendas is very much associated with the priorities of funding agencies such as the EU, Swedish International Development Cooperation Agency, Norwegian Agency for Development Cooperation, Canadian International Development Agency and the Heinrich Böll Foundation (Rumelili and Boşnak 2015; Kuzmonavic, 2010). For example, a human rights-focused CSO employee states how

Table 12.3: Election process of executive board members in CSOs

Election process	%
No election was carried out	2.3
Nobody ran as a candidate, current members were 'convinced' to run	2.6
Elections carried out with single lists	66.9
Elections carried out with multiple lists	7.5
Respected members chose the candidates	3.9
Another organisation determined the candidates	1.9
Previous board members chose the candidates	1.9
More than one candidate ran for presidency	1.7

Source: Reproduced from YA DA (2015)

acquiring EU grants is determined by the subject matters of the proposed projects, as follows:

> [The] EU loves projects on children, women and environment. If you write a project on such issues you are much more likely to receive funds, let's say in comparison to a proposal that focuses on the Kurdish issue. And they favour the organisations that embrace the state discourse. At the end of the day, they do not want to be at odds with the government officials. (quoted in Ertan, 2011, p 15)

Furthermore, international funds are transferred to CSOs on a project basis. CSOs that aim to secure grants are incentivised into shaping their agendas around projects. Project-based activities with well-thought-through logic models that outline the mechanisms through which project inputs are transformed into outputs and outcomes are overall considered to increase the effectiveness of organisations. However, many experts criticise the recent domination of a 'project culture' among CSOs in Turkey, since project-based operations pull civil society towards profit-driven private sector values and workplace practices (Kuzmonavic, 2010), raising more questions regarding the attributes of CSOs associated with democratic outcomes. These concerns are put into perspective in the following statement of a human rights activist:

> We do not get money from EU anymore, we used to in the past. But we gave up. Because they force you to turn your all work in to "projects".... We do so many things that cannot be written as projects or predicted a head. We provide lawyers free of charge to so many different social groups; we cannot simply label them. One day it is a member of a minority religious group discriminated in the workplace, next day it is a woman beaten up by her husband. How are we supposed to turn such services into written projects? The work we do, you simply cannot breakdown it to narrow projects with objectives and measurable outcomes. (quoted in Ertan, 2011, p 14)

International funding may be leading to the professionalisation of some CSOs, and generating some problematic affects on the agenda formation processes in CSOs; considering the low capacity and infrastructure[7] commonly observed in CSOs in Turkey, the net effect of these funds can be still considered positive in terms of empowering non-state actors in a context that has been dominated by a strong state.

Another crucial policy analysis tool for CSOs is programme evaluation. The main goals of evaluation practices are to increase the quality of programmes and to enhance the societal impact of CSOs by revealing what works and what is not. When asked whether they follow up on the impact of their programmes and activities, 85 per cent of CSO representatives stated that they do (YA DA,

2015). However, when we look into the techniques utilised by CSOs in Turkey, most organisations lack systematic evaluation programmes, relying on informal, customary and irregular approaches.

As Figure 12.4 displays, about 20 per cent of interviewed CSO representatives indicated using research-based evaluation methods whereas the majority of organisations utilise less systematic evaluation techniques such as informal exchange of ideas with stakeholders, following the media coverage of an organisation's activities and getting feedback from programme participants and beneficiaries.

Figure 12.4: Approaches to evaluation

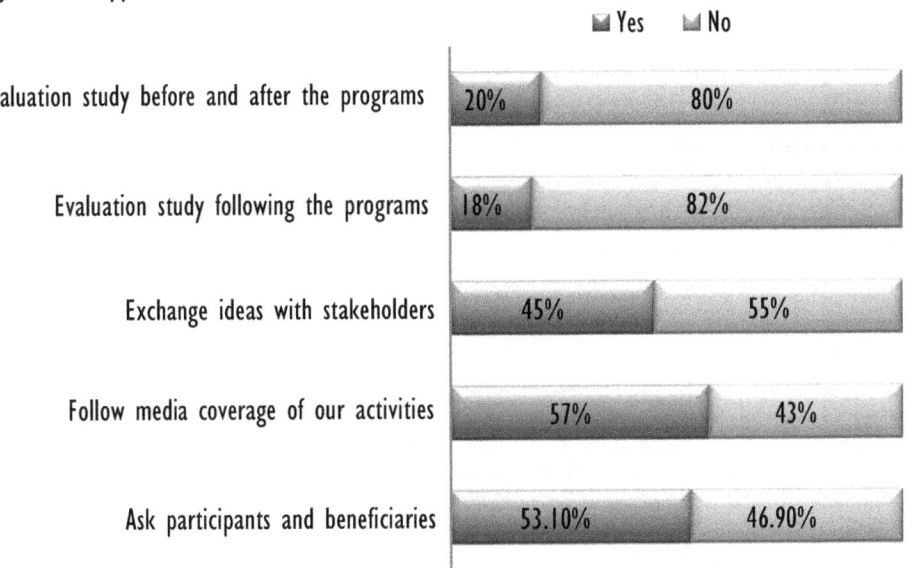

Source: YA DA (2015)

Conclusion

Turkey is historically characterised by a weak civil society and an omnipresent state. While Turkish civil society is considerably sparse in comparison to other OECD countries, since the 1990s, CSOs have increased in number and are becoming more visible and effective. Among various reasons, the EU accession process has been imperative in both reforming the legal structures in which CSOs operate and strengthening their capacity by imposing policy analytic techniques through EU funds and training programmes.

A review of existing empirical studies shows that most CSOs in Turkey have very few members, their executive boards mostly consist of married older males, and administrators tend to dominate decision-making processes through top-down managerial structures. In other words, Turkish CSOs are limited in their representativeness of different social groups in society, lack the capacity to mobilise large populations for collective action, and are far from acting as schools of democracy through their inner workings.

Among the CSOs that are involved in providing programmes and services to various beneficiaries, many depend on international funds to sustain their activities. While these funds reinforce the adoption of policy analytic techniques among recipient organisations, they also enable international donors to shape the agendas of many CSOs. Nevertheless, most CSOs still rely mostly on informal approaches to most stages of policy analysis, as exemplified in the high number of CSOs that rely on unsystematic approaches to programme evaluation.

Despite recent positive trends, the capacity of Turkey's CSOs to promote democracy remains quite limited. The political climate and ongoing State of Emergency following the July 2016 coup attempt further suggests that prospect of a civil society won't be progressing any time soon.

Acknowledgements

I would like to thank Yasama Dair (YA DA) Foundation for sharing invaluable data for this study. I am also indebted to Ugras Ulas Tol for providing feedback and suggestions on early drafts of this chapter.

Notes

[1] Integration of Turkish CSOs into policy-making processes is still a work in progress, and their effectiveness varies significantly among policy issues. For example, while women's CSOs achieved significant gains in terms of legislative change since the mid-2000s, urbanisation policies have been mostly indifferent to the demands of urban-focused CSOs. In terms of service delivery, humanitarian CSOs have been very active, especially in oversees operations, working closely with public organisations. See TUSEV (2015) for a further discussion of the state of relations between CSOs and the state in Turkey.
[2] While Metin Heper and Serif Mardin's views on civil society during the Ottoman era tend to dominate the literature, other views have a much more favourable view of civil society for the same era. See, for example, Zencirci (2014).
[3] Some of the major works based on these assumptions include, but are not limited to, Uhlin (2009) and Paxton (2002).
[4] Many scholars have criticised these assumptions (for example, Armony, 2004).
[5] See Greenacre (1991) for more on MCA.
[6] This may also be due to a lack of interest in running for the board, or due to a limited number of existing members, as mentioned before.
[7] For example, almost 10 per cent of CSOs do not have any office space, with almost half renting their offices. Only 32 per cent of CSOs have paid employees, and these positions are almost overwhelmingly secretarial or janitor types of work. About half of all CSOs have a functioning website and the majority of these organisations are located in Istanbul, Ankara and Izmir (YA DA, 2015). About 18 per cent of CSOs have regular publications and outreach programmes. Consequently, despite the professionalisation trend in the last few decades, CSOs are still mostly characterised by low capacity.

References

Armony, A. (2004) *The dubious link: Civic engagement and democratization*, Stanford, CA: Stanford University Press.

Aydın-Düzgit, S., and Kaliber, A. (2016) 'Encounters with Europe in an era of domestic and international turmoil: Is Turkey a de-Europeanising candidate country?', *South European Society and Politics*, vol 21, no 1 (March), pp 1-14.

Aydın-Duzgit, S. and Keyman, F. (2007) 'Europeanization, democratization and human rights in Turkey', in E. LaGro and K.E. Jorgensen (eds) *Turkey and the European Union: Prospects for a difficult encounter*, London: Palgrave Macmillan, pp 69-89.

Aytac, E., Carkoglu, A. and Ertan, G. (2017) 'Determinants of interpersonal trust in Turkey', *METU Studies in Development*, vol 44, no 1 (April), pp 1-24. [in Turkish]

Baban, F. (2005) 'Community, citizenship and identity in Turkey', in F. Keyman and A. Icduygu (eds) *Citizenship in a global world: European questions and Turkish experiences*, Oxford: Routledge.

Decamoğlu, S. (2008) 'Sosyal sermaye kuramı açısından Türkiye'de demokrasi kültürü uzerine bir değerlendirme', Unpublished thesis, Pamukkale University.

Ertan, G. (2011) 'Civil society as informal networks', Paper presented at the 6th ECPR General Conference, 25-27 August, Reykjavik, Iceland.

Greenacre, M.J. (1991) 'Interpreting multiple correspondence analysis', *Applied Stochastic Models and Data Analysis*, vol 7, no 2, pp 195-210.

Heper, M. (2000) 'The Ottoman legacy and Turkish politics', *Journal of International Affairs*, vol 54, no, pp 63-82.

Heper, M. and Yıldırım, S. (2011) 'Revisiting civil society in Turkey', *Southeast European and Black Sea Studies*, vol 11, no 1, pp 1-18.

Kalaycıoglu, E. (2002) 'Civil society in Turkey: Continuity or change?', in B. Beeley (ed) *Turkish transformation: New century – New challenges*, Huntingdon: Eothen Press, pp 59-78.

Karaman, L. and Aras, B. (2000) 'The crisis of civil society in Turkey', *Journal of Economic and Social Research*, vol 2, no 2, pp 39-58.

Keyman, F.E. and Düzgit, S. (2007) 'Europeanization, democratization and human rights in Turkey', in E. LaGro and K.E. Jørgensen (eds) *Turkey and the European Union: Prospects for a difficult encounter*, Basingstoke: Palgrave Macmillan, pp 69-89.

Keyman, F.E. and Icduygu, A. (eds) (2005) *Introduction citizenship in a global world: European questions and Turkish experiences*, Oxford: Routledge.

Kirisci, K. (2004) 'Between Europe and the Middle East: The transformation of Turkish policy', *Middle East Review of International Affairs*, vol 8, no 1, pp 39-51.

Kubicek, P. (2005) 'The European Union and grassroots democratization in Turkey', *Turkish Studies*, vol 6, no 3, pp 361-77.

Kuzmanovic, D. (2010) 'Project culture and Turkish civil society', *Turkish Studies*, vol 11, no 3, pp 429-44.

Mardin, S. (1969) 'Power, civil society and culture in the Ottoman Empire', *Comparative Studies in Society and History*, vol 11, no 3, pp 258-81.

Muftuler-Bac, M. (2005) 'Turkey's political reforms and the impact of the European Union', *South European Society and Politics*, vol 10, no 1.

Nelson, B.J., Carver, K.A. and Kaboolian, L. (2007) 'Creating concord organizations: Institutional design for bridging antagonistic cultures', in H.K. Anheier and Y. Raj Isar (eds) *Conflicts and tensions*, London: Sage, pp 283-95.

OECD (Organisation for Economic Co-operation and Development) (2011) *Statistics/Society at a Glance* (www.oecd-ilibrary.org/sites/soc_glance-2011-en/08/01/index.html;jsessionid=6ar6hdgtbgtmd.x-oecd-live-02?itemId=%2Fcontent%2Fchapter%2Fsoc_glance-2011-26-en&_csp_=7d6a863ad60f09c08a8e2c78701e4faf).

Öniş, Z. (2003) 'Domestic politics, international norms and challenges to the state: Turkey–EU relations in the post-Helsinki Era', *Turkish Studies*, vol, no 1, pp 9-34.

Paxton, P. (2002) 'Social capital and democracy: An interdependent relationship', *American Sociological Review*, vol 67, no 2, pp 254-77.

Rumelili, B. and Boşnak, B. (2015) 'Taking stock of Europeanization of civil society in Turkey: The case of NGOs', in A. Tekin and A. Gunay (eds) *The Europeanization of Turkey: Polity and politics*, Oxford: Routledge, pp 127-44.

Rumford, C. (2001) 'Human rights and democratization in Turkey in the context of EU candidature', *Journal of European Area Studies*, vol 9, no 1, pp 93-105.

Salamon, L.M. (2002) *The tools of government: A guide to the new governance*, Oxford: Oxford University Press.

Sarigil, Z. (2007) 'Europeanization as institutional change: The case of the Turkish military', *Mediterranean Politics*, vol 12, no 1, pp 39-57.

Schimmelfennig, F., Engert, S. and Knobel, H. (2003) 'Costs, commitment and compliance: The impact of EU democratic conditionality on Latvia, Slovakia and Turkey', *JCMS: Journal of Common Market Studies*, vol 41, no 3, pp 495-518.

TUSEV (2015) *Sivil toplum izleme raporu*, Istanbul: TUSEV Yayinlari.

Uhlin, A. (2009) 'Which characteristics of civil society organizations support what aspects of democracy? Evidence from Post-Communist Latvia', *International Political Science Review*, vol 30, no 3, pp 271-95.Usul, A.R. (2010) *Democracy in Turkey: The impact of EU political conditionality*, Oxford: Routledge.

YA DA (Yasama Dair Vakfi) (2015) *Verilerle sivil toplum kuruluslari*, OFSET Matbaacilik: Ankara.

Zencirci, F.G. (2014) 'Civil society's history: New constructions of Ottoman heritage by the Justice and Development Party in Turkey', *European Journal of Turkish Studies*, vol 19, pp 1-17.

Part Five
Academic, bureaucratic and advocacy-based policy analysis

THIRTEEN

Policy analysis and capacity in the Central Bank of Turkey

Caner Bakır and Mehmet Kerem Coban[1]

Introduction

Central banks are at the centre of macroeconomic policy-making. This is because, within the state apparatus, they design and implement monetary policy and advice governments. Following the global financial crisis (GFC), central banks and bank regulators embraced a macroprudential approach as a new conventional wisdom aiming to limit and contain systemic financial risk through macroprudential regulation (Baker, 2013). The Central Bank of the Republic of Turkey (hereafter CBRT) is no exception (Kara, 2016).

The GFC, as a *structural ideational context*, opened a window of opportunity for a change in the prevailing central banking assumptions at national and international levels that price stability is not sufficient to ensure financial stability. Unsurprisingly, macroprudential regulation that aimed at financial stability emerged as one of the top policy issues among central banks worldwide (Goodhart, 2011; Baker, 2013).[2]

In the post-GFC *structural material context*, the quantitative easing and low interest rate policies adopted by major central banks in developed economies accelerated capital inflows to emerging and developing countries. Turkey already had first-hand experience with the adverse effects of such capital flows in the past leading to economic and financial crises. This included appreciation of the Turkish lira due to the short-term, speculative and unproductive nature of those inflows, along with increasing financialisation in the economy with excess bank credit growth and high leverage (Bakır and Öniş, 2010). The result has been the widening current account deficit that increased the macroeconomic vulnerability to capital flows, signalling a risk of financial/economic crisis. Similar factors had resulted in the 1994 and 2001 Turkish financial crises, which were triggered by sudden stops of capital inflows followed by capital outflows.

In this environment, central banks in developing countries including Turkey used various monetary (for example, interest rate corridor) and macroprudential policy tools (for example, required reserves ratio) to limit and contain macroeconomic and financial stability risks arising in a surge in capital flows (IMF, 2011; Lim et al, 2011). Specifically, the leadership at the CBRT *proactively* engaged in policy design aimed at ensuring financial and macroeconomic stability triggered by policy instruments (for a discussion based on causal mechanisms, see Akgunay and Bakır, 2016). It experimented with what Hakan Kara, Chief Economist of CBRT,[3] called a 'new policy mix', or 'an unconventional approach in monetary policy' in November 2010 (see Kara, 2012, p 2). The policy mix involved an asymmetrical interest rate corridor and reserve option mechanism to manage capital (in)flows more proactively. As such, the CBRT lowered its policy rate, widened the interest rate corridor and increased reserve requirements to slow capital inflows.[4] The aim was to enhance the resilience of the economy against volatility in capital flows through influencing excess credit growth and exchange rate appreciation.

In this context, between September 2010 and August 2015, the CBRT used its existing monetary policy tools, aiming to smooth financial cycles, excess credit growth in particular, and to stabilise the economy in the medium term (Kara, 2016). The new policy mix included four policy instruments: 'the joint use of the interest rate corridor between overnight borrowing and lending rates, liquidity policies and required reserves in addition to short-term policy rates' (Kara, 2012, pp 2, 3; see also Akcelik et al, 2013).

It is widely held that 'the Turkish state is weak and cannot adopt a proactive approach in the financial services industry by steering and coordinating policy community' (Bakır, 2006a, p 204; see also Bakır, 2015a). This is due to 'fragmentation' and 'a lack of coordination and institutionalised consensus building' among key actors, and lack of 'shared vision' and 'policy coherence' in the state apparatus (see Bakır, 2006a, 2015a).

The Turkish experience in policy design and implementation in macroeconomic and financial stability shows otherwise. As Kara (2012, p 1) concluded, 'the new policy framework has been quite effective in reducing the macro financial risks related to a sudden reversal of capital flows by engineering a "soft landing" of the Turkish economy' in 2011. It is puzzling that a seemingly weak state acted strong by adopting a proactive monetary policy to effectively address the macro-financial risks. This issue deserves investigation because it shows that weak state capacity (see Bakır, 2006a) in the macroeconomic and financial policy sector in Turkey can be complemented via a strong bureaucratic policy capacity.

If, as Kara notes, '[o]ur implementation of unorthodox policies, and our courage to engage with such issues following [the global financial crisis] were due to our infrastructure' (Ceyhun, 2011), then it is legitimate to take a modest step to investigate that infrastructure, what we call *the policy capacity in central banking*. The CBRT's experience in policy analysis and design offers an opportunity to examine its innovative policy mix to deal with the build-up of macro-financial risks associated with capital flows that started in November 2010.

This chapter examines policy capacity and policy analysis in the context of the CBRT's role in policy design and implementation that relate to macroeconomic and financial stability in Turkey. Specifically, it focuses on agency-level (that is, individual and organisational) complementarities that relate to the Bank's policy capacity. These are related to the Bank's knowledge and expertise, human capital, recruitment and career development prospects, its ability to collect and analyse data, its formal organisation and departments related to policy analysis, its organisational culture emphasising measured risk-taking in policy design and implementation (see also Bakır, 2007, 2012a) and its policy entrepreneurship linking its bureaucratic agenda with its governmental agenda due mainly to its strong analytical, operational and political capacity.

This chapter argues that proactive behaviour in monetary policy design and implementation is most likely when a central bank has strong analytical, operational and political policy capacity. The contribution of this chapter to the literature on policy analysis is threefold. First, it relates policy design, analysis and capacity literatures to central banking, which has been grossly neglected so far. Although policy analysis of the Central Bank of Israel was introduced in *Policy analysis in Israel* (see Flug, 2016), there has not been any engagement with policy analysis and capacity literatures. Second, it responds to the calls that there is 'little empirical evidence or systematic research' in policy analytical capacity, 'the ability of an organisation to produce valuable policy-relevant research and analysis on topics of their choosing' (Oliphant and Howlett, 2010, pp 439-40; see also Howlett, 2009). The literature presented below is tested against the findings from interviews, personal communications with policy analysts and documentary analysis. Third, this chapter, to our knowledge, is the first in public policy literature on Turkey that focuses on *policy analysis* in the public sector.

This chapter is informed by interview data gathered for our earlier individual studies on the Turkish macroeconomic and financial regulatory bureaucracies over the last 10 years, analyses of secondary literature, newspapers, official reports (for example, annual reports, working papers, etc) and websites published by the public bureaucracies and written correspondence with policy advisers.

The remainder of this chapter is organised as follows. The next section introduces some of the key concepts and approaches adopted in the literature on policy analysis and capacity at organisational (that is, bureaucratic) level. This is followed by organisational analytical and operational capacity and then political capacity at the CBRT. The conclusion summarises the main findings and arguments.

Policy analysis, policy capacity and central banking

It is widely accepted that the 'aim of policy analysis is to permit improvements in decision making and policymaking by allowing a fuller consideration of a broader set of alternatives, with a wider context, with the help of more systematic tools' (Dror, 1971, p 232, cited in Jordan and Turnpenny, 2015, p 13). It is also characterised as 'a method for structuring information and providing opportunities for the development of alternative choices for the policymaker' (Gill and Saunders, 1992, pp 6-7, cited in Howlett et al, 2015). As such, policy tools are at the heart of policy analysis, which are important parts of the policy formulation process.

Policy tools and policy capacity

There are three main types of policy tools that inform policy design and analysis in the policy formulation process:

> *Simple tools* such as checklists, questionnaires, impact tables or similar techniques for assisting expert judgement. *More formal tools*, such as scenario techniques, [cost benefit analysis], risk assessment and multi-criteria analysis, which entail several analytical steps corresponding to predefined rules, methods and procedures. *Advanced tools* which attempt to capture the more dynamic and complex aspects of societal or economic development by performing computer-based simulation exercises. (Jordan and Turnpenny, 2015, p 18; emphasis added)

We adopt this taxonomy in our discussion on policy tools and analysis. However, such a discussion would be incomplete without linking it to policy capacity, which relates to the ability of bureaucracy to identify policy objectives and tools, as well as to manage their implementation to achieve policy outcomes. As defined by Wu et al (2015, p 166), policy capacity is '[t]he set of skills and resources – or competences and capabilities – necessary to perform policy functions.' Howlett and Ramesh (2014, p 322) refer to policy capacity with a focus on 'governance capacity' as 'the resources and skills a government requires to steer a governance mode so as to make sound policy choices and implement them effectively.' Following Howlett and Ramesh (2014), policy capacity is defined here as an organisation's sources of making and implementing sound policy decisions. Here, the capacity of bureaucracy is crucial in the design and implementation of public policies (Howlett and Ramesh, 2016), so that the given public sector actor can fulfil its public role in society.

There are three dimensions of policy capacity at bureaucratic level (Wu et al, 2015, p 167). These are *organisational analytical capacity*, *organisational operational capacity* and *organisational political capacity*. Analytical policy capacity requires 'a recognized requirement or demand for research (a market), a supply of qualified researchers, ready availability of quality data, policies and procedures to facilitate productive interactions with other researchers, and a culture in which openness is encouraged and risk taking is acceptable' (Riddell, 2007, p 5, cited in Oliphant and Howlett 2010, p 440). It 'help[s] to ensure policy actions are *technically sound* in the sense they can contribute to attainment of policy goals' (Wu et al, 2015, pp 167-8; original emphasis). In the context of central banking, we consider analytical capacity as the capacity to collect, process and analyse relevant information and data that translate to policy actions. Policy analytical capacity is related to policy learning and is not limited to organisational competence in use and command over data collection and analysis, but to the broader organisational context:

> ... a recognized requirement or demand for [analysis]; a supply of qualified [analysts]; ready availability of quality data; policies and procedures to facilitate productive interactions with other [analysts]; and a culture in which openness is encouraged and risk-taking is acceptable. (Riddell, 2007, p 7, cited in Howlett, 2009, p 156)

Organisational operational capacity 'allows the alignment of resources with policy actions so that they can be *implemented* in practice' (Wu et al, 2015, p 168; original emphasis). In this regard, for an organisation to implement policies, the organisation needs strong intellectual leadership and human capital, which are also indispensable assets for any central bank.

Finally, organisational political capacity 'helps to obtain and sustain *political support* for policy actions' (Wu et al, 2015, p 168; original emphasis). Analytical and operational capacities refer to internal sources of policy capacity, while political capacity relates to an external source of policy capacity (Pal and Clark, 2015; Wu et al, 2015). Internal and external sources of policy capacity are also crucial for effective and robust monetary and financial stability-related policies.

Central banking and policy capacity

Fragile banking and financial sectors (Minsky, 2008 [1986]; Calomiris and Haber, 2014) require a high level of policy capacity. The high level of opaqueness of financial institutions' balance sheets (Flannery et al, 2004, 2013) and increasingly complex financial and banking services and products (Campbell et al, 2011) are two main sources of motivation for central banks and regulatory agencies to closely supervise and robustly regulate the financial services industry. Thus, policy capacity and policy analysis become indispensable for a central bank in the conduct of monetary policy and/or regulation of the financial system.

Quaglia (2005a, p 554) offers an excellent analysis of the micro-institutional foundation of a central bank's resources and strategies: 'Central banks can be skilful and influential political actors, depending on the resources they possess, first and foremost, tangible assets, such as existing degrees of independence [from the government in implementing monetary policy], and intangible assets, such as expertise, authority, and the strategies of the bank' (see also Quaglia, 2005b). This organisational institutionalist perspective informs the policy capacity discussion in this chapter.

Policy capacity relates to a central bank's legal independence to conduct policy analysis and thereby implement monetary policy without major interventions from the government. Overcoming the time-inconsistency problem (Kydland and Prescott, 1977), whereby enabling a central bank to act according to an economic rationale, central bank independence (CBI) became popular around the world in the 1990s (Alesina and Summers, 1993; Cukierman, 2008; Fernandéz-Albertos, 2015). Rather than being focused on the political feasibility of a policy (Meltsner,

1972), formal and informal independence from political pressures allow the central bank to focus on designing and implementing an appropriate monetary policy.

Domestic and international structural shocks such as the 2001 Turkish economic crisis and the GFC opened a window of opportunity for institutional change in central banking. Given the politicised nature of the central banking tradition in Turkey, the legal reform in 2001 that supplied formal independence to the CBRT is conceived as an institutional milestone, a product of institutional policy entrepreneurship (Bakır, 2007, pp 71-88; 2009). Legal independence increased the formal organisational operational capacity of the CBRT, as the government's access to its funds for deficit financing was prohibited. Increased legal independence strengthens the CBRT's capacity because it contributes to insulate monetary policy design and implementation from political interference (Bakır, 2007). Further, the CBRT's increased transparency and accountability (Bakır, 2006b) contributed especially to its analytical and operational policy capacity. To sustain this capacity, the CBRT and the government established channels for communication for better policy coordination.

Organisational analytical and operational capacity at the Central Bank of Turkey

A comparative analysis of organisational change in macroeconomic bureaucracies (the CBRT, Treasury and Ministry of Finance) in Turkey has shown that the CBRT moved to a central position in macroeconomic policy-making from the periphery along with the Treasury, while the Ministry of Finance lost its place at the centre and moved to the periphery in the 1990s (Bakır, 2012a, b). Specifically, the CBRT and the Treasury have been successful in building organisational capacity that resonates with organisational adaptation to the changing structural and institutional contexts since the deregulatory 1980s (Bakır, 2012a, b).

Any organisation needs analytical and operational capacity so as to produce knowledge, make (informed) decisions, and then implement and evaluate those decisions. Knowledge has a critical role in the policy process, from analysis and design to evaluation (MacRae, 1991; Radaelli, 1995). Thus in any central bank, the organisational structure somehow relates to production of knowledge based on data collection and analysis.

Human capital

If analytical capacity relates to the ability to produce and process data leading to knowledge, there is a need for a discussion on the quality of human resources. Various annual reports of the CBRT show that while the total number of staff at the CBRT fluctuated between 1997 and 2015, the ratio of employees holding Master's and PhD degrees has almost doubled since the adoption of an inflation-targeting regime in 2006.

Various departments, the Research and Monetary Policy Department in particular, have benefited from recruitment and career development policies. In addition to its organisational credibility and reputation, the CBRT has strong career patterns that relate to selection and promotion of its staff within an organisational hierarchy. Specifically, it used to attract graduates from various disciplines in the social sciences, economics in particular, with strong quantitative skills. In addition to a competitive salary and fringe benefits, the horizontal organisational structure dismantling the rigid hierarchical structure in the post-2001 period prioritised policy analytic 'knowledge and skills' over 'seniority' (interviews). The result was the promotion of a much younger generation of policy workers over old cadres.

In regard to human capital investments for policy workers, there are four main policies and venues at the Bank. The first is the Bank's policy to allow an increasing number of personnel to go abroad for postgraduate studies. For example, 24 researchers working in the CBRT were sent abroad by the Bank between 1997 and 2011 to do a PhD (Ceyhun, 2011). As to the impact of education abroad on bank personnel, senior officials observed significant contributions such as self-empowerment, a rise in productivity and a wider policy perspective among staff (Gürler, 2013). More importantly, staff who went abroad claimed that the graduate education enabled them to analyse the issues through various perspectives, qualifying them to do better analyses (Gürler, 2013, p 82). Matching the right skills with requirements for robust policy analysis and implementation contributes to the Bank's policy analytical capacity.

The second is on-the-job training, in which personnel receive training on panel data, Stata and other statistical methods. The third source of professional training contributing to policy analysis is attendance at international academic conferences and workshops at which the staff present research findings. Finally, the International Monetary Fund (IMF) and The World Bank seminars on formal modelling serve as important workforce development opportunities providing new learning experiences and skills (interviews). There is also a further opportunity in professional and academic training in the context of knowledge transfer that came with the establishment of the Istanbul School of Central Banking. The School aims to provide an environment for interaction on central banking in emerging and developing economies, conducting analyses and, more importantly, organising conferences and workshops while training central bankers from around the developing world.[5]

Policy tools, data collection, analysis and knowledge production

In regard to monetary policy, the Research and Monetary Policy Department generates several policy alternatives and then tries to narrow them down to a few solutions. One of the *simple* policy tools used at the outset of policy analysis is brainstorming that facilitates active and open discussions on policy problems, alternatives, objectives and tools. Policy options are narrowed down via several strategies where discussions at interdepartmental meetings and seminars are of utmost importance (interviews).

The CBRT has a system-wide perspective in data collection and analysis.[6] It collects and uses data on macro and micro-economic analyses ranging from economic growth, the labour market and the balance of payments to consumer behaviour and business cycles. Like advanced country central banks, the Bank uses *more formal* econometric and statistical tools. In this regard, inflation and output gap forecasts are of the utmost importance in inflation targeting, where interest rates are used as policy instruments to stabilise prices and minimise output volatility. In a similar vein, expectation surveys, designed and analysed in coordination with the Statistics Department, are one of the key tools that the CBRT uses in designing monetary policy. For example, the Bank uses formal tools such as structural Vector Auto Regressions (VAR), panel VAR and Autoregressive Distributed Lag (ADL) models for analysing the effects of monetary policy on prices and inflation. As noted above, it also engages with a wide range of micro-level analyses on, for example, labour markets, the impact of economic reforms on labour supply, income distribution, poverty and health topics. Most of these are cross-section analyses while panel data analyses are also used.

Macroeconomic models of applied general equilibrium theory are to analyse macroeconomic variables such as economic growth, business cycles and the effects of monetary policy. Examples include theoretical models such as Dynamic Stochastic General Equilibrium (DSGE) and Dynamic General Equilibrium (DGE) models for modelling actor behaviour, as well as panel data and estimation techniques and the Generalised Method of Moments (GMM) to estimate parameters in these models, to name but a few. These models may be considered as *advanced tools* used for monetary policy formulation.

Although the Banking Supervision and Regulation Authority (BRSA) is the principal prudential regulator, the CBRT also has a duty to take measures to ensure stability in the financial system, money and foreign exchange markets. Thus, it analyses the systemic risk and resilience of the financial system. Its related policy analyses include:

> ... [r]egular daily and weekly reports of credit developments, credit and liquidity risks, FX [foreign exchange] net position etc and the monthly report submitted to MPC meetings are used in systemic risk assessments. Vintage analysis of retail loans, interest rate risk scenarios, DuPont analysis (decomposition of banks' profitability), stress tests, and impact studies of macroprudential tools are also employed. The Financial Conditions and Financial Strength Indices [that] provide information about the overall strength of the financial sector. (FSB, 2015, p 18)

Within the Financial Stability Committee (FSC), the CBRT uses a heat map as a risk assessment tool that 'is utilised to illustrate how a financial shock can affect financial stability and the real economy both quantitatively and qualitatively' (FSB, 2015, p 17).

> [It is] a useful first step in expanding their risk assessment toolkit to facilitate more objective and efficient discussions of financial stability risks within the SRAG [Systemic Risk Assessment Group]. The authorities [both the CBRT and BRSA] aim to use this analysis as the basis for developing early warning models that can provide a more forward-looking perspective. Such models are expected to supplement stress test analyses and quantitative impact studies with observed data as well as qualitative assessments that incorporate financial system intangibles. (FSB, 2015, p 17)

In a similar vein, the CBRT collects data and analyses leverage and the FX risk of the non-financial corporate sector with particular emphasis on 'unhedged corporate net short FX positions' (FSB, 2015 p 16). In this respect,

> It also initiated in 2013 a corporate sector monitoring project ('RESIM'), comprising a mostly qualitative survey of corporate sector representatives, which includes data on FX borrowing and its motivation. In addition, the CBRT began to publish the Financial Accounts Report in 2012, which includes flow of funds data for the household and corporate sectors. (FSB, 2015 p 16)

The CBRT also works with outside experts whose knowledge and expertise in some of the formal techniques complement the Bank's policy analytical capacity (interviews). This is because in-house knowledge and expertise may not always be adequate to design new policies and their implementation. Here the department benefits from external consultation, knowledge transfer and learning from national and international experts. Our interviews also reveal that there are consultation meetings with other central bankers and deliberate learning from others' experiences who have faced similar policy challenges (for policy learning and policy capacity linkages, see Bennett and Howlett, 1992; Borrás, 2011). Further, IMF, the Bank for International Settlements and the European Central Bank also offer technical assistance in organisational capacity-building. For example, 'the foundations' of the CBRT's stress-testing framework was based on the technical assistance of the European Central Bank in 2011 (FSB, 2015, p 17). Moreover, there are occasions when the CBRT needs external advice and lesson-drawing from other countries' experiences. For example, the successful Mexican experience in foreign exchange auctions was examined and de-contextualised by the CBRT. Consulting the academic literature and central banking publications, as well as discussions at BIS meetings, also provide policy inputs to the CBRT (see Bakır, 2007, pp 76-7).

It should be noted that communication strategy is a policy instrument used by the Central Bank to inform its target audience and influence their expectations. Monetary Policy Committee announcements and the Inflation Report are the two main instruments in this regard. The CBRT also publishes working papers and policy briefs. Without the capacity to use more sophisticated methods and techniques, let alone the availability of data collected or accessed, monetary policy analysis is less likely. Moreover, it is worth noting that the CBRT launched an academic journal, *Central Bank Review*, in 2001, which also publishes pieces from leading central banking experts. The widely analysed issues in these publications reflect some of the key financial economic and monetary policy issues in Turkey, such as consumer credit, inflation, and capital flows management. An overview of the content of these publications over the last two decades shows increasingly technical language and high-powered econometrics and modelling tools, demonstrating the increased policy analytical capacity of CBRT personnel over time.

Organisational culture that relates to policy analysis

It should be noted that following the 2001 CBI legal reform, the CBRT has gradually moved from a hierarchical organisational structure to a horizontal structure that facilitates more interdepartmental interactions and collaboration, and promotes a culture based on open discussions and risk-taking (Bakır, 2012a). The CBRT's culture of decision-making appears to be very open, inclusive and encouraging of new ideas and innovative thinking, suggesting strong policy analytical capacity. Further, conflicting views among various departments over a policy are resolved through the arbitration of the CBRT governor and deputy governors (interviews).

Formal organisational structure that relates to policy analysis and capacity

The formal organisation of the CBRT relates to its analytical and operational organisational capacity. The Research and Monetary Policy Department, the Statistics Department and the Banking and Financial Institutions Department contribute to the analytical and operational capacity of the CBRT in support of price stability and financial stability. These departments play significant interrelated and complementary roles in policy analysis at the CBRT.

Research and Monetary Policy Department

The Research and Monetary Policy Department is the key department in policy analysis at the CBRT, which also hosts the Monetary Policy Support Division. This department is placed at the centre of monetary policy-making due to the inflation-targeting regime adopted by the CBRT in 2006 after the 2001 legal reform (Bakır, 2012a, pp 158-61; see also Bakır, 2017). As such, the number of its staff doubled from 46 in 2000 to 101 in 2011 (Ceyhun, 2011). It hosts about 70 researchers with MA degrees and 30 researchers with PhDs.

The primary mandate of the department is to compile data on several financial economic indicators and to conduct research that informs monetary policy decisions.[7] For example, it collects and analyses data on prices and various indicators related to pricing behaviours, the pricing of loans, inflation and inflation expectations. It is primarily responsible for producing evidence-based research related to monetary policy based on formal modelling and forecasting.

Members of the Monetary Policy Committee (MPC) are informed by members of the General Directorate of Research and Monetary Policy through presentations on various topics ranging from inflation, financial markets and the labour market to macroeconomic conjectural developments in domestic and global markets and fiscal policy in the morning sessions of the MPC meetings (interviews). This is followed by presentations made by the General Directorates of Research and Monetary Policy, Banking and Financial Organisations and Markets (see Ceyhun, 2011).

Further, this department is active in dissemination of its analyses. For example, it produces working papers and research reports along with the Research Notes in Economics Series published by the CBRT. Some of the topics covered include capital mobility, consumer credit, cultural issues and consumer behaviour, inflation rate, economic growth projections, unemployment rate and yield curve, as well as ex-post analyses of implemented policies, such as the reserve option mechanism.[8]

Statistics Department

Data collection and analysis are important for any central bank.[9] As such, the CBRT collects and uses data on prices, the payments system, public finance and trade statistics, among other areas. Thus, another key department that contributes to policy analysis in the CBRT is the Statistics Department. It hosts three divisions: Monetary and Financial Data Division, Balance of Payments Division and Real Sector Data Division. This department is tasked with the production or gathering of data necessary for the functioning of the CBRT.[10] Since it has a mandate to prepare tables of monetary and financial statistics, the Statistics Department plays a crucial role in the collection and dissemination of data within the CBRT. It also compiles data produced by other bureaucracies, such as the Ministry of Finance (for example, on central government expenditures) or consumer price data produced by the Turkish Statistical Institute (TURKSTAT).

Banking and Financial Institutions Department

The third critical department in policy analysis is the Banking and Financial Institutions Department.[11] It hosts six divisions: Macro Financial Analysis Division, Financial Stability Division, Financial Tools and Regulations Division,

International Institutions and Regulations Division, Financial Data and Monitoring Division and Currency Legislation Division.

The new consensus among central bankers that price stability does not guarantee financial stability and that there is a need for a macroprudential approach to financial regulation to address systemic financial risk (Baker, 2013) increased the importance of policy design and implementation with macroprudential intent in the CBRT. Unsurprisingly, the Banking and Financial Institutions Department has gained significance following the establishment of the Financial Stability Committee in June 2011. It is the key unit within the CBRT on financial stability-related policy analysis and design. In addition to publishing the *Financial stability report* twice a year, and presenting financial stability-related issues to MPC meetings monthly, and informing the CBRT semi-annually, it participates in SRAG (Systemic Risk Assessment Group) meetings. As such, it been reconfigured to strengthen its focus on financial stability analysis with the establishment of Financial Stability Division in August 2013. Further, this division initiated 'a "Financial Data Project" to identify evolving data needs for banking sector, non-financial corporations and household analysis' (FSB, 2015, p 16).

Regarding financial stability, the CBRT collects data on banks' balance sheets, focusing especially on the data on foreign exchange exposure of non-financial corporations to assess the risk arising from unhedged corporate net short FX positions. In regard to containing macro-financial risk, it operates in collaboration with other bureaucracies such as the Treasury, the BRSA, Capital Markets Board and the Deposit Insurance Fund.

The CBRT has several Memoranda of Understanding (MoU) with the BRSA to cooperate on data-related issues and share databases.[12] As such, it can have access to specialised databases that are managed by the BRSA. For example, the it has access to offsite supervisory data from the BRSA rather than using its own power to collect these data directly from banks. The CBRT can monitor the quality and performance of credit allocation by gathering data from the BRSA. It also contributes to risk assessment tool development and data gap identification at the SRAG under the FSC.

One of its other crucial roles is to disseminate knowledge produced by the department on financial stability. The *Financial stability report* is the flagship publication prepared by this department where the CBRT also signals the financial economic challenges ahead. The CBRT publishes macro stress test results in the report. The stress test framework 'evaluates the impact of economic growth, FX and interest rate shocks on the banking sector via the channels of credit risk, re-pricing risk, income risk and FX risk' (FSB, 2015, p 18). Although previous issues of the report used to be more concerned with interpreting indicators of financial stability, such as household indebtedness or the credit volume in the Turkish economy, more recent issues involve analyses of trends in those variables.

Organisational political capacity: strong interpersonal ties matter

In regard to containing macro-financial risk, the 'new policy mix' noted above faced its limitations in early 2011. The CBRT did not have a formal mandate to oversee or take measures to address system-wide risks. Thus, facing difficulties in limiting commercial bank credit growth with its monetary policy instruments (Gurkaynak et al, 2015), it needed supplementary and complementary macroprudential instruments implemented by the BRSA.[13] However, the BRSA had a microprudential approach to financial regulation and supervision focusing on the financial soundness of individual banks rather than systemic financial stability focusing on the financial system as a whole. The CBRT was acting properly vis-à-vis its cultural environment (that is, macroprudential regulation became an informal and common programmatic idea among central banks) rather than limiting itself instrumentally vis-à-vis its official objective of price stability. Such a cultural environment was lacking as the legitimate context for the BRSA.

Some senior officials at the CBRT and BRSA noted at our interviews that these strong personal ties facilitated the establishment of the FSC in June 2011 that became a venue where the CBRT translated its macro-financial stability agenda to a governmental agenda. *Strong interpersonal ties* between the then CBRT Governor, Erdem Başçı,[14] and the then Deputy Prime Minister for Economic and Financial Affairs, Ali Babacan,[15] have been one of the key temporal sources of political capacity enhancing both the CBRT's and Turkish state's policy capacity in this instance. The strength and content of the interpersonal ties included a shared neighbourhood, childhood and schooling (*Hürriyet*, 2011). The policy entrepreneurship of the CBRT, under the leadership of the then Governor, Basci, defined the problem (that is, macro-financial risks) and its solution (that is, macroprudential policy), and linked them with the political leadership. The FSC became a venue for close cooperation and collaboration between the CBRT, BRSA, Ministry of Economy, as well as the Treasury. The central bureaucratic agenda of the CBRT that had been translated to the governmental agenda with the establishment of the FSA was to facilitate the BRSA's use of its prudential policy tools to complement the policy mix (interviews). The BRSA eventually became a vital contributor to policy design and implementation processes to limit bank credit growth (IMF, 2016, pp 60-2).

Conclusions

Central banking in an interdependent world involves a technical and complex policy design and implementation. The GFC has shown that maintaining price stability does not guarantee financial stability. Based on the CBRT's experimentation with the new policy mix between 2010 and 2011, this chapter has argued that policy design and implementation to achieve financial and macroeconomic stability requires rigorous policy analysis and relies on a high level of policy capacity including analytical, operational and political dimensions.

It was these dimensions of policy capacity that enabled the CBRT to translate its policy design and implementation preferences for a governmental agenda. As such, a seemingly weak Turkish state acted proactively to contain and limit macro-financial risks arising from a surge in capital inflows.

We showed that various dimensions of the CBRT's policy capacity contributed to policy design and implementation. Indeed, a central bank with internal and external sources of policy capacity can dominate the policy process that relates to macroeconomic bureaucracy. This, in turn, calls our attention to a need for linkages between policy entrepreneurship and policy capacity to design and implement policies.

This chapter finds that policy analysis at the CBRT is informed by six key internal sources of policy capacity. These are (1) ready availability of quality data; (2) human capital with high technical knowledge and expertise in evidence-based policy analysis and advice; (3) recruitment and career development practices enhancing policy analysis; (4) horizontal organisational arrangements that facilitate more interdepartmental interaction, communication and collaboration; (5) an organisational culture that is based on open discussions and risk-taking, promoting policy innovation; and (6) policy learning and transfer capabilities arising from interactions with a transnational epistemic community of central bankers.

This chapter also finds that the much-neglected political support given to the CBRT's policy design and implementation is the most critical type of capacity. This is an external source of policy capacity. In particular, this chapter highlights the significance of *strong* social ties between central bankers (knowledge producers and brokers) and key politicians (decision-makers) in enhancing the policy capacity (for actors in policy formulation, see Howlett, 2009, 2011). In a world of complex monetary policy-making, central banks around the world need to have high analytical and implementation capacities. They also need to have a political capacity to translate their policy preferences to governmental policy.

This finding offers a valuable insight into the CBI literature that has overemphasised central banks' independence from politicians. This dominant paradigm in central banking ignores the fact that central bankers need the support of politicians to translate their policy preferences into government actions. Further, politicians are not homogenous entities sharing the same beliefs. For example, some politicians have a tendency to intervene in monetary policy, while others are committed to the CBI and advance a central bank's policies in bureaucratic and political arenas. Thus, based on evidence from Turkey, we also argue that political capacity is of the utmost importance in translating a central bank's bureaucratic agenda on financial stability to the governmental agenda, strengthening state capacity by steering policy formulation and implementation.

Capitalising on the sources of organisational capacity (that is, analytical, operational and political), central banks design and implement monetary policy that is attentive to both macroeconomic and financial stability. To contain macroeconomic and systemic risks without compromising price stability, policy capacity is vital. However, politicians should note that policy capacity that contains macrofinancial risks is not a substitute for overdue structural reforms in Turkey.

Further, policy capacity in Turkey in general and at the CBRT in particular is contextually and temporally contingent. Thus, it is volatile. This has been more visible with Turkey's seismic regime change taking place at a structural level. The CBRT's policy capacity has been eroding in recent years since its introduction of a 'new policy mix'. Its statutory independence is not internalised by the government, as evidenced by senior politicians' fierce partisan campaigns for lower interest rates and their efforts to *blame* the CBRT's interest rate policy for causing inflation, lower economic growth and investment rates (see Bakır, 2015b; *Financial Times*, 2015). Arguably, monetary policy formulation and implementation are now subject to partisan challenges that have been more severe than that of the pre-2001 period. This undermines the CBRT's confidence, ability and willingness to provide innovative policy advice and its implementation. Further, politicians increasingly intervene in senior appointments, staff recruitment, career development and promotion that are relatively influenced by political criteria (interviews). This adversely affects the CBRT's ability to recruit and retain analysts with the requisite skills, knowledge and expertise, staff morale and horizontal intra-personal relations. Not only will these accelerating challenges erode the policy capacity of the CBRT, but also that of the Turkish state. Failures in policy design and implementation, poor policy outcomes and increased socioeconomic costs in various policy sectors should be no surprise in Turkey if these tendencies are not reversed.

Notes

[1] We are grateful to Sinan Akgunay for his comments and suggestions.
[2] Ghosh et al (2017, p 18), in a recent survey, find that in 53 developing and emerging market economies, macroprudential regulations are the third most used policy instrument used to counter surges in capital inflows that led to financial stability concerns in these economies; 16 per cent of 223 surges in capital inflows have been countered by tightening macroprudential regulations. These economies depend more on foreign exchange interventions and monetary tightening (that is, increasing or lowering policy rates).
[3] Kara, a career central banker, was former Director General of the Research and Monetary Policy Department and Head of the Economic Modelling and Forecasting Division.
[4] Our concern here is not to offer a discussion of the policy mix or its effects. See Kara (2012); Akcelik et al (2013); Gurkaynak et al (2015).
[5] There have been frequent conferences and workshops since 2005. The conference themes have included inflation targeting, globalisation, Islamic banking and systemic financial risks, all of which demonstrate that the CBRT is observing international policy challenges alongside its own policy needs such as dollarisation and inflation targeting, important in the mid-2000s. For more information, see http://imb.tcmb.gov.tr/
[6] We thank Mehmet Soytas for his comments on formal techniques used in the CBRT.
[7] For further information, see the mandate of the department online at www.tcmb.gov.tr/wps/wcm/connect/TCMB+EN/TCMB+EN/Bottom+Menu/About+The+Bank/Organizational+Structure/Head+Office
[8] See research papers written by CBRT personnel online at www.tcmb.gov.tr/wps/wcm/connect/TCMB+EN/TCMB+EN/Main+Menu/PUBLICATIONS/Research

9 The data produced and/or compiled by the CBRT is accessible online via the Electronic Data Dissemination System (EVDS) at https://evds2.tcmb.gov.tr/. Furthermore, summary data are also accessible in annual reports and other CBRT publications such as the *Inflation report* and *Financial stability report*.
10 For further information, see the mandate of the department online at www.tcmb.gov.tr/wps/wcm/connect/TCMB+EN/TCMB+EN/Bottom+Menu/About+The+Bank/Organizational+Structure/Head+Office/Statistics+Department
11 For further information, see the mandate of the department online at www.tcmb.gov.tr/wps/wcm/connect/TCMB+EN/TCMB+EN/Bottom+Menu/About+The+Bank/Organizational+Structure/Head+Office
12 The key macroeconomic bureaucratic actors that relate to the financial services industry signed a protocol for information sharing and cooperation over financial issues on 31 October 2012.
13 Turkey has a multiple regulatory framework. The BRSA is in charge of regulating and supervising bank and non-bank financial institutions. The Capital Markets Board steers the capital markets. The Treasury supervises the insurance market. Along with these regulatory bodies, the CBRT acts as the monetary authority whose main function is to gather data from these bodies and process them for policy analysis of monetary policy. For more information, refer to the institutional structure of governance in financial stability at http://tcmb.gov.tr/wps/wcm/connect/TCMB+EN/TCMB+EN/Main+Menu/MONETARY+POLICY/FINANCIAL+STABILITY/Institutional+Framework
14 Erdem Başçı served as Deputy Governor (2003-11) and Governor of the CBRT (2011-16).
15 Ali Babacan served as Deputy Prime Minister for Economic and Financial Affairs (2009-15) in the 61st and 62nd governments of the Republic of Turkey; see www.tbmm.gov.tr/develop/owa/milletvekillerimiz_sd.bilgi?p_donem=26&p_sicil=6063

References

Akcelik, Y., Aysan, A.F. and Oduncu, A. (2013) 'Central banking in the making during the post crisis world and the policy-mix of the Central Bank of the Republic of Turkey', *Journal of Central Banking Theory and Practice*, vol 2, no 2, pp 5-18.

Akgunay, S. and Bakır, C. (2016) 'From a micro-prudential framework to macroprudential mechanisms: Analysis of the banking mechanisms in the post-2011 Turkish experience', Paper presented at Turkish Political Economy Society (TPES) 2nd International Conference, 9 December, Istanbul: Istanbul Policy Centre.

Alesina, A. and Summers, L. H. (1993) 'Central bank independence and macroeconomic performance: Some comparative evidence', *Journal of Money, Credit and Banking*, vol 25, no 2, pp 151-62.

Baker, A. (2013) 'New political economy of the macroprudential ideational shift', *New Political Economy*, vol 18, no 1, pp 112-39.

Bakır, C. (2006a) 'Governance by supranational interdependence: Domestic policy change in the Turkish financial services industry', in J. Batten and C. Kearney (eds) *Emerging European financial markets: Independence and integration post-enlargement*, London: Elsevier, pp 179-211.

Bakır, C. (2006b) 'Türkiye Cumhuriyet Merkez Bankası'nın 1930-2001 arasında siyasal ve ekonomik bağımsızlığı: Siyasal-ekonomik etkileşime ilişkin karşılaştırmalı bir çözümleme ['The political and economic independence of the Central Bank of the Republic of Turkey between 1930-2001: A comparative analysis'], *METU Studies in Development*, vol 33, no 1, pp 1-31.

Bakir, C. (2007) *Merkezdeki Banka ve uluslararasi bir karsilastirma* [*Bank in the centre: The Central Bank of the Republic of Turkey and an international comparison*], Istanbul: Bilgi University Press.

Bakır, C. (2009) 'Policy entrepreneurship and institutional change: Multilevel governance of central banking reform', *Governance*, vol 22, no 4, pp 571-98.

Bakır, C. (2012a) 'Organizational change in economic bureaucracy in Turkey, 1980-2010: Interactions with national and global dynamics', TUBITAK Project No 108K511, Unpublished report.

Bakır, C. (2012b) 'Maliye burokrasisinde orgutsel degisim ve vergi denetim kurulu baskanliginin kurulmasi' ['Organisational change in fiscal bureaucracy and the establishment of Tax Inspection Board], *Amme Idaresi Dergisi* [*Journal of Public Administration*], vol 45, no 2, pp 81-102.

Bakır, C. (2015a) 'Bargaining with multinationals: Why state capacity matters', *New Political Economy*, vol 20, no 1, pp 63-84.

Bakır, C. (2015b) 'Merkez bankasi baskanlari ve siyasetciler' ['Central bankers and politicians'], *Kurumsal Yatirimci Dergisi (Nisan-Haziran)*, pp 56-7.

Bakır, C. (2017) 'How can interactions among interdependent structures, institutions, and agents inform financial stability? What we have still to learn from the global financial crisis', *Policy Sciences*, vol 50, no 2, pp 217–39.

Bakır, C. and Öniş, Z. (2010) 'The emergence and the limits of the regulatory state: The political economy of Turkish banking reforms in the age of the post-Washington Consensus', *Development and Change*, vol 41, no 1, pp 77-106.

Bennett, C.J. and Howlett, M. (1992) 'The lessons of learning: Reconciling theories of policy learning and policy change', *Policy Sciences*, vol 25, no 3, pp 275-94.

Borrás, S. (2011) 'Policy learning and organizational capacities in innovation policies', *Science and Public Policy*, vol 38, no 9, pp 725-34.

Calomiris, C.W. and Haber, S.H. (2014) *Fragile by design: The political origins of banking crises and scarce credit*, Oxford: Princeton University Press.

Campbell, J.Y. Jackson, H.E. Madrian, B.C. and Tufano, P. (2011) 'Consumer financial protection', *The Journal of Economic Perspectives*, vol 25, no 1, pp 91-113.

Ceyhun, E. (2011) 'Merkez'in 100 kişilik araştırma ordusu var!', *Dünya*, 5 October (www.dunya.com/gundem/merkez039in-100-kisilik-arastirma-ordusu-var-haberi-155642).

Cukierman, A. (2008) 'Central independence and monetary policymaking institutions – Past, present and future', *European Journal of Political Economy*, vol 24, no 4, pp 722-36.

Dror, Y. (1971) *Ventures in policy sciences*, New York: Elsevier.

Fernandéz-Albertos, J. (2015) 'The politics of central bank independence', *Annual Review of Political Science*, vol 18, pp 217-37.

FSB (Financial Stability Board) (2015) *Peer review of Turkey*, Review report, 19 November (www.fsb.org/2015/11/peer-review-of-turkey/).

Financial Times (2015) 'Erdogan backs off in battle with Turkish Central Bank', 12 March (www.ft.com/content/205c72f6-c89d-11e4-8617-00144feab7de).

Flannery, M.J., Kwan, S.H. and Nimalendran, M. (2004) 'Market evidence on the opaqueness of banking firms' assets', *Journal of Financial Economics*, vol 71, no 3, pp 419-60.

Flannery, M.J., Kwan, S.H. and Nimalendran, M. (2013) 'The 2007-2009 financial crisis and bank opaqueness', *Journal of Financial Intermediation*, vol 22, no 1, pp 55-84.

Flug, K. (2016) 'Policy analysis at the Bank of Israel', in G. Menahem and A. Zehavi (eds) *Policy analysis in Israel*, Bristol: Policy Press, pp 141-52.

Ghosh, A., Ostry, J.D. and Qureshi, M.S. (2017) *Managing the tide: How do emerging markets respond to capital flows?*, IMF Working Paper, No 17/69. Washington, DC: International Monetary Fund.

Gill, J.I. and Saunders, L. (1992) 'Toward a definition of policy analysis', *New Directions for Institutional Research*, vol 76, pp 5-13.

Goodhart, C.A.E. (2011) 'The changing role of central banks', *Financial History Review*, vol 18, no 2, pp 135-54.

Gurkaynak, R., Kantur, Z., Tas, M.A. and Karaman, S.Y. (2015) 'Monetary policy in Turkey after Central Bank independence', *Iktisat, Isletme ve Finans*, vol 30, no 356, pp 9-38.

Gürler, E. (2013) 'Türkiye Cumhuriyet Merkez Bankası yurt dışı lisansüstü eğitim uygulamaları: 1996-2011 Döneminin analizi ve değerlendirmesi', Yayımlanmamış Uzmanlık Tezi, Ankara: TCMB, Şubat (www.tcmb.gov.tr/wps/wcm/connect/6194dbed-81f6-42f7-9cbc-ea0f5662c3e4/evrimguler.pdf?MOD=AJPERES&CACHEID=ROOTWORKSPACE6194dbed-81f6-42f7-9cbc-ea0f5662c3e4).

Howlett, M. (2009) 'Policy analytical capacity and evidence-based policy-making: Lessons from Canada', *Canadian Public Administration/Administration Publique du Canada*, vol 52, no 2, pp 153-75.

Howlett, M. (2011) *Designing public policies: Principles and instruments*, Abingdon: Routledge.

Howlett, M. and Ramesh, M. (2014) 'The two orders of governance failure: Design mismatches and policy capacity issues in modern governance', *Policy and Society*, vol 33, no 4, pp 317-27.

Howlett, M. and Ramesh, M. (2016) 'Achilles' heels of governance: Critical capacity deficits and their role in governance failures', *Governance*, vol 10, no 4, pp 301-13.

Howlett, M., Tan, S. L., Migone, A., Wellstead, A. and Evans, B. (2015). 'Policy formulation, policy advice and policy appraisal: The distribution of analytical tools', in A. Jordan and J. Turnpenny (eds), *The tools of policy formulation: Actors, capacities, venues and effects*. Cheltenham: Edward Elgar Publishing, pp 163-83.

Hürriyet (2011) 'Babacan 5 yıl bekledi Çıkrıkçılar'dan Arkadaşını Merkez'in başına taşıdı' ['Babacan waited for 5 years to carry his friend to the top of the Central Bank'] (www.hurriyet.com.tr/babacan-5-yil-bekledi-cikrikcilar-dan-arkadasini-merkez-in-basina-tasidi-17550789).

IMF (International Monetary Fund) (2011) *Recent experiences in managing capital inflows – Cross-cutting themes and possible policy framework*, IMF Policy Paper, Washington, DC: IMF.

IMF (2016) *2016 Article IV consultation – Staff report*, IMF Country Report No 16/104, April, Washington, DC: IMF.

Jordan, A. and Turnpenny, J. (2015) *The tools of policy formulation: Actors, capacities, venues and effects*, Cheltenham: Edward Elgar Publishing.

Kara, H. (2012) *Monetary policy in Turkey after the global crisis*, Working Paper No 12/17, Ankara: Central Bank of the Republic of Turkey.

Kara, H. (2016) *Turkey's experience with macroprudential policy*, BIS Papers 86, Basle: BIS.

Kydland, F.E. and Prescott, E.C. (1977) 'Rules rather than discretion: The inconsistency of optimal plans', *Journal of Political Economy*, vol 85, no 3, pp 473-92.

Lim, C., Columba, F., Costa, A., Kongsamut, P., Otani, A., Saiyid, M., Wezel, T. and Wu, X. (2011) *Macroprudential policy: What instruments and how to use them? Lessons from country experiences*, IMF Working Papers 11/238, Washington DC: International Monetary Fund.

MacRae, D., Jr (1991) 'Policy analysis and knowledge use', *Knowledge and Policy*, vol 4, no 3, pp 27-40.

Meltsner, A.J. (1972) 'Political feasibility and policy analysis', *Public Administration Review*, vol 32, no 6, pp 859-67.

Minsky, H.P (2008 [1986]) *Stabilizing and unstable economy*, Foreword with Henry Kaufman, New York & London: McGraw Hill.

Oliphant, S. and Howlett, M. (2010) 'Assessing policy analytical capacity: Comparative insights from a study of the Canadian environmental policy advice system', *Journal of Comparative Policy Analysis: Research and Practice*, vol 12, no 4, pp 439-45.

Pal, L.A. and Clark, I.D. (2015) 'Making reform stick: Political acumen as an element of political capacity for policy change and innovation', *Policy and Society*, vol 35, no 3-4, pp 247-57.

Radaelli, C.M. (1995) 'The role of knowledge in the policy process', *Journal of European Public Policy*, vol 2, no 2, pp 159-83.

Riddell, N. (2007) *Policy research capacity in the federal government*, Ottawa: Policy Research Initiative.

Quaglia, L. (2005a) 'An integrative approach to the politics of central bank independence: Lessons from Britain, Germany and Italy', *West European Politics*, vol, 28, no 3, pp 549-68.

Quaglia, L. (2005b) 'Civil servants, economic ideas, and economic policies: Lessons from Italy', *Governance*, vol 18, no 4, pp 545-66.

Wu, X., Ramesh, M. and Howlett, M. (2015) 'Policy capacity: A conceptual framework for understanding policy competences and capabilities', *Policy and Society*, vol 35, no 3-4, pp 165-71.

FOURTEEN

Think tanks and policy analysis in Turkey

Göktuğ Morçöl, Özer Köseoğlu, Mehmet Zahid Sobacı and Ömer Faruk Köktaş

Introduction

Think tanks are informal actors that play pivotal roles in public policy-making processes. They are mostly non-governmental organisations (NGOs) that have the capacity to set their own research agendas and produce policy-relevant knowledge. The increased complexity and changing nature of societal problems governments encounter and the need for more analytical capacity to deal with such problems has increased their importance in policy processes.

The origins of think tanks can be traced back to the early 20th century, when governments in the US and UK were forced to respond to problems created by urbanisation, industrialisation and economic growth (Stone and Garnett, 1998). After the first wave of think tanks created in the first decades of the century, another wave came in the US, after the Second World War. Beginning with the 1980s, think tanks proliferated, not only in the countries they originated in, but also around the world.

Turkey is among those countries where think tanks have proliferated and participated in policy-making processes in recent decades. In this chapter, we trace the history of think tanks in Turkey, and present the results of the findings of our content analyses of policy papers produced by the most prominent think tanks in the 2000s. In these analyses we investigated two sets of issues. First, we categorised and tracked the policy areas and topics covered in the papers produced by think tanks (international relations, education, etc). The topics they covered and emphasised have parallels with the prevalent policy issues of their time. Second, we assessed to what extent the authors of the reports followed academic and analytical conventions that are used in the policy analysis and evaluation literature, and applied policy-analytical methods. Although no universal norms or formats exist for policy analysis papers, there are some conventions and methods that are commonly covered in the main textbooks of policy analysis and evaluation (see, for example, Dunn, 2012; Rossi et al, 2004) and promoted by professional organisations (see, for example, the Society for Benefit-Cost Analysis, https://benefitcostanalysis.org/ and the Campbell Collaboration, www.campbellcollaboration.org/). The extent to which these conventions and methods are covered in the papers provides an indication of the level of development not only of the think tanks in Turkey, but also that of the policy analysis practice in the country.

There is no commonly accepted definition of think tanks (Smith, 1991; Stone, 2004), but Rich's generic definition captures the common elements most scholars would agree with: think tanks are 'independent, non-interest based, non-profit organisations that produce and principally rely on expertise and ideas to obtain support and to influence the policy-making process' (Rich, 2004, p 11). Ladi (2000) points out that organisational independence and stability, the capacity to self-determine the research agenda, policy orientation and expertise of the employees and professionalism are fundamental characteristics of think tanks. While they may be organisationally independent, they can also be organised within an institution such as a ministry, political party or university. They may be ideologically and politically neutral, but may also carry out their activities within an ideology or movement.

The most basic function of think tanks is to provide the information and expertise policy-makers need. They perform policy and programme evaluations to measure the successes of policies that are implemented. Thus they function as a bridge between information and policy-making (McGann, 2011). Think tanks may also be policy actors: they may promote their views on policy issues and even issues to be placed on policy agendas (Rich, 2004). They may be actors in 'policy networks' that help create or implement policies (Stone, 2000; Weaver and McGann, 2009).

Think tanks use various methods and tools to disseminate their ideas and positions, for example, publishing books and policy issue papers, organising forums, conferences, panels and symposia and participating in internet blogs and social media (Abelson, 2002; Weaver and McGann, 2009). In this chapter we focus primarily on the papers produced by think tanks in Turkey.

A brief history of think tanks in Turkey

There is no consensus on when the first think tanks emerged in Turkey, but there are studies that trace the first ones as far back as the 1960s (Aydın, 2006; Uzgel, 2006; Bağcı and Aydın, 2009, p 86; Ediger, 2009; Kantarcı, 2009; Aras et al, 2010). Aydın (2006) identifies four periods of development of think tanks in Turkey: the 1960s and 1970s, the post-1980 military coup period until the end of the Cold War in the early 1990s, the 1990s and the period since 2000.

The basic characteristic of the 1960s is the liberal atmosphere created by the 1961 Constitution. The provisions of the Constitution guaranteed freedoms of thought, expression and organisation, and facilitated the participation of new actors in political life (Özbudun, 1995; Karatepe, 2016), which together enabled the creation of independent organisations that would contribute to policy processes. The Constitution also established the framework of a planned and mixed economic model. Specialised policy analysis institutions were needed to inform policy-making in this model. Another important development in this period was the beginning of the process of Turkey's economic integration into the European Economic Community, with the signing of the Ankara Agreement in 1963. This process also brought about the requirement for policy analyses, and thus contributed to the establishment of the first generation of think tanks: the Turkish Economic and Social Studies Committee[1] (Ekonomik ve Sosyal Etüdler Heyeti, 1961), Economic Research Foundation (İktisadi Araştırmalar Vakfı, 1962) and Economic Development Facility (İktisadi Kalkınma Tesisi, 1965)[2] (Güvenç, 2007; Bağcı and Aydın, 2009; Bulut and Güngör, 2009).

The 1980 military coup was a milestone in the development of think tanks in Turkey. Under the military administration, all kind of voluntary initiatives, associations and foundations were restricted, which also affected think tanks. Nevertheless, new think tanks were founded in the 1980s: the Foundation for Political and Social Research (Siyasi ve Sosyal Araştırmalar Vakfı, SİSAV), Foundation for Middle East and Balkan Studies (Orta Doğu ve Balkan İncelemeleri Vakfı, OBİV), Islamic Studies Centre (İslam Araştırmaları Merkezi, İSAM) and Turkish representative institutions of two German Foundations, Konrad Adenauer Stiftung (KAS) and Friedrich Ebert Stiftung (FES). These new think tanks were the products of the political and economic environment. The economic liberalisation that was promoted by the economic decisions made on 24 January 1980, which started a neoliberal era in Turkey, encouraged the creation of think tanks that represented private sector interests (for example, SİSAV). Others were created with the support of the post-coup government to promote its policy positions (for example, OBİV). The German foundations that were affiliated with German political parties collaborated with the Turkish political parties with worldviews and policy positions close to theirs. For example, KAS, which is affiliated with the Christian Democratic Union in Germany, collaborated with the Anavatan Party of Prime Minister Özal and those think tanks that represented similar worldviews (Güvenç, 2007; Bağcı and Aydın, 2009).

The post-Cold War period led to the liberalisation of policy-making processes in Turkey and accelerated the foundation of think tanks. The general need to understand the new world order that emerged following the Cold War, and the specific need for systematic information-gathering and analysis to implement the reforms required by the European Union (EU) integration process, were the causes of the increase in the number of think tanks in this period (Bulut and Güngör, 2009). The Turkish Economic and Social Studies Foundation (Türkiye Ekonomik ve Sosyal Etüdler Vakfı), ARI Movement (ARI Hareketi), Association for Liberal Thinking (Liberal Düşünce Derneği), Root Foundation for Political and Social Research (Kök Sosyal ve Siyasal Araştırmalar Vakfı) and Centre for Eurasian Strategic Research (Avrasya Stratejik Araştırmalar Merkezi) were some of the think tanks that were founded in this period (Güvenç, 2007; Aras et al, 2010).

In the 2000s, not only the number of think tanks increased, but also the policy fields and activities they organise diversified, similar to developments in other countries. McGann (2016) cites the following among reasons for the increase in their number around the world: the information and technological revolution, the end of national governments' monopoly on information, the increasing complexity and technical nature of policy problems, increasing sizes of governments, the crisis of confidence in governments and elected officials, globalisation and the growth of state and non-state actors, and the need for timely and concise information and analysis. Aydın (2006) cites similar global trends as the background for their increased numbers and dissemination in Turkey. Another important reason was the mass media's increased demand for policy expertise. As the media's solicitation of the opinions of the experts affiliated with think tanks increased, so did their visibility, and new think tanks were formed (Bağcı and Aydın, 2009). In this period, state institutions such as the Grand National Assembly of Turkey, the Ministry of Internal Affairs and Turkish Armed Forces established their own think tanks. As part of the development of civil society in Turkey, some private sector organisations and interest groups also established think tanks.

Functions and types of think tanks in Turkey

The think tanks in Turkey have similar functions in policy processes and use similar tools as their counterparts in other countries (Aydın, 2006; Aras et al, 2010). They aim to carry out research on various policy problems such as foreign affairs, democratisation, human rights, energy and migration. They contribute to policy-making processes by producing policy-relevant information (Arslan, 2009; Aras et al, 2010; Gül and Yemen, 2016).

However, there is not sufficient information about the extent to which each think tank in Turkey has the above-cited functions and which specific tools its uses, and neither is there systematic information available about whether and to what extent they have influenced policy processes. Toktaş and Aras' (2012) interviews with small numbers of think tank directors indicate that the directors thought that they did influence policy processes in a few policy areas: national security, human rights, women's rights, ecology, crime and immigration. Aydın's (2006) earlier interviews with think tank directors, politicians and academics indicate that such influences were limited and indirect, primarily because of the reluctance of politicians to listen to think tanks. Gül and Yemen's (2016) more recent interviews with eight think tank representatives show that even those that are relatively close to government complain about bureaucracy's predominance in policy-making processes.

Despite these difficulties, their number has grown, and they have become more active in publishing policy papers, particularly in the last two decades. In the study whose results we present in the following sections, we focused particularly on the papers and reports published online by prominent think tanks in Turkey. The content and authorship of the papers are the most tangible indicators of the current state of think tanks in the country.

Papers produced by think tanks in the 2000s

As noted earlier, we analysed the contents of a sample of papers produced by the most prominent think tanks in Turkey since 2000, the last phase in the evolution of these organisations in Turkey. In the 2000s not only the number of think tanks increased globally, but also the technological advances in these years enabled them to disseminate their ideas and products far and wide, particularly through the internet. The think tanks in Turkey began to publish their papers on their websites in the early 2000s. This accessibility of their papers allowed us to retrieve them and analyse their content. In our analyses we specifically categorised and tracked the policy areas and topics covered in the papers, and investigated the extent to which the authors of the reports followed academic and analytical conventions that are used in the policy analysis and evaluation literature and applied policy-analytical methods.

To identify the papers to be analysed in our study, we referred first to McGann's (2016) list of 32 active think tanks in Turkey. Our initial searches indicated that we could include only 10 think tanks, because they were the only ones that published papers on the internet and did so frequently. We excluded those that published sporadically and those whose papers were not available on the internet. The think tanks that are included in our study are the Turkish Economic and Social Studies Foundation (Türkiye Ekonomik ve Sosyal Etüdler Vakfı, TESEV), International Strategic Research Organisation (Uluslararası Stratejik Araştırmalar Kurumu, USAK), Turkish Asian Centre for Strategic Studies (Türk Asya Stratejik Araştırmalar Merkezi, TASAM), Economic Policy Research Foundation of Turkey (Türkiye Ekonomi Politikaları Araştırma Vakfı, TEPAV), Foundation for Political, Economic and Social Research (Siyaset, Ekonomi ve Toplum Araştırmaları Vakfı, SETA), Wise Men Centre for Strategic Studies (Bilge Adamlar Stratejik Araştırmalar Merkezi, BİLGESAM), Institute of Strategic Thinking (Stratejik Düşünce Enstitüsü, SDE), Centre for Middle Eastern Strategic Studies (Ortadoğu Stratejik Araştırmalar Merkezi, ORSAM), Education Reform Initiative (Eğitim Reformu Girişimi, ERG) and Istanbul Policy Centre (İstanbul Politikalar Merkezi, IPM) (see Table 14.1).

Think tanks in Turkey publish their policy analyses under different names: reports, analyses, policy analyses and policy notes. They also use these names quite interchangeably. For instance, a publication type labelled as a 'report' by one think tank may correspond to that labelled as 'analysis' by another. Think tanks also publish comments and views, which are brief and in the form of commentaries, like newspaper columns.

In our study we first identified 990 papers published in all forms by the above-mentioned think tanks. Then we excluded the ones that were too brief (shorter than 15 pages), those that were written as commentaries and those did not include any references. After these exclusions, we had 476 papers in total. (We use the term 'paper' for all types of reports, analytical reports, etc, included in our study.)

We selected a sample of 94 papers systematically from the chronological listings of the papers published by the think tanks (roughly 20 per cent of the total 476).

Table 14.1: Think tanks included in the study

Think tank name (abbreviation)	Type	Year founded	Total number of papers (year of first publication)	Number of papers in sample	Website
BILGESAM	Independent	2008	36 (2009)	7	www.bilgesam.org
ERG	University	2003	31 (2006)	6	www.egitimreformugirisimi.org
IPM	University	2001	31 (2006)	6	http://ipc.sabanciuniv.edu
ORSAM	Independent	2009	103 (2009)	21	www.orsam.org.tr
SDE	Independent	2009	15 (2010)	3	www.sde.org.tr
SETA	Independent	2006	127 (2008)	25	www.setav.org
TASAM	Independent	2002	16 (2005)	8	www.tasam.org
TEPAV	Independent	2004	40 (2005)	3	www.tepav.org.tr
TESEV	Independent	1994*	43 (2002)	8	www.tesev.org.tr
USAK	Independent	2004	34 (2008)	7	www.usak.org.tr**
Total			476	94	

Note: * The predecessor of this think tank was founded in 1961, noted in this paper.
** The link www.usak.org.tr was active by the time we collected the data for this paper (March 2016). It is currently broken because the think tank USAK was shut down by a government decree later in 2016.

Table 14.1 presents the breakdown of the total number of papers published by the 10 think tanks (476) and of the sample papers selected for our content analyses (94). The column 'Number of papers in sample' also indicates, in parentheses, the years in which the think tanks published their first papers online. There is typically a time lag between the founding of a think tank and the first online paper it published.

The information about 'Type' is based on Bağcı and Aydın's (2009) categorisation of think tanks in Turkey. They propose the following: (1) independent and semi-independent organisations; (2) state-funded organisations; and (3) university-based organisations. The independent and semi-independent organisations are think tanks that operate either completely or largely free from the influence of any pressure group or non-governmental organisation (NGO). State-funded think tanks are established within public institutions. University-based think tanks have organic relations with universities. Table 14.1 shows that 8 of the 10 think tanks in our study are independent/semi-independent organisations and only two (ERG and IPM) are university-affiliated. None of the state-funded think tanks cited above (those that were established by the Grand National Assembly of Turkey, Ministry of Internal Affairs and Turkish Armed Forces) is among the 10 listed in Table 14.1, because we could not locate papers that they published online and that met our selection criteria mentioned above.

In the increasingly politicised world of policy analysis in the late 20th and early 21st centuries (Radin, 2013), many think tanks take openly ideological positions (liberal, conservative, etc) and some of them are directly or indirectly related to political parties (Stone and Garnett, 1998). Several German think tanks, such as those mentioned earlier (Konrad Adenauer Stiftung and Friedrich Ebert Stiftung), have affiliations with political parties (Aydın, 2006). No think tanks have direct ties with political parties in Turkey (Yıldız et al, 2013, p 196), but some do have political orientations. For instance, Yıldız et al (2013) note that the Wise Men Center For Strategic Studies (Bilge Adamlar Stratejik Araştırmalar Merkezi, BİLGESAM) is considered liberal, the Institute of Strategic Thinking (Stratejik Düşünce Enstitüsü, SDE) conservative democrat and the International Strategic Research Organisation (Uluslararası Stratejik Araştırmalar Kurumu, USAK) liberal nationalist. We did not include this information in Table 14.1 because of difficulties in pinpointing the political and ideological positions of all 10 think tanks.

In the following section we present the results of the content analyses of the 94 papers mentioned in Table 14.1. We first read and analysed a small sample of papers to refine and calibrate our interpretations of them in a pilot study. After coding all the papers, we re-read the ones that there were disagreements on the codes until reaching full consensuses on all categories. Finally, the results of the content analyses were tabulated and further analysed using Excel and SPSS.

Content analyses of the papers

It should be noted first that although we aimed to cover the years between 2000 and 2015 in our study, we found that the 10 think tanks listed in Table 14.1 began publishing their papers online in 2005. Before that year, only TESEV had published one paper, in 2002.

Table 14.1 shows that there is a variation in the numbers of papers produced by think tanks in the 2005-15 period. This can partly be explained by the fact that some of the think tanks were founded later and therefore did not have the same number of years to generate as many papers as the older ones. For example, SDE was founded in 2009 and produced only 15 papers. ORSAM was founded in the same year, but it generated the second largest number of papers. SETA, founded in 2006, produced the largest number of papers. TESEV, the oldest think tank, generated a moderate number of papers in the 2000s. It is also noteworthy that even the earlier think tanks (for example, IPM) did not begin publishing their papers online until a few years after their founding.

Trends, areas and topics

Figure 14.1 shows the trends in the number of papers produced by the 10 think tanks since 2002 (total 476), with an overall increase in the total number of papers published between 2005 and 2015. The spike in 2011 may be an outlier: there were a large number of papers written on issues in the Middle East in that year. Figure 14.1 also shows the relative contributions of each think tank thank in each year. It shows, for example, that ORSAM's paper production declined after 2011, whereas SETA's increased.

Figure 14.1: Papers published per year, 2002–15

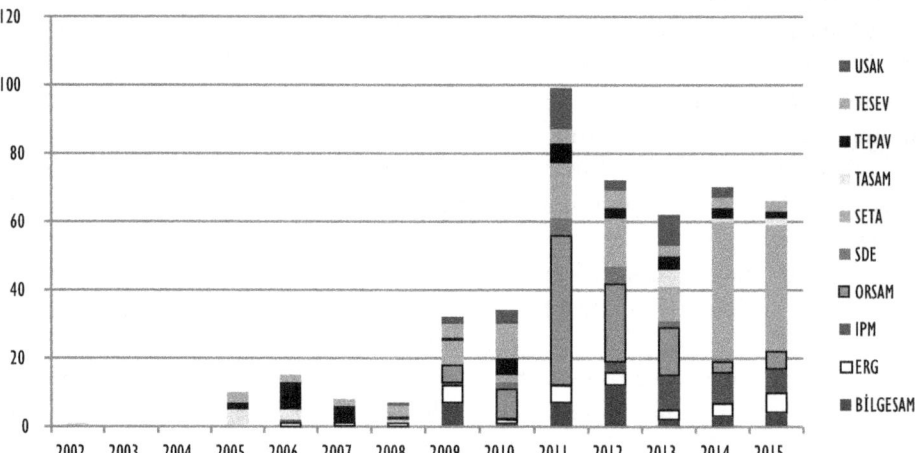

The results of our analyses of the policy areas covered in the papers we analysed (94 papers) are presented in Figure 14.2. We categorised those that focused on issues such as nationalism, political parties and elections, constitution-making and democratisation (including the Kurdish problem) as 'politics'. Under the category of 'others' we included areas such as strategic planning and local and regional governments. The most popular areas are international relations (39.4 per cent), politics (21.3 per cent), education policy (11.7 per cent) and economic policy (7.4 per cent). The less popular policy areas are energy policy (2.1 per cent), migration policy (2.1 per cent), social policy (2.1 per cent), health policy (1.1 per cent) and religion policy (1.1 per cent). The low number of papers in the areas of energy, health and social policy, which have been increasingly important in recent years, is noteworthy.

Figure 14.3 illustrates the trends in publications in the more popular policy areas: international relations, politics, education policy and economic policy. It shows that the numbers of papers in all four areas increased over the years, but particularly in international relations. The main reason for the increase in papers published on politics in 2014 is that both the local election and presidential election were held in that year.

Figure 14.2: Policy areas covered in 94 papers

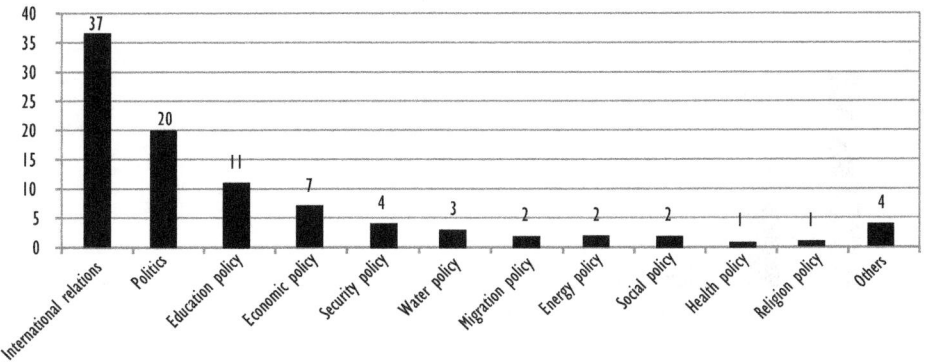

Figure 14.3: Trends in more popular policy areas

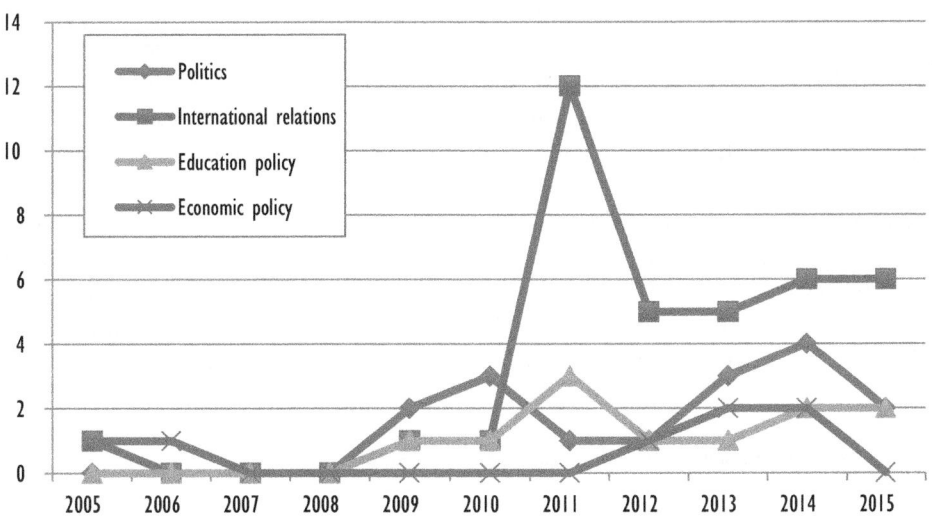

Figure 14.4 illustrates the distribution of the geographic loci of the 94 papers analysed. It shows that although the most popular policy area is international relations (see Figure 14.3), a majority of the papers (50 out of 94) are about problems in Turkey. Still, the remaining papers (44) are about international problems. The most popular topic is the Middle East (25 papers), followed distantly by Europe, Africa and others. The fact that 60 per cent of the papers produced in 2011 are on international relations (Figure 14.3) and that the Middle East is the second most popular topic, after Turkey (Figure 14.4), indicates that

Policy analysis in Turkey

the think tanks were interested in the developments that had begun in the Arab countries in December 2010 (the 'Arab Spring').

Figure 14.4: Geographic loci of papers

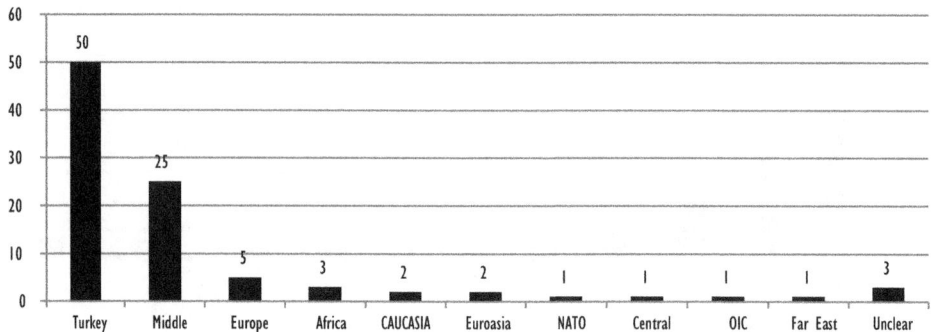

Authors of the papers

As noted earlier, we investigated the extent to which the authors of the reports followed academic and analytical conventions that are used in the policy analysis and evaluation literature and applied policy-analytical methods. The first step in our analyses was to identify the authors' institutional affiliations. It is noteworthy that a quarter of the papers did not include any information regarding the authors' affiliations. These are displayed as 'unknown' in Figure 14.5, which shows the distribution of the authors' institutional affiliations: university, think tank and public institution. We observed that the 94 papers we analysed had been written by a total of 143 authors. Of these, 45 papers had one author (48 per cent), 38 had two authors (40 per cent) and 11 had three authors (12 per cent). Figure 14.5 displays the affiliations of all the authors, which is why the total is 143, not 94.

Figure 14.5: Institutional affiliations of authors

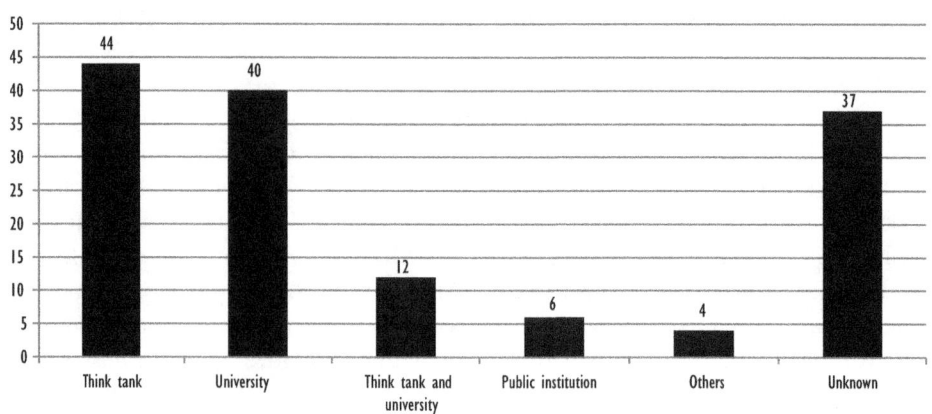

Figure 14.6 shows that the largest number of authors have doctoral degrees, followed by those with Master's and Bachelor's degrees. Once again, however, there was a lack of information about the authors in a large number of papers. The fact that a large number have doctoral degrees indicates the close connection between the think tanks and universities in Turkey.

Figure 14.6: Academic degrees of authors

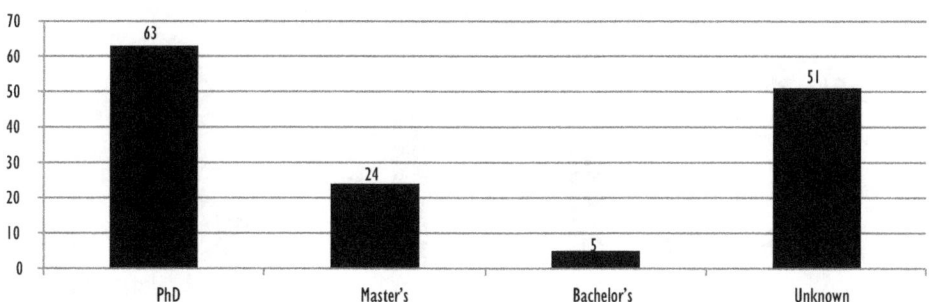

Summary, purpose statement and problem definition

One could expect that those authors with academic degrees would follow academic conventions in their papers. We investigated particularly whether the papers included abstracts/executive summaries, purpose statements and problem definitions. We found that a majority (66 per cent) did include an abstract or an executive summary. Figure 14.7 shows that the practice of writing an abstract or executive summary is not equally distributed among the think tanks. This is common practice for some think tanks, but not for others. The think tanks can be divided into four groups: (1) those that include an abstract/executive summary in all of their publications (SETA and SDE); (2) those that include an abstract/executive summary in most of their publications (USAK, ORSAM, IPM); (3) those that have very few abstracts/executive summaries (TESEV and TEPAV); and (4) those that include no abstracts or executive summaries (TASAM and BİLGESAM). It is also noteworthy that there has been an increase in the number of papers that included an abstract or executive summary over the years: while only 30 per cent of the papers between 2005 and 2010 included one of them, 76 per cent of those between 2011 and 2015 did so.

Almost half of the 94 papers we read (44.7 per cent) included a clearly stated purpose for their studies. Also, we could discern some purpose, but with some difficulty, in 20.2 per cent. (This second group of papers are indicated as the 'maybe' category in Figure 14.8.) Additionally, it is noticeable that one-third of the reports (35.1 per cent) did not have any statement of purpose. Figure 14.8 shows the distribution of the three categories on whether or not there is a clearly stated purpose: yes, not very clear, and no. The think tanks that include a clear statement of purpose in their reports respectively are TESEV (75 per cent), IPM (66 per cent), ERG (67 per cent) and SETA (52 per cent). There are think tanks that include a clear statement of purpose in their reports relatively less often: TASAM (33 per cent), ORSAM (29 per cent), USAK (14 per cent) and SDE (0 per cent). We also found that the percentage of papers that included a statement of purpose increased over time: it was included in only 9 per cent of papers between 2005 and 2009, but 90 per cent of papers published between 2010 and 2015 had statements of purpose.

Figure 14.7: Use of abstract/executive summary in papers by think tank

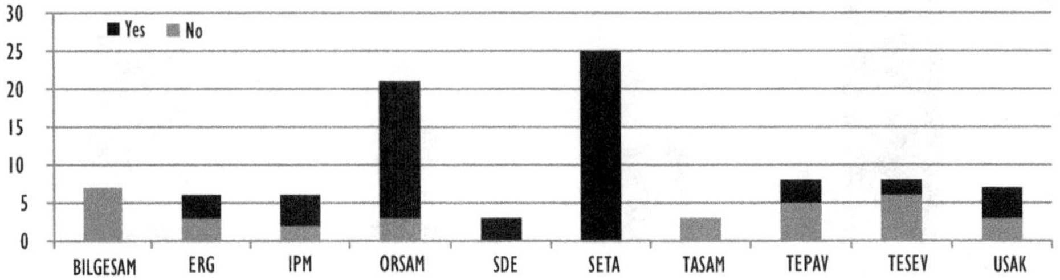

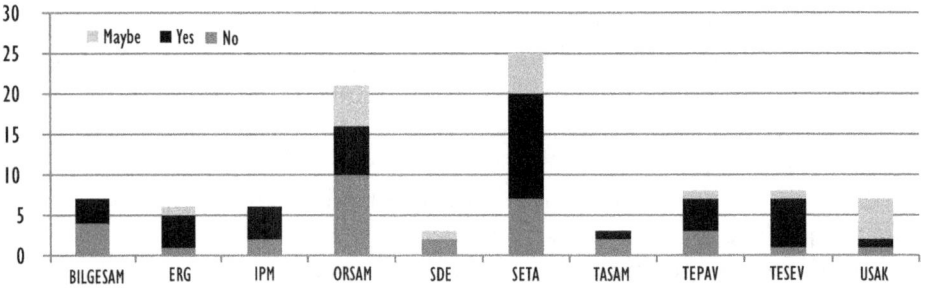

Figure 14.8: Use of statement of purpose in papers by think tank

Our content analyses indicate that only 17 per cent of the papers in our sample have a clear problem definition. Figure 14.9 shows that the think tanks that have a clear problem definition in their reports are: SETA (37 per cent), ERG (19 per cent), ORSAM (12 per cent), TEPAV (12 per cent), TESEV (6 per cent), USAK (6 per cent), BİLGESAM (6 per cent), IPM (0 per cent), SDE (0 per cent) and TASAM (0 per cent). We also found that the percentage of papers with a clear problem definition increased over the years: it was included in only 19 per cent of papers between 2005 and 2010, but 81 per cent of papers published between 2011 and 2015 had a problem definition.

Analytical approaches and tools

Dunn (2012) points out that policy analysis may be descriptive or normative, or both. Descriptive policy analysis identifies categories and patterns with the purpose of explaining policy situations and predicting policy outcomes. Normative

Figure 14.9: Use of problem definition in papers by think tank

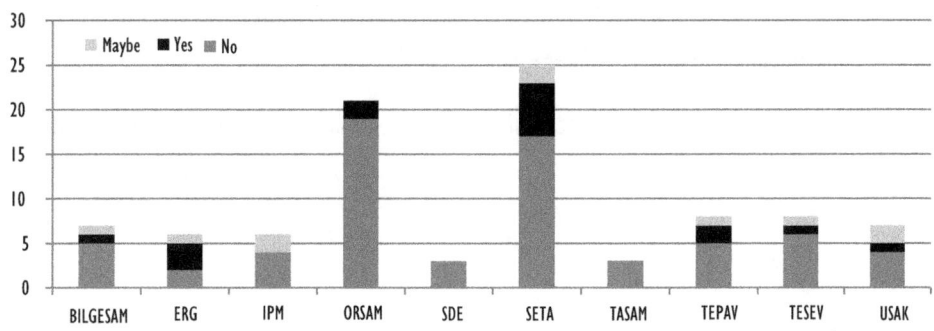

policy analysis, on the other hand, prescribes policy options or evaluates policy performance based on values. In our study we assessed whether the orientation of each paper was descriptive, normative or both.

Figure 14.10 displays our findings for each think tank. Among the papers we analysed, 97.9 per cent were either descriptive or both normative and descriptive. About half (51.1 per cent) were descriptive only, and 46.8 per cent were both descriptive and normative. Descriptive analysis is predominant in the reports of SDE (100 per cent), TASAM (67 per cent), ORSAM (67 per cent) and TEPAV (62 per cent). On the other hand, USAK (86 per cent), ERG (67 per cent) and TESEV (63 per cent) employ both descriptive and normative analyses at higher percentages.

According to Dunn (2012), policy analysis may be prospective or retrospective. Prospective policy analysis produces ex-ante policy information. This kind of information can be created by identifying/constructing policy alternatives and preferences and synthesising qualitative and quantitative information that could be used to make policy decisions. Retrospective policy analysis produces ex-post policy information. We investigated in our study which of these two forms of policy analysis was used in the papers. We found that only 9 studies (9.6 per cent) used either a prospective or retrospective form of policy analysis. Figure 14.11 shows the distribution of these 9 papers among only 5 of the 10 think tanks

Figure 14.10: Descriptive and normative analyses in papers by think tank

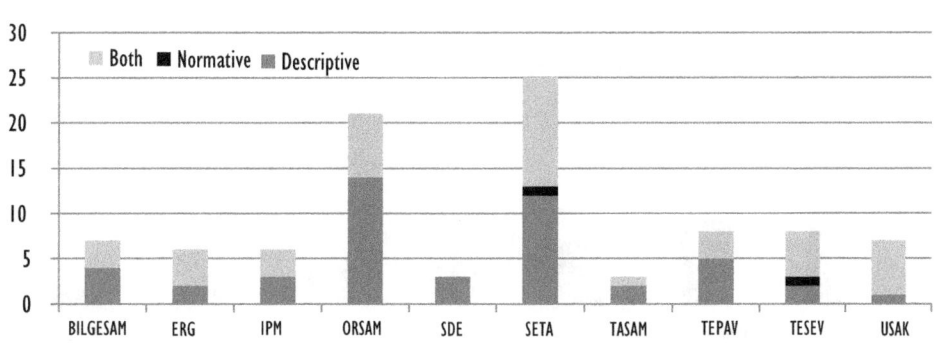

Policy analysis in Turkey

whose papers we analysed. We should note that the two forms of policy analysis Dunn defines demand high levels of conceptual and analytical rigour, and the papers we analysed did not achieve those levels.

Figure 14.11: Retrospective and prospective forms of policy analysis in papers by think tank

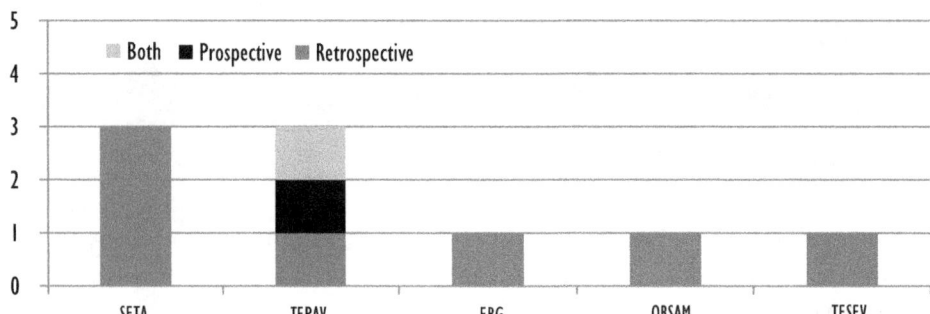

To further investigate the analytical quality of the papers, we asked which methods of data collection and analyses their authors used. We found that only in 27 papers (28.7 per cent) was a data collection method used; the authors of the remaining 67 papers did not use any data collection method. Figure 14.12 shows the distribution of data collection methods used in the remaining papers. The total number of data collection methods is higher than 27 because some of the papers used multiple methods. Interview is the most popular method, followed by secondary data, focus groups and surveys.

The total number of papers that used any data analysis methods is 15 (16 per cent). Figure 14.13 shows the distribution of data analysis methods used in these papers. Once again, the total number of data analysis methods is higher than 15 because some of the papers used multiple methods. Descriptive statistics are the most popular method. More complex methods (qualitative or quantitative) are rarely used.

We also compared the use of data collection analysis methods used in the earlier period of 2005 to 2010 and the later period of 2011 to 2015. Because the total numbers for both were low, it is difficult to make comparisons, but we found that there is a slight increase in the percentages of the data collection and analysis methods used over time.

Figure 14.12: Data collection methods used in papers

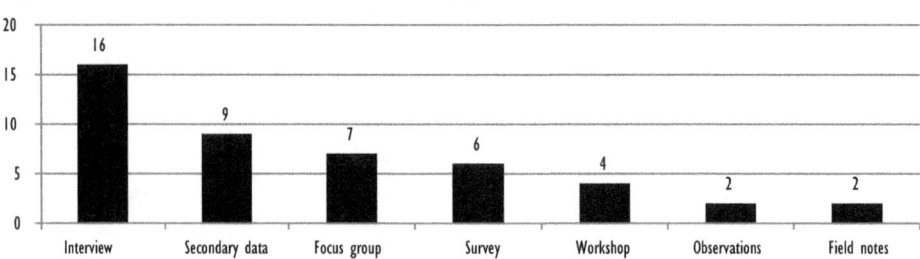

Figure 14.13: Data analysis methods used in the papers

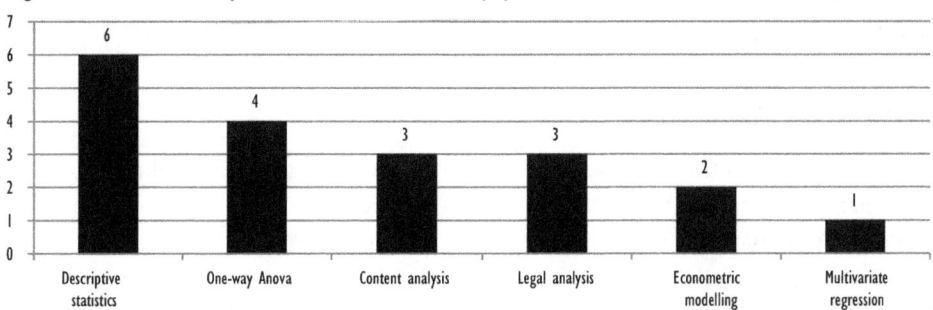

Direct data collection or analysis is not always expected in policy analysis papers. Analysts may gather information from other (secondary) sources and interpret them to make policy proposals or evaluate policy outcomes. So we asked to what extent the authors of the papers used academic literature, government statistics, legal documents or policy documents (policy analysis papers, reports, books produced by other analysts) as secondary sources of information. Figure 14.14 presents our findings. A majority of the authors (69 per cent) referred to academic literature in their papers. This is not surprising, given the fact that large numbers have doctoral degrees and are affiliated with universities (see Figures 14.5 and 14.6). More than half of the papers (56.4 per cent) interpreted official statistics. The percentage of papers that used policy documents, such as development plans, government programmes and European Union (EU) progress reports, is relatively low (36.2 per cent). The authors of only 28 per cent of the papers interpreted legal documents. We should note that these were not in-depth legal interpretations, but brief references to various laws and regulations.

Figure 14.14: Number of secondary sources used in papers

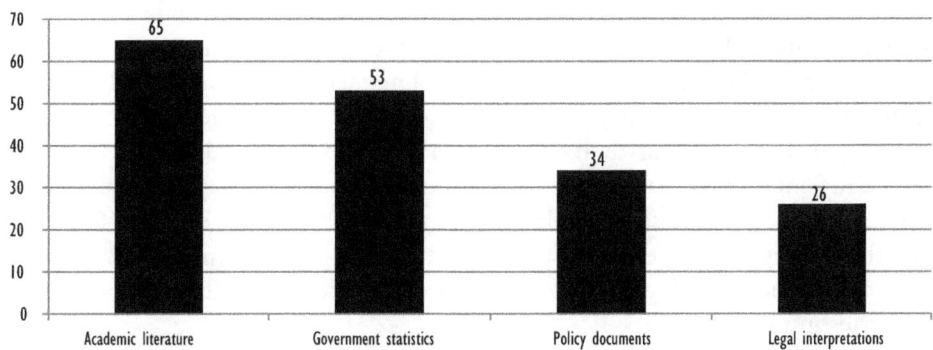

We also compared the earlier period of 2005 to 2010 and the later period of 2011 to 2015 in the uses of the four types of secondary sources of information. The use of academic literature increased from 55 per cent in the first period to 73 per cent in the second period. Similarly the use of official statistics increased from 45 to 59 per cent. The use of legal documents and policy documents, on the other hand, dropped, from 40 to 24 per cent and from 45 to 34 per cent respectively.

Discussion and conclusion

The discussions in the previous section show that think tanks in Turkey followed a similar path to their counterparts in many other countries. They emerged in response to increasing demands for policy-relevant information in the increasingly complex societies of the 20th and 21st centuries. The changes in the political environment in the country, such as the democratisation process of the 1960s, the restrictive politics of the 1980s and internationalisation in the post-Cold War era affected their creation and development. The specific demands for policy-relevant information that were created by the long-term planning framework set up by the 1961 Constitution and the EU accession process were particularly important drivers.

Our content analyses of the think tanks' papers indicate that they follow the policy agendas and trends in Turkey and the world. The most popular area of policy in the papers is international relations. This is not surprising, given the fact that a majority of the think tanks in Turkey were established as international affairs and strategic research centres. The increasing globalisation of the world in the early 21st century and the increasing interest of the Turkish government in international relations in this period provides the background to the popularity of this policy area. McGann (2016) notes that most of the influential think tanks in the US also operate in the field of international affairs.

The papers we analysed provide some indications of the particular policy priorities in international relations in Turkey and how they have changed over time. The most frequently studied international relations issue is the Middle East. The social movements that began in the Middle Eastern countries in 2010 (the 'Arab Spring') had a direct impact on the priorities of the think tanks in Turkey. Sixty per cent of the reports written in 2011 focused on international affairs and 45 per cent on the Middle East as a region. The fact that terrorism and refugee problems had direct impacts on Turkey also attracted the attention of think tanks and forced them to focus their agendas on the Middle East. It seems that the decreasing interest in Europe in Turkish politics and public opinion in recent years has led to a decrease in the interest in papers written on Europe. The fact that the papers written on Africa increased in number beginning in 2013 is a reflection of the Turkish government's intensified diplomatic initiatives in African countries in recent years.

The second most popular policy area in the papers analysed is what we call 'politics', which includes topics like democratisation, elections, nationalism and the Kurdish question. These were prominent issues in the political agenda of the country in the period we studied, and were intertwined with the international relations of the country, particularly with countries in the Middle East. In recent years, think tanks that have expertise in more specific policy areas such as education, health and social policy have been established, and in our study we observed that education policy was among the top areas of interest.

In our analyses we also investigated the formats of the papers and the methods used by their authors. These are potentially important indicators of the development of policy analysis practices in the country – at least the policy analysis that is practised in think tanks. What we see is a mixed picture. On the one hand, some of the expected format requirements (purpose statement and problem definition) are lacking, and in a very small percentage data collection and analysis methods are applied. The fact that a large majority of the papers were written by university-affiliated academics or think tank experts with advanced degrees (Master's and PhD degrees) makes these deficiencies even more noteworthy. It is also noteworthy that the papers produced by the two university-affiliated think tanks in our study (ERG and IPM) are no better than the independent think tanks (all the others in our study) in terms of deficiencies in paper format (lack of purpose statement and problem definition) or lack of data collection and analysis methods used. On the other hand, there seems to be some improvement in aggregate, at least in the formats of the papers: more included purpose statements in the later years we analysed.

We observed that there were no format/style standards in the papers. While some do include sections such as an abstract/executive summary, which directly appeals to policy-makers, others do not. The increase in the number of reports that include abstracts/executive summaries, purpose statements and research questions indicate that common formatting conventions are beginning to emerge.

A large majority of the papers we analysed are descriptive and lack normative elements (recommendations, evaluations). More often than not, it is expected that policy issue papers include some recommendations and/or evaluations, although this is not a requirement – a paper may be descriptive only, it may lay out policy options without making a recommendation, for example (for different models and options, see Dunn, 2012). The fact that a large majority of the papers we analysed are descriptive is not a problem in itself. If a paper is descriptive in the broadest sense of the term (that is, it identifies categories and patterns with the purposes of explaining policy situations and predicting policy outcomes using appropriate models and methods), that would be well within the realms of expectation for a policy paper. The findings in our study show that very few of the papers used data collection or analysis methods, and that very few were constructed within a prospective or retrospective framework, which are indications of deficiencies. Most of the papers we read were mere narratives; they did not include any discernible frameworks or analytical approaches.

The slight increases over the years in the applications of methods, together with the noticeable improvements in the format of the papers (summary, purpose and research questions) are noteworthy for the future of work done by think tanks. These developments and improvements are important because think tanks can play significant roles in the development of policy analysis in a country. In Korea, policy analysis developed as an independent academic discipline, apart from political science and public administration, thanks to the significant contributions of think tanks and research institutes (Mo, 2007). Think tanks can play a similar role in Turkey. The number of think tanks has increased considerably in Turkey in the last few decades, particularly in the last decade, and there is also a growing community of public policy scholars who have played roles in think tanks. All these developments may be harbingers of the emergence of public policy as a distinct academic discipline in Turkey.

Notes

[1] Its name was changed to the Turkish Economic and Social Studies Foundation (Türkiye Ekonomik ve Sosyal Etüdler Vakfı, TESEV) in 1994. TESEV is still one of the most influential institutions in policy-making processes.

[2] Its name was changed to the Economic Development Foundation (İktisadi Kalkınma Vakfı, IKV) in 1967.

References

Abelson, D.E. (2002) *Do think tanks matter?*, London: McGill-Queen's University Press.

Aras, B., Toktaş, Ş. and Kurt, Ü. (2010) *Araştırma merkezlerinin yükselişi*, Ankara: SETA Report.

Arslan, E. (2009) 'Düşünce kuruluşlarının Türkiye serüveni', in H. Kanbolat and H.A. Karasar (eds) *Türkiye'de stratejik düşünce kültürü ve stratejik araştırma merkezleri: Başlangıcından bugüne Türk düşünce kuruluşları*, Ankara: Nobel Yayınları, pp 31-8.

Aydın, A. (2006) 'The genesis of think-tank culture in Turkey: Past, present and future?', Unpublished Master's thesis, Ankara: Middle East Technical University.

Bağcı, H. and Aydın, A. (2009) 'Dünyada ve Türkiye'de düşünce kuruluşu kültürü', in H. Kanbolat and H.A. Karasar (eds) *Türkiye'de stratejik düşünce kültürü ve stratejik araştırma merkezleri: Başlangıcından bugüne Türk düşünce kuruluşları*, Ankara: Nobel Yayınları, pp 57-125.

Bulut, A.T. and Güngör, F. (2009) 'Think tankler ve dış politika: Türkiye ve ABD örneği', in H. Kanbolat and H.A. Karasar (eds) *Türkiye'de stratejik düşünce kültürü ve stratejik araştırma merkezleri: Başlangıcından bugüne Türk düşünce kuruluşları*, Ankara: Nobel Yayınları, pp 262-81.

Dunn, W.N. (2012) *Public policy analysis* (5th edn), Boston, MA: Pearson.

Ediger, V.Ş. (2009) 'Türk think tankı'nın olgunlaşma dönemine doğru', in H. Kanbolat and H.A. Karasar (eds) *Türkiye'de stratejik düşünce kültürü ve stratejik araştırma merkezleri: Başlangıcından bugüne Türk düşünce kuruluşları*, Ankara: Nobel Yayınları, pp 197-208.

Gül, H. and Yemen, A. (2016) 'Türkiye'de düşünce kuruluşlarının kamu politikası süreçlerindeki rolü ve etkisi', in M.A. Çukurçayır, H.T. Eroğlu, H. Sağır and M. Navruz (eds) *Kayfor 13 Bildiriler kitabı: Kamu yönetiminde değişimin yönü ve etkileri*, Konya: Selçuk Üniversitesi, pp 656-82.

Güvenç, S. (2007) 'Türkiye'nin dış politikası ve düşünce kuruluşları', in S.C. Mazlum and E. Doğan (eds) *Sivil toplum örgütleri ve dış politika: Yeni sorunlar, yeni aktörler*, İstanbul: Bağlam Yayınları, pp 159-80.

Kantarcı, Ş. (2009) 'Yirmi birinci yüzyıl Türkiyesi'nde doğan sivil tabanlı yeni kurumlar: Stratejik araştırma merkezleri', in H. Kanbolat and H.A. Karasar (eds) *Türkiye'de stratejik düşünce kültürü ve stratejik araştırma merkezleri: Başlangıcından bugüne Türk düşünce kuruluşları*, Ankara: Nobel Yayınları, pp 323-31.

Karatepe, Ş. (2016) *Türk anayasa hukuku*, Ankara: Savaş Yayınevi.

Ladi, S. (2000) 'Globalization, think tanks and policy transfer', in D. Stone (ed) *Banking on knowledge: The genesis of the global development network*, London: Routledge, pp 215-22.

McGann, J.G. (2011) 'Think tanks: The global, regional and national dimensions', in *Think tanks in policy making – Do they matter?*, Friedrich Ebert Stiftung Briefing Paper Special Issue, pp 8-15.

McGann, J.G. (2016) *2015 global go to think tanks index report*, University of Pennsylvania Scholarly Commons.

Mo, C. (2007) 'Korean policy analysis: From economic efficiency to public participation', in F. Fischer, G.J. Miller and M.S. Sidney (eds) *Handbook of public policy analysis: Theory, politics and methods*, New York: CRC Press, pp 617-24.

Özbudun, E. (1995) *Türk anayasa hukuku* (4th edn), Ankara: Yetkin Yayınları.

Radin, B. (2013) *Beyond Machiavelli: Policy analysis reaches midlife*, Washington, DC: Georgetown University Press.

Rich, A. (2004) *Think tanks, public policy and the politics of expertise*, New York: Cambridge University Press.

Rossi, P.H., Lipsey, M.W. and Freeman, H.E. (2004) *Evaluation: A systematic approach* (7th edn), Thousand Oaks, CA: Sage.

Smith, J. (1991) *The idea brokers*, New York: The Free Press.

Stone, D. (2000) 'Think tank transnationalisation and non-profit analysis, advice and advocacy', *Global Society*, vol 14, pp 153-72.

Stone, D. (2004) 'Introduction: Think tanks, policy advice and governance', in D. Stone and A. Denham (eds) *Think tank traditions*, Manchester: Manchester University Press, pp 1-19.

Stone, D. and Garnett, M. (1998) 'Introduction: Think tanks, policy advice and governance', in D. Stone, A. Denham and M. Garnett (eds) *Think tanks across nations*, Manchester: Manchester University Press, pp 1-21.

Toktaş, Ş. and Aras, B. (2012) 'National security culture in Turkey: A qualitative study on think tanks', *Bilig*, vol 62, pp 245-64.

Uzgel, İ. (2006) 'Düşünce kuruluşları (think tank'lar)', in F. Başkaya (ed) *Kavram sözlüğü*, İstanbul: Türkiye ve Orta Doğu Vakfı Yayını, pp 141-9.

Weaver, R.K. and McGann, J.G. (2009) 'Think tanks and civil societies in a time of change', in J.G. McGann and R.K. Weaver (eds) *Think tanks and civil societies*, New Brunswick, NJ: Fourth Paperback, Transaction Publishing, pp 1-37.

Yıldız, M., Çelik, D., Arslan, N., Çiftçi, L., Eldemir, S. and Sinangil, S. (2013) 'Kamu politikalarında düşünce üretim kuruluşlarının rolü: Genel çerçeve ve Türkiye'den örnekler', in M. Yıldız and M.Z. Sobacı (eds) *Kamu politikası: Kuram ve uygulama*, Ankara: Adres Yayınları, pp 188-220.

FIFTEEN

Public policy and media in Turkey

Başak Yavçan and Hakan Övünç Ongur[1]

Introduction

There is a growing literature on the relationship between mass media and policy-making, and how mass media is crucial in terms of drawing and keeping public attention on policy processes. As Strömberg (2001, p 653) puts it, 'the logic why mass media should influence policy is simple. If more informed voters receive favourable policies, then mass media should matter because they provide most of the information people use in voting.' However, if we consider politics beyond a simple voting practice, and rather as an ever-expanding sphere of power relations that involves the direct participation of people in daily issues, the degree that mass media matters should increase. With both online and print media becoming more accessible to everyone and the flow of information growing incrementally, the mediation of information between people and policy-makers is becoming more important. Therefore in this chapter we explore this relationship between media and policy-making in the Turkish case.

Our contribution to the existing literature is twofold. On the one hand, we address the three different roles played by mass media in its relationship to policy-making in Turkey – (1) agenda-setting; (2) framing; and (3) panoptical, and being reflected by public policy – and, based on Pierre Bourdieu's field theory, we point out the way media as a semi-autonomous field can reflect and refract public policy with respect to varying conditions. On the other hand, methodologically, we suggest a template for media content analysis for the Turkish media and its role in policy-making across different Turkish media outlets over 20 years, as a framework for future studies.

We first review the literature explicating the relationship between mass media and policy-making. Then we engage with this literature, complementing it with the 'field theory' framework suggested by Bourdieu (Benson, 2006), exploring the Turkish case through this perspective. We then lay out our time series media content analysis methodology as a way to understand the scope of the media coverage of policy processes and the way they are framed across different Turkish media outlets in regards to various policy areas, namely, domestic politics/ideology, economics, internal security and foreign policy. In doing this, we further elaborate different sub-policy areas encompassed by each field such as the executive vs the opposition, corruption, Turkey and its engagement with international organisations and so on. Illustrating trends of the role of the media in setting the agenda and framing the policy processes with the help of this data, we further describe the distribution of each policy field across newspapers with varying economic and cultural capital, as manifested by their sales and readership base. Finally, we illustrate how the content of news changes based on the policy area with respect to the critical tone towards policy-makers. Rather than testing any set of hypotheses with this data, our aim is to describe how each of the processes laid out in the literature are at play for this period under investigation in Turkey.

Literature review

The literature on the media's role in policy-making is vast but converging, in attributing similar roles for the media to play (see, for example, McCombs and Shaw, 1972; Kingdon, 1984; Nacos et al, 2000; McCombs, 2004; Walgrave and van Aelst, 2006; Scheufele, 2007; Koch-Baumgarten and Voltmer, 2010). Lattman-Weltman (2013) suggests that there are three different roles that mass media plays in its relations with policy-makers. First, as an agenda-setter, 'the media interfere with the contingent process that defines what themes are important for the wider public agenda' (Lattman-Weltman, 2013, p 4). The coverage of news, the tone that is used to introduce a story, the physical space that a story occupies in print or online media platform, the frequency of repetition that a particular news possesses, and many other related factors directly affect how the public 'consumes' a story and how it is ranked among other stories. This also explains why media ownership is important, especially where democratic pluralism is demanded. 'Concentrations of media ownership can lead to overrepresentation of certain political opinions or forms of cultural output (those favoured by powerful media owners, whether on commercial or ideological grounds) and to the exclusion of others' (Doyle, 2002, p 26).

Second, as a provider of framing, mass media has 'the power to determine a particular focus, certain associations of sense, a certain meaning for each event, version or subject' (Lattman-Weltman, 2013, p 4). Accordingly, the narration of news is just as important for the public to consume a story as how it is defined. By framing, the media puts constraints on the way the public is presented with a story; in other words, the presentation or characterisation of a story is important in how the public understands it. 'Framing an issue involves selecting some aspects of a perceived reality ... in such a way as to promote a particular problem definition, causal interpretation, moral evaluation, and/or treatment recommendation' (Soroka et al, 2013, p 204). The link between reality and the public is determined or mediated by the means of mass media, hence it is vulnerable to the way it is framed (McCombs, 2004, pp 21-35).

Third, mass media plays a panoptical role, where it is capable of exposing 'public figures in practices considered morally inadmissible or simply illegal.... [W]hen fulfilling its self-defining functions of "guardian" or "watchdog" of the public democratic interest, the mass media thus interfere directly in the political capital of public figures' (Lattman-Weltman, 2013, p 5). Modelled first by Jeremy Bentham in the 19th century, panopticon implies the architecture of ring-shaped prison cells, at the centre of which there is a tower with an observer. It is used to describe what Michel Foucault calls the 'disciplinary society' of today where 'there would no longer be inquiry, but supervision (*surveillance*) and examination. It was no longer a matter of reconstituting an event, but something – or, rather, someone – who needed total, uninterrupted supervision' (Foucault, 1994, p 59). This constant supervision of the public as well as policy-makers is conducted by media outlets nowadays, and this also shows why the media as a producer or representing knowledge is critical for power relations in any society. On the other hand, the panoptical role of the media could also be reserved. 'While policymakers pay attention to the media as a manifestation of public opinion, they also follow the news as a way of monitoring the political environment in which they operate' (Voltmer and Koch-Baumgarten, 2010, p 3).

The question remains if it is possible to jointly benefit from these three conceptualisations. There is a recent tendency in a brand of media studies that is particularly interested in explaining the relationship between media and politics by integrating the French sociologist Pierre Bourdieu's field theory into their work (Benson, 1998; Benson and Neveu, 2004; Yavcan and Ongur, 2016). In developing our methodological approach for this chapter, we benefit from this line of work and conceptualise media as a 'semi-autonomous field', sometimes reflecting and at other times refracting the positions of other fields it engages with, that is, external influences, for a given issue area (Benson, 2006, p 196; Benson, 2010).

It was Bourdieu (1984, pp 220-6) himself who first used the concept of a field – a social or institutional area of struggle among agents over the appropriation of the related form of (economic, political, cultural, intellectual, etc) capital – to demonstrate the substantial link between the fields of politics and of journalism, stating that 'the journalistic field produces and imposes on the public a very particular vision of the political field' (Bourdieu, 1998, p 2). Within each field, agents who (re-)act according to their dispositions (*habitus*) that develop out of their position in social classes and not of calculated interests are objectively structured and hierarchically organised. Agents, in other words, both reflect and reproduce their positions within fields. Although they are independent spaces of struggle, fields constantly interact with each other, and are therefore regarded as semi-autonomous, that is, constantly affecting and being affected by other fields, and subordinate to the greater field of power (Bourdieu, 1993, pp 29-73).

It is not only the panoptical power of the media, previously highlighted by Lattman-Weltman, that directly interferes with the political capital of public figures, but also the agenda-setting and framing abilities of the agents of the field of journalism (media) over the social construction of 'reality' which make Bourdieu's field theory a very useful tool for analysing media and policy-making. As shown elsewhere (Yavcan and Ongur, 2016, p 2426), Rodney Benson (2010) mentions three other advantages provided by the application of field theory to this particular type of analysis. First, field theory allows inquiring about the dynamics of media outlets' relations with other fields; second, it shows how different media outlets are positioned within the field of journalism; and finally, it bypasses common sense regarding the direct proportion of political power and news making.

In the following, our data make use of field theory with an eye on the relationship between different media outlets and their relationship to the nexus of power, especially the changing dynamics via its consolidation through the Justice and Development Party's (Adalet ve Kalkınma Partisi, AKP) consecutive election victories. Yet, as elaborated by Benson (2004) and Yang and Ishak (2012), it is not only cross-national variation among different media systems but also within-country variation across media institutions that should be considered as possible variables affecting the output of the field. These are, in fact, factors that mediate the aforementioned structural impact, and include the media field's positioning of itself vis-à-vis other fields in relation to the consumer/reader base, also resulting in different editorial room norms. For instance, according to Hanitzsch et al (2011), media outlets closest to the intellectual pole have relatively high autonomy and emphasise cultural capital over economic capital.

For our application of these different approaches to the Turkish case, we make use of these interactions of the field of media with other fields, and suggest that the role that media assumes in terms of its ability to set the agenda, to frame or be panoptically relevant may depend on these interactions and should therefore be investigated through this perspective. We show that for the past 20 years, four particular newspapers selected from the Turkish mass media are engaged in agenda-setting in terms of public policy-making (especially during the period of coalitions in the 1990s, as well as the political rise of the AKP in the early 2000s). However, especially after the consolidation of political power in the late-2000s, these newspapers show a tendency to be affected by this consolidation as the level of criticism towards policy-making has been in steady decline since then. Nevertheless, as suggested by Bourdieu, this decline does not diffuse in sync, because different media outlets are shown to pursue different dispositions towards criticism even though they share the same field of journalism and are similarly affected by the political pressure over them.

Data description and methodology

In order to illustrate different forms of public policy covered by the media and to analyse its content with regards to criticism directed at the government (or lack thereof), we selected five different Turkish newspapers. These represent both the mainstream, centrist, widely circulated tabloid media, namely, *Hürriyet*, *Milliyet* and *Sabah*, with an average circulation of 400,000, 200,000 and 300,000 respectively. We also selected the prestige papers of the leftist paper *Cumhuriyet*, with an average daily circulation of 60,000, and the conservative paper *Zaman*,[2] with an average daily circulation of about 850,000.

While we are hesitant to attribute any ideological affinity to the papers *a priori*, existing literature has illustrated the voting biases of their readers and their parallelism with political parties via content analysis prior to elections (Çarkoğlu et al, 2014). We therefore used this cue to create variety in our selection of newspapers. Other potential papers that fit the selection criteria either did not have archives (as in the case of *Sözcü* and *Radikal*) or were not available for the entire 19 years of our analysis (such as *Habertürk*, *Star* and *Posta*). Table 15.1 illustrates the circulation, year of establishment, ownership information and the conglomerate sectors associated with each owner.

Table 15.1: Basic data on newspapers selected

	Daily circulation (August 2014)*	Year established	Owners (Christensen, 2007, p 188)	Company activity areas
Zaman	940,000	1985	Feza/Samanyolu	Broadcasting, indirectly education, health, construction
Hürriyet	386,000	1948	Doğan (since 1994)	Media, finance, energy, industry, commerce
Cumhuriyet	56,000	1924	Cumhuriyet Foundation	Education
Milliyet	162,000	1926	Doğan (1980-2011) Demirören (2011+)	Energy, real estate, commerce, industry
Sabah	313,000	1985	Dinç Bilgin (1985-2000) Ciner Group (2000-07) Turkuvaz/Çalık (2007+)	Textile, energy, construction, finance, telecommunication

Note: *For the daily circulation numbers, please see www.medyatava.com/tiraj/2014-08-11

For the content analysis the sampling was conducted based on the selection of the full front pages of these papers for the 5th, 15th and 25th of each month for 20 years, yielding to 36 front pages from each paper with each year. Most of the newspapers were photocopied and scanned from hardcopies from the archives of the library of Turkish General National Assembly and National Library in Ankara. Some newspapers provided us with the newspapers selected from their own electronic archives. When, for a particular reason, the paper for the predetermined date was not available in the archives, the following day's paper was included in the sample.

For this analysis, hard copies of the newspapers were selected for investigation. While sales of newspapers are not very impressive in Turkey, other ways of consuming the informational material provided by newspapers are very prevalent, including online readership. As we have argued elsewhere, in Turkey, newspaper reporting is the main source of reporting in that the headlines and main stories are covered as part of the morning news on most TV channels (Yavcan and Ongur 2016). This pattern compares well with cases such as in Argentina, where news broadcasting is mostly via newspaper journalism (Waisbord, 1994). An alternative could be to analyse the content of the online versions of the newspapers; however, several challenges prevented us from pursuing this option, such as the fact that not all the newspapers had extensive online content with well-developed websites. Partly related to this, the search engines of the online websites did not cover the entire period under investigation, and some papers only allow for a one-year search on their databases. Furthermore, the online archives are not fully dependable, as content is sometimes deleted due to various concerns ranging from data storage costs to removal of content criticising the government.

In terms of methodology, we trained a team of coders on a structured codebook and met regularly to address ambiguities in coding. We coded the content of the news stories concerning public policy with the following categories of 'politics/ideology', 'economy', 'society, culture and sports', 'security/terrorism', 'Turkey and international organisations' and 'Turkish foreign policy (vis-à-vis states, hence not international organisations)'. We then constructed detailed subheadings for each of these categories, some set *a priori,* and some as aggregations of common themes coded as open-ended. We excluded editorial excerpts as our interest lies in news reporting by journalists.

Furthermore, in order to better understand the potential criticism of the government, as a proxy for the media's direct attempt to set the agenda and affect public policy, we measured the nature of the criticism in the Turkish context, searching across various forms, issues and direction of criticism elaborated on by Benson (2010). Accordingly, we first identified articles from each paper's front page targeting public policy or a government agency. We identified whether or not there was extant criticism in a given news story, which we labelled as *general criticism*. Following that, we measured criticism based on its source (through an outside source or the journalist themself), and created a scale of criticism.

Analysis

Distribution of public policy news

Table 15.2 demonstrates the distribution of public policy news over 19 years (between 1995 and 2013) by subject area. As stated, one of the primary functions of mass media is to define what themes or subjects are important or worth being presented for the attention of the public. Regardless of the character of media outlets, this agenda-setting function plays a critical role in determining what matters in public policy processes for policy-makers. Accordingly, five newspapers with the largest number of nationwide sales selected the themes of 'politics/ideology', 'economics', 'society, culture and sports', 'security/terrorism', 'Turkey and international organisations' and 'foreign policy' over other subjects for policy-making. It should be noted that these common categories only cover articles directly concerning the government.

Looking at all news stories over the time period considered, over 6,000 articles relate to public policy. The first finding in terms of agenda-setting is that Turkish newsreaders are exposed to a heavy news content that is predominantly domestic.

Table 15.2: Distribution of public policy news by subject area, 1995–2013

Subcategory	Number of news stories	%
Politics/ideology	3,198	51.14
Economy	768	12.28
Society, culture and sports	373	5.97
Security/terror	682	10.91
Turkey and international organisations	328	5.25
Foreign policy	824	13.18
Other	80	1.28
Total	6,253	100

Only 18 per cent of news content is related to Turkish foreign policy, either to a specific country or an international organisation. This is surprising in that the period between 1995 and 2005 in particular, in which Turkey was accepted as a European Union (EU) candidate, is marked with Turkey's negotiations with the EU that had a direct impact on the country's domestic political formation – out of 1,152 articles on foreign policy, only 200 concern EU–Turkey relations. While this is perplexing for the Turkish case, the comparative lack of attention to foreign policy-making is common in news coverage, mostly because in EU member states these are framed as domestic politics (de Vreese, 2003), and the general popularity of international news is rather weak (Wanta et al, 2004).

Among the majority of articles that are directly related to the domestic political context, the subcategory of 'politics/ideology' has the highest share. If we include the subcategories of 'society, culture and sports' and 'security/terrorism', economics is set to have the least concerned theme in Turkey. It is also quite interesting given that this 19-year period is marked by three different economic crises and their immediate impacts on society, in 1994, 2001 and 2008. Figure 15.1, on the distribution of these different categories over the years, further accentuates these points.

Despite being a country of transition with an unstable economy, where discussing economic policies constitutes a big part of daily conversations (Öniş, 2009), this is not reflected in the news coverage. It was only in 2001 that news about economics outnumbered news about other realms of public policies. The economic crisis in 2008, which had a devastating effect on the world economy as a whole, did not, for instance, lead to a significant increase in the number of related news stories. It is possible to assume from this data that the framing of the economic crises might be said to impact greatly on how the public perceives and reacts to their severity.

On the contrary, coverage on security/terrorism almost directly reflects domestic events surrounding the Kurdish issue, in particular. The capture of Abdullah

Figure 15.1: Distribution of public policy news over 19 years

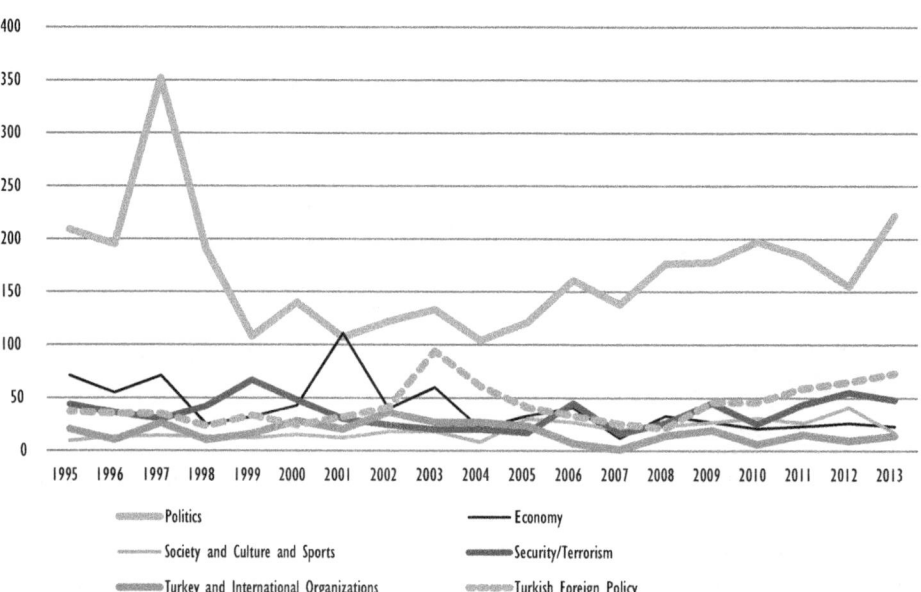

Öcalan, leader of the Kurdistan Workers' Party (PKK), in 1999 signifies a peak in security news, followed by a major decline in the number of stories until 2009, when the so-called Kurdish Opening Process was launched (Çakır, 2010). After that point, news coverage started to be framed as less of a security/terrorism issue and more of a democratisation/minority rights issue. The change in framing resulted in the shifting of the Kurdish issue from the subcategory of 'security/terrorism' to that of 'domestic politics' under the subheading of 'minority rights'.

The aforementioned relations between Turkey and the EU is also supported here by the trend in data that shows a radical drop in the number of stories regarding international organisations in the media by 2006. In terms of foreign policy in general, news coverage of international affairs and organisations peaks, expectedly, in 2003, with the US invasion of Iraq and domestic debates on whether Turkey should send in troops, with a steady rise in 2011 with the 'Arab Spring', the Syrian Civil War and the growing number of refugees in the country (Ayata, 2015).

Thus far, Table 15.2 and Figure 15.1 have illustrated that there is little evidence to suggest Turkish media's proactive agenda-setting powers other than reflecting actual public policy, except for the subject of the economy, where its limited coverage, especially during times of crises, implies that the issue is low down on the agenda.

Subcategories of public policy news

The most prominent news category shown in Table 15.2 and Figure 15.1 is 'politics/ideology'. In order to grasp the content of this category in detail, we further analysed its subcategories. Among 19 of them, we selected 5 that are

Figure 15.2: Five specific subcategories of public policy with political content across 19 years

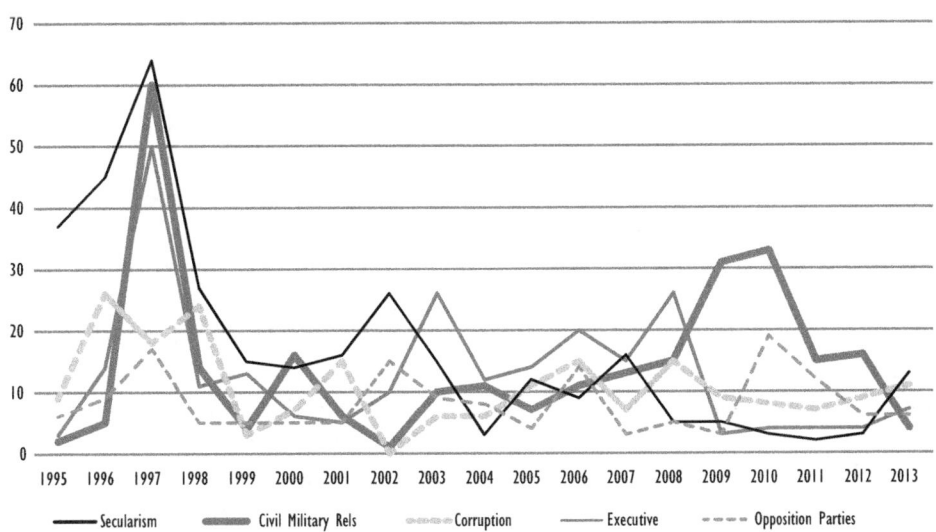

directly related to policy-making, namely, 'secularism', 'civil–military relations', 'corruption', 'executive' and 'opposition parties', explored here and shown in Figure 15.2.

In terms of news coverage regarding secularism, a peak is found in 1997 with the so-called February 28 Process and the subsequent military intervention into domestic politics. At a National Security Council meeting on this date the Turkish military leadership initiated a process that would eventually result in the end of the coalition government and the closing down of one of its parties, the Welfare Party, based on the proposed danger to the secular character of the Republic (Cizre and Çınar, 2003). This discussion was again heated when former members of the Welfare Party took power in 2003 with the newly founded Justice and Development Party (Adalet ve Kalkınma Partisi, AKP), and lasted until 2009, when high-profile military officers were charged with an alleged coup against the government (known as the Ergenekon Process; see Aydın-Düzgit, 2012). National and international (EU) support for the AKP government during these trials was also reflected in the news coverage.

These same debates might also be tracked by the increase in the number of stories covered in terms of civil–military relations. However, unlike 1997, these relations were no longer framed within the realm of secularism, but shifted, in fact, to civilian control of the military. The dying out of the secularism debate, following the adaptation of the EU Acquis limiting the military's role in politics (Gürsoy, 2011), and the 2010 referendum that helped the AKP government's consolidation of power, signifies the further subordination of the majority of mass media in terms of agenda-setting.

When it comes to corruption, reporting during coalition times intensified. Given that there was a flux of votes of no confidence and government changes during this era (Heper and Keyman, 1998), this should be read as a clear example of media setting the agenda and affecting public policy. The only exception to the relative silence during the AKP's consecutive governments is in 2013. On 17 and 25 December 2013, there were a series of corruption allegations via social media against some members of the AKP government (Özbudun, 2015), resulting in a certain degree of increase in the share of corruption-related news in mainstream outlets.

During the 19 years under investigation, news concerning the executive action has the highest frequency of reporting overall, yet at the same time, declines dramatically over the years. This illustrates the clear reluctance of most news outlets to report on the executive, either negatively or positively (except for election years), a trend overlapping with the AKP's consolidation of power. This is illustrative of the media's – as a field – changing relationship with external influences, in this case, the strengthened power nexus. The year 2013 represents again an exceptional year in terms of reporting on the executive body. The Gezi Park Movement in June was a social movement that started as a protest for the protection of the environment, but extended to politics, due to the disproportionate use of force by the police (Farro and Demirhisar, 2014). The government came under the radar first of social media and then of mass media, albeit reluctantly.

There is no such declining or increasing trend of reporting with regards to the opposition or other political parties. The general coverage of the opposition remains rather stable and limited, which indicates the tendency (habitus) of the Turkish mass media to put less importance on it. Yet a detailed analysis of different news outlets is necessary at this point in order to illustrate potential differences in the field of journalism, as suggested by Bourdieu's emphasis of 'within field' variation.

Framing public policy across newspapers

As illustrated in Table 15.3, there are considerable differences across newspapers in terms of framing public policy processes. The shares in total number of stories show that those related to the executive are the most covered, whereas those related to the opposition are the least covered for the time period under investigation. Nevertheless, almost half of the stories related to the opposition are to be found in *Cumhuriyet*, the most critical newspaper within this sample, while the others (especially *Zaman* and *Sabah*, the most pro-government for the time covered) tend not to report on the views of the opposition regarding policy-making.

A similar trend can be observed in relation to the coverage of corruption in policy-making processes. This is not particularly surprising in that corruption news is expected to point out the wrongdoing of governments, eliciting the media's watchdog character. *Cumhuriyet*, again, covers more than half of the news in this subject area, whereas *Hürriyet* and *Milliyet*, the tabloid mainstream media, have limited coverage, and *Zaman* and *Sabah* remain rather silent. What sets *Cumhuriyet* apart from the other newspapers is that it is regarded as a quality paper. Compared to the others, *Cumhuriyet* carries no characteristics of being a tabloid paper, as suggested by its lower number of sales and lesser usage of pictures and it could be argued that the newspaper does not have organic political engagements that interfere with its potential of attracting advertisements directly from the market. Furthermore, as evidenced by several market research reports, the readership base of this media outlet is much more educated, and reading the paper takes a lot longer.[3] These characteristics are also important in understanding its critical content, discussed in the following section.

Table 15.3: Framing public policy news across five newspapers, 1995–2013

	Zaman (%)	Hürriyet (%)	Cumhuriyet (%)	Milliyet (%)	Sabah (%)	Total number of stories
Secularism	11.5	26.9	27.3	25.6	8.8	227
Civil-military relations	11.7	21.9	23.7	23.0	19.7	274
Corruption	8.7	13.6	55.3	15.0	7.3	206
Executive	18.2	21.2	34.8	13.9	11.8	330
Opposition	4.5	26.3	45.5	16.7	7.1	156
Total	143	260	427	224	139	1,193

The coverage of news related to secularism and civil-military relations shows a different pattern. The two tabloid newspapers, *Hürriyet* and *Milliyet*, and *Cumhuriyet*, tend to treat these two areas of policy-making as if they are overlapping, mostly due to the fact that the earlier interventions of the military to the legislation or the executive were justified in ideological terms, implying damage to the secular character of the state. However, *Zaman*, the newspaper funded by the former supporter of the AKP government, the Gülen Movement, abstains from framing news in this fashion ('secularism'). However, after the Ergenekon trials, both *Zaman* and the pro-government *Sabah* start referring to civil-military relations, a different way of framing secularism.

The distribution of policy subjects across these newspapers is not only indicative of their agenda-setting preferences and framing issues jointly under different subcategories, but also manifestations of a bigger picture with regards to the newspapers' levels of criticism towards policy-making. We take criticism as the media's attempt as an independent facility to affect the power nexus in shaping public policy.

Distribution of criticism towards public policy

In order to measure the concept of criticism in news stories and its encompassing dimensions, we borrowed from Benson (2010), where he compared the US and French press in terms of their criticism of government regarding immigration policy. Accordingly, we identified whether there was existing criticism in a given news story, which was labelled as general criticism. Subsequently, we focused on the source of criticism in an attempt to understand whether it is directed at the government directly by the reporter of the newspaper or via an external actor/source such as an opposition MP or an expert. Finally, an additive index of both of these measures was created by adding them up. Figures 15.3 and 15.4 clarify how criticism is distributed across newspapers and policy issues, respectively.

Figure 15.3 illustrates the percentage share of critical stories to all policy-related news across the selected newspapers over 19 years. Overall, the first half of the 1990s was considered a period of rather extended journalistic freedom and criticism with a variant media environment by academics and practitioners alike. This is also supported by the declining trend of criticism from that point onwards, thus justifying our deliberate selection of 1995 as a starting point for analysis. Although there is great variation between the newspapers, from the zero criticism of *Sabah* to full criticism by *Cumhuriyet*, this general decline is reflected in Figure 15.3 for all outlets. While it is quite intriguing to explore, explaining the reasons for this decline is beyond the scope of this chapter, although the way this criticism correlates with different realms of public policy is worth mentioning. Figure 15.4 shows the distribution of criticism towards public policy by the six issue areas initially discussed.

Figure 15.3: Distribution of criticism towards public policy across five newspapers over 19 years

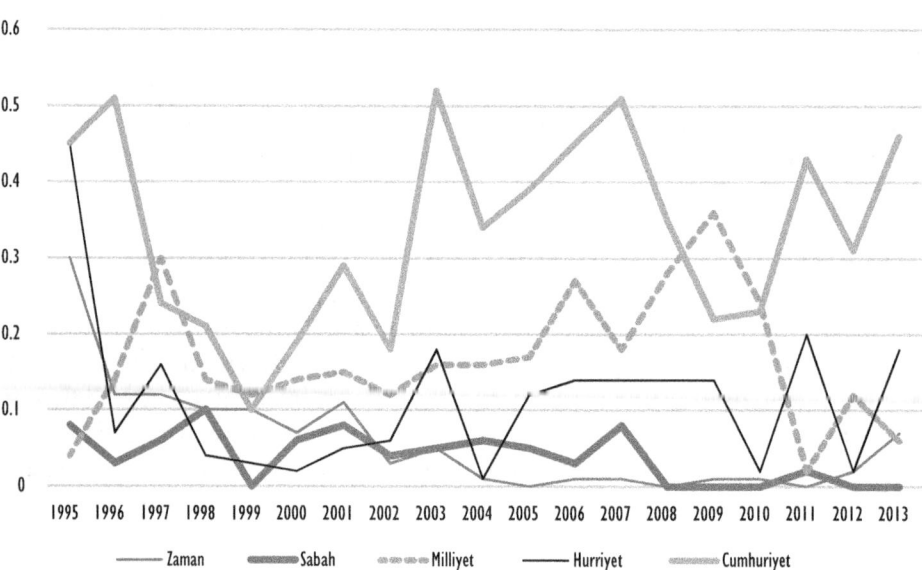

Accordingly, economic policy is subjected to most criticism among all newspapers for the 19 years. It is not only the fact that Turkey went through a series of economic crises during these years that explains this phenomenon, but the non-ideological character of criticism on economic grounds also plays an important role in the relative increase in criticism. On its mirror image, politics/ideology is the second most criticised policy area, although most of its source is the most critical newspaper, *Cumhuriyet*.

Figure 15.4: Distribution of criticism towards public policy by subject area (1995-2013)

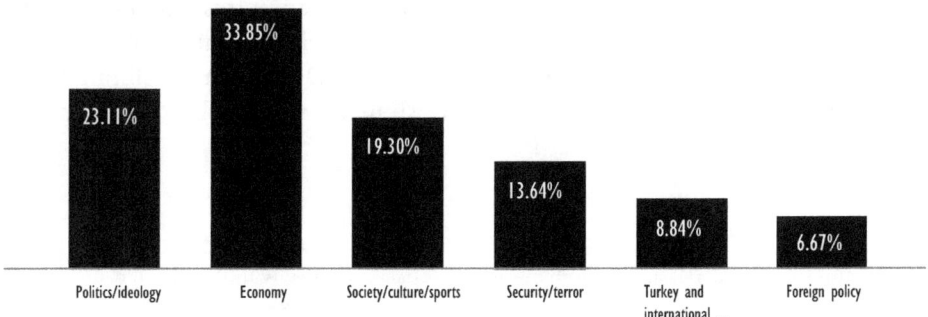

The second most striking outcome that can be derived from Figure 15.4 is the low share of critical stories about security/terrorism and Turkey's relationship with international organisations as well as foreign policy. It could be argued that regardless of the source or time, although not shown in Figure 15.4, all kinds of Turkish press are reluctant to be critical of high politics. In other words, the ability of the Turkish press to set the agenda to affect public policy through criticism depends on the issue, and is mostly visible regarding the economy, albeit declining over time in politics. On the other hand, when it comes to foreign policy and security, the line between the government and the state starts to blur, and then the media sees a lesser role for itself in influencing policy-making.

Conclusion

In this chapter we explored the role of Turkish media vis-à-vis public policy-making by suggesting a methodology of content analysis that is framed within Pierre Bourdieu's field theory. We selected five different newspapers based on their ideological orientation and their cultural capital, either intellectual or mainstream media outlets. We presented a study over 19 years (1995-2013) in an attempt to show the way they framed public policy. We argued that the three different roles played by mass media in its relationship to policy-making – (i) agenda-setting; (ii) framing; (iii) panoptical, and being reflected by public policy – depends on the level of consolidation of governmental power, the ideological positioning of the media outlet and the issue area under discussion.

The findings mostly support our hypotheses. In terms of the agenda-setting ability of Turkish media, areas outside domestic politics and ideology, even including the economy, are limited, as evidenced by their low coverage. This trend is also shown as consistent over time. When it comes to framing the area of politics and ideology, as state power is consolidated, the number of reports regarding the executive begins to decline. On the other hand, the debates around secularism shift to be framed under civil-military relations, reflecting the state discourse. Here, mass media might be said to be solely panoptical and reflective. Coverage of corruption and opposition, furthermore, is mostly left to the already critical outlets, with a clear attempt to influence policy-making, whereas the mainstream and pro-government outlets remain limited in this role. Finally, this trend is also visible in different papers' levels of criticism towards public policy, which overlaps with attention paid to policy areas. Overall, the declining trend of reporting – let alone criticising – in Turkish media suggests little evidence for an attempt to change in the near future.

Notes

1. We are thankful to Melis Zeynep Uz, Büşra Efe, Kadir Akalın, Emrah Gülsunar, Hüseyin Zengin, Ömer Giderler and Emre Ünür for their data assistance with this chapter.
2. *Zaman* was closed by a decree as a part of the AKP government's struggle with the so-called parallel state, after the coup attempt on 15 July 2016.
3. Refer to the MediaCom BIAK Turkey report at www.slideshare.net/MediaComInsights/presentations/2 and www.mediacom.com/en/contact-us/global-offices/europe,-middle-east-africa/turkey/istanbul.aspx

References

Ayata, B. (2015) 'Turkish foreign policy in a changing Arab world: Rise and fall of a regional actor?', *Journal of European Integration*, vol 37, no 1, pp 95-112.

Aydın-Düzgit, S. (2012) 'No crisis, no change: The third AKP victory in the June 2011 parliamentary elections in Turkey', *South European Society and Politics*, vol 17, no 2, pp 329-46.

Benson, R. (1998) 'Field theory in comparative context: A new paradigm for media studies', *Theory and Society*, vol 28, no 1, pp 463-98.

Benson, R. (2001) 'News media as a "journalistic field": What Bourdieu adds to new institutionalism, and vice versa', *Political Communication*, vol 23, no 2, pp 187-202.

Benson, R. (2004) 'Bringing the sociology of media back in', *Political Communication*, vol 21, no 3, pp 275–292.

Benson, R. (2006) 'News media as a "journalistic field": What Bourdieu adds to new institutionalism, and vice versa', *Political Communication*, vol 23, no 2, pp 187–202.

Benson, R. (2010) 'What makes for a critical press? A case study of French and US immigration news coverage', *International Journal of Press/Politics*, vol 15, no 1, pp 3-24.

Benson, R. and Neveu, E. (2004) *Bourdieu and the journalistic field*, London: Polity Press.

Bourdieu, P. (1984) *Distinction: A social critique of the judgment of taste*, translated by R. Nice, Cambridge, MA: Harvard University Press.

Bourdieu, P. (1993) *The field of cultural production*, translated by R. Johnson, New York: Columbia University Press.

Bourdieu, P. (1998) *On television*, translated by P. Ferguson, New York: The New Press.

Christensen, C. (2007) 'Breaking the news: Concentration of ownership, the fall of unions and government legislation in Turkey', *Global Media and Communication*, vol 3, no 2, pp 179-99.

Cizre, Ü. and Çınar, M. (2003) 'Turkey 2002: Kemalism, Islamism, and politics in the light of the February 28 process', *The South Atlantic Quarterly*, vol 102, no 2/3, pp 309-32.

Çakır, R. (2010) 'Kurdish political movement and the "democratic Opening"', *Insight Turkey*, vol 12, no 2, pp 179-92.

Çarkoğlu, A., Baruh, L. and Yıldırım, K. (2014) 'Press-party parallelism and polarization of news media during an election campaign: The case of the 2011 Turkish elections', *The International Journal of Press/Politics*, vol 19, no 3, pp 295-317.

de Vreese, C. (2003) *Framing Europe: Television news and European integration*, Amsterdam: Aksant Academic Publishers.

Doyle, G. (2002) *Media ownership: The economics and politics of convergence and concentration in the UK and European media*, London: Sage.

Farro, A. and Demirhisar, D. (2014) 'The Gezi Park movement: A Turkish experience of the twenty-first-century collective movements', *International Review of Sociology*, vol 24, no 1, pp 176-89.

Foucault, M. (1994) *Power*, translated by R. Hurley et al, New York: The New Press.

Hanitzsch, T., Hanusch, F., Mellado, C., Anikina, M., Berganza, R., Cangoz, I., et al (2011) 'Mapping journalism cultures across nations: A comparative study of 18 countries', *Journalism Studies*, vol 12, no 3, pp 273-93.

Heper, M. and Keyman, E. (1998) 'Double-faced state: Political patronage and the consolidation of democracy in Turkey', *Middle Eastern Studies*, vol 34, no 4, pp 259-77.

Gürsoy, Y. (2011) 'The impact of EU-driven reforms on the political autonomy of the Turkish military', *South European Society and Politics*, vol 16, no 2, pp 293-308.

Kingdon, J. (1984) *Agenda-setting, alternatives and public policies*, New York: HarperCollins.

Koch-Baumgarten, S. and Voltmer, K. (eds) (2010) *Public policy and mass media: The interplay of mass communication and political decision making*, London: Routledge.

Lattman-Weltman, F. (2013) 'Media and policy analysis in Brazil: The process of policy production, reception and analysis through the media', in J. Vaitsman, J.M. Ribeiro and L. Lobato (eds) *Policy analysis in Brazil*, Bristol: Policy Press, Chapter 13 (http://policypress.universitypressscholarship.com/view/10.1332/policypress/9781447306849.001.0001/upso-9781447306849-chapter-13).

McCombs, M. (2004) *Setting the agenda: The mass media and public opinion*, London: Polity Press.

McCombs, M. and Shaw, D. (1972) 'The agenda-setting function of mass media', *Public Opinion Quarterly*, vol 36, no 2, pp 176-87.

Nacos, B., Shapiro, R. and Isernia, P. (eds) (2000) *Decision making in a glass house: Mass media, public opinion, and American and European foreign policy in the 21st century*, Lanham, MD: Rowman & Littlefield.

Öniş, Z. (2009) 'Beyond the 2001 financial crisis: The political economy of the new phase of neo-liberal restructuring in Turkey', *Review of International Political Economy*, vol 16, no 3, pp 409-32.

Özbudun, E. (2015) 'Turkey's judiciary and the drift toward competitive authoritarianism', *The International Spectator: Italian Journal of International Affairs*, vol 50, no 2, pp 42-55.

Scheufele, D. (2007) 'Framing, agenda setting, and priming: The evolution of three mass media effects models', *Journal of Communication*, vol 57, no 1, pp 9-20.

Soroka, S., Farnsworth, S., Lawlor, A. and Young, L. (2013) 'Mass media and policymaking', in E. Araral, S. Fritzen, M. Howlett, M. Ramesh and X. Wu (eds) *Routledge handbook of public policy*, London: Routledge, pp 204-14.

Strömberg, D. (2001) 'Mass media and public policy', *European Economic Review*, vol 45, no 1, pp 652-63.

Voltmer, K. and Koch-Baumgarten, S. (2010) 'Mass media and public policy – is there a link?', in S. Koch-Baumgarten and K. Voltmer (eds) *Public policy and mass media: The interplay of mass communication and political decision making*, London: Routledge, pp 1-14.

Waisbord, S.R. (1994) 'Television and election campaigns in contemporary Argentina', *Journal of Communication*, vol 44, no 2, pp 125-35.

Walgrave, S. and van Aelst, P. (2006) 'The contingency of the mass media's political agenda setting power: Towards a preliminary theory', *Journal of Communication*, vol 56, no 1, pp 88-109.

Wanta, W., Golan, G. and Lee, C. (2004) 'Agenda setting and international news: Media influence on public perceptions of foreign nations', *Journalism & Mass Communication Quarterly*, vol 81, no 2, pp 364-77.

Yang, L.F. and Ishak, M.S.A. (2012) 'Framing interethnic conflict in Malaysia: A comparative analysis of newspapers coverage on the Hindu Rights Action Force', *International Journal of Communication*, vol 6, no 1, pp 166-89.

Yavcan, B. and Ongur, H.O. (2016) 'Determinants of media criticism in a democracy in transition: Applying field theory to Turkey', *International Journal of Communication*, vol 10, no 1, pp 2422-41.

SIXTEEN

Public policy education in Turkey

Mete Yıldız and Cenay Babaoğlu

Introduction

Complementary to public policy research, the teaching of the subject in its modern sense began in the US in the 1960s (Allison, 2006, p 64; Mead, 2013, p 389; Vesely and Zelinkova, 2015, p 51). Public policy research and teaching became transnational by gradually diffusing into other countries with the help of international organisations and think tanks (McGann, 2007, p 67) and other agents of change and transfer. Sanabria-Pulido et al (2016), in their study, emphasise the isomorphism of public affairs education and public policy implementation in the world. They trace the roots of the transfer process, and point at the relationship between the countries with developed and developing economies. Their study shows that the changes in public affairs education in developed countries trigger dissemination in Latin America countries, as in many developing countries (Sanabria-Pulido et al, 2016, p 2).

Turkey is also one of many examples of the transnationalisation and global diffusion of public policy. Although the first academic journal articles and books date back to the 1970s and 1980s (Olgun, 2015), the main increase in public policy teaching, observable in the increasing numbers of public policy courses, teaching materials and academic activities, had begun in the 1990s. Although there were no public policy courses in the undergraduate curriculum recommended for public administration departments by the Turkish Higher Education Agency in 2000 (Şaylan and Sezen, 2000, pp 75-6), public policy education gained further momentum during the 2000s (Orhan, 2007, p 302; Yıldız et al, 2011).

Although the topic of public policy studies is multi-disciplinary by nature, and many specific public policy courses are likely to be taught in various social sciences disciplines, since there is no systematic analysis of such classes in the literature, this chapter focuses on public policy education based only on data collected about public policy courses taught in political science and public administration departments.

Within this framework, this chapter examines the development and current state of public policy education in Turkey, based on the teaching of the subject mostly in political science and public administration departments. As such, the objective of the study is to analyse and explain the conditions under which public policy classes – among other relevant developments such as the production of teaching materials, the creation of new organisational units, such as public policy Master's programmes and sub-departmental units/concentrations, and the organisation of scholarly activities, such as public policy workshops – have emerged and evolved over time, and the motivations of the faculty to introduce, develop and maintain public policy courses. To this end, studies on the teaching of public policy in the political science and public administration departments in Turkish universities at undergraduate and graduate levels are reviewed.

The results of these analyses provide data to compare and contrast public policy education in Turkey with other nationwide practices that can be found in the literature, such as in the case of the Czech Republic. The study concludes with a discussion of current and future challenges facing public policy education in Turkey, and recommendations for addressing these.

Brief overview of public policy studies in Turkey

When public policy analysis is defined basically as a simple advisory function, as 'speaking truth to power', there are numerous examples of the existence of public policy documents in the Turkish administrative history. Some selected examples from different periods are the 'Orkhon inscriptions/monuments' (8th century, Göktürk Empire), Yusuf Has Hacip's *Kutadgu bilig* (11th century, Karahan Empire), Nizam-ul Mulk's *Siyasetname* (11th century, Seljuk Empire) and Treasurer Sari Mehmet Pasha's *Advice to government officials* (18th century, Ottoman Empire) (Yıldız et al, 2016b).

With the founding of the Turkish Republic in 1923, there was a new era in which contemporary public policy analysis theory and practice, with its accompanying scientific methods and procedures, was transferred to Turkish academia. Akdogan (2011) has utilised John Kingdon's 'multiple streams model' in order to identify and analyse the windows of opportunity when scientific study of public policy analysis could have taken root, achieved maturity and depth, and become institutionalised in Turkey. These four windows of opportunity, as proposed by Akdogan, are:

- 1924: John Dewey was invited to Turkey by the Turkish Ministry of Education for the purpose of preparing a report for the overhaul of the education system of the newly-formed Republic, just a year earlier.
- 1950-65: the influence of social scientists conducting empirical studies that would provide empirical data for further scientific analyses, decision-making and planning.
- 1961: the establishment of the State Planning Organization (SPO) after the 1960 military intervention, for the purpose of introducing a nationwide social and economic planning system.1975: the establishment of the Operations Research Society, as the name suggests, aimed at promoting the use of an operations research methodology.

Akdogan also made a case to include the enactment of Law no 5018 on Public Financial Management and Control in 2002, as a window of opportunity to further rationalise the public finance system, as a tool of more rational decision-making and planning, but he argued that at the time of writing the article (2010 or 2011), it was too early to evaluate. For the previous four windows of opportunity, however, Akdogan's verdict is that they all fully or partially failed to create a long-lasting effect. Therefore, these opportunities for public policy studies to take root and get institutionalised in Turkey were all missed.

Unlike Akdogan's hopeful start but grim conclusion for the current state of maturity and depth of public policy studies in Turkey, Robins (2009) concluded that the cause was lost from the very beginning. By examining and explaining a case study of how the national drug prevention policy is organised in Turkey, Robins argued that at the time of writing his manuscript (probably in 2007 or 2008), there were no systematic, lengthy academic studies of public policy-making in Turkey, either in any major European language or in Turkish. Robins also argued that public policy analysis theory and practice failed to penetrate into the political and administrative systems of developing countries (countries other than 'mature democracies', he explained) such as Turkey. According to him, these studies were unable to gain maturity and depth, due to the problems of these countries' economic and political systems. The main outcome of this situation, he argued, is that even important policy areas are poorly understood due to a lack of compelling and detailed empirical evidence.

More recently, Köseoğlu (2013), Erat (2014), Çiner (2015a) and Olgun (2017) documented the numerical increase in academic studies of public policy. Olgun (2017) documented this by examining policy-related articles published in the leading public administration journal of Turkey, *Amme İdaresi Dergisi*, in her analysis of its almost 50 years of publication (1968-2015), as shown in Figure 16.1 below.

Figure 16.1: Policy-related articles in Amme İdaresi Dergisi, 1969–2014

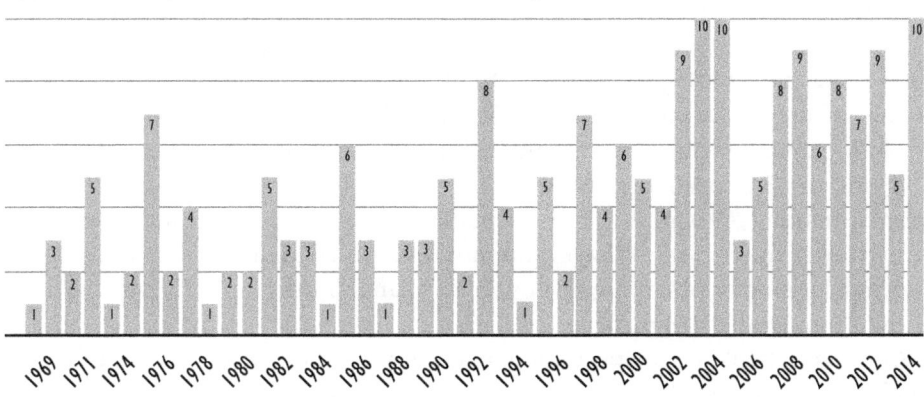

Source: Olgun (2017).

In the same time period, the numbers of scientific studies in the field of public policies has gone up. In 2006, *Public policy practices in Turkey from the establishment of the Republic until the present* by Erkul and Gökdemir; in 2008, *Public policy* by Çevik and Demirci; in 2011, under the editorship of Kartal, *Public administration and public policy in Turkey*; in the same year, under the editorship of Kaptı, *Public policy process*; in 2013 *The transformation in public policies* by Bekir Parlak and *Public policy: Theory and practice* by Yıldız and Sobacı were published. In various journals, numerous articles written by many authors were published in the same time period (Olgun, 2015). Special issues should also be mentioned. A number were edited on public policy first by Köseoğlu (2013) in the journal *Bilgi*; and then by Çiner (2015b) in the journal *Memleket: Siyaset ve Yönetim* (issue 19-20). More recently, Babaoğlu (2016) edited two special issues in the *Journal of Legislation*. These were titled 'Theoretical background of public policy' and 'Public policy analysis in Turkey'. However, it may be too early to tell these studies' usefulness and relevance to the practice and instruction of public policy in Turkey.

Public policy teaching in Turkey: literature review

Studies of public administration and policy teaching have always been a popular activity in the public administration discipline in Turkey (Ergun, 1983; Mıhçıoğlu, 1988; Aykaç, 1995; Kaya, 1995; Sezen, 1995; Şaylan and Sezen, 2000; Omurgonulsen, 2004, 2007a, b; Onder and Brower, 2013; Parlak et al, 2015). For example, Omurgonulsen (2010) conducted a detailed analysis of the current state (in terms of organisation and numbers), problem areas and development trends (in terms of educational programmes, academic publishing efforts and teaching materials) in undergraduate-level public administration education in Turkey. He concluded that it has been affected by both global developments in public administration research and practice, such as the new public management ideas, and Turkey's own/specific problems, such as the demand for higher education surpassing supply due to demographic trends, pressures emanating from this supply–demand disequilibrium in terms of the quantity and quality of the educational infrastructure and university faculty, and finally, grim job prospects after graduation (2010, pp 155-6). Omurgonulsen also emphasised the hybrid nature of public administration education in Turkey, due to its formation and evolution under the mixed and sometimes conflicting influences of the Ottoman, Continental European and more recently, Anglo-American schools of public administration (2010, p 157). He concludes by stating that public administration departments have failed to shape administrative reform, but have become passive bystanders, merely observing the ongoing change in the administrative system (Omurgonulsen, 2010, p 158).

Omurgonulsen's observations on public administration education can be easily applied and transferred to the area of public policy education. Findings of studies delving into the emergence and development of public policy education in Turkey provide a striking parallel in terms of public policy education as a response to both global and local conditions and trends, having a hybrid nature, and failing to influence or shape practice.

Within this context, public policy teaching in Turkey began in the 1990s and gained momentum during the 2000s (Yıldız et al, 2011). The first undergraduate course was offered in the Middle East Technical University (Orta Dou Teknik Üniversitesi, ODTU) by Goktug Morcol in 1991, while the first graduate-level public policy course was offered during the early 1990s[1] by Turgay Ergun in the Public Administration Institute for Turkey and the Middle East (TODAİE). We added the syllabi of this first undergraduate level public policy course to the Appendix section at the end of this chapter, as it constitutes a historical record for the development of public policy teaching in Turkey.[2]

These humble beginnings in the 1990s quickly turned into a trend of increasing numbers of undergraduate, Master's and doctoral-level courses, as well as newly emerging programmes such as Master's programmes or concentrations/sub-departments in the area of policy analysis. Figure 16.2, presented below, depicts this continuous increase in the numbers in Turkey since the 1990s. The slight decrease in 2016 is due to the closing of some universities linked to subversive activities after the attempted military coup on 15 July 2016.

As of March 2011 there were 165 universities in Turkey. Out of these 165 universities, 57 of them had public administration or political science departments (Yıldız et al, 2011, p 345). In 2014, the number of Turkish universities increased to 179, and the number of public administration departments reached 95 (Usta and Çelik, 2015, pp 316-17).

Figure 16.2: Courses and graduate programmes of public policy, 1990–2017

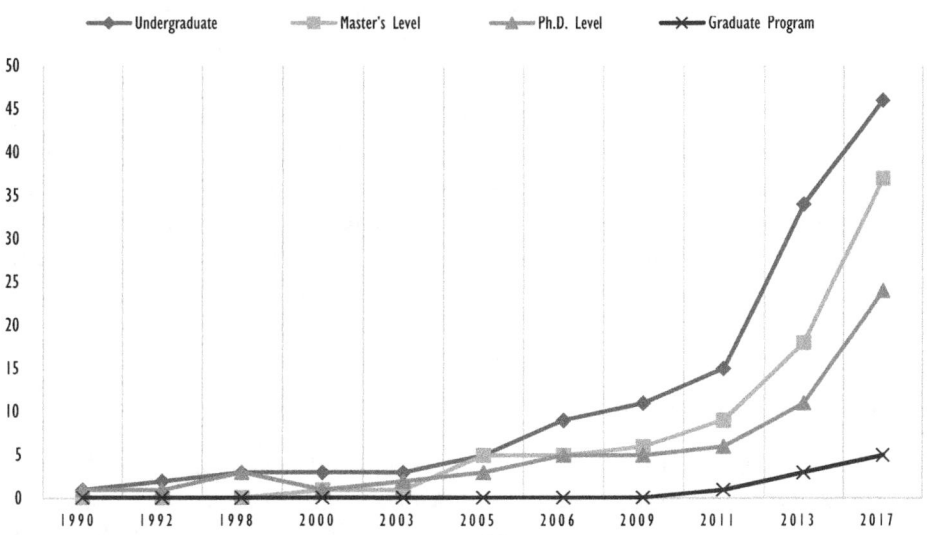

Sources: Yıldız and Babaoğlu (2012); Akyıldız and Akman (2013); Yıldız et al (2017)

Although the increase in the numbers of public administration departments was apparent, the reasons behind the increase were not well known. With the Europeanisation and internationalisation of public administration education worldwide (Demir, 2015, pp 37-9), in order to understand the reasons behind the increasing interest in public policy education, Yıldız et al (2011) studied the factors that played a part in the creation, development and numerical increase of public policy courses in Turkish political science and public administration departments. Their findings show that four main factors were influential in the introduction and diffusion of public policy courses at undergraduate level. These factors are:

- A beginning to mid-career generation of academicians who received their Master's and doctorate degrees in countries such as the US, UK and France, prior to returning to Turkey as young academics, transferring their interest in public policy analysis courses to the Turkish universities that employed them on their return to Turkey.
- An older generation of academicians, in their mid or late-career phases, who discovered the importance of public policy analysis during sabbatical year visits abroad in developing countries, transferring these courses back to their home departments/universities in Turkey.
- Another group of academicians, neither educated nor having visited developed countries through graduate studies or sabbatical visits, but who clearly understood the benefits of employing public policy analyses tools for examining and understanding current administrative functioning and reforms in Turkey.
- The homogenising influence of scientific interactions with European universities through academic change programmes such as Erasmus and Socrates (and through shared or common degree programmes, various types of scientific collaborations with US universities as well) (Yıldız et al, 2011, pp 352-4).

Another recent study by Yıldız et al (2016a) showed that similar reasons were effective in the creation and diffusion of graduate-level e-government classes in the political science and public administration departments of Turkish universities.

It is now necessary to have a closer look at current developments that pertain to the state of public policy education in Turkey today. These include academic activities that stimulate public policy research and teaching, the production of teaching materials and the creation of new organisational units.

Public policy workshops

Scientific/academic activities such as conferences and workshops not only serve the transfer of research and mingling of academicians; they are also important exchange arenas of ideas and educational practices. For example, the public policy workshops, which have been organised by a different academic unit/university each year since 2009, provide such a chance for exchange and collaboration that stimulates public policy research and teaching. Table 16.1 provides detailed information about these workshops. And also in 2012, the Public Administration Forum, the largest academic public administration conference in Turkey, announced its annual theme as the 'Transformation of public policies', further contributing to the popularity of and academic interest in the topic of public policy.

Table 16.1: List of public policy workshops organised in Turkey

Workshop number	Year	Location	Organiser	General theme(s)	Number of presentations[b]	Availability of Discussants for each paper	Funding
1	2009	Mersin	Mersin University	Concept and methodology	7	–	Self-funding
2	2010	Ankara	TODAİE	Methods of analysis by examples	10	–	Self-funding
3	2011	Bandırma, Balıkesir	Balıkesir University	Public policies and democracy	6	–	Self-funding
4	2012	Ankara	Hacettepe University	Higher education policies	5[c]	+	Self-funding
5	2013	Ankara	Yıldırım Beyazıt University	Analysis/case studies in which policy analysis models and methods are being used	10[d]	+	Funding support from government (TUBITAK)
6	2015	Sakarya	Sakarya University		9[d]	+	Funding support from TUBITAK
7	2016[a]	Artvin	Artvin Çoruh University	Method and Implementation	NA	NA	NA

Notes: [a] Cancelled on 2 August 2016.
[b] Numbers were taken from the conference programmes. Some presentations may not have been made, although they were on the programme. Introductory speeches and final/general evaluation sessions are not included in the count.
[c] Plus two workshop/discussion roundtable sessions.
[d] Started by a seminar on research methods in policy analysis, presented by Göktuğ Morçöl.
Source: Data are compiled from the Public Policy Analysis Study Group website, at http://kamupolitikalari.org/index.php/Calistaylar

Production of teaching materials

An important limiting factor for the teaching of public policy to flourish in non-Western, developing countries is the relative lack of teaching materials in native tongues that are relevant to the local conditions. In Turkey, this limitation has been felt less and less during the last decade, as more and more teaching materials have been produced, albeit with some exceptions.

The topic of public policy teaching materials can be examined under several subtopics. First of all, a significant number of Turkish-language textbooks had been written since the early 2000s, such as those written by Göksu et al (2003), Erkul and Gökdemir (2006), Çevik and Demirci (2008), Kartal (2011), Kaptı (2011) and Yıldız and Sobacı (2013). These include both translations and adaptations of theoretical material and sectoral/topical studies such as education, health and transportation policies.

As a second subcategory, online lecture notes (Yıldız, 2011) on public policy are also available.[3] These notes, written with the support and sponsorship of the Turkish Academy of Sciences' (TÜBA) National Open Course Materials Programme, aim to provide the general public with the means of accessing course materials on a wide array of social and applied sciences through a website, free of charge. The lecture notes provide semester-long (15 weeks) materials of instruction for undergraduate-level courses.

Third, articles in refereed academic journals constitute an increasing corpus of research, which includes both the theoretical and practical dimensions of public policy analysis. Olgun (2015), in her review of the oldest and most prestigious academic journal in the area of public administration (*Amme Idaresi Dergisi*, AID, indexed by the Social Sciences Citation Index), traces articles back to the 1970s. She also reports an increasing frequency in the number of articles concerning public policy studies in AID that can also be used as teaching materials.

Fourth, graduate students' interest in public policy analysis has grown in the last few years. A recent study that focused on the institutionalisation of public policy education in Turkey shows an increase in the number of Master's theses and dissertations about public policy (Yıldız et al, 2017: p 685). Data from the Turkish Higher Education Council thesis catalogue can be seen in Figure 16.3.

Fifth, an encyclopaedia of public policy (Altunok and Gedikkaya, 2016) was recently published. This 400-page long encyclopaedia contains detailed definitions and examples of many concepts and practices of public policy. The usefulness of such a reference material for both novice and seasoned public policy students is beyond measure.

The last sub-category of public policy teaching materials, case studies, presents an exception to this list of improvements. To the best of our knowledge, there is no extensive and systematic repository of public policy case studies comparable, for example, to the in-depth, data-driven reports of the CQ Researcher, published by CQ Press[4] and the Harvard Kennedy School's case database.[5] Creating such a pool of in-depth, data-driven case studies with a sound pedagogical approach is an important need of public policy teaching, which is waiting for an able contributor.

Figure 16.3: Master's and PhD theses about public policy in the Turkish Higher Education Council Thesis Catalogue

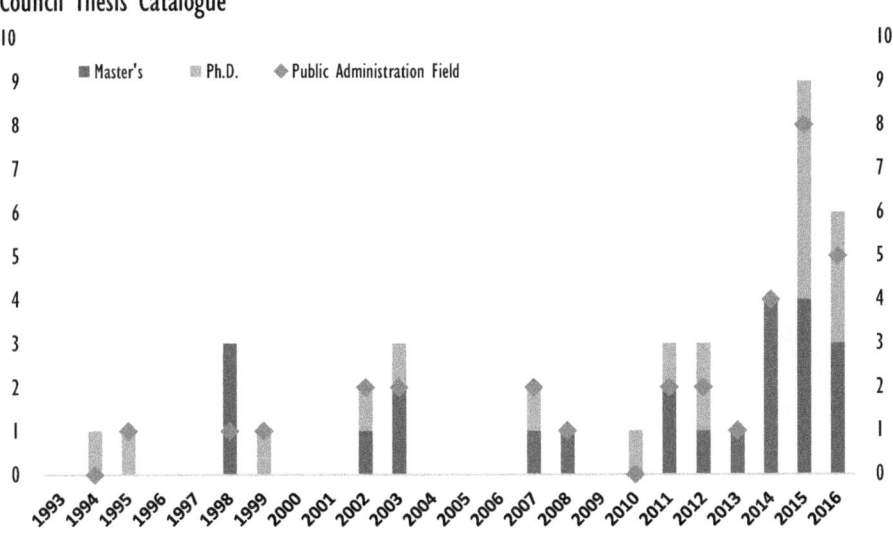

Source: Yıldız et al (2017: 672)

Creation of new Master's programmes and sub-departments/ concentrations of public policy

While during the 2000s there was a substantial increase in the number of public policy courses, the 2010s has been witnessing a new phase of institutionalisation efforts in public policy education in Turkey, exemplified by the creation of sub-departments/concentrations (*anabilim dalı*) and Master's programmes about public policy. Yıldız et al (2017) examined the reasons for and the creation processes of these new organisational units for public policy teaching by conducting in-depth interviews with the founding and current faculty members of these concentrations and programmes, listed in Table 16.2. They also aimed at determining the problems of these institutionalisation processes and the solutions proposed for addressing them.

Yıldız et al's (2017, p 686) results show that there is an evolutionary trend in public policy teaching in Turkey that starts with the introduction of elective public policy courses. The second phase is the transformation of elective courses to introductory level compulsory courses (e.g. Public Policy, Public Policy Analysis). The third phase is the addition of a few elective courses to supplement the introductory level compulsory Public Policy course (e.g. Comparative Public Policy, Social Policy). The fourth and current phase is the founding of Master's programmes or sub-departments/concentrations of public policy that brings these newly created Public Policy courses under the roof of one organisational unit. A fifth phase that may occur in the future may be the creation of public policy departments, independent from the current organisational units of political science and public administration departments, which have hosted most of the Public

Table 16.2: New Master's programmes and sub-departments/concentrations of public policy in Turkey

University	Type of programme	Year of introduction	Website
Sabancı	Master's	2011	http://mpp.sabanciuniv.edu/tr
Hacettepe	Sub-department/concentration	2013	www.sbky.hacettepe.edu.tr/
Marmara	Sub-department/concentration	2013	http://kamu.siyasal.marmara.edu.tr/genel-bilgiler/ana-bilim-dallari/
Gazi	Master's	2014	http://iibf.gazi.edu.tr/posts/view/title/kamu-yonetimi-3622?siteUri=iibf
Nevşehir	Master's	2014	http://iibf.nevsehir.edu.tr/tr/bolumler_kamu_yonetimi

Source: Yıldız et al (2017: 675)

Policy courses so far. The findings of Yıldız et al (2017) show that respondents do not perceive the creation of separate public policy departments as highly likely.

The problems of institutionalisation being faced by these new organisational units can be summarised as a lack of qualified instructors, the missing link between teaching public policy concepts and theories and applying them to real-life cases and problems, inadequate application of quantitative methods in public policy studies, lack of international and/or interdisciplinary collaboration efforts in public policy research and teaching, low levels of student awareness about the nature and content of the topics of public policy and finally, a lack of adequate teaching materials (Yıldız et al, 2017, pp 686-7).

Discussion and conclusion

We conclude with a discussion of the current and future challenges facing public policy education in Turkey, and recommendations for how to address these challenges. To that end, we discuss the results of previous analyses, and compare and contrast them with public policy education in a comparable case, namely, with Central European countries in general, and specifically the Czech Republic. These countries provide a comparable case to Turkey in terms of public policy education, since both regions are recipients of developments in public policy research and instruction from developed countries through similar means of transfer such as graduate students educated abroad. The timing of the transfer was also almost simultaneous, beginning in the 1990s. However, the parameters of comparison between these two cases do not match completely; for example, while students' ability gains from taking public policy courses were examined in the Czech Republic case, no such evaluation has been conducted in the Turkish case.

Vesely and Zelinkova (2015, p 51) document in detail the development and problems of public policy education in the Czech Republic. They started a timeline for the creation and development of public policy programmes in Central

European countries such as Hungary, the Czech Republic and Slovenia in the 1990s, after the fall of communism.

They argue that certain problems make the teaching of public policy difficult in the Czech Republic, and state these problems as: (1) the dependence on instructors with a public policy education, experience and expertise, with a therefore lack of institutionalisation for public policy studies (2015, pp 52, 63-4); (2) the nesting of public policy courses in social science disciplines, such as sociology, rather than policy studies having its own institutional home, therefore its inability to become an autonomous discipline (2015, pp 56-7); (3) the lack of systematic public policy teaching, which exists only in three institutions (2015, pp 58-9); and (4) the lack of methodological diversity, with the dominant methodological orientation being quantitative, due to the dominance of the sociological tradition in public policy studies (2015, pp 63-4).

Vesely and Zelinkova (2015, pp 58-9) also point to some strengths of public policy education in the Czech Republic. These can be listed as: (1) a strong professional orientation, since some of the public policy courses were always based on application, heeding Geva May's (2005) recommendation of public policy studies being a 'clinical profession'; and (2) the production of Czech-language teaching materials such as textbooks, although these books were modified versions of foreign-language books adapted to the Czech case.

They also report some mixed findings. Former students of public policy courses in Charles University in Prague state that while some skills gained in public policy courses such as the ability to orient oneself and acquire new knowledge, communication skills, argumentation and critical thinking skills and strategic and analytical thinking were quite useful, some other skills/knowledge areas such as policy analysis skills, professional theoretical knowledge, policy design skills, political analysis, cost-benefit analysis and statistics were not extensively used, and were therefore not that useful in these former students' work environments. These students were also least satisfied with acquiring organisational skills, practical professional experience and skills and computer literacy (Vesely and Zelinkova, 2015, pp 60-2).

Based on the growing literature on public policy education in Turkey, current developments and trends, and comparisons with cases such as public policy education in the Czech Republic reported above, the following suggestions can be made regarding the further improvement of the quality and quantity of public policy education in Turkey.

First, similar to the findings presented in the Czech Republic case, a significant increase in the quality and quantity of public policy teaching in Turkey is still very much dependent on the availability of able instructors with a public policy education, experience and expertise. This problem has been partially solved by the inclusion of new academicians to the ranks of the public policy research community in Turkey, easily observed by the increasing attendance figures in the Public Policy Workshops, as mentioned above. Attracting more scholars to the field, on the other hand, depends on the future level of institutionalisation, as also discussed above.

Second, the problem of lack of teaching materials, such as lecture notes, books and case studies, has been partially solved both in the Turkish and Czech Republic cases. As explained, Turkish-language public policy textbooks, journal articles based on empirical data analysis and online lecture notes are growing in number, albeit rather slowly. Most of the material being produced is descriptive and based on qualitative analysis. Here the current issue is to increase the amount of original research findings in the teaching materials, by going beyond the translation and adaptation of foreign texts. The only area in which the development of teaching materials is rather slow (or non-existent?) is in the production of detailed/in-depth, data-driven cases to use in public policy classes as case studies.

Third, unlike the Czech Republic, the connection between public policy teaching and its practice is not very strong in Turkey. One way to remedy this may be to establish better institutional links between universities on the one hand, and public agencies and think tanks on the other. The exchange of both public policy academicians/researchers and students between universities and think tanks can be especially useful. Such experiences in the past proved fruitful for both parties (for a detailed account of the Avrasya Stratejik Araştırmalar Merkezi [ASAM] example, the most prominent think tank in Turkey during the late 1990s and early 2000s, see Karasar, 2012, pp 47-69).

All these above-mentioned reasons coming together contribute to the relatively continuing lack of institutionalisation of public policy teaching and to the inability of public policy studies to become an autonomous academic discipline in Turkey. However, as presented in detail above, there are positive developments that support both the institutionalisation of teaching and autonomy of the academic studies of public policy.

First, as showcased by Yıldız et al (2017, p 686), new Master's programmes and sub-departments/concentrations of public policy emerge as a sign of higher levels of demand and supply for teaching and research. Second, six consecutive meetings of the Public Policy Workshops drew larger crowds each time. These serve as a hub of activity and as a pool for sharing experiences of both research and teaching. Third, as shown above, course numbers indicate an upward trend in public policy teaching at both undergraduate and graduate levels.

Although these positive developments are good news for public policy researchers and students alike, there are still many shortcomings to overcome. First of all, both research on and practice of public policy teaching had been supply-based. In other words, the demand for public policy courses or their impact on graduates' job-related skills has not yet been examined. Future researchers of public policy education in Turkey should conduct such demand-based studies.

Second, more research has to be conducted to establish a better link between teaching and research on the one side, and the practice of public policy by various non-university policy actors on the other. Joint national and international level policy research projects may serve this purpose well.

Third, one of the most important factors that would increase student interest in and demand for public policy education is the relevance of public policy studies in the job entrance process and beyond. In other words, if the topic of public policy becomes part of the job entrance and promotion examinations, demand is likely to rise. There are positive developments in Turkey to that effect: university graduates need to take a centrally administered test entitled the Public Personnel Selection Exam (Kamu Personeli Seçme Sınavı, KPSS) as part of the required procedure to apply for government jobs. The addition of questions about public policy analysis to this test increases awareness about and interest in the topic of policy analysis among the students coming from various disciplinary backgrounds. According to the answer provided by the Office of the Prime Minister[6] to a right to know request, a total of five public policy-related questions were asked in the KPSS exams between 2011 and 2016, out of a total of 210 public administration questions (2 per cent).

To sum up, public policy studies and its teaching have gained some momentum and reached some level of maturity, contrary to Robins' (2009) claims otherwise. Tallying all the supporting and limiting factors about public policy education, as well as the opportunities and tasks that lie ahead, there are reasons to be hopeful about the future.

Notes

[1] While the first official record in the Registrar's Office of the Public Administration Institute for Turkey and the Middle East belongs to 1998, Professor Ergun, in an interview, pointed to the early 1990s for the introduction of this first graduate-level public policy course in Turkey.

[2] We would like to thank Professor Gokhan Orhan for locating and sharing the undergraduate course's syllabus from his personal records.

[3] These online lecture notes are available in Turkish at www.acikders.org.tr/course/view.php?id=66

[4] For more information, see http://library.cqpress.com/cqresearcher/

[5] For more information, see http://case.hks.harvard.edu/

[6] The information was provided by the BİMER (Prime Ministry Communications Centre) Unit of the Office of the Prime Minister, according to the Freedom of Information Act, Application Number 1600275372, dated 13 October 2016.

References

Akdogan, A.A. (2011) 'Türkiye'de kamu politikası disiplinin tarihsel izleri ['Historical steps of public policy discipline in Turkey'], in F. Kartal (ed) *Türkiye'de kamu yönetimi ve kamu politikaları* [*Public administration and public policy in Turkey*], Ankara: TODAİE, pp 75-98.

Akyıldız, F. and Akman, E. (2013) 'Dünyada ve Türkiye'de kamu politikaları öğretimi' ['Public policy education in the world and Turkey'], in B. Parlak (ed) *Kamu politikalarında dönüşüm* [*Transition in public policy*], 373, Ankara: TODAIE, pp 291-328.

Allison, G. (2006) 'Emergence of schools of public policy: Reflections by a founding dean', in R.E. Goodin, M. Moran and M. Rein (eds) *The Oxford handbook of public policy*, Oxford: Oxford University Press, pp 58-79.

Altunok, H. and Gedikkaya, F. (2016) *Kamu politikaları ansiklopedisi* [*Public policy encyclopaedia*], Ankara: Nobel.

Aykaç, B. (1995) 'Türkiye'de kamu yönetimi öğretiminin gelişimi' ['The development process of public administration education in Turkey'], *Kamu Yönetimi Disiplini Sempozyumu Bildirileri – II* [*Proceedings of the Symposium of Public Administration Discipline in Turkey – II*], Ankara: TODAİE, pp 271-9.

Babaoğlu, C. (ed) (2016) Special Issue, 'Public policy and public policy analysis', *Journal of Legislation*, nos 29 and 30.

Çevik, H.H. and Demirci, S. (2008) *Kamu politikası* [*Public policy*], Ankara: Seckin.

Çiner, C.U. (2015a) 'Kamu yönetimi eğitimi ve öğretimi literatürü üzerine bir çözümleme' ['An analysis of public administration education and teaching literature'], in M. Okcu, B. Parlak and E. Akman (eds) *Kamu yönetimi eğitimi* [*Public administration education*], Bursa: Ekin, pp 3-24.

Ciner, C.U. (ed) (2015b) Special Issue, 'Public Policy', *Memleket: Siyaset ve Yönetim* [*Land, Politics and Administration*], issue 19-20.

Demir, F. (2015) 'Europeanization in higher education', in M. Okcu, B. Parlak and E. Akman (eds) Public administration education, Bursa: Ekin, pp 37-50.

Erat, V. (2014) 'Türkiye'de kamu politikaları alan yazını üzerine bir inceleme', *Gumushane University Social Science e-Journal*, vol 10, pp 92-117.

Ergun, T. (1983) 'Yüksek yöneticilerin yetiştirilmesi sorunu' ['The problem of educating high level officials'], *Amme İdaresi Dergisi*, vol 16, no 2, pp 23-36.

Erkul, H. and Gökdemir, L. (eds) (2006) *Türkiye'de cumhuriyetin kuruluşundan günümüze uygulanan kamu politikaları – 1* [*Public policy practices in Turkey from the establishment of the Republic until the present*], Ankara: Detay.

Geva May, I. (2005) 'Thinking like a policy analyst: Policy analysis as a clinical profession', in I. Geva May (ed) *Thinking like a policy analyst: Policy analysis as a clinical profession,* New York: Palgrave MacMillan, pp 15-50.

Göksu, T., Çevik, H.H., Baharçiçek, A. and Şen, A. (eds) (2003) *1980-2003: Türkiye'nin dış, ekonomik, sosyal ve idari politikaları* [*1980-2003 Turkish foreign, economic, social and administrative policies*], Ankara: Siyasal.

Kaptı, A. (ed) (2011) *Kamu politika süreci* [*Public policy process*], Ankara: Seckin.

Karasar, H.A. (2012) 'Türk düşünce kuruluşlarının "Anası": Avrasya Stratejik Araştırmalar Merkezi' ['The Mother' of Turkish think tanks: Eurasia Stratejical Research Centre'], in H.A. Karasar and H. Kanbolat (eds) *Avrasya'da stratejik düşünce kültürü ve kuruluşları* [*Strategical thinking culture and institutions in Eurasia*], Ankara: Nobel, pp 47-69.

Kartal, F. (2011) *Türkiye'de kamu yönetimi ve kamu politikaları* [*Public administration and public policy in Turkey*], Ankara: TODAİE.

Kaya, Y.K. (1995) 'Türkiye'de kamu yönetimi öğretimi', in *Kamu Yönetimi Disiplini Sempozyumu Bildirileri – II* [*Proceedings of the Symposium of Public Administration Discipline in Turkey – II*], Ankara: TODAİE, pp 249-69.

Köseoğlu, Ö. (2013) 'Meslek, sanat ve disiplin olarak kamu politikası: Türkiye'ye izdüşümleri' ['Public policy as a profession, art and discipline: Reflections to Turkey'], *Bilgi*, vol 2, no 6, pp 4-36.

McGann, J.G. (2007) *Think tanks and policy advice in the US: Academics, advisors and advocates*, New York: Routledge.

Mead, L.M. (2013) 'Teaching public policy: Linking policy and politics', *Journal of Public Affairs Education*, vol 19, no 3, pp 389-403.

Mıhçıoğlu, C. (1988) *Türkiye'de çağdaş kamu yönetimi öğretiminin başlangıç yılları* [*The beginning years of contemporary public administration education in Turkey*], Ankara: Ankara University SBF.

Olgun, B. (2015) 'Amme İdaresi Dergisi'nde kamu politikası çalışmalarının izini sürmek' ['Tracking public policy Studies in Amme İdaresi journal'], Unpublished Conference Presentation, 6th Public Policy Workshop, 17-18 September, Sakarya University, Sakarya, Turkey.

Olgun, B. (2017) 'Türkiye'de kamu politikaları çalışmalarının gelişiminin Amme İdaresi Dergisi'nde yayımlanmış makaleler üzerinden analizi: 1968-2015', Unpublished Master's Thesis, Hacettepe University, Ankara.

Omurgonulsen, U. (2004) 'Dünyada kamu yönetimindeki dönüşümün Türkiye'deki lisans düzeyi kamu yönetimi öğretimine yansımaları', in M.K. Öktem and U. Ömürgönülşen (eds) *Dünya'da kamu yönetimindeki dönüşüm ve Türkiye'de kamu yönetimi öğretimine yansımaları, II*, Kamu Yönetimi Forumu (KAYFOR II), Ankara: Hacettepe Üniversitesi, pp 120-65.

Omurgonulsen, U. (2007a) 'Türkiye'de lisans düzeyi kamu yönetimi öğretiminde yakın dönemde yaşanan gelişmeler (1982-2006)', in A. Goktork, M. Ozfidaner and G. Unlu (eds) *Kamu Yönetimi Forumu (Kayfor IV): Kuramdan uygulamaya yönetim ve reform* [Public Administration Forum: Administration and reform, 8-10 Kasım 2006], Mugla: Mugla Üniversitesi, pp 361-86.

Omurgonulsen, U. (2007b) 'Türkiye'de lisans düzeyi kamu yönetimi öğretiminin kurumsallaşma derecesi: 2000'li yıllarda bölüm ve öğrenci sayıları ile akademik kadronun durumu' (basılmamış bildiri), *V. Kamu Yönetimi Forumu (KAYFOR V): Kamusal Bilinç, Kent ve Çevre: Güncel Sorunlar ve Çözümler*, 18-20 Ekim 2007, Izmit: Kocaeli Üniversitesi IIBF Kamu Yönetimi Bölümü.

Omurgonulsen, U. (2010) *Türkiye'de lisans düzeyi kamu yönetimi öğretiminde yakın dönemde yaşanan gelişmeler: Mevcut Durum, Sorun Alanları ve Gelişme Egilimleri* [Recent developments in public policy instruction in Turkey], *Ankara Üniversitesi SBF Dergisi*, vol 65, no 3, pp 123-61.

Onder, M. and Brower, R.S. (2013) 'Public administration theory, research, and teaching: How does Turkish public administration differ?', *Journal of Public Affairs Education*, vol 19, no 1, pp 117-39.

Orhan, G. (2007) 'Kamu politikalarıyla ilgili sorunlar nasıl çözülür? Disiplinler arası bir yaklaşım olarak kamu politikaları analizi ve getirdiği açılımlar' ['How can the problems of public policy be solved?'], in S. Aksoy and Y. Ustuner (eds) *Kamu yönetimi: Yöntem ve sorunlar*, Ankara: Nobel, pp 287-304.

Parlak, B. (ed) (2013) *Kamu politikalarında dönüşüm* [*Transition in public policies*], 373, Ankara: TODAIE.

Parlak, B., Okçu, M. and Akman, E. (eds) (2015) *Kamu yönetimi eğitimi* [*Public administration education*], Bursa: Ekin.

Robins, P. (2009) 'Public policy making in Turkey: Faltering attempts to generate a national drugs policy', *Policy & Politics*, vol 37, no 2, pp 289-306.

Sanabria-Pulido, P., Rubaii, N. and Puron, G. (2016) 'Public affairs graduate education in Latin America: Emulation or identity?', *Policy and Society* (http://dx.doi.org/10.1016/j.polsoc.2016.11.004).

Şaylan, G. and Sezen S. (2000) 'The paradigmatic crises of public administration and teaching curriculum: The Turkish case', *Turkish Public Administration Annual*, vol 24, no 26 pp 59-76.

Sezen, S. (1995) 'Kamu yönetimi öğretimi: Özellikler ve sorunlar grup raporu', *Kamu Yönetimi Disiplini Sempozyumu Bildirileri*, C II, Ankara: TODAİE, pp 245-7.

Usta, S. and Çelik, V. (2015) 'Türkiye'de cumhuriyet sonrası kamu yönetimi eğitiminin gelişimi' ['Public administration education in Turkey after the establishment of the Republic'], in M. Okcu, B. Parlak and E. Akman (eds) *Public administration education*, Bursa: Ekin, pp 297-326.

Vesely, A. and Zelinkova, A. (2015) 'Public policy programmes and policy analysis instruction in the Czech Republic', *Central European Journal of Public Policy*, vol 9, no 1, pp 50-77.

Yıldız, M. (2011) *Kamu politikası*, Türkiye Bilimler Akademisi (TÜBA), Ulusal Açık Ders Malzemeleri (www.acikders.org.tr/course/view.php?id=66).

Yıldız, M. and Babaoğlu, C. (2012) 'Türkiye'de lisansüstü düzeyde kamu politikası öğretimi konusunda düşünce ve öneriler', *9 Kamu Yönetimi Forumu (KAYFOR)*, Yayınlanmamış Bildiri, Gazi Üniversitesi, Ankara.

Yıldız, M. and Sobacı, M.Z. (eds) (2013) *Kamu politikası: Kuram ve uygulama* [*Public policy: Theory and practice*], Ankara: Adres.

Yıldız, M., Babaoğlu, C. and Demircioglu, M.A. (2016a) 'Graduate level e-government education in public administration departments: Current state and future prospects in Turkey', *Journal of Public Affairs Education (JPAE)*, vol 22, no 2, pp 287-302.

Yıldız, M., Babaoğlu, C. and Şahin, B. (2016b) 'Kamu politikasını Türk idare tarihi *üzerinden çalışmak*' ['Studying public policy by using Turkish administrative history'], *Hacettepe Üniversitesi IIBF Dergisi*, vol 34, no 2, pp 133-58.

Yıldız, M., Babaoğlu C. and Tugan, E.N. (2017) 'Türkiye'de kamu politikaları öğretiminde kurumsallaşma çabaları' ['Institutionalisation efforts in public policy teaching in Turkey'], Accepted for publication in *Ankara Üniversitesi SBF Dergisi*. vol 72, no 3, pp 669-688.

Yıldız, M., Demircioglu, M.A. and Babaoğlu, C. (2011) 'Teaching public policy to undergraduate students: Issues, experiences, and lessons in Turkey', *Journal of Public Affairs Education*, vol 17, no 3, pp 343-65.

Appendix: Syllabus of the first undergraduate-level public policy course in Turkey, ODTU, 1991

```
Middle East Technical University
Department of Public Administration
Adm-487 Public Policy Analysis I: Analysis of Policy
Course Outline
Fall Semester 1991-1992

Instructor: Göktuğ Morçöl
Office No: 142

1.  What is public policy analysis?
    Basic concepts: policy, knowledge, politics.
    Related areas: planning, budgeting.
    A brief history.
    Readings:

    -   Harold Laswell, "The Policy Orientation" in Daniel
        Lerner and Harold Laswell, The Policy Sciences.

    -   Thomas Dye, "Models of Politics: Some Help in Thinking
        About Public Policy," chapter 2 in Understanding
        Public Policy.

    -   Christopher Ham and Michael Hill, "Policy and Policy
        Analysis," chapter 1 in The Policy Process in the
        Modern Capitalist State.

    -   Tom Burden and Mike Campbell, "Marxism and Public
        Policy," chapter 1 in Capitalism and Public Policy in
        the U.K.

    -   Arnold J. Heidenheimer, Hugh Heclo and Carolyn T.
        Adams, "The Politics of Social Choice," chapter 1 in
        Comparative Public Policy.

2.  Economic Policy:
    Readings:

    -   Heidenheimer, Heclo and Adams, chapter 5.

    -   Abel Aganbegyan, "Economic Reforms" in Perestroika
        1989.

    -   George Gilder, "The Supply Side" in Wealth and Poverty.

3.  Education Policy:
    Readings:

    -   Heidenheimer, Heclo and Adams, chapter 2.
    -   TUSIA  Türkiye'de Eğitim: Sorunlar ve Değişime Yapısal
        Uyum  Önerileri, chapters 1 and 9.
```

4. Health Policy:
   Readings:

   - Heidenheimer, Heclo and Adams, chapter 3.

5. Housing Policy:
   Readings:

   - Heidenheimer, Heclo and Adams, chapter 4.
   - Ruşen Keleş, "Konut Politikalarımız", A.Ü. S.B.F. Dergisi, Ocak-Haziran 1989.

6. Environmental Policy:
   Reading:

   - Frederick N. Bolotin, *International Public Policy Sourcebook*, Part II.

Students' final grades will be determined by:

1. Policy paper (40%)
2. Final examination (40%)
3. Class participation (20%)

Index

A

Abdullah Gul Government (58th government) 73–4
abusive constitutionalism, concept of 82
academics
   activities of 26–8
   collaboration with politics 131
   community of policy researchers 28
   teaching policy-related courses 30
administrative system *see* public administration
advanced policy tools 218, 222
advice giving, practice of 19, 22
advocacy coalition framework 29
Agriculture and Rural Development Institution 25
Amme İdaresi Dergisi (AID) 26–7, 273
analytic-level capacities 157
analytical capacity 220
analytical policy capacity 218
Anavatan Party 237
Ankara Agreement (1963) 237
applied general equilibrium theory 222
Arab Spring 244, 250, 262
ARI Movement (ARI Hareketi) 237
Association for Liberal Thinking (Liberal Duşunce Derneği) 237
Association Law (2004) 201
Autoregressive Distributed Lag (ADL) models 222

B

Babacan, Ali 227
Başçı Erdem 227
Bank for International Settlements 223
Banking and Financial Institutions Department 224, 225–6
   Currency Legislation Division 226
   Financial Data and Monitoring Division 226
   Financial Stability Division 225, 226
      Financial Data Project 226
   Financial stability report 226
   Financial Tools and Regulations Division 225
   International Institutions and Regulations Division 226
   Macro Financial Analysis Division 225

Banking Supervision and Regulation Authority (BRSA) 222, 226, 227
Barker Report (1950) 23, 25
Basic approaches in political science (Saybaşılı) 62
behaviouralism 125
Bentham, Jeremy 257
Bergama Gold Mine dispute 136
BİLGESAM (Wise Men Centre for Strategic Studies) 239, 240, 241, 245, 246
boomerang effect metaphor 35–48
   in communication studies 43–4
   explanations 44–7
      ambiguity of measurable performance targets 44–5
      deceleration of administrative reform 46–7
      incompatibility of private sector methods 44
      new public management approach 45–6
   policy evaluation of 43–4
Border Management Bureau 155
Bourdieu, Pierre 255, 257, 258
Brewer, Gary 105
BRSA (Banking Supervision and Regulation Authority) 222, 226, 227

C

Canadian International Development Agency 207
capital flows 215, 216
capital inflows 148, 215, 216, 228
Capital Markets Board of Turkey (CMB) 71, 226
capitalism 89, 94
   investments in urban settings 109
CBRT (Central Bank of the Republic of Turkey) 3, 13, 73, 145
   advanced policy tools 222
   Banking and Financial Institutions Department 224, 225–6
   capital inflows 215, 216
   Central Bank Review 224
   central position in macroeconomic policy-making 220
   communication strategy 224
   data collection and analysis 222–3, 225, 226, 228

FX risk 223
expectation surveys 222
external technical assistance 223
financial and macroeconomic stability
  215–16
horizontal organisational structure 224, 228
human capital 220–1, 228
  higher education qualifications 220, 221
  IMF and World Bank seminars 221
  international academic conferences and
    workshops 221
  on-the-job training 221
  postgraduate studies abroad 221
  recruitment and career development
    policies 221, 228
increased transparency and accountability
  220
independence 145, 147, 148, 157, 158,
  220, 229
macroeconomic models of applied general
  equilibrium theory 222
Memoranda of Understandings (MoUs) 226
more formal policy tools 222
outside experts 223
policy analysis 216, 217–20, 221, 224–6,
  227, 228
policy capacity 218–20, 227, 228, 229
policy design and implementation 215–16,
  227–8, 229
  policy mix 216, 227, 229
price stability objective 145, 146
Research and Monetary Policy Department
  224–5
  policy tools 221–2
Research Notes in Economic Series 225
responsibility for financial stability 222–3
Statistics Department 224, 225
censuses 20
central bank independence (CBI) 219–20,
  224, 228
Central Bank of Israel 217
Central Bank of the Republic of Turkey
  (CBRT) see CBRT (Central Bank of the
  Republic of Turkey)
central banks/banking 215
  analytical capacity 218
  low interest rates 215
  managing macroeconomic and financial
    stability risks 215
  micro-institutional foundation of 219
  monetary policy design and implementation
    217
  policy capacity and 216, 219–20
  legal independence 219–20
  politicians and 228
  politicised nature of 220
  quantitative easing 215
  see also CBRT (Central Bank of the
    Republic of Turkey)
central government
  creation of new ministries 75–6
  historical development
    1924 Constitution 69
    during the 1940s and 1950s 69
    1961 Constitution 69–70
    1982 Constitution 70
    adoption of presidential government
      system 72
    Budget Law no 6767 (2016) 71
    institutional transformation during 2000s
      72, 75
    neoliberal policies 70–1
    privatisation of public economy enterprises
      71–2
  key changes since 2001 73
  and local government
    ambiguous relationship with 91–2
    dialectical relationship with 9, 96–9, 100
    re-centralisation process 72, 76
  see also local government; presidency; Prime
    Minister; prime ministry
Centre for Eurasian Strategic Research
  (Avrasya Stratejik Araştırmalar Merkezi)
  237
Centre for Middle Eastern Strategic Studies
  (Ortadoğu Stratejik Araştırmalar Merkezi,
  ORSAM) see ORSAM (Centre for Middle
  Eastern Strategic Studies)
Centre for Policy Studies (UK) 46
Chambers of Turkish Architects and
  Engineers 42
Charles University 281
cities 94
  investment in 107
citizenship, republican model of 201
city councils 5
City Planning and Coordination Directorates
  98–9
civic activism 115–16
civil society
  current overview of 202–5
  categories of CSOs 204–5
  low levels of social trust 203–4
  membership of CSOs 202–3
  historical overview of 199–202
    centralised state 200
    detrimental political events 202
    EU influence in shaping 201–2
    impact of EU accession process 201, 209
    independence claims by minorities 200
    institutional reforms 201
    structural transformations of state and
      society 200–1
    unitary state 200

professionalisation of 202
relationship with democracy 205–6
weakness of 199–200, 203, 209
  roots of 199–200
see also CSOs (civil society organisations); Ottoman Empire
civil society organisations (CSOs) *see* CSOs (civil society organisations) 12–13
climate change 129
combined methods of research 56–7, 58, 61, 63
competitiveness 149
complex network governance framework 29
concord organisations 204
Constitutional Court 42, 70, 185
Constitutions
  (1924) 69
  (1961) 236
  (1982) 70, 77, 80, 81, 89, 90, 106
    changes to 201
coordination 6
Copenhagen Summit (2002) 201
Council of Ministers 70
coups 263
  (1980) 23, 24, 115, 237
  (2016) 79, 115, 138, 202
    State of Emergency 202, 210
Court of Accounts 8, 35, 74
  evaluation of public organisations 38, 39
    compliance audits 38
    financial audits 38
    reports 38
  judicial powers 39
  legal changes to organic law 41, 42–3, 43
  performance audits 41, 42–3
    pilot studies 41
  The planning and control of seashores report 41–2
  role of 38
  see also performance auditing
crazy projects 109
critical theory 55
CSOs (civil society organisations) 5, 199
  agendas 207, 208
  Association Law (2004) 201
  categories by legal status 204
    associations 204, 205
    cooperatives 204
    foundations 204
    professional associations 204
    unions 204
  closure of 202
  decision-making structures
    election process of executives 207
    hierarchical norms and principles 207, 209
    lack of diversity 207, 209

profiles of executives 206–7, 209
divided structure of networks 204
EU support for 201–2
  restricted groups 202
formation of 200
grants and funds 207–8, 210
  project-based activities 208
institutional reforms 201
membership
  art organisations 202, 203
  environmental organisations 202, 203
  humanitarian organisations 202, 203
  labour unions 203
  low levels of social trust 203–4
  mutual aid 202, 203
  OECD vs Turkey 202–3
  political parties 202, 203
  professional associations 203
  recreational organisations 202, 203
  religious organisations 202, 203
  numerically by country 204
policy analysis in 205–9
political polarisation 204
professionalisation of 208
programme evaluation 208–9
  goals of 208
  methods and techniques 209
representation of different social groups 207–8, 210
see also civil society
Cumhuriyet 14, 258, 259, 264–5, 266, 267
Czech Republic 280–1

D

Dahl, Robert A. 183
Dalan, Bedrettin 108
data collection methods 20, 22–3
  of research 58
Davutoğlu, Prime Minister Ahmet 78–9
decentralisation 72, 87, 88, 90, 100, 101, 107
decree laws 88
democracy
  full 55
  ideals 20, 21
  strengthening of 83
  values 20
Democrat Party 23, 24, 25–6
  attempted reduction of bureaucratic privilege 69
Democratic People's Party (Demokratik Halk Partisi, DEHAP) 185, 194
Democratic Society Party (Demokratik Toplum Partisi, DTP) 185
  election manifestos 187, 188, 189
  policy categories 193–4, 195
Denizli 92–3

Deposit Insurance Fund 226
deputy prime ministers 76
Derviş, Dr Kemal 73, 145, 147, 157
descriptive policy analysis 246, 251
design methods of research 58
Development Agencies (DAs) 150, 151, 157, 158
developmental projects 123
developmentalism 137
Dewey, John 3, 23, 272
Directive on Methods and Principles of Legislative Processes 5, 30
Directorate General for Migration Management (DGMM) 153, 154, 156, 157
discursive policy analysis 128
district municipalities 91, 93, 95, 106
Downs, Anthony 183
Durak, Aytac 112
Dynamic General Equilibrium (DGE) model 222
Dynamic Stochastic General Equilibrium (DSGE) model 222

E

economic crises 35, 166
 (2001) 24, 145, 193, 195
 AKP'S attempts to overcome 35, 45
 see also financial crises
Economic Development Facility (İktisadi Kalkınma Tesisi) 13, 237
Economic Policy Research Foundation of Turkey (Turkiye Ekonomi Politikaları Araştırma Vakfı, TEPAV) see TEPAV (Economic Policy Research Foundation of Turkey)
Economic Research Foundation (İktisadi Araştırmalar Vakfı) 13, 237
Economic Stability Decisions (1980) 70, 71
Economy Coordination Board 71
economy, the
 crises 24, 35, 45, 145, 166, 193, 195
 election manifestos 186, 187, 188
 public concern for 6–7, 11–12, 166, 167
 public policy news 260, 261, 266, 267
education
 4+4+4 reforms 133
 policy analysis
  academic activities 26–8
  expansion of courses 26
  language textbooks 27
  problems in teaching and research 28–30
  teaching of 25–6
 policy preferences 166, 167, 172–4
  of educational groups 172–3
  by gender 172, 173

public evaluation of 173–4
reform of system 173
Turkish students studying abroad 25, 26
see also public policy education
Education Reform Initiative (Eğitim Reformu Girişimi, ERG) see ERG (Education Reform Initiative)
election manifestos
 policy categories 189–94, 195
  agriculture and farmers 189, 190, 191, 192
  civic mindedness: positive 193, 194
  culture: positive 191
  decentralisation: positive 193, 194
  democracy 189, 190, 191, 192, 193, 194, 195
  economic goals 191
  economic growth 189, 190, 191, 192, 194, 195
  economic planning: positive 189, 190, 192, 193
  education expansion 189, 190, 191, 192, 194
  equality: positive 191, 193, 194, 195
  free enterprise: positive 189, 190, 191, 194
  freedom and human rights: positive 193, 194
  governmental and administrative efficiency 192–3, 194
  incentives: positive 189, 190, 191, 192
  labour groups: positive 193, 194
  law and order 189, 190
  military: negative 193, 194
  multiculturalism: positive 193, 194
  national way of life: positive 192
  peace: positive 193, 194
  political corruption: negative 191
  technology and infrastructure: positive 189, 190, 191, 192, 193–4, 194
  welfare state expansion 189, 190, 191, 192, 193, 194, 195
 policy domains 186–9
  economy 186, 187, 188
  external relations 186, 189
  fabric of society 186, 188, 189
  freedom and democracy 186, 188
  political system 186, 187–8, 189
  social groups 186, 189
  welfare and quality of life 186, 187, 188
 relationship with public opinion 195
elections
 legislative 184, 185
  (2002) 185, 195
  (2015) 185
 mandate view of 183, 184
electoral competition 183

empirical evidence 52–3, 55
Energy Support Commissions (Enerji Destek Komsiyonlari) 99
Enlightenment, the 19, 20, 124
environmental policy 30, 123
  disputes 128–9, 134–8
    Bergama Gold Mine dispute 136
    bureaucratic fragmentation 134–5
    climate change 129
    confrontations and contestations 135, 137
    development paradigms 134
    emotional and irrational movements 135
    hydro plant, Sakarya River 137
    problems facing scientists 137
  environmental discourses 137
  environmentalists
    challenges to new development projects 137–8
    government opposition to 137
    new policy discourses 136–7
    professional organisations 137–8
Erdoğan, Recep Tayyip 24, 35, 74, 137
ERG (Education Reform Initiative) 239, 240, 246, 247, 251
Ergun, Turgay 275
Eroğlu, Veysel 137
EU (European Union) 4, 8, 43, 46
  support for CSOs 201–2
  triggering policy change 11
  see also Europeanisation of policy-making in Turkey
European Central Bank 223
European Charter of Local Self-Government 96
European Social Survey (ESS) 165
  complexity of politics 165
Europeanisation of policy-making in Turkey 71, 87, 143–4
  civil society 201–2
  confirmation as an EU candidate country 24, 36, 143, 149
    administrative reforms 36
    membership negotiations 73
  EU accession report 36
  EU financial assistance programmes 149
  formal intensity 157
  immigration policies and governance 156–7
    civilian authority 155
    control of movement, public security and human rights 153
    in flux from 1990s to 2000s 152–3
    legal framework and institutions 153–4, 155
    procedural changes 154
    regional policy instruments 155
    Syrians, influx of 153, 154
    transformative role of the EU 155, 158

instrument density 156
international pressures and influences 143
macroeconomic policies and governance 156, 157–8
  balanced budgets 146, 156
  changing regime from 1990s to 2000s 145–6
  fiscal rules 147–8, 156
  monetary policy 147
  multi-annual programming 147–8
  stability culture 146, 156
  transformative role of the EU 148, 158
  Treasury as 'Super Ministry' 147, 157
policy density 144, 156, 158
policy intensity 144, 156–7, 158
regional development policies and governance 156, 158
  in flux from 1990s to 2000s 149
  partnership 150
  procedural changes 150–1
  programming 150
  regional convergence versus regional competitiveness 149, 156
  regional policy instruments 151
  strategic planning 150
  transformative role of the EU 151–2, 158
evidence-based policy analysis 125
executive commission 111
executive government, personnel positions 2
expectation surveys 222
experts and expertise 10–11, 123–4
  education 133
  environmentalists
    challenges to new development projects 137–8
    government opposition to 137
  new law on metropolitan municipalities 133
  relationship with policy-makers 132–3
  role in environmental policy disputes 128–9, 134–8
    Bergama Gold Mine dispute 136
    bureaucratic fragmentation 134–5
    confrontations and contestations 135, 137
    development paradigm 134
    hydro plant, Sakarya River 137
    new policy discourses 136–7
    problems facing scientists 137
    professional organisations 137–8
  role in the policy process 124–7, 131–2, 134
    authority challenged 125
    evolution of 124–5
    ideologies and values 133
    influence of Second World War 124–5
    interpretive methods 125–6
    problems 131
    research 131

top-down tradition 131–2, 133, 135
in Turkey 130–4
see also science

F

farmers' goods protection councils 99
field theory 255, 257–8
  advantages of 258
  agents 257
financial crises 24, 35, 43, 47, 166
  in 2001 73, 220
  global 75, 189, 215, 220, 227
Financial Stability Committee (FSC) 222, 226, 227
Financial stability report 226
Foucault, Michel 257
Foundation for Middle East and Balkan Studies (Orta Doğuve Balkan İncelemeleri Vakfı, OBİV) 237
Foundation for Political and Social Research (Siyasi ve Sosyal Araştırmalar Vakfı, SİSAV) 237
Foundation for Political, Economic and Social Research (Siyaset, Ekonomi ve Toplum Araştırmaları Vakfı, SETA) *see* SETA (Foundation for Political, Economic and Social Research)
framing 256
Friedrich Ebert Stiftung (FES) 237

G

Gaebler, Ted 46
GEGP 73, 74
General Directorate of Research and Monetary Policy 225
Generalised Method of Moments (GMM) model 222
Gezi Park Movement 264
global financial crisis (GFC) 75, 189, 215, 220, 227
global warming 129
globalisation 21, 29, 94, 95, 134
governance 199
governance capacity 218
governments, responsiveness of 183
Grand National Assembly of Turkey (TBMM) 37, 38, 75
  elections to 80
  increased members of 80
  powers to investigate President 81, 82
  reform packages, passing of 201
  supervisory tools 80
  term of office 80
Gülen Movement 265

H

Habermas, Jürgen 55
HABITAT-II Summit (1996) 116
Hamzaoğlu, Professor Dr Onur 137
healthcare services 166, 167, 170–2, 176
Heinrich Böll Foundation 207
Helsinki Summit (1999) 201
hermeneutics approaches 55
Housing Development Agency 107
human capital 220–1, 228
human dignity 20, 21
Human Resources Development Programme Authority 25
Hürriyet 14, 258, 259, 264, 265, 266

I

IMF (International Monetary Fund) 4, 8, 11, 23, 24, 35, 46, 73, 87, 148, 221, 223
  deficit rule 147
implementation
  challenges 5–6
  failures 6
  performance auditing 41–3
  strategic planning 39–41
    macro problems 40
    micro problems 40
  see also public policy tools
Industrial Revolution 19–20
Inflation Report 224
İnsan Kaynaklarının Geliştirilmesi Program Otoritesi (Human Resources Development Programme Authority) 25
Institute of Economic Affairs (UK) 46
Institute of Strategic Thinking (Stratejik Duşunce Enstitusu, SDE) *see* SDE (Institute of Strategic Thinking)
institutional rational choice framework 29
international financial loan agreements 35–6
International Monetary Fund (IMF) *see* IMF (International Monetary Fund)
International Social Survey Programme (ISSP) 168, 195
  Health and Healthcare Model 171
International Strategic Research Organisation (Uluslararası Stratejik Araştırmalar Kurumu, USAK) *see* USAK (International Strategic Research Organisation)
interpretivist methods in policy analysis 54–6, 125–6, 128
Investment Monitoring and Coordination Presidencies (IMCP) 95, 97–8
IPM (Istanbul Policy Centre) 239, 240, 245, 246, 251
Islamic Studies Centre (İslam Araştırmaları Merkezi, İSAM) 237
issue of saliency 163, 165–6, 174, 175

Istanbul Canal 109
Istanbul Policy Centre (İstanbul Politikalar Merkezi, IPM) *see* IPM (Istanbul Policy Centre)
Istanbul School of Central Banking 221

J

Journal of Legislation (*Yasama Dergisi*) 62
judiciary 82
Justice and Development Party (Adalet Kalkinma Partisi, AKP) 8, 12, 24, 263
 booklet on service delivery 112
 closure of small local administrations 92
 corruption allegations 264
 election manifestos 187, 188, 195
  policy categories 189–90
 electoral promises 47
 electoral successes 258
  (2002) 201
  (2015) 78–9
 foundation of 184
 goal to end economic crisis 35
 in government (2002-2015) 184
 domestic advice and expertise, ignoring 45–6
 legislation 175
 neoliberal reform policies 24, 35–6
 new law for Court of Accounts 41, 42–3, 43
 public administration reform 35–6, 35–9
 public policy analysis methods and techniques 36
 responses to public opinion 175
 reversion of public policy methods and techniques 35, 43, 44, 46–7
 strengthening power base 47
 see also boomerang effect metaphor

K

Kara, Hakan 216
Kemal, Mustafa Atatürk 23
Kingdon, John 272
knowledge 220
 see also human capital
knowledge transfer 19
Konrad Adenauer Stiftung (KAS) 237
KÖYDES Allowance Commissions 99
Kurdish Opening Process 262
Kurdish political movement 185, 194
 Democratic People's Party (Demokratik Halk Partisi, DEHAP) 185, 194
 see also Democratic Society Party (Demokratik Toplum Partisi, DTP); Peace and Democracy Party (Barış ve Demokrasi Partisi, BDP); People's Democratic Party (Halklarin Demokratik Partisi, HDP)

L

Lasswell, Harold 3, 105, 124, 125
 objective knowledge generation 20, 21
 see also policy sciences
Latour, Bruno 128
Law no 657 on Civil Servants (1965) 89
Law no 3046 (2011) 75, 76, 84
Law no 4749 on Regulating Public Finance and Debt Management (LRPFDM, 2002) 145, 146, 147
Law no 4817 on Work Permits for Foreigners (2003) 152, 153
Law no 5018 on Public Financial Management and Control (PFMCL, 2003) *see* PFMCL (Law no 5018 on Public Financial Management and Control, 2003)
Law no 5019 on the Administration of Metropolitan Municipalities (2003) 93, 94
Law no 5025 (2003) 93, 94
Law no 5026 on the Annexation of Municipalities and Villages to Denizli Municipality (2003) 93
Law no 5216 on Metropolitan Municipalities (2004) 88, 93, 94
Law no 5227 on the Fundamental Principles and Restructuring of Public Administration (2003) 74
Law no 5302 on Special Provincial Administration (2005) 88, 97
Law no 5449 on the Establishment, Coordination and Duties of Development Agencies (2006) 88
Law no 5683 on Residence and Travel of Foreigners in Turkey (1950) 152
Law no 5747 (2008) 93, 94
Law no 6360 (2012) 94, 95–6
Law no 6458 on Foreigners and International Protection (LFIP, 2013) 152, 153, 154
Law no 6771 (2017) 80–1
LFIP (Law no 6458 on Foreigners and International Protection, 2013) 152, 153, 154
loans 35–6
local government 74
 and central government
  ambiguous relationship with 91–2
  dialectical relationship with 9, 96–9, 100
 centralist character 91
 closure of administrations 92
 definition of 106
 and the law 90–1
 and public administration 91
 reform of 87, 88
 structure of 106–7

types of 90, 91
see also mayors; metropolitan municipalities; municipalities; villages
LRPFDM (Law no 4749 on Regulating Public Finance and Debt Management, 2002) 145, 146, 147

M

macroeconomic bureaucracies 220
macroeconomic policies and governance 145–8
macroeconomic policy-making 215, 220
macroprudential regulation 215, 227
mandate view of elections 183, 184
Manifesto Project (CMP/MARPOR) 186–94
mass media *see* media
mayors 9–10, 95, 108
  election of 110, 115
  empowerment of 110, 117
  influence in local government 105–6
  as one-and-only decision-makers 110–12
    determining council agendas 111, 117
  political relationships 111–12
  supervision of 114, 117
  suspension of 115
media 14, 255–6
  agenda-setting 256, 258, 260, 262, 267
  framing 256, 258, 264–5, 267
  literature review 256–8
  ownership of 256, 259
  panoptical role 256–7, 258, 268
  public policy news
    civil-military relations 263, 265, 268
    corruption 263–4, 265, 268
    distribution of 260–2
    distribution of criticism 265–7
    economy 260, 261, 266, 267
    executive 263, 264, 265
    framing across newspapers 264–5
    minority rights 262
    newspapers, analysis of 258–60
    opposition parties 263, 264, 265
    politics/ideology 260, 261, 262, 266–7
    secularism 263, 265, 268
    security/terrorism 260, 261, 261–2
    society, culture and sports 260, 261, 267
    subcategories 262–4
    Turkey and international organisations 260, 261, 262, 267
    Turkish foreign policy 260, 261, 262, 267
  as a semi-autonomous field 257
mega-projects 107–9
  Istanbul Canal 109
  relief in Buca/İzmir 109
  theme park, Istanbul 109

mesne profits 41
methodological pluralism 57
metropolisation 94–6
metropolitan councils 95
metropolitan governments 106
metropolitan municipalities 90, 92, 94–5, 96, 106, 133
  boundaries 95
Middle East and North African (MENA) states 202
Middle East Technical University (Orta Dou Teknik Universitesi, ODTU) 275
Milliyet 14, 258, 259, 264, 265, 266
ministerial system 75–7
Ministry of Development (formerly State Planning Organization, SPO) 75
  guidelines for investment proposals 24–5
  Investment Circular and Investment Programme Preparation Guide 75
Ministry of Economy 74, 227
Ministry of Environment and Urban Planning 76, 107
Ministry of EU Affairs 73
Ministry of Finance 38, 40, 220
  monitoring of fiscal policy 75
Ministry of Interior 114
Ministry of Internal Affairs 94
monetary policy 219, 220, 229
  price stability 145, 146
  proactive behaviour 216, 217
  Research and Monetary Policy Department (CBRT) 221
  responsibility of the CBRT 147
    advanced policy tools 222
    expectation surveys 222
    formal policy tools 222
    inflation targeting 148
  transparency 147
Monetary Policy Committee (MPC) 148, 156, 157, 224, 225
Money Credit Board 71
Morcol, Goktug 275
more formal policy tools 218, 222
multiple streams model 272
municipal councils 5, 110–11
  agendas 111
municipalities 9–10, 90, 91, 92, 96
  capitalist pressures 107
  closing down policy 92–3
  conversion to villages 93–4
  duties 106
  evaluation of policies 114–16
    civic activism 115–16
    civic inspections 114–15
    elections of candidates 115
    juridical supervision 114
    media information 116

non-evaluation of policies 115–16
participatory mechanisms 116
public opinion 115
faster implementation of policies 112–14
new public management (NPM) principles 112
outsourcing of service delivery 113
privatisation of public services 112–13
mega-projects 107–9
referential of service delivery 107–8
Municipality Law no 5393 (2005) 88, 93
mysticism 19

N

national developmentalism 201
National Security Council 70
National Strategy of Regional Development (NSRD) (MoD, 2014) 149, 150
Nationalist Movement Party (Millliyetci Hareket Partisi, MHP) 12
election manifestos 187, 188, 195
policy categories 191–3
foundation of 184
nature 128
nepotism 2
new public management (NPM) approach 36, 37, 44, 45–6, 71, 72
in local government 112
non-governmental policy actors 4
normative policy analysis 246–7, 251
Norwegian Agency for Development Cooperation 207

O

objective analysis 21, 29
objective knowledge 20, 21
Öcalan, Abdullah 261-2
OECD (Organization for Economic Co-operation and Development) 4, 8, 43
influence on Turkish regional development policies 152
regulatory reform programme 36
operational capacity 220
operational-level capacities 157
Operations Research Society 272
organisational operational capacity 218, 219, 228
organisational political capacity 218, 219, 227, 228
ORSAM (Centre for Middle Eastern Strategic Studies) 239, 240, 241, 242, 245, 246, 247
Osborne, David 46
Ottoman Empire 7
centralised state 200
data collection methods

expansion of scope 23
nationwide census (1831) 22–3
dissolution of 200
European scientific knowledge and practices 19
intermediary structures 200
land ownership 200
meritocracy 22
polity-relevant knowledge 22
power of 200
reforms 22
Özal, Turgut 24, 130, 237
Özay, Ismail 114

P

panel VAR 222
parliamentary system 77, 78, 79, 83
comparison with presidential government system 82
participatory practices 29, 30
Passport Law no 5682 (1950) 152
Peace and Democracy Party (Barış ve Demokrasi Partisi, BDP) 185
election manifestos 187, 188, 189
policy categories 193–4, 195
People's Democratic Party (Halklarin Demokratik Partisi, HDP) 12, 185
election manifestos 187, 188, 189
policy categories 193–4, 195
performance auditing 35, 37, 38, 41–3
boomerang effect metaphor 44–7
immunity of public managers 42
purpose of 44
performance budgeting 37, 37–8, 40
performance measurement 36–7
'Measurement of output and performance in central government' report 37
public sector organisations 38
PFMCL (Law no 5018 on Public Financial Management and Control, 2003) 3, 36, 37, 39, 88, 145, 146, 147, 148, 273
significance of 74–5
policy analysis
aim of 217
characterisation of 217
definition 1, 51, 124
emergence of 1
failed opportunities for 3
future of 28
historical and global context 19–22
historical practice of 22–5
institutional and agency-level constraints 3–4
see also policy research and analysis
policy analytical capacity 218–19
policy analytical methods 23, 24, 28

policy capacity 216
  central banking and 216, 218–20, 227, 228, 229
  definition 218
  organisational analytical capacity 218, 228
  organisational operational capacity 218, 219, 228
  organisational political capacity 218, 219, 227, 228
  see also CBRT (Central Bank of The Republic of Turkey); central banks/banking
policy cycle approach 105
  stages 105–15
    decisive stage 110–12
    evaluation stage 114–16
policy entrepreneurs 3
policy entrepreneurship 73, 217, 220, 227, 228
policy learning 96, 143, 218, 223, 228
policy-making
  caricatured image of 4
  central role of prime ministry 76, 84
  creation of agencies 24
  empirical study on 2–3
  and media 255–68
  policy analytical methods 23, 24, 28
  presidential government system 84
  US influence on 23
  values in 29
  see also Europeanisation of policy-making in Turkey
policy outcomes 143
policy outputs 143, 157
policy professionals 59, 63
policy research and analysis 8, 52
  classified list of methods of social enquiry 58
  combined methods in public policy 56–9
    Master's programmes 57
    review of literature (US) 57–9
  internet survey (Turkey)
    books 61–2
    combined methods 61, 63
    courses 61
    findings 59–62
    frequency distribution 61
    literature review/analysis 60
    methodology and data sources 59
    methods and techniques of policy research 60
    methods of policy analysis 61
    qualitative methods 61, 63, 64
    quantitative methods 61, 63
  positivist tradition 52–3, 55
  post-positivist (interpretivist) approaches 54–6

quantitative methods 52, 53
skills 64
policy responsiveness 183
policy sciences 1–2, 3, 19, 20–1
  of democracy 1–2, 19, 20
  theoretical challenges to 21–2
policy studies 7–8, 25, 28, 51
  comparison between Turkey and the US 63–4
policy tools 218–19
  advanced tools 218
  more formal tools 218, 222
  simple tools 218
political capacity 227
political-level capacities 157–8
political parties 183–4
  election manifestos see election manifestos
  policy issues 184
  R&D departments 185
  responsiveness of 183–4
  transmitting popular preference into policy 183
  Turkish political landscape (2002-2015) 184–6
  vote shares and seats in parliament 185
politics of service 112
positivist approaches 20, 52–3, 55
post-positivist (interpretivist) approaches 54–6
power of the purse 43
prefects 97, 98
Preliminary National Development Plan (PNDP) (SPO, 2003) 149, 150
presidency
  centralisation of power 77–80
  'counter signature rule' 78
  establishing government and appointing ministers 72
  President
    appointment of vice-presidents 81
    budgetary power 81
    executive duties and powers 80–1
    'general criminal responsibility' of 81
    powers of 79, 80, 81–2, 82
    presidential decree (Article 106) 81
    public election of 72, 77, 78
    term of office 81
  presidential government system 78–9
    comparison with parliamentary system 82
    legal adoption of 80, 89
    support for 79
    term of office 80
    Turkish model 79
  semi-presidential system 78, 83
  strengthened powers and duties 70
price stability 145, 215, 226, 227
Prime Minister 77
  abolition of role 72

economic administration 71
  role and power of 70
    impact of 1982 Constitution 70
prime ministry
  central role in policy-making process 76, 84
  centralisation of 72–7
  coordination boards 77
  hierarchical structure of 76
  increased public institutions and
    organisations 70
Prime Ministry Higher Audit Board 74
private sector companies 44
privatisation policies 169–70, 176
Programmatic Financial and Public Sector
  Adjustment Loan Agreement (PFPSAL-1)
  37–8
project credits 36
prospective policy analysis 247
provincial administrations 90
provincial community health councils 99
provincial coordination councils 98–9
provincial councils 106
  governors 106, 107
provincial traffic commissions 99
public administration
  centralist character 91
  characteristics of 2, 6
  integral unity of 90
  legal principles of 90
  reform of 8, 35, 35–9, 36–7, 87, 88–9
    deceleration 46–7
    Draft Law no 5227 88
    new public management approach 72
  reorganisation of 70
  strategic plans 75
  US influence on 23
  reports 23
  see also strategic planning
Public Administration Department (Faculty of
  Political Science at Ankara University) 7
  US influence 25
Public Administration Forum (KAYFOR)
  27–8, 277
Public Administration Institute for Turkey and
  the Middle East (TODAİE) 7, 46, 70, 275
  goal of 25
Public Finance Management and Control
  Law no 5108 (PFMCL) (2003) *see*
  PFMCL (Law no 5018 on Public Financial
  Management and Control, 2003)
Public Finance Management Credit 88
public finance management reform 87, 88
public management movement 36
public opinion 11–12, 115, 163–4, 174–5
  economic issues 6–7, 11–12
  general attitudes towards politics 164–7
    crime 166, 167

economic problems 166, 167
educational and healthcare policy 166,
  167
educational groups 164–5
gender differences 164, 165
terrorism 166, 167
unemployment 166, 167
on government expenditure 47
issue of saliency 163, 165–6, 174, 175
policy preferences 167–74, 176
  economic policies 167–8, 170, 176
  educational policies 172–4
  healthcare policies 170–2, 176
  income inequality 168, 176, 195
  privatisation of state-owned businesses and
    industry 169–70, 176
  taxation 168–9, 171–2, 176
relationship with election manifestos 195
public organisations 24, 35, 37
  accountability 39
  defining tangible and measurable
    performance targets 44–5
  five-year development plans 38
  performance measurement and auditing 38,
    39
  seashore management and responsibilities
    41–2
  strategic planning 39–41
    budgets 40–1
    incompatibility of private sector methods
      44
    performance indicators and measurable
      outputs 39, 40
public personnel management reform 87,
  88–9
Public Personnel Selection Exam (Kamu
  Personeli Seçme Sınavı, KPSS) 283
public policy
  complexity of 127
  definition 21, 124
  diversity of contributors 127
  education and training 3–4
  limited capacity to solve problems 56
  and media 255–68
  problems 29, 30
  research and analysis methods 56–9
  see also experts and expertise;
    implementation; territorialisation policies
Public Policy Analysis Study Group 28
public policy education 14, 271–2, 280–3
  in the Czech Republic 280–1
    problems of teaching 281
    strengths of 281
  improvements
    availability of quality instructors 281–2
    institutional links between universities and
      think tanks 282

teaching materials 282
institutionalisation 278, 279, 280, 281, 282
literature review 274–6
  public administration 274, 276
Master's and PhD theses 279
Master's programmes and sub-departments/concentrations 279–80, 282
overview 272–4
  documents 272
  scientific studies 274
  special issues 274
  window of opportunity 272–3
production of teaching materials 277–9
  articles in refereed academic journals 278
  case studies 278
  encyclopaedia 278
  growing interest of graduate students 278
  online lecture notes 278
  since the early 2000s 278
Public Administration Forum (KAYFOR) 27–8, 277
shortcomings
  demand-based studies 282
  link between teaching/research and practice 282
  relevance of studies to job entrants 283
teaching 275
undergraduate courses and graduate programmes 275
  academics returning from abroad 276
  influence of European universities 276
  older generation of academicians 276
workshops 28, 272, 276–7, 281, 282
public policy studies 28, 29, 62, 272–4
Public policy: Theory and practice (Yildiz and Sobaci) 62
public policy tools 25, 35, 47
  new, design and transfer of 37–9
  performance budgeting 36, 37
  see also strategic planning
Public Policy Workshops 28, 272, 276–7, 281, 282
public programmes 25
public sector
  five-year development plans 37–8
  performance measurement 38
  reorganisation of 36
public services 90, 91, 95
  public-private partnerships 113
  see also service delivery

Q

qualitative methods of research 55–6, 57–9, 58, 59, 61, 63, 64
quantitative easing 215

quantitative methods of research 20, 52, 53, 54, 57–8, 59, 61, 63

R

rational approaches 54–5
rational choice theorists 21–2
rational thinking 20–1
referendums 72, 77, 80
regional development agencies 99–100
Regional Development Committee 151
Regional Development High Board 151, 156
regulatory authorities/organisations 71
  limited authority 76
  ongoing issues in 76
Republic of Turkey
  administrative system 89–92
  centralised state 2, 200, 201
  Constitutional Articles 90
  constitutional issue 79–80
    Law no 6771 80–1
  coups 263
    (1980) 23, 24, 115, 237
    (2016) 79, 115, 138, 202
    State of Emergency 202, 210
  decentralisation 72, 87, 88, 90, 100, 101, 107
  legal-institutional preparation process 82–3
  liberalisation process 87, 89
  'lost' years of 1990s 72–3
  national developmentalism 201
  populist policies of coalition governments 24
  re-centralisation 72, 76, 138
  republican model of citizenship 201
  scientific methods in policy-making 23
  state/governmental reform 87–9
  state's territory 89–90
  as a unitary state 89, 90, 200
  see also Europeanisation of policy-making in Turkey
Republican People's Party (Cumhuriyet Halk Partisi, CHP) 12, 93, 175
  election manifestos 187, 188
  policy categories 189–90, 194, 195
  foundation of 184
research 28–30
  funding and dissemination of 131
  see also policy research and analysis
Research and Monetary Policy Department 221, 224–5
  brainstorming 221–2
Research and Monetary Policy Department (CBRT)
  mandate 225
  staffing 225
retrospective policy analysis 247

Root Foundation for Political and Social Research (Kok Sosyal ve Siyasal Araştırmalar Vakfı) 237

S

Sabah 14, 258, 259, 264, 265, 266
saliency, issue of 163, 165–6, 174, 175
science
  authority of 125
  BSE crisis 126
  experts and the general public 127
  'problem of extension' 126–7
  scientific evidence 129
  second wave of science studies 126
  social character of 126
  third wave of science and technology studies 126–7
scientific methods 19–20
scientific research 131
scientificity 21
SDE (Institute of Strategic Thinking) 239, 240, 241, 245, 246, 247
seashores 41–2
Secretariat-General of EU Affairs 71, 73, 76
security 6, 7
service delivery 108, 109, 112
  outsourcing 113
  privatisation of 112–13
SETA (Foundation for Political, Economic and Social Research) 239, 240, 241, 242, 245, 246
Sezer, President Ahmet Necdet 93
Social Assistance and Solidarity Foundations 99
social problems 20, 21
social science methodology 52
social trust 203–4
Special Expert Commission 145
special provincial administrations 95, 97
SPO (State Planning Organization, later Ministry of Development) 3, 23, 39, 70, 71, 76, 272
  9th and 10th Development Plans 149, 150
  strategic management working group 40
  strategic planning 40
SRAG (Systemic Risk Assessment Group) meetings 226
stability culture, principle of 146
State of Emergency 202, 210
State Planning Organization (SPO) *see* SPO (State Planning Organization, later Ministry of Development)
state, the
  centralised 2, 200, 201
  hierarchical power structure 2, 4
  unitary 89, 90, 200

statistical data analysis methods of research 58
Statistics Department 224, 225
  Balance of Payments Division 225
  Monetary and Financial Data Division 225
  Real Sector Data Division 225
STEP programme 73, 145, 146, 147
strategic planning 13, 30, 31, 35, 36, 37, 38
  boomerang effect metaphor 44–7
  public organisations 39–41
survey methods 20
Swedish International Development Cooperation Agency 207
symbol specialists 19

T

Tarim ve Kirsal Kalkınmayı Destekleme Kurumu (TKDK) (Agriculture and Rural Development Institution) 25
TASAM (Turkish Asian Centre for Strategic Studies) 239, 240, 245, 246, 247
Task Force on Migration and Asylum Action Plan (2004) 155
taxation 166, 168–9, 171–2, 176
teaching *see* education
TEKEL (Monopoly on Tobacco and Alcoholic Products) 73
TEPAV (Economic Policy Research Foundation of Turkey) 239, 240, 245, 246, 247
territorialisation policies 88, 89, 92–6, 100–1
  closing down policy 92–3
  conversion of municipalities to villages 93–4
  metropolisation 94–6
terrorism 6, 7, 166, 167, 260, 261–2
TESEV (Turkish Economic and Social Studies Foundation 239, 240, 241, 245, 246, 247
think tanks 13, 132, 235–6, 250–2, 282
  definition 236
  functions of 235, 236, 238
  growth of 237–8, 250, 252
  history of 236–8
  independence of 236
  liberalisation in Turkey 237
  origins of 235, 236, 250
  papers (produced during 2000s), analysis of
  analytical approaches and tools 246–50
  authors 244–5, 249, 251
  data collection and analysis 248–9, 251
  descriptive policy analysis 246, 247, 251
  economic policy 242
  education policy 242, 251
  energy policy 242
  groups 245
  health policy 242, 251
  international relations 242, 250
  internet 239

Middle East 243, 250
normative policy analysis 246–7, 251
politics 250–1
prospective policy analysis 247–8
religion policy 242
retrospective policy analysis 247–8
selected organisations 240
selection criteria 239–40
social policy 242, 251
summary, purpose statement and problem definition 245–6
trends, areas and topics 242–4
political ideologies 241
types of 238
town municipalities 95
TR02-JH-03 Asylum-Migration Twinning Project (2002) 155
transportation coordination centres 99
Treasury 145, 220, 226, 227
as 'Super Ministry' 147, 157
Turkey see Republic of Turkey
Turkish Academy of Sciences (TÜBA) 3, 24
National Open Course Materials Programme 278
Scientific research and policy interface 131, 132
Turkish Asian Centre for Strategic Studies (Turk Asya Stratejik Araştırmalar Merkezi, TASAM) see TASAM (Turkish Asian Centre for Strategic Studies)
Turkish Citizenship Law no 403 154
Turkish Economic and Social Studies Committee (Ekonomik ve Sosyal Etudler Heyeti) 13, 237
Turkish Economic and Social Studies Foundation (Turkiye Ekonomik ve Sosyal Etudler Vakfı, TESEV) see TESEV (Turkish Economic and Social Studies Foundation
Turkish Higher Education Agency 271
Turkish National Assembly see Grand National Assembly of Turkey (TBMM)

U

unemployment 166, 167
United States of America (USA)
federal agencies 21
Government Performance Results Act (1993) 37
influence on policy-making 23
research and analysis methods 57–9
Master's programmes 57
University of Chicago 46
urban land rent 94
urbanism 94, 107

USAK (International Strategic Research Organisation) 239, 240, 241, 245, 246, 247
utilitarian approaches 54–5

V

value-laden politics 21, 29
Vector Auto Regressions (VAR) 222
vice-ministers 76, 77
vice-presidents 81
vice-prime ministers 77
Village Infrastructure Support Project (KÖYDES) 99
villages 90, 92, 95, 106
closing down policy 92–3
conversion from municipalities 93–4
villages Services Department 106

W

Welfare Party 263
Wise Men Centre for Strategic Studies (Bilge Adamlar Stratejik Araştırmalar Merkezi, BİLGESAM) see BİLGESAM (Wise Men Centre for Strategic Studies)
workshops, public policy see Public Policy Workshops
World Bank 4, 8, 23, 24, 35, 36, 37, 87, 221
World Values Survey (WVS) 11, 164, 203

Z

Zaman 14, 258, 259, 264, 265, 266